KIRKSTA BEY

VOLUME I

The 1950-64 excavations: a reassessment

by

Stephen Moorhouse and Stuart Wrathmell

West Yorkshire
Archaeology Service

ISBN 1 870453 01 8

Published by: West Yorkshire Archaeology Service, 14, St. Johns North, Wakefield, WF1 3QA, on behalf of West Yorkshire Archives and Archaeology Joint Committee.

Printed by: Arthur Wigley & Sons, Ltd., Bradford BD1 4SS

CONTENTS

LIST OF FIGURES

LIST OF TABLES

LIST OF PLATES

ACKNOWLEDGEMENTS

This report is based upon excavation archives and artefacts held by Leeds City Museums. The first and principal acknowledgement is, therefore, to the staff of the Museums, and in particular to Peter Brears (Director) and Elizabeth Pirie (Curator of Archaeology). Without their whole-hearted co-operation in making the material available for study, and in locating finds which had become dispersed from the main collection, the project would have been impossible. The Yorkshire and Humberside Schools Museum Service readily gave permission for the Kirkstall artefacts in its travelling exhibition to be returned to the collection for study; and the staffs of the Yorkshire Archaeological Society, the Thoresby Society and the West Yorkshire Archive Service have assisted in various aspects of the research. Mrs Jean Le Patourel has very kindly given advice and provided information on the pottery.

The tasks of processing the original records, redrawing the site plans and sections, cataloguing and drawing the finds and typing the draft texts were funded largely by the Manpower Services Commission, through the Kirkstall Abbey Excavation Scheme. They were carried out under the supervision of Michael Haynes and Andrea Smith, who themselves provided the initial structural descriptions and finds catalogues. The primary drawings were by Roman Biegonowski, Brian Connor, Kathleen Crawshaw, John Herbert, Maureen Lea, Andrew Nicholson and Philip Robertson. The draft texts were typed by Joan Clarkson, Avril Dunn and Kathy Fairbourne. The plans and sections which appear in this volume were drawn by Chris Philo, Jon Prudhoe and Andy Swann. The small-find drawings are by Chris Bishop, Debbie Marshall and Teresa Widera. The pottery and clay tile illustrations are, respectively, by Anna Slowikowski and Stephen Moorhouse; and the final text has been typed by Anne Smith and Elaine Tyndall.

The authorship of the various chapters and sections of this volume is recorded under the appropriate headings. The specialists who contributed to Chapter 16, The Small Finds, provided information as follows: on the funerary letter (no. 208), Dr J. Blair; on the decorated window glass, Dr L. A. S. Butler; on ironwork, Dr I. H. Goodall; on copper alloy artefacts, Mrs A. Goodall; on the composition and condition of the window glass, Dr J. Henderson; on petrology, Dr G. F. Hornung. The text of Part One: The Excavated Structures, is by Stuart Wrathmell, who is responsible for the reinterpretations of the evidence. Work on Part Two: The Finds, has been supervised and edited by Stephen Moorhouse. Dr Wrathmell has carried out the final editing of the whole report.

FOREWORD by John D. Hedges, County Archaeologist

In the eighteenth and nineteenth centuries Kirkstall Abbey was regarded as one of the finest picturesque sites in the English landscape: impressive, crumbling, ivy-clad walls, blending into a tranquil pastoral background. The background has changed; but the Abbey remains one of the most notable monuments to twelfth-century monastic architecture, thanks to the decision by Leeds City Corporation, in 1890, to take reponsibility for its maintenance and conservation.

The ruins have, of course, attracted the attention of antiquarians and archaeologists for several centuries. In the early eighteenth century Ralph Thoresby, Leeds' most renowned antiquarian, examined floor tiles and coffins at the Abbey. During the nineteenth century the custodians of the site, employed by the owners, the earls of Cardigan, cleared rubble from various buildings and uncovered buried foundations. In the 1890s, after the purchase by Leeds City, the standing walls were consolidated, and the Abbey precincts were laid out as a public park. It was in the course of this work that various ancillary structures, including the Guest House, were located.

The first archaeological excavations were carried out for Leeds City Museum between 1950 and 1964. These, the subject of this volume, concerned principally the southern claustral ranges and the Infirmary. In 1979 the West Yorkshire Archaeology Unit excavated the main Guest House buildings, to prepare the wall foundations for consolidation, and to allow the site to be displayed more coherently to the public. Since 1981 this project has been expanded, thanks to the involvement of the Manpower Services Commission, to cover most of the Guest House precinct. During the same period the Leeds City Museum has embarked upon an important programme of structural conservation, linked to a photographic survey of the standing buildings.

The present volume is the first of a series designed to encompass not only the Unit's own excavations, but also many of the earlier investigations which are either unpublished or, as in this case, in need of fuller publication and reassessment. The publication has been made possible by the support of the Leisure Services Committee, Leeds City Council, under the chairmanship of Councillor Elizabeth Nash; of Leeds City Museums, under the direction of Peter Brears, and of the Recreation and Arts Committee, West Yorkshire Metropolitan County Council, under the chairmanship of County Councillor John M. Sully. The series as a whole will provide Kirkstall Abbey with the kind of detailed archaeological publication appropriate to such an important landmark of our medieval heritage.

ABBREVIATIONS

For abbreviated area excavation codes, see Table 1.

C	century
c.	*circa*, 'about'
Cl-	context (one, onwards)
cms	centimetres
Dl-	drain (one, onwards)
E	east
fig.	figure
figs	figures
illust.	illustrated/illustration
km.	kilometre
mm.	millimetre
N	north
no.	number
nos	numbers
p.	page
pl.	plate
pls	plates
pp.	pages
S	south
Sl-	section (one, onwards)
SF	small find
unstrat.	unstratified
vess.	vessel
W	west
Wl-	wall (one, onwards)

BIBLIOGRAPHY

Brakspear, H., 1905. *Waverley Abbey* (Guildford).

Burton, J., 1758. *Monasticon Eboracense* (York).

Crossley, D. W. (ed.), 1981. *Medieval industries*, Counc Br Archaeol Res Rep 40.

Duncan, H. B., and Wrathmell, S., forthcoming. 'Bell moulds from Kirkstall Abbey', *Hist Metallurgy*.

Dunning, G. C., 1968. 'Medieval bronze tap-handles from Lewes and Kirkstall Abbey', *Antiq J*, 48, pp. 310-11

Dunning, G. C., 1969. 'A medieval pottery roof-finial found at Portsmouth', *Proc Hampshire Field Club*, 25, pp. 95-101.

Eames, E. S., 1980. *Catalogue of medieval lead-glazed earthenware tiles* (London), 2 vols.

Gathercole, P. W., 1955. 'Excavations at Castle Hill, Thurgarton', *Archaeol Newsletter*, 5, no. 9, pp. 181-2.

Godfrey, W. H., 1952. 'English cloister lavatories as independent structures', *Archaeol J*, 106 (for 1949), supplement, pp. 91-7.

Goodall, I. H., 1981a. 'The medieval blacksmith and his products', in Crossley 1981, pp. 51-62.

Goodall, A. R., 1981b. 'The medieval bronzesmith and his products', in Crossley 1981, pp. 63-71.

Greeves, T., 1980. 'Interim report on the excavation of a tin mill on Bodmin Moor, Cornwall, in 1979', *Hist Metallurgy*, 14, pp. 104-5.

Haynes, R., 1956. 'Thirteenth century smelting residues from Kirkstall Abbey', *J Iron Steel Instit*, 183, pp. 359-61.

Hope, W. H. St. J., 1900. 'Fountains Abbey', *Yorkshire Archaeol J*, 15, pp. 269-402.

Hope, W. H. St. J, 1903. 'The London Charterhouse and its old water supply', *Archaeologia*, 58, pp. 293-312.

Hope, W. H. St. J., 1907. 'Kirkstall Abbey', in Hope, W. H. St. J., and Bilson, J., *Architectural description of Kirkstall Abbey*, Publ Thoresby Soc, 16.

Hope, W. H. St. J., and Fowler, J. J., 1903. 'Recent discoveries in the cloister of Durham Abbey', *Archaeologia*, 58, pp. 437-60.

Hunter, J. R., 1981. 'The medieval glass industry', in Crossley 1981, pp. 143-50.

Manby, T. G., 1973. 'Building materials', in H. E. J. Le Patourel, *The moated sites of Yorkshire*, Soc Medieval Archaeol Monog Ser, no. 5, pp. 83-8.

Micklethwaite, J. T., 1982. 'On a filtering cistern of the fourteenth century at Westminster Abbey', *Archaeologia*, 53, pp. 161-70.

Moorhouse, S., 1983a. 'The medieval pottery', in P. Mayes and L. A. S. Butler, *Sandal Castle excavations 1964-1973* (Wakefield), pp. 83-212.

Moorhouse, S., 1983b. 'The medieval pottery', in D. Williams, *Excavations at Gargrave (1877-1981)*, Craven Dist Counc Occas Publ (Skipton), pp. 33-48.

Moorhouse, S., 1984. 'Documentary evidence and its potential for understanding the inland movement of medieval pottery', *Medieval Ceramics*, 7, pp. 45-88.

Owen, D. E., n.d. *Kirkstall Abbey* (Leeds).

Perkins, J. B. W., 1940. *London Museum, medieval catalogue* (London).

Paiskowski, J., and Haynes, R., 1957. 'Thirteenth-century smelting residues from Kirkstall Abbey', *J Iron Steel Instit*, 185, p. 531.

Rahtz, P. A., 1979. *The Saxon and medieval palaces at Cheddar*, Brit Archaeol Rep, Brit Ser no 65 (Oxford).

Report 1. T. A. Hume and D. E. Owen, *Kirkstall Abbey excavations, first report, 1950*, Publ Thoresby Soc (1951).

Report 2. T. A. Hume and D. E. Owen, *Kirkstall Abbey excavations, second report, 1951*, Publ Thoresby Soc (1952).

Report 3. T. A. Hume and D. E. Owen, *Kirkstall Abbey excavations, third report, 1952*, Publ Thoresby Soc (1953).

Report 4. L. Alcock and D. E. Owen, *Kirkstall Abbey excavations, fourth report, 1953*, Publ Thoresby Soc (1954).

Report 5. D. E. Owen, *Kirkstall Abbey excavations, fifth report, 1954*, Publ Thoresby Soc (1955).

Report 6. C. V. Bellamy and D. E. Owen, *Kirkstall Abbey excavations, sixth report, 1955*, Publ Thoresby Soc (1956).

Report 7. D. E. Owen, *Kirkstall Abbey excavations, seventh report, 1956*, Publ Thoresby Soc (1957).

Report 8. D. E. Owen, *Kirkstall Abbey excavations, eighth report, 1957*, Publ Thoresby Soc (1958).

Report 9. C. M. Mitchell and C. V. Bellamy, *Kirkstall Abbey excavations, ninth report, 1958*, Publ Thoresby Soc (1959).

Report 10. C. V. Bellamy and C. M. Mitchell, *Kirkstall Abbey excavations, tenth report, 1959*, Publ Thoresby Soc (1960).

Report 11. E. J. E. Pirie, *Kirkstall Abbey excavations, 1960-1964*, Publ Thoresby Soc, 51, no. 112.

Rostoker, W., McNallan, M., and Gebhard, E. R., 1983. 'Melting/smelting of bronze in Isthmai', *Hist Metallurgy*, 17, pp. 23-27.

Salzman, L. F., 1967. *Building in England down to 1540: a documentary history*, 2nd ed. (Oxford).

Tylecote, R. F., 1962. *Metallurgy in archaeology* (London).

Tylecote, R. F., 1980. 'Calenick: a Corinth tin smelter, 1702 to 1891', *Hist Metallurgy*, 14, pp. 1-16.

Tylecote, R. F., 1982. 'Early copper slags and copper-base metal from the Agadez region of Niger', *Hist Metallurgy*, 16, pp. 60-64.

Watson, R., 1800. *Chemical essays*, 7th ed. (London).

Webster, J., 1671. *Metallographia*, 2nd ed. (London).

Willis, R., 1869. *Architectural history of Christ Church, Canterbury* (London).

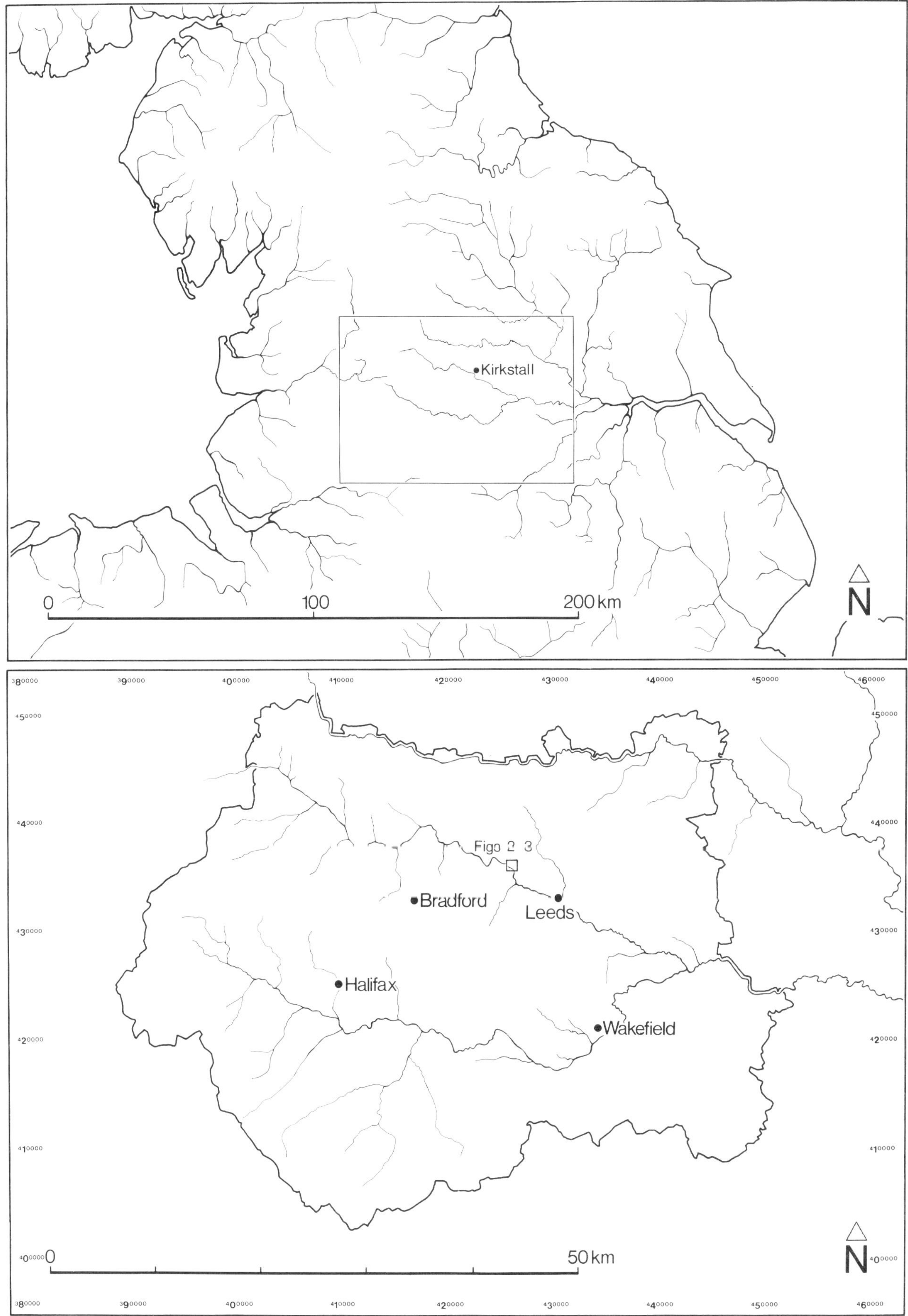

Fig. 1. Location map.

Plate 1. General view of the southern ranges of the Abbey, from the south. The buildings extend from the *Cellarium* (left) to the Abbot's Lodging (right).

Plate 2. A similar view to that in Pl. 1, published in the *Universal Magazine*, after an engraving of 1723 by Samuel Buck.

Chapter 1
Introduction

Kirkstall Abbey, a Cistercian house, lies on the north bank of the River Aire, about 5 km. (3 miles) west of the centre of Leeds (Figs 1 and 2). It was founded in the year 1152 by a group of monks from Fountains, and the primary building programme is said to have been completed before the death of the first abbot, Alexander, in 1182.[1] A substantial proportion of the late twelfth-century buildings survives, along with the well-preserved Abbot's Lodging of the thirteenth century. On the other hand, many of the structures which surrounded them had been reduced to foundation level after the Dissolution, and had become lost to view.

To the east of the claustral ranges, the Infirmary buildings were rediscovered in the later nineteenth century. To the west, the Guest House and ?Malt House (among others) were uncovered in the 1890s, when the Abbey precincts were landscaped as a public park (Figs 2 and 3). Between 1950 and 1964 the first properly conducted archaeological excavations were carried out under the auspices of Leeds City Museums. These, the subject of this present volume, revealed more buildings and yards to the south of the claustral ranges. Since 1979 the current excavations of the Guest House buildings have added further details to the picture, including stretches of two substantial roadways.

Yet there is no doubt that many more structures await discovery: the ancillary craft and agricultural buildings which should lie in the Outer Precinct, west of the Guest House; and the Lay Brothers' Infirmary, which ought to be sited south or west of their Reredorter. Other, broader

Fig. 2. The modern setting of the Abbey and its precinct.

questions have been raised, and not fully answered, by the various excavations. To what extent has the river changed its course since the twelfth century, and how much of the riverside ground was reclaimed in monastic times? How extensive were the fishponds, and how much of them was filled in before the Dissolution? Where did the main drain originate before and after the erection of the Guest House? What were the principal components of the water-supply system?

Set against these larger issues, the aim of the present volume is a modest one. It is to publish in a new format and to re-interpret the available evidence from the 1950-64 excavations. The reason for doing so is, paradoxically, in part due to the exemplary speed with which the excavations were originally published: in a series of annual reports from 1950 to 1959 (hereafter *Reports 1-10*), and in a further volume covering the years 1960-64 (*Report 11*).

The medium of the annual report gave little opportunity for drawing general conclusions, particularly when various parts of a building or yard might be excavated over a number of seasons. Though the final report includes some reconsideration of earlier work, it is primarily concerned with the results of excavation since 1960. The only general plan of excavated structures was published at a very small scale,[2] as were many of the detailed plans; and there was, for example, no attempt to provide integrated phase plans of standing and excavated structures.

A further reason for this new report is that it provides an opportunity to publish a significant quantity of evidence for the first time. New details have been added to the plans and sections from archive drawings and photographs. The published texts have been augmented by archive notes. Many artefacts are here illustrated and described for the first time, although many more objects have disappeared in the years since excavation (see Chapter 16). The surviving pottery has now been subjected to complete quantitative analysis (see Chapter 14). Moreover the significance of this newly published material has been enhanced by the experience gained in the more recent, Guest House excavations. The investigations of the 1950s and 1960s were mainly carried out

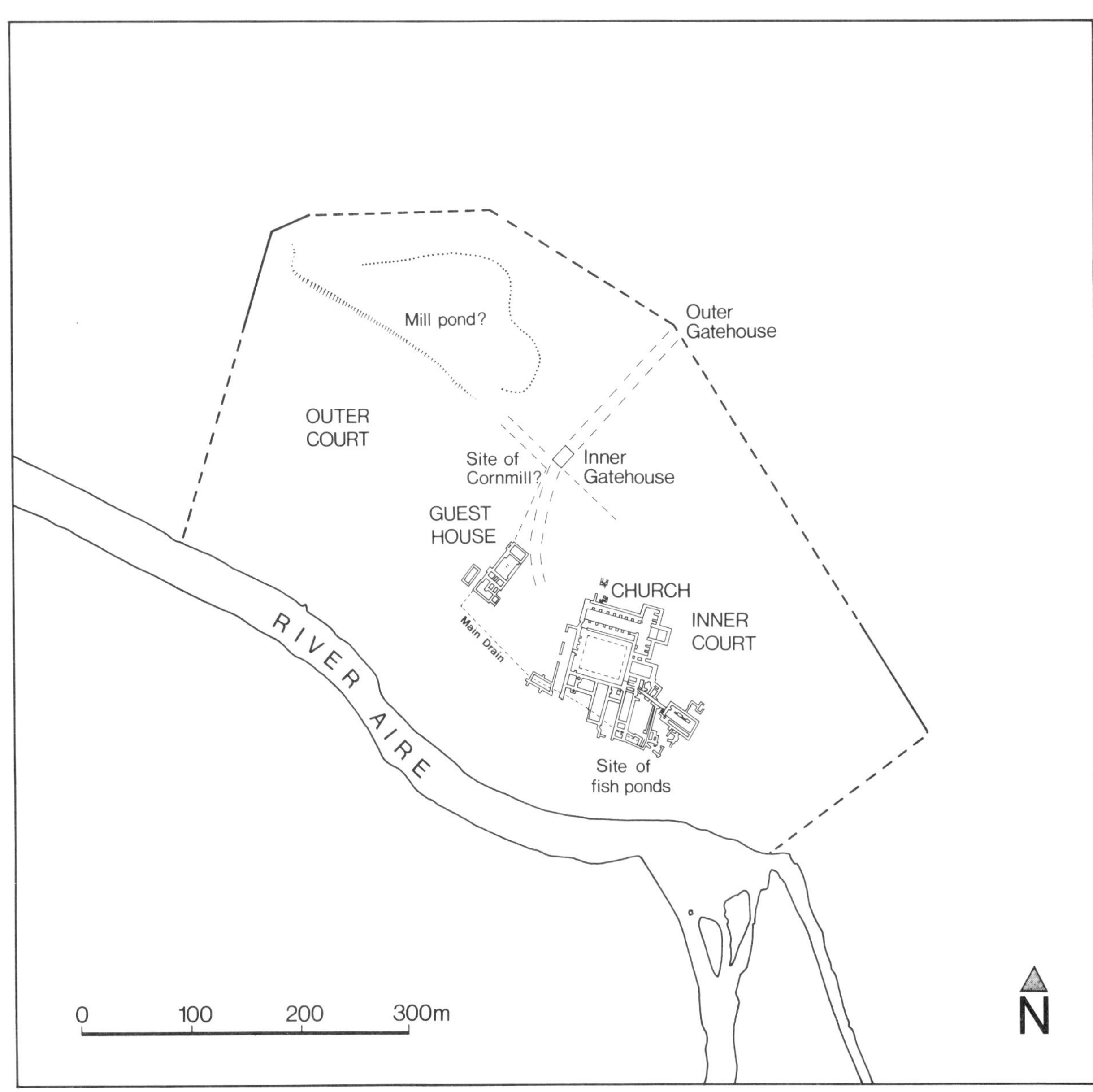

Fig. 3. Monastic structures within the precinct, covering the same areas as Fig. 2.

within the confines of small box trenches; whereas the work at the Guest House has been undertaken on a much larger scale, by open-area techniques. Where original interpretations have been radically altered through a re-valuation of evidence, this has been done with the information from the Guest House in mind.

The original aim of the excavations seems to have been to recover pottery which could be dated closely, by reference to dateable architectural features.[3] As work progressed, new structures were discovered, and new objectives emerged. In the later seasons much effort was expended in tracing parts of the drainage system. The somewhat piecemeal development of the work was inevitably reflected in the annual reports; but the information has now been regrouped into building units (Fig. 4).

It will be clear from Appendices A and B that the survival of original site records is very uneven. Nevertheless, a full discussion has been attempted for all areas except the sub-Dorter, and for all materials except the metal-working debris, the animal remains and the floor tiles. The sub-Dorter excavations apparently revealed no medieval features.[4] The metal slags and animal bones were fully treated in the original

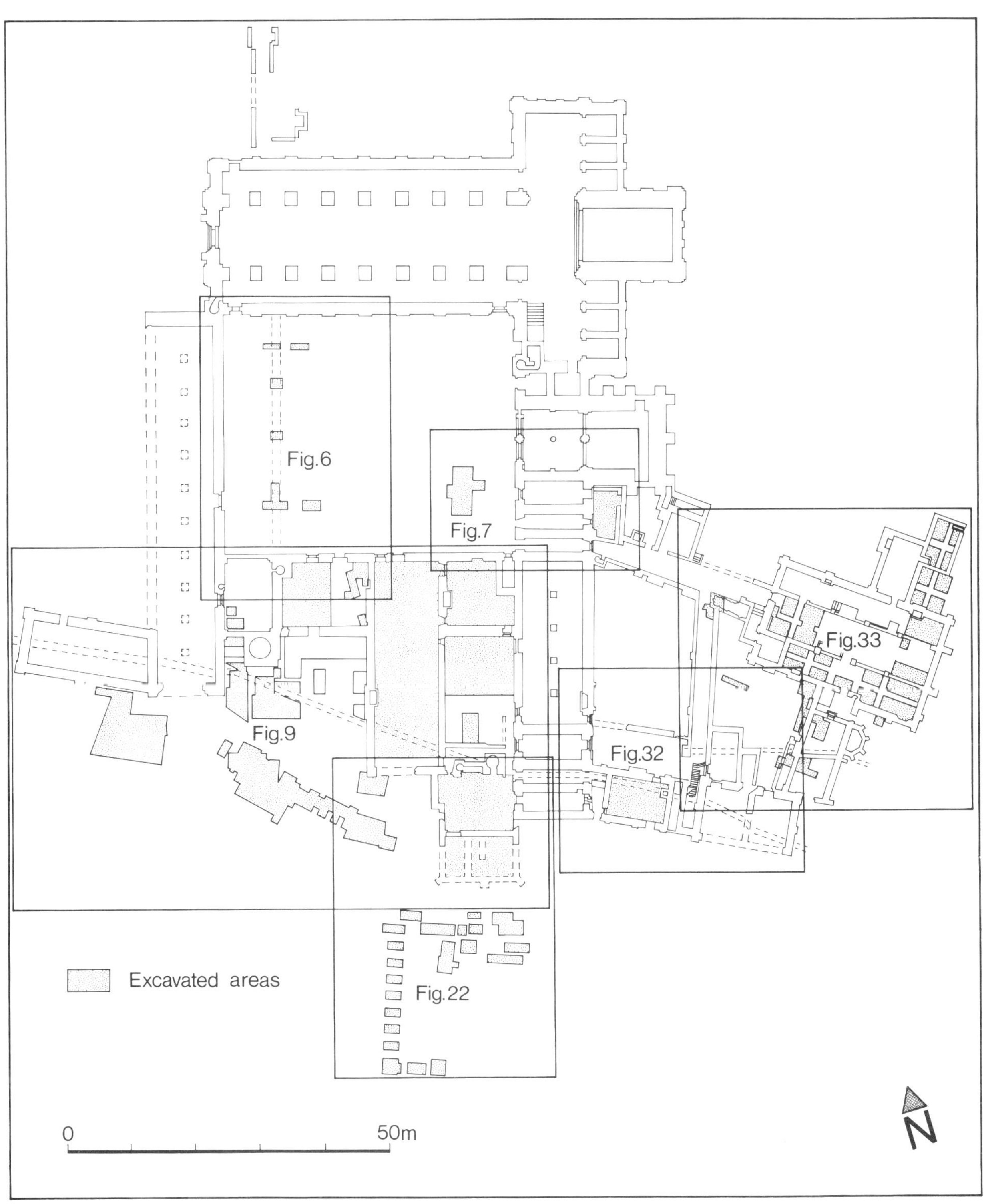

Fig. 4. Location of excavated areas.

reports, and the material no longer survives. The evidence is summarised briefly here (Chapters 17 and 18).

The floor tiles have been omitted for a different reason. The principal find of inlaid tiles *in situ* was in the fifteenth-century Misericord,[5] but the floor in question contained parts of a mosaic tile floor which had originally been laid elsewhere in the Abbey. Many other tiles are known to have been found during the building conservation programme of the 1890s, and some were relaid in the Abbey Church. Other tiles were dumped on the Guest House site during the contemporary park landscaping, and these have been recovered in recent excavations. It seems, on balance, best to reserve discussion of floor tiles to a later volume, when the whole Abbey assemblage can be treated as a single body of material.

A final point concerns the detailed area plans which appear in this volume. These usually show the relationships of excavation trenches and standing buildings, and in such matters as in others, they follow the original site and publication plans. Yet there are undoubtedly inaccuracies in the location of trenches, and in the location of doors, windows and other features occurring in the surviving masonry. The reason is that the excavations were not accompanied by a large-scale survey of adjacent standing walls. The only ground-plan available then, and now, is the 'historical' plan, at a scale of 1:300, published in 1907 by Sir William St. John Hope.

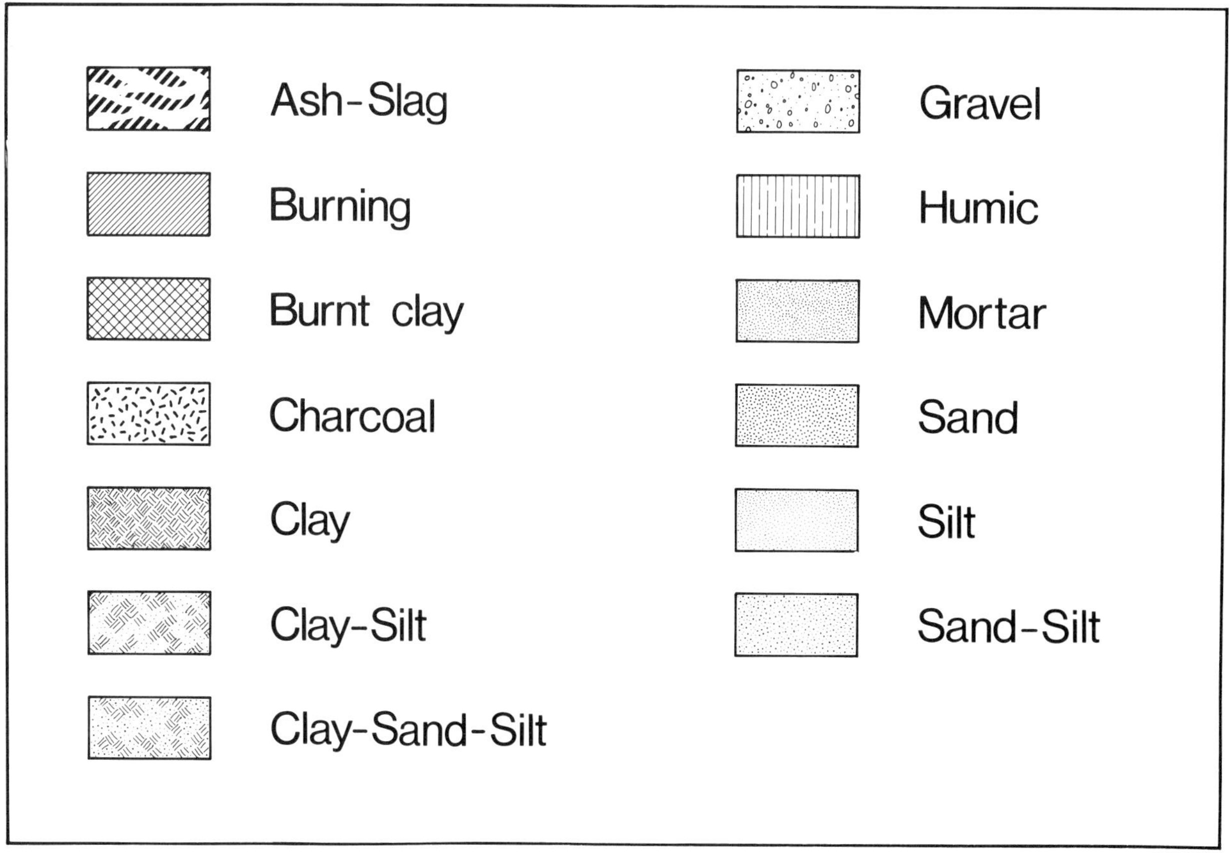

Fig. 5. Drawing conventions for plans and sections (Figs 6-36).

PART ONE

THE EXCAVATED STRUCTURES

by Stuart Wrathmell

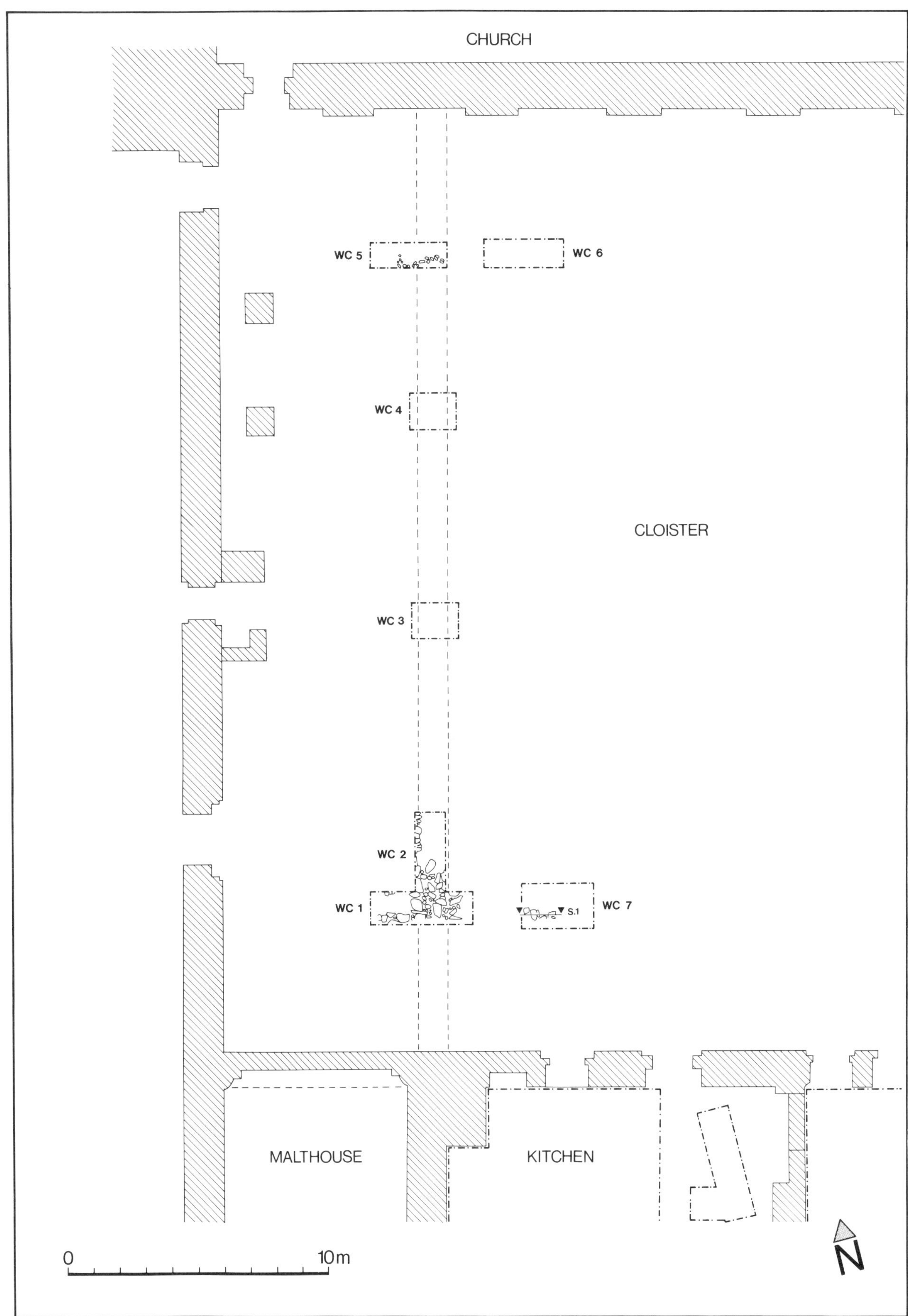

Fig. 6. Plan of Cloister Lane structures. For section see Fig. 8.

Chapter 2
The Cloister Lane

An open space about 8 metres wide, running along the east side of the *Cellarium*, was walled off from the rest of the Cloister area. It formed the Cloister Lane, a feature included in the plans of some, but not all Cistercian houses. The dividing wall had been completely demolished, but its former junctions with the Church on the north, and with the Kitchen on the south, were noted by St. John Hope.[6] He was also able to identify this wall as a primary monastic feature, and to ascribe its demolition to the late fifteenth century. In 1963 a series of five trenches was excavated along the assumed line of the wall; and two others, to the east, were intended to locate the north and south Cloister arcades.[7] The trenches were numbered WC1 to WC7. Original plans and section drawings survive.

The results of these investigations were not spectacular (Fig. 6). Trench WC1 revealed the rubble foundation of the demolished wall and, on the west side only, a course of dressed, mortared masonry belonging to an east to west wall. Its alignment (but not its character) matched that of a further length of masonry in WC7 (Fig. 8, S1). It has been interpreted as the footing for the extended Cloister arcade, laid after the Lane wall had been demolished.

Further north the remains of the Lane wall were even more depleted; but amongst the debris in WC2 was a coin weight dated to between 1464 and 1471 (SF 407). Trench WC6, placed on the assumed line of the north Cloister arcade, produced no features at all.

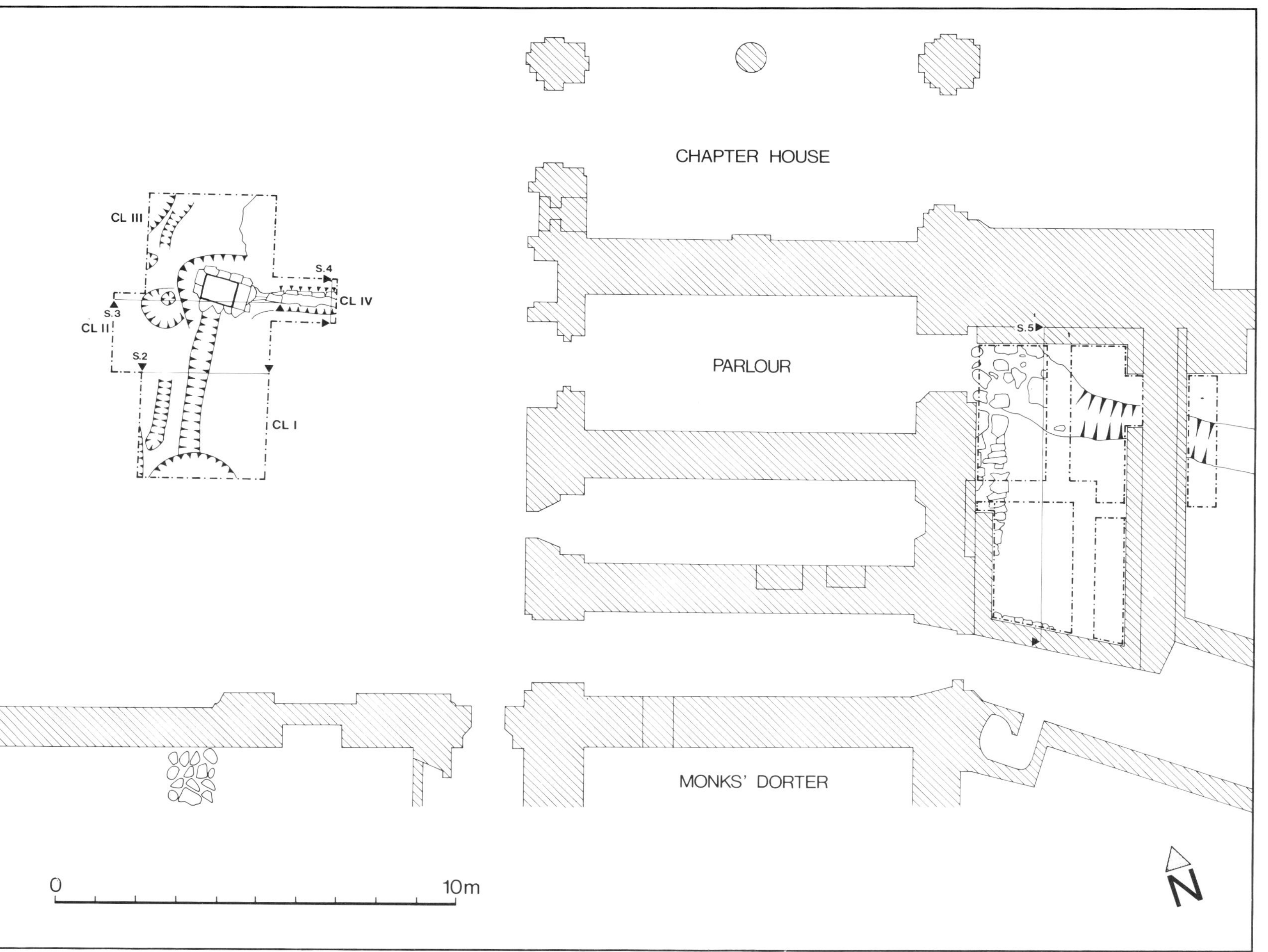

Fig. 7. Plan of Cloister cistern and East Room. For sections see Fig. 8.

Chapter 3
The Cloister Cistern

Introduction

In 1953 an attempt was made to trace the 'rubble foundation' which crossed the Warming House northwards into the Cloister area (Chapter 5, p.14). Ultimately four contiguous trenches, numbered CL I to CL IV were excavated. They revealed a cistern with an inlet conduit running from the east, and an outlet conduit extending south towards the Warming House. These features cut the remains of a metal-working site. Archive plans, sections and notes survive, and have been used to amplify the earlier, published description. In particular, the pre-cistern features omitted from the previously published plan[8] are now illustrated (Fig. 7). The general stratigraphic sequence in these trenches was, in chronological order: natural clay; charcoal, burnt clay and metal-working features of the primary construction phase; the twelfth-century cistern and conduits; a layer of yellow clay containing late medieval pottery, and patches of cobbles set in the surface of this clay (Fig. 8, S2-S4).

First phase

The metal-working phase of activity was marked by a spread of charcoal (C3), lying mainly to the north and west of the conduits. It contained a large quantity of iron slag, and was thought to be consistent with bloomery operations.[9] The charcoal filled a north to south gully in the surface of natural, and overlay patches of burnt clay. Immediately west of the cistern was a hollow, which cut through the charcoal and had itself been cut by the cistern foundation trench. Above its surviving east end was the start of another layer of charcoal. The fill of the depression, oversimplified on the only available section (Fig. 8, S3), contained burnt stones and baked clay. It is not clear whether the sides and bottom of the hollow were themselves burnt; but in general the evidence points to the hollow having been associated with the metal-working phase. A smaller, deeper hole had been cut through the hollow, packed with cobbles and capped with a large stone. This, too, may have been a metal-working feature.

Second phase

The foundation trench of the cistern cut the depression and the secondary charcoal layer. The cistern itself measured internally 1.1 metres by 0.9 metres, and was 2.8 metres deep. It was lined with dressed masonry, and was provided with a step-like projection on the east (Pl. 3). The inlet conduit entered the cistern on the same side: though there was no clear opening in the cistern lining, the depth of the channel indicated that it would have emerged just above or beneath the step. The conduit was set in a trench. It comprised side-stones set on edge, tilted inwards towards the top and capped by smaller flags (Fig. 8, S4). The outlet conduit was of very similar form (Fig. 8, S2; Pl. 4). It began with a funnel-shaped hole in the south side lining of the conduit, about 0.3 metres above the level of the inlet. It cut through the charcoal and extended south as far as a large, deep intrusion, circular or semi-circular in plan, with vertical sides and a loose rubble and earth filling (Pl. 5). A piece of lead gutter or sink fitting (SF 250) was found in this area. Both conduits, and the cistern construction trench, were sealed by yellow clay (C 2A) which contained late medieval pottery. The clay did not, however, cross the cistern fill: it ended immediately behind the lining stones. This implies that the cistern continued in use during the last half century of the Abbey's existence, an implication confirmed by the pottery from its fill (pp. 78, 100).

Plate 3. The Cloister cistern, from the west, showing the step and possible inlet hole.

Plate 4. The Cloister cistern from the south-west, showing the stones of the outlet conduit, from the north-west.

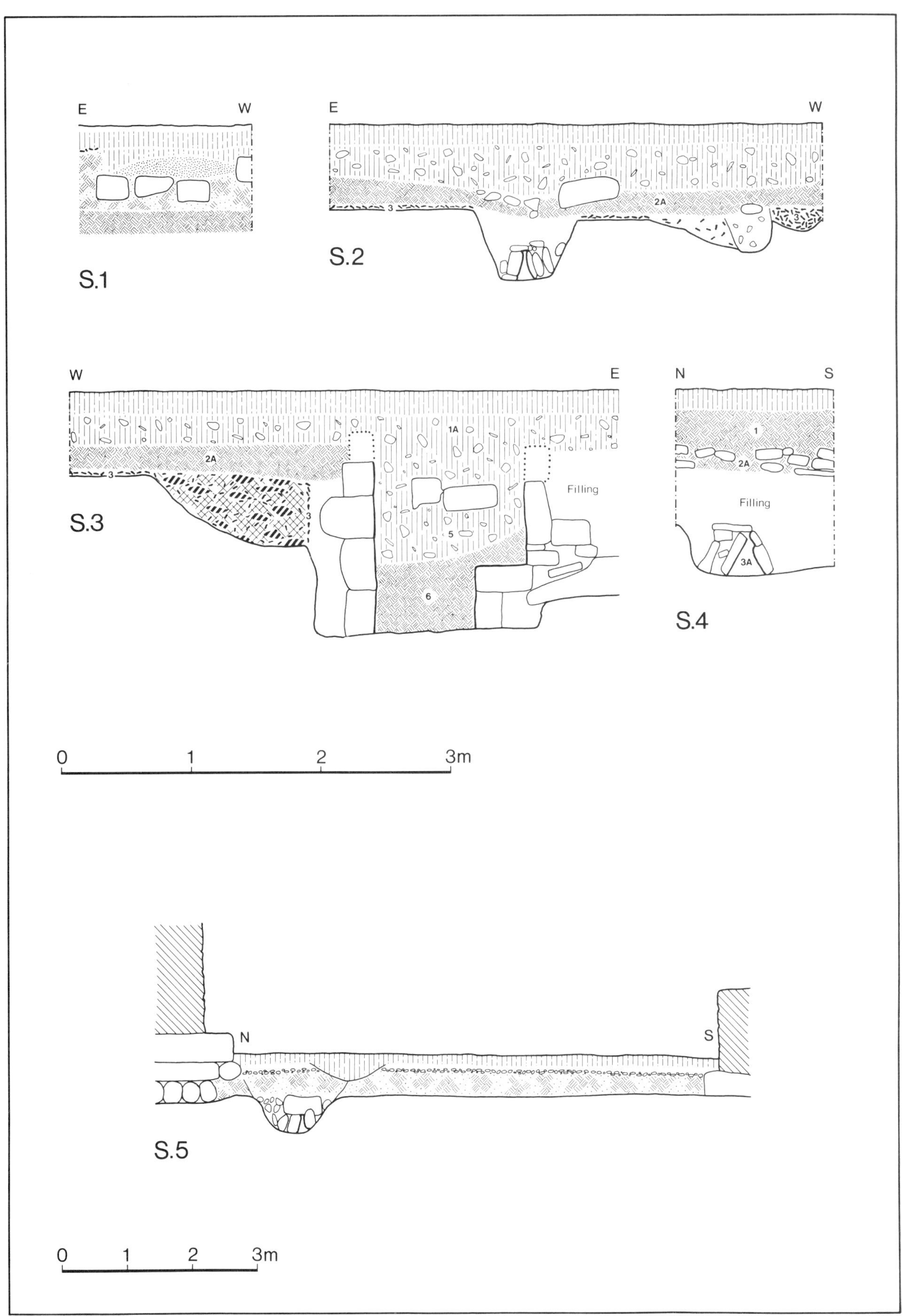

Fig. 8. Cloister and East Room: sections.

The remaining questions about the cistern - the date of its construction and its precise function in the Abbey water-supply system - are less easy to answer. It has previously been supposed that the conduits were simply stone-lined channels; and that the outlet channel had continued beneath the Cloister alley (now a tarmac path) to link with the rubble-filled trench which ran beneath the Warming House and pre-dated its twelfth-century north and south walls. There are reasons for disputing both these suppositions. In the first place, the depth of the inlet - 0.3 metres below the outlet - indicates that water was brought to the cistern under pressure, in a pipe; and that the triangular arrangement of side and cap stones was used to protect the pipe from disturbance. The outlet conduit, having a similar arrangement of stones, may well also have housed a pipe. Secondly, although the outlet conduit has been described as similar in form to the Warming House feature,[10] it does not seem from the photographs to have had anything other than a very general resemblance to it. The Warming House trench was much wider, and was packed with pitched stones (Pl. 6); and if it was used in this form as a 'drain', it can only have been a soakaway, designed to disperse excess water in a particular direction, rather than to convey water - either fresh or foul - from one point to another. The possible functions of the Warming House trench are discussed in Chapter 5.

The final pieces of evidence which have a bearing on these questions are the alignment of the cistern and the intrusion at the south end of CL I. The cistern and its conduits follow a near-rectangular alignment, but the whole complex is set obliquely to the axis of the Cloister. It seems unlikely that such a discrepancy was accidental; rather, that it was conditioned by the position of some other feature in the water supply system. A possible candidate is the deep pit at the south end of the outlet conduit. This was thought to have been a disturbance caused by digging out a tree;[11] but it may instead have been a circular cistern or well which was robbed out in recent times.

If the outlet conduit and the Warming House trench are not, in fact, two parts of the same feature, then the dating of the cistern must be reassessed; for its attribution to the primary building work depended partly upon the fact that the Warming House trench and its rubble fill ran beneath the original wall foundations in the south claustral range. The one remaining link between the cistern and datable structures is provided by the inlet conduit. If, as is probable but not certain, the trench in the East Room is a continuation of the inlet line (Chapter 4), then the water supply and therefore the cistern can still be regarded as primary features, since the East Room trench passes beneath the Dorter range foundations.

Plate 5. The pit (?cistern or ?well) at the south end of the Cloister cistern outlet conduit, from the north-west.

Chapter 4
The East Room

The 1954 season witnessed the excavation of a room on the east side of the east claustral range, fronting the Parlour and the early Dorter stairs (Fig. 7). It was built in the angle between the Parlour and the thirteenth-century Chapter House extension. On the south it cut into the north side of the corridor leading from the Cloister to the Infirmary. The room has been dated by St. John Hope to the fourteenth century.[12] As well as the published account,[13] a number of original section drawings, plans and notes survives.

The earliest remains comprised a trench running east to west beneath the floor. It was about 1 metre wide. Where it crossed the east half of the room and extended beyond the room to the east, it was filled with clay and charcoal. Further west, however, it contained large stones, set on edge and capped with flags, surrounded by smaller stones (Fig. 8, S5). It passed beneath the offset foundation course of the east range wall, and can be dated thereby to the primary, twelfth-century construction period, or to an earlier time. There is, in fact, little reason to doubt that the feature is a continuation of the inlet conduit for the Cloister cistern (Chapter 3). Though the published description is not entirely clear, the archive section drawing of the trench indicates a form of conduit closely comparable to that of the cistern inlet (Fig. 8, S4, S5). In addition, the trench was said to contain 'rubbery' clay, probably puddled clay used to seal the robbed pipe. The absence of stonework in the eastern part of the trench may indicate that the pipe was provided with a solid conduit only where it ran beneath and in the vicinity of contemporary buildings.

At the south-east corner a small area of rubble projected into the room, apparently from beneath the south end of the east wall. It is thought to have been part of the foundation of the stretch of north corridor wall demolished when the room was built.

The earliest flooring of the room was marked by a layer of pebbles in the surface of brown clay, itself presumably the former soil horizon. The pebbles extended over the whole room, and continued beneath the stone benches which were set on all four sides. The benches were associated with a secondary flooring of mortar, on a thin clay base which survived only in patches but which ran up to the sides of the benches. A piece of Cistercian ware[14] was apparently found beneath the south end of the west side bench, and indicates that both the benches and the mortar flooring can be dated to the last century of monastic occupation. However, the pottery from this room cannot now be identified amongst the surviving assemblage.

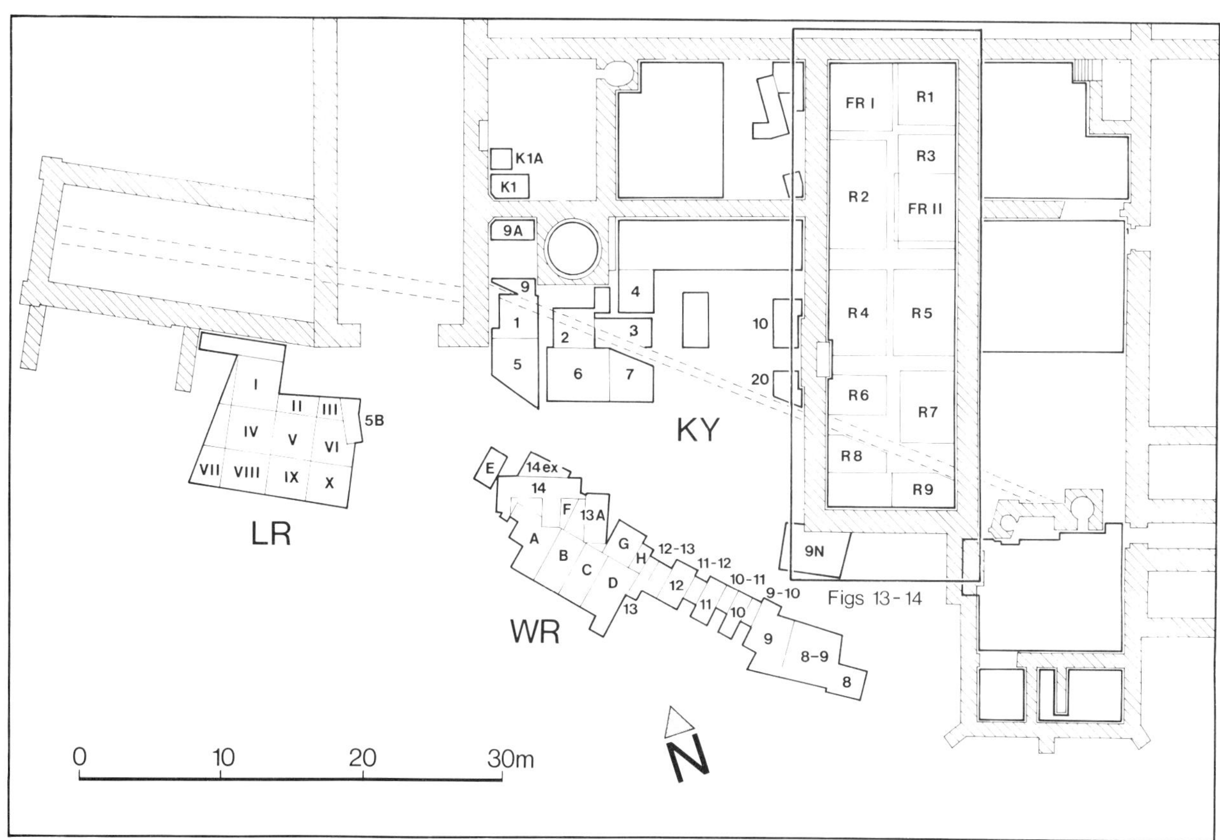

Fig. 9. South of Cloister: key to excavation area codes.

Chapter 5
The Warming House and Warming House Courtyard

Introduction

In 1952 excavations took place in the Warming House, at the east end of the south cloister range.[15] The room originally measured 9 metres by 6 metres, and occupied the space between the earliest, east to west Refectory, and the Dorter range (Figs 10 and 29). The reorientation of the Refectory in the thirteenth century allowed the Warming House to be expanded westwards, to about double its initial size. Its original west wall was demolished to foundation level, and its Cloister entrance was moved from the east end of the north wall to a point further west.[16] This transfer was probably made in order to insert in the original entrance position a new opening, with a higher, two-centred arch, to give access to a new flight of stairs to the dormitory. The linking of these two events - the repositioning of the Warming House entrance and the erection of the new Dorter stairs - resolves neatly a conflict of evidence recorded by St. John Hope.[17] It has been made possible by the new, early thirteenth-century dating for the reorientation of the Refectory (Chapter 6).

In the fifteenth century there was a further phase of rebuilding. The Cloister archway to the Dorter stairs was reduced to a doorway, and the lower stairs were turned west to give access directly to the Warming House.[18] At the same time, the floor area beneath the staircase was partitioned off by a new wall, effectively reducing the size of the Warming House by a significant amount. Other than the photographs and two section drawings, no original records of the excavation have survived.

South of the Warming House was a courtyard, defined as a distinct space when the thirteenth-century Refectory was built. There were traces of a fifteenth-century pentice in its

Plate 6. Warming House: rubble-filled trench, from the south, with possible westward extension just beyond the baulk. The late medieval fireplace, overlying the charcoal layer of its predecessor, is on the left.

north-east corner, overlying a water cistern. Most of the excavation took place in 1951;[19] but the water cistern was later re-excavated,[20] and subsequently reinterpreted.[21]

First phase

The earliest feature within the Warming House (or more correctly, in the east end of the primary Refectory) was a rubble-filled trench which ran from north to south across the room (Fig. 10; Pl. 6). The trench was cut through clayey loam (C8), into natural clay. It passed beneath both the north and south walls of the room, and can therefore be identified as the primary feature in this part of the Abbey. Southwards, it extended across the Warming House courtyard, where a stretch of it had been removed by later disturbance. It ran as far as the main drain, where its course was cut by the main drain lining. It followed a slightly sinuous course, and there was a distinct change in line about 2 metres from the north wall. At that point, both the published plan[22] and the archive photographs (Pl. 6) hint at a junction with a similar rubble-filled trench running west, at right-angles. If the westerly line of rubble extended through the Refectory, it may have been represented by the early rubble feature discovered in the north-west corner of that building.[23]

As to the function of this feature, there are several possibilities. In the first place, it may have been a pre-monastic ditch, of the kind more recently discovered in the Guest House area, which was packed with rubble to avoid subsidence when the claustral buildings were erected. Secondly, it may have been a temporary drainage gully, used during the primary work of construction before the permanent drainage system was operative. Again, the rubble in this case would mark its disuse. Thirdly, it may have been an enclosure wall foundation, of a period before the present claustral layout. The character of the pitched rubble, with small stones packed in the gaps, is readily paralleled in the foundations of the Guest House West Hall. Finally, and as suggested in previous reports, it may have been some form of

Plate 7. Warming House Courtyard: continuation of rubble-filled trench shown on Pl. 6, from the south.

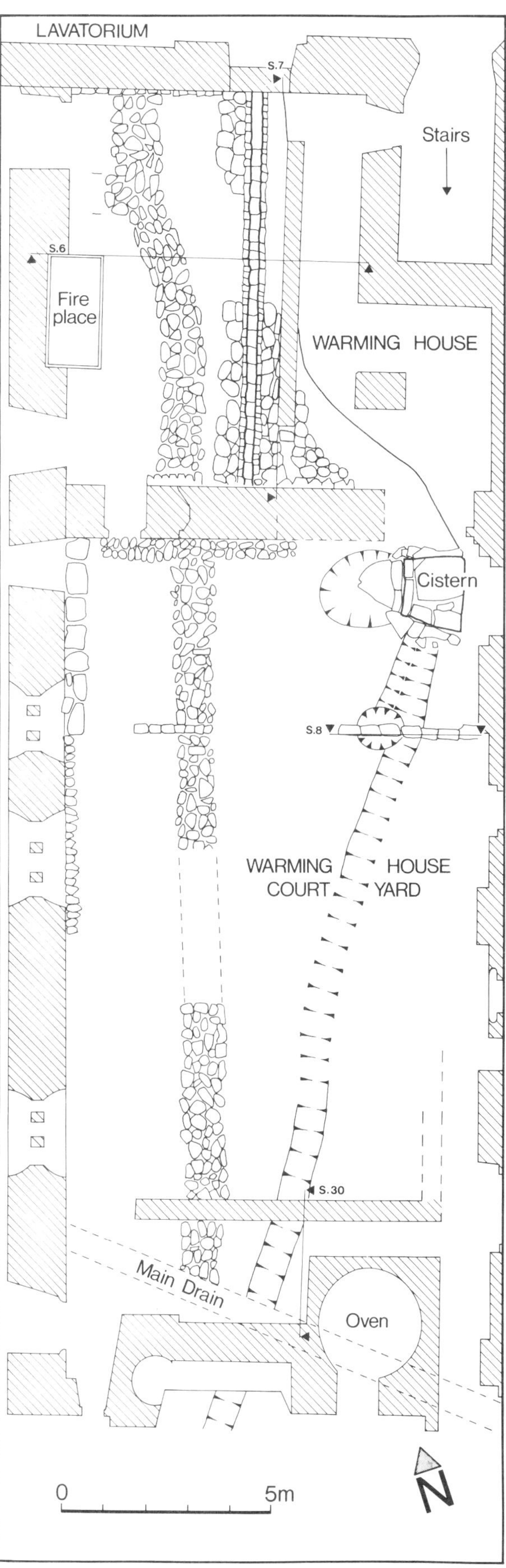

Fig. 10. Plan of Warming House and Courtyard. For sections see Figs 11, 12.

soakaway to rid the Cloister area of surface water, or of excess water derived from the supply system. The photographs (Pls 6 and 7), if not the section drawings (Fig. 11, S6) point most strongly to a pitched rubble foundation.

Two other areas of rubble to the east undoubtedly mark the original line of the Refectory — Warming House partition. Their west edges were in line, and they conformed precisely to the position of the partition wall which St. John Hope adduced on the basis of the surviving structure. The gap between these stretches of foundation may have been an original feature. The southern area of rubble was far more extensive than would have been needed for a wall alone. Originally, it was probably a rectangular base, occupying the south-west corner of the Warming House; but its north-east corner had been disturbed by a water-pipe trench (Fig. 11, S7). It may have been the fireplace foundation.

Second phase

The pipe trench which disturbed the first-phase foundations was part of a water-supply system which extended from the Cloister to the area south of the Meat Kitchen. To the north the pipe (SFs 322, 323, 326) probably originated at a cistern which served the thirteenth-century Lavatory basins. It was traced from a point beneath the early thirteenth-century Warming House doorway, when it curved through the Warming House to its south-east corner. It cut through part of the first-phase rubble foundation and took a course to avoid the supports of the thirteenth-century Dorter stairs. It passed beneath the threshold of the twelfth-century doorway in the south wall of the Warming House, and disturbed the foundations there. The pipe-line is indisputedly linked to the second phase of construction. The claim in a previous report,[24] that the pipe was a primary monastic feature, can be discounted. The pipe itself, set in the bottom of a deep, V-shaped trench, was encased in puddled yellow clay, and dropped about 0.4 metres in level along its course southwards (Fig. 11, S6). The trench backfill contained both iron and lead slag (Chapter 17),[25] and had been disturbed by a secondary cut of unknown purpose.

The south end of the pipe fed a cistern which was located in the north-east corner of the Warming House courtyard. The cistern was sited immediately in front of the sub-Dorter doorway: the boulder clay had been cut back vertically against the entrance to accommodate it. Like the Cloister cistern, the structure was lined with stone and had a flagged floor. It had been provided with steps on its west side (Pl. 8). It measured about 1.7 metres by 1.5 metres, and its floor was about 2 metres below the present ground level. Only the bottom six courses of stonework remained, and the partly robbed structure had been filled with a succession of earth, charcoal and clay layers. Their deposition seems to have occurred at a late period: fifteenth-century pottery was recovered from all levels, and a coin of *c.* 1424 is said to have been found in the lower fill.[26] Unless the coin was intrusive, its association with some near complete pottery vessels of Type 7 (Northern Gritty Ware) is an important one, since it extends the currency of the type into the fifteenth century.

The inlet pipe entered the cistern at its north-east corner, close to the floor. An outlet was sited in the south-west corner, apparently also at floor level. It fed a stone-lined conduit, 120mm. wide (D1), which extended south-west across the courtyard area (Fig. 12, S8). The conduit ran beneath the Warming House pentice, beneath the Meat Kitchen and under the main drain. It was obviously intended to provide fresh water to a point further south, and its precise function is considered below (Chapter 9, p. 36).

Two other possible channels may have been linked to the cistern. One of these extended between the cistern and a 'sump', or robbed-out feature located about 3 metres west of the Dorter range, beneath the surface drain associated with the Warming House court pentice (Fig. 12, S8).[27] A second channel may have run east through the sub-Dorter doorway, for the archive photographs (Pl. 9) seem to show the cross-section of a trench with a distinct fill immediately behind the robbed east lining of the cistern. The published account does not, however, refer to such a feature.

Within the Warming House, the pipe trench for this water supply was sealed (along with the earlier features) by a mortar surface (C6) which extended across the whole of the room, and which marks the completion of the second-phase alterations. The surface was based partly on sandy make-up (C7), and was itself probably the base for a tiled floor. It was on a level with the tops of both the twelfth- and thirteenth-century wall foundations, and it skimmed the surface of the footings of the demolished west wall. The flooring ran

Plate 8. Warming House Courtyard cistern, from the east, showing steps.

Plate 9. Warming House Courtyard cistern, from the south-west showing the fill of the inlet conduit on the left section, and a possible outlet conduit trench on the right.

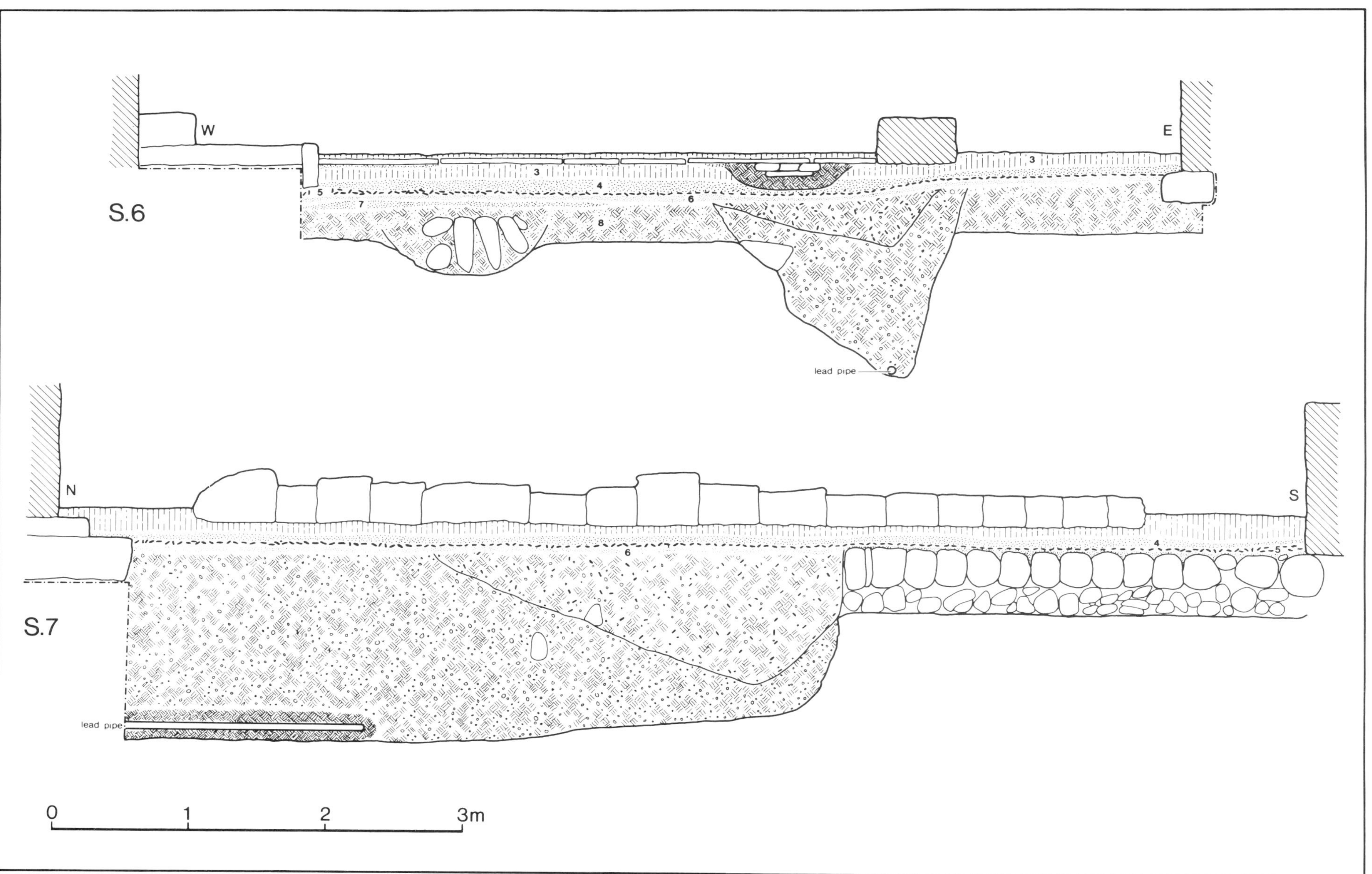

Fig. 11. Warming House: sections.

beneath the third-phase fireplace in the new west wall, as did an extensive spread of charcoal (C5). There were signs that an area of tiles, set in burnt clay, also underlay the fireplace:[28] these probably represented the second-phase hearth in the same position.

Third phase

The final alterations to the Warming House were made in the fifteenth century, and involved a reduction in the size of the room. The existing mortar floor was covered by sand, soil and clay (C2-C4), forming the base of a new flagged floor (C1) which survived largely intact. A new north to south wall was set in the clay and soil, to create a room beneath the Dorter stairs. The surviving fireplace was built against the west wall, probably on the site of its predecessor (Pl. 6). On the east side of the Warming House, and running parallel to the new east wall, a small stone-lined channel was constructed beneath the pavement (Pl. 10). It is said to have originated at a stone trough,[29] set in the blocked north doorway of the second phase; but it was probably a conduit or drain linked to the Cloister Lavatory system. It ran through a hole chiseled out of the south wall, and extended across the northern part of the courtyard. The excavated dating evidence of this phase conforms with that adduced from architectural features. In the make-up layer beneath the channel was a coin of *c.* 1420 (SF 394);[30] and a coin dated *c.* 1470 was found in the channel itself, sealed by the flagging (SF 396).[31]

The cistern in the courtyard was probably disused and backfilled at the same time. Its topmost filling was gravel flooring material,[32] probably a part of the floor belonging to a pentice which was erected in the north-east part of the courtyard. The roof line of the pentice is visible in the Dorter range wall, but there is no similar evidence in the Refectory wall. On the west the gravel flooring was, indeed, confined to the east side of the Warming House channel; and on the south it was delimited by an east to west surface drain.

Plate 10. Warming House: remains of fifteenth-century flagged floor and drain from the south.

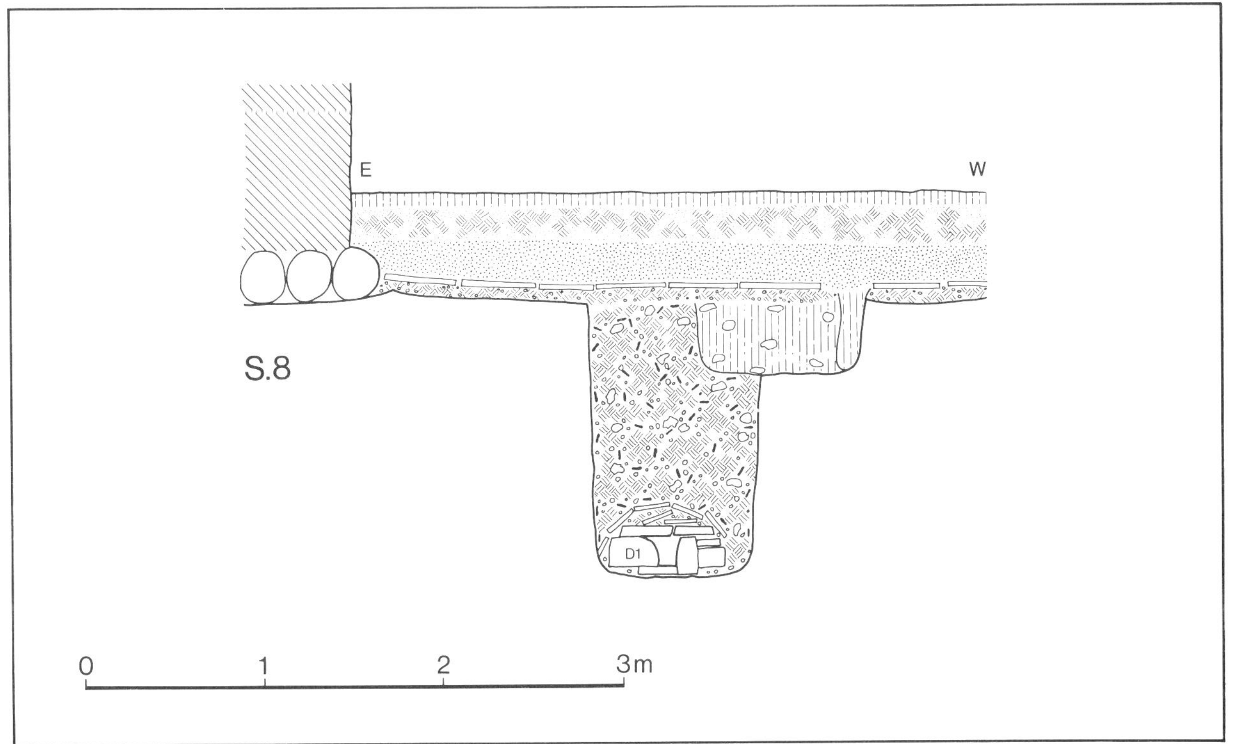

Fig. 12. Warming House Courtyard: sections.

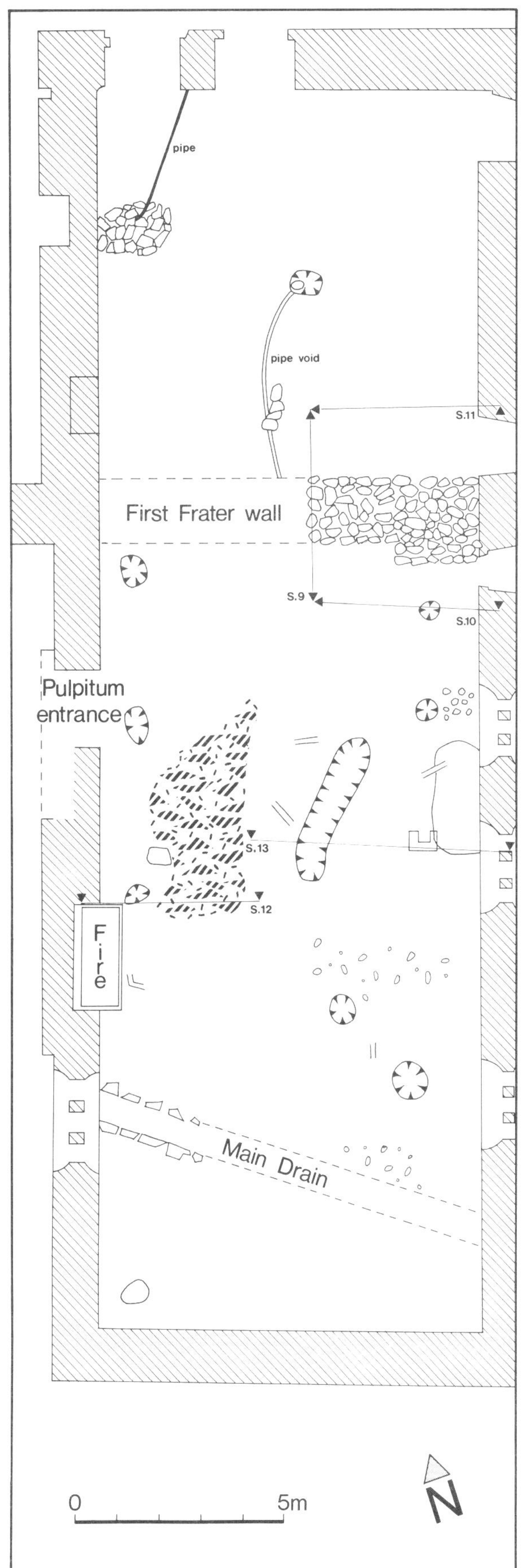

Fig. 13. Plan of features beneath tiled floor in the Refectory, located on Fig. 9. For sections see Fig. 15.

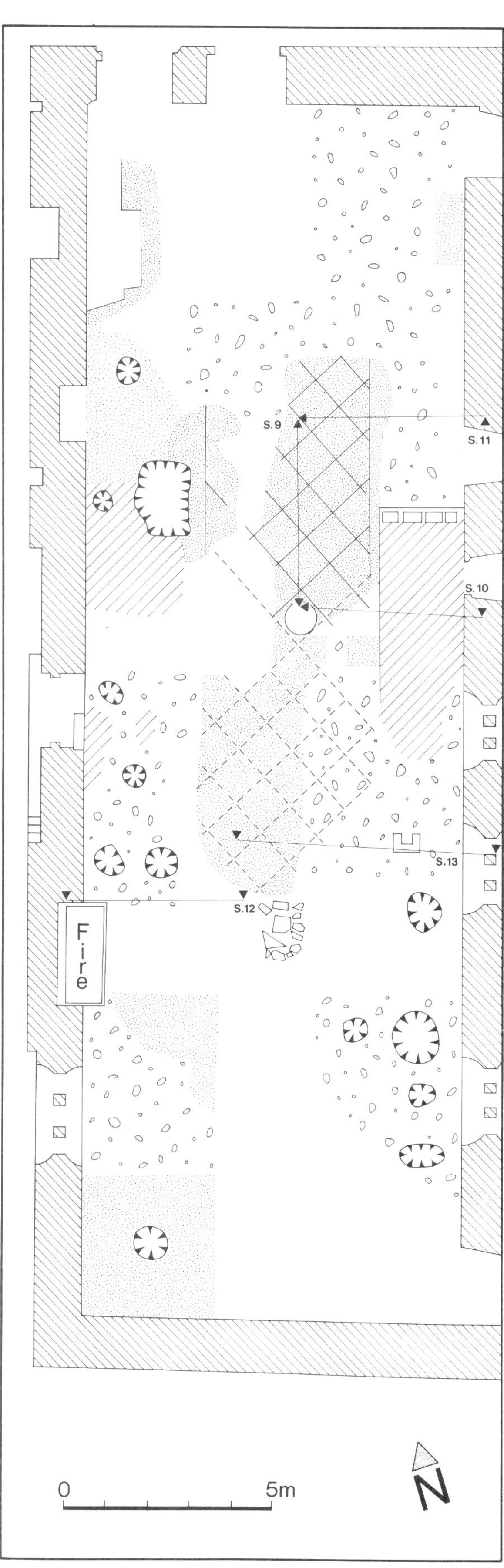

Fig. 14. Plan of tiled floor and later features in the Refectory, located on Fig. 9. For sections see Fig. 15.

Chapter 6
The Refectory

Introduction

The monastic dining hall, the Frater or Refectory, was originally aligned east to west in the centre of the southern claustral range, and measured 21.3 metres by 9.4 metres internally. In the early thirteenth century, however, it was rebuilt on a north-south axis, to a length of over 30 metres (Fig. 13). This enlargement and change in orientation is a development also seen at other Cistercian houses.[33] Further modifications took place in the fifteenth century. They are seen to have resulted from a relaxation of the rule prohibiting the eating of meat. The Refectory was converted into a two-storey building: the ground floor became the Misericord, a hall where meat could be eaten, and the Refectory itself was moved to the first floor.

In 1953 two trenches were excavated in the Refectory area, FRI and FRII (Fig. 9). The second of these was cut across the presumed south wall line of the original, east-west dining hall. They were followed two years later by more extensive operations, a grid of trenches encompassing the whole area enclosed by the extant walls of the second-phase Refectory (R1 to R9). Results were published in *Report 4,* pp. 56-60, and *Report 6,* pp. 1-11. None of the original 1953 records has survived, but three note books of 1955 describe trenches R1 to R8. The only available plan of the whole area is that published as *Report 6,* fig. 1. It appears from the records that some trenches were taken down to the natural clay, or at least to the pre-Refectory ground surface. Others were not; or if they were, the records have not survived. The original layout of the grid areas provided for a central baulk running on the axis of the building. Before the end of operations several stretches of this baulk and some of the transverse ones had been removed.

The observed architectural sequence indicates that excavated features should be grouped into three phases: those belonging to the original east-west Refectory and to the external area on its south side; those which represent primary occupation of the rebuilt, north-south Refectory, and those related to the fifteenth-century alterations. In practice, the method of site recording has necessitated only two plans: one indicating features sealed by the fifteenth-century flooring; and the other showing the flooring itself and features cut into it (Figs 13 and 14).

Refectory Phase 1

The principal remains of the first Refectory comprised the rubble foundation of the demolished south wall (Pl. 11). Only the eastern half was planned (in outline), although at least part of the western half seems to have been uncovered. It was set in a shallow trench cut down to the natural boulder clay (Fig. 15, S9). An external expansion of the foundation at its east end may mark the position of the original *pulpitum.* On the north side of the foundation there was no sign of the primary Refectory floor; but a layer of clayey loam (C3) containing bands of sand and mortar, had been dumped to a height level with the top of the surviving foundation (Fig. 15, S9), and this was interpreted as primary floor make-up. A discontinuity in the strata immediately above foundation level was seen to mark the position of the floor itself.[34] The presence of late medieval pottery in FR I, C3, is presumably due to the disturbance caused when the wall laver was removed (see below, p. 22).

The relationship of these make-up layers to the successive builds of the Refectory is fundamental to the interpretation of this site. The material defined as original make-up in 1953 was thought in 1955 to contain two sand and mortar floors,[35] one of them belonging to the second-phase Refectory. The available evidence of relationships nevertheless points to the 1953 interpretation as being the correct one. To the south of the original building, all the make-up layers, including the lowest sand and mortar band, lapped over the rubble footings of the new Refectory east wall (e.g. Fig. 15, S12 and S13). Further north, within the area of the original building, the foundation of the new east wall was set in a trench which cut through all the surviving make-up layers (Fig. 15, S11).

This conclusion provides the first Refectory with one internal feature: a void running beneath the make-up layers, which marked the former position of a north-south lead water-pipe. Its south end abutted the original south wall foundation. Its north end emerged vertically through a hole which appears to have been cut into the clay make-up, and which presumably signifies the point at which the pipe was pulled out. It is possible that, during its period of use, the pipe rose up from the floor at this point, to connect with a free-standing laver or cistern. There is no recorded evidence of its continuation northward or of any connecting pipe-line.

To the south of the primary building a number of features can be ascribed to the first phase, sealed beneath the floor make-up of the second-phase Refectory. On the east side a patch of burnt clay with charcoal and calcined bones (C10) was found to be cut by the Refectory wall (Fig. 15, S13). To

Plate 11. Refectory: the foundation of the primary south wall, from the west, seen disappearing beneath the east wall of the second-phase Refectory. The enlargement in the external face of the foundation may indicate the site of the *Pulpitum.*

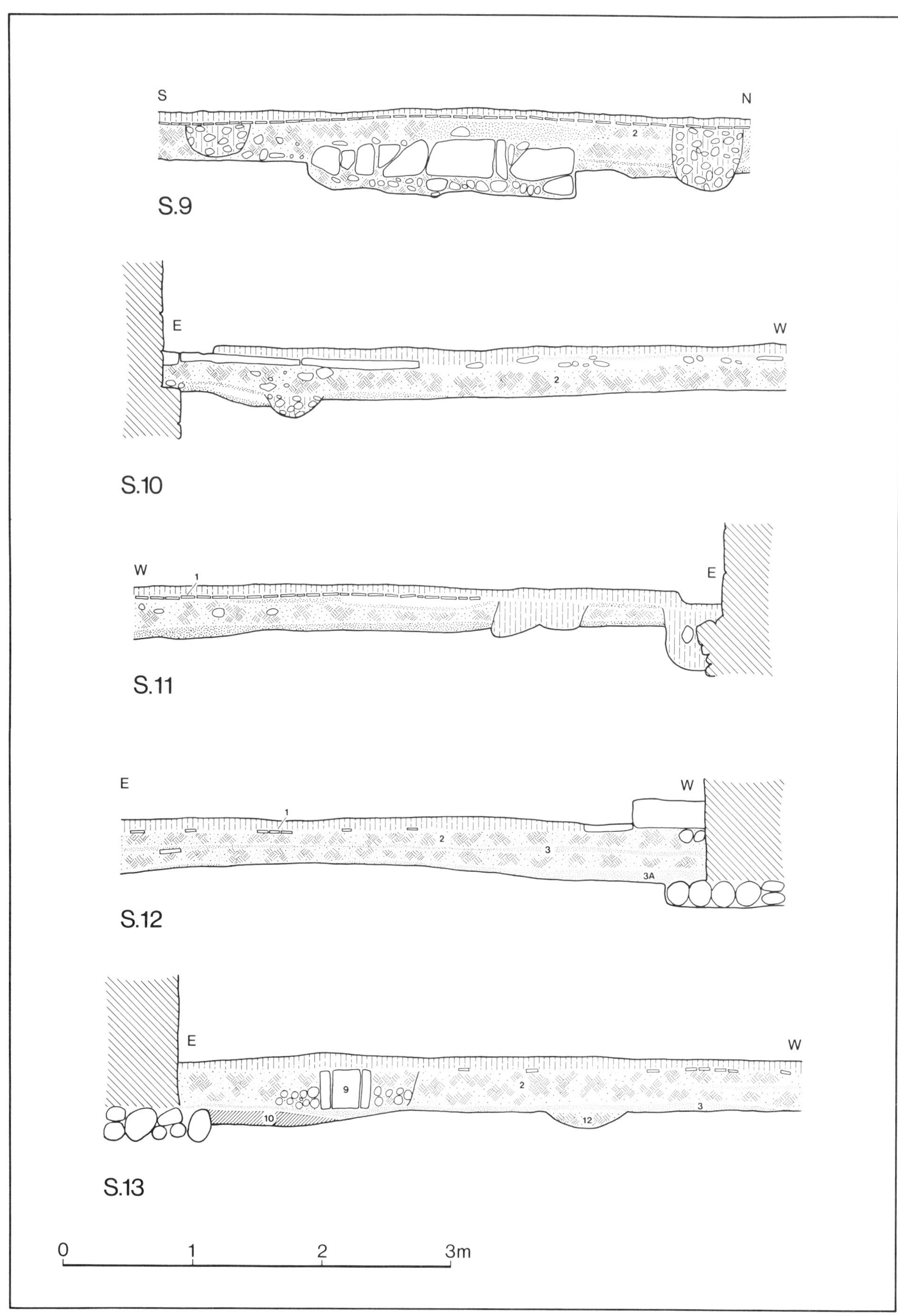

Fig. 15. Refectory: sections.

the west of it a shallow gully (C12) containing soft clay and horse bones lay beneath the floor make-up. Some at least of the cobbles occurring between these features seem also to have been primary: pot sherds from the same vessel came from the cobbling the sand layer and the trench,[36] although most of the cobbling in this area is best assigned to a later phase.

The dating of these primary features is not precise, but generally within the late twelfth and early thirteenth centuries. The floor make-up of the primary Refectory possibly contained a Type 1 jar of twelfth-century date. The floor and the water-pipe should have been in place before the end of the 1180s, when the main building campaign was complete.[37] The external features can be dated to any time before the erection of the second-phase Refectory which, it is argued below, took place soon after *c.* 1220.

Refectory Phase 2

The rebuilding of the Refectory on a north-south axis caused a stretch of the original Frater south wall to be reduced to floor level. The new walls were built on shallow rubble footings. Towards the south end, where the east and west walls bridged the main drain, they were set on large flagstones. The drain itself changes alignment where it passes beneath the extended Refectory walls. It was probably rebuilt at the time of Phase 2 construction. The suggestion in *Report 11*, pp. 16-20, that this section of the main drain did not exist before the reorientation of the Refectory, is discussed further in Chapter 11.

The interpretation offered in 1955[38] proposed a series of floor levels below the surviving fifteenth-century tiled surface. 'Natural' is described in the records as brown boulder clay: it was probably the pre-Refectory soil layer. Upon this was a layer of sand and mortar (C3A), separated in places from a higher, similar band (C3) by brown clayey loam (Fig. 15, S12). Above C3 was more clayey loam and rubble (C2) and above this, the mortar base for the tiled floor. Several indications point to the sequence C3A to C2 being of a single deposition. In the first place, the lowest band of sand was in some parts below the top of the footings, an uneven deposit upon the pre-existing surface. Secondly, any such floor would have been at a lower level than the surviving top of the primary Frater foundation. Finally, joining sherds from a number of vessels were scattered through these layers (see p. 95, Table 10). The interpretation proposed here is the one made in 1953:[39] that the entire make-up below the tiles was laid down for the north-south Refectory during its construction. Equally, the coins from the clay and sand layers above the Phase I floor level at the north end (SFs 390 and 391) can be reinstated as dating evidence for the construction of Phase 2. They give a *terminus post quem* of *c.* 1220.[40] The pottery from the floor make-up layers is consistent with such a date. The flagstones above the make-up may have been second-phase flooring, reused in Phase 3. These, and an associated stub of walling, are described in Phase 3.

Several internal features are possibly to be assigned to the construction or use of the Phase 2 Refectory. The first is a setting of vertical slabs (C9), forming three sides of a square, which was founded upon the lowest band of sand (C 3A; Fig. 15, S13). Its top was level with the base of the fifteenth-century floor (the presumed second-phase floor level). Yet an associated area of cobbles extended only half-way up through the clay make-up. The function of the setting is unknown. It may have been built during the floor construction. On the other hand, the published section drawing[41] shows the line of a cut on its west side (only), which suggests that the feature may post-date the make-up: it may in fact belong to Phase 3. The stratigraphic position of a second feature is equally

Plate 12. Refectory: the fifteenth-century tiled floor, from the north-east. The squares of tiles are set diagonally to the axis of the room, and to the border tiles. On the left are patches of stone flagging.

ambiguous. It comprised an area of burnt lime, charcoal, burnt sandstone, clinker and iron which seems, from the site records, to have been cut through the floor make-up down to natural. This, again, could belong either to second-phase or to third-phase construction.

Some short lengths of lead pipe void were recorded within the floor make-up, none of them obviously linked to the others or to any structural feature. One of these, in front of the fifteenth-century hearth, was sealed by the lowest sand C3A and therefore belongs to or predates Phase 2 construction. The only intact length of piping was found in the north-west corner of the building (Pl. 14). It had probably served a wall laver of Phase 2; but its relationships to surrounding features are discussed under Phase 3 below.

Refectory Phase 3

The walls of the Refectory were later heightened to accommodate an upper floor. This activity can be ascribed to the later fifteenth century on the basis of the architectural form of the associated windows.[42] At the same time the floor of the lower storey was replaced with glazed earthenware tiles (Pl. 12). Some of them were derived from an inlaid mosaic tile floor datable stylistically to *c.* 1240, and presumably removed from another building.[43] As relaid, the main area of tiles comprised a central panel divided into squares of 64 tiles each, set diagonally to the axis of the building and separated by borders formed from triangular (halved) tiles (Pl. 13). The mosaic tiles were thought by the excavators to have been laid as a centre-piece in the four central squares. The axial square immediately north of these was part of a ring of tiles, defining an untiled circle of about 0.58 metres diameter. This was interpreted as the position of a first-floor support. About 7.2 metres to the south, again on the axis of the building, was a setting of stones. They apparently lay below the mortar base for the tiles, and were associated with a second group of curved tiles. The precise relationship of stones and tiles is not clear from the records; but this feature is very probably another post base. Two sherds of Cistercian ware, only one of which survives, were found beneath the tiles, and were presumably deposited when the floor was laid.

Plate 13. Refectory: detail of the inlaid and border tiles used in the fifteenth-century floor.

The tiled floor was framed on both sides, and possibly also at the south end, by sandstone flags. Irregularities in the edge dividing the flags from the tiles may indicate that the former were, in fact, remnants of the second-phase floor, replaced in the centre because of wear. Very little flooring survived at either end of the room; but it is certain that at the north end the pattern changed. The flagging ceased on the line of the first-phase wall foundation, and seems to have been replaced by tiles extending the full width of the room. On the east side, the northern edge of the flagstones was marked by a short length of wall or edging[44] set upon the first-phase foundations. This, too, may have been a feature originating in Phase 2, perhaps the foundation of a partition wall.

In the north-west corner of the room the tiling stopped short of the west wall, and the 1.2 metre gap between them was thought to mark the position of the staircase. In the gap, but also extending beneath the tiles, was a rubble-filled depression which contained the water pipe referred to under Phase 2. The rubble seems to have marked two distinct features, the upper part being attributed to the staircase foundation.[45] The pipe seems to have lain at the bottom of the upper rubble, against the side of the hollow (Pl. 14). Its end had been folded back to create a water-tight seal; and in the filling above were found parts of two bronze taps (Chapter 16, SF 187).

The pipe, which had presumably served a wall laver, was ascribed by its excavator to Phase 3 on the basis of its relationship to the fifteenth-century doorway in the north wall.[46] Yet it seems more likely to have been a second-phase fitting, for two reasons. In the first place, there would hardly have been room for both the staircase and a laver. Secondly, the pipe end was sealed as if, when the laver was removed, the rest of the supply was to continue. This would be an understandable measure if a second-phase laver were being removed to accommodate a third-phase staircase; but it would hardly seem necessary if the laver was being robbed out after the Dissolution.

Plate 14. Refectory: disturbance in the north-west corner, from the south-west, showing the rubble beneath the floor tiles and the lead water pipe with its sealed end.

Chapter 7
The Malthouse, Kitchen and Kitchen Yard

Introduction

In its original form the principal building of the southern range, the Refectory, was aligned east-west, and occupied much of the space between the *Cellarium* and Dorter range. Within a century of the foundation, however, the Refectory had been reoriented north to south. The realignment enabled the Kitchen to be extended eastwards, into what was formerly the west end of the Refectory.[47] It also created a Kitchen Yard enclosed on three sides, bounded on the west by the *Cellarium* and on the east by the new Refectory. The area between the Kitchen and *Cellarium* was originally an open space, a continuation of the Cloister Lane which extended northwards along the east side of the *Cellarium* as far as the Church. In the later twelfth century it was spanned by two arches which left the ground floor open, but allowed the Kitchen and Cellarium to be linked at first-floor level. The arches were walled up during the thirteenth century; and in the fifteenth century the ground floor seems to have been occupied by a Malthouse, with the stone base of a Vat attached to the south.[48]

Excavations in this area began in 1950 along the north side of the Kitchen Yard, between the Vat and Refectory (Fig. 9).[49] They revealed the flooring of a pentice attached to the Kitchen, as well as two drains running south from the Kitchen towards the main drain. Exploratory holes confirmed the lines of the drains southwards; and to the north the more easterly drain was examined within the area of the (extended) Kitchen. The only unpublished site records now available are photographs. In 1954 there was more extensive work within the Kitchen. The west half of the building (that is, the whole of the original Kitchen) was examined, although the published account concentrates upon the sequence of open hearths.[50] Once again, unpublished photographs are the only archive material available.

During the final series of excavations, in 1960-61 and in 1963, further work was undertaken in the Kitchen and Malthouse, and more extensively in the Kitchen Yard.[51] The primary aim was to establish the development of the Abbey's main drainage system. Trenches KY 1-7, 9 and 9A were excavated immediately south, east and west of the Vat. KY8, 10 and 20 re-examined the two drains first recorded in 1950. Additional small-scale trenching took place in the south-west corner of the Malthouse (K1, K1A) and in the north-east corner of the Kitchen (K2). Plans, sections and site notes have survived for most of these areas, providing useful additional information to that already published.

The Malthouse and areas south of the Malthouse

During the 1960s a series of trenches was excavated alongside the *Cellarium* (Fig. 16). The most northerly of these was confined to the threshold of the *Cellarium* doorway. It revealed, beneath paving, two lengths of lead piping. These had obviously been robbed out east of the entrance, though no robber trench was recorded; they were not traced further into the building. The archive photograph shows that the more northerly pipe was the earlier of the two. It was set in a wad of yellow clay; but neither this nor its successor was channelled through the *Cellarium* foundation, in the manner of the primary Guest House pipes. This suggests that both were laid after the *Cellarium* was constructed. The doorway would have provided the only convenient route for them once the *Cellarium* walls had been erected. One of the pipes may formerly have been connected to the piping which extended beneath the Vat and which probably served the Scullery.

The remaining trenches against the *Cellarium* produced a number of drains running north-south. To the north of the main drain, D10A comprised a flagged floor, set in clay, and substantial side and cap stones. Its point of origin was northwards of the *Cellarium* doorway, and may well have been in the Cloisters. Southwards, it was accommodated beneath the south wall of the Malthouse (ascribed by St. John Hope to the thirteenth century), and extended as far as the main drain. Its construction can, therefore, be assigned to the late twelfth or thirteenth century.

Immediately east of D10A was a second linear feature, D12, also running north-south, though in a less sinuous fashion. It comprised a trench 0.6 metres wide at its north end. Its rubble fill is recorded to have cut through an area of mortar flooring within the Malthouse. The feature was identified by its excavators as a soakaway, 'probably of comparatively modern date'.[52] Yet a published photograph[53] seems to show the trench extending beneath, and therefore pre-dating, the thirteenth-century south wall of the Malthouse. Indeed, its line was continued by a 0.3 metre wide trench as far as the main drain, and possibly beyond (as D10B). D12 bears many of the characteristics of the rubble-filled trench which ran through the Warming House and Warming House Courtyard (see Chapter 5). It seems likely that both would have had the same function, whatever that was; the range of possibilities is discussed on p. 14. There are few records of floor levels in this area. It seems in general that the interior of the Malthouse was mortared, presumably as a base for a tile floor, whilst to the south were the remains of extensive flagging.

On the south side of the main drain were two other north-south drains, D10 and D10B. Both passed beneath a late, perhaps post-monastic wall which linked the south end of the *Cellarium* to the building added on to the south wall of the Vat. The sequence at this point is illustrated in Fig. 18, S17. The earliest feature, D10, was cut into natural clay and overlain by successive layers of black earth and grey soil. A smaller drain, D10B, was cut into the grey layer, and was itself overlain by the late wall.

Drain D10 was of similar construction to the north side drain D10A. It ran south until it had cleared the south end of the *Cellarium*, and then ran west towards the structures located south of the Lay Brothers' Reredorter (see Chapter 8 below). It evidently drained from, rather than to, the main drain, and was suggested in the earlier report[54] as the original course of the main drain, running from the east end of the *Cellarium* conduit and linked to D10A. The general layout of the earliest drainage system is reconsidered below (Chapter 11). Here, it need only be said that the interpretation in *Report 11* is by no means the only one feasible. It seems equally possible that the south drain D10 was a southern branch from the main drain; and that D10A was merely the first convenient line along which surface water could be drained from the Cloister area. The dating of D10 is unknown. It was certainly constructed after the south end of the *Cellarium*, but not necessarily much later. The smaller drain above, D10B, was ascribed by its excavators to post-monastic times; but the reasons for this are unclear. It was said to be a flimsy structure of tile 'which broke off short' as it reached the wall running east from the south-east corner of the *Cellarium*.[55] Yet the site records and photographs[56] show it disappearing beneath that wall. Although there is no record of its re-emergence on the south side of the wall, it seems at least possible that D10B had formerly continued on the same line as D10, to become D11, the smaller drain which served the buildings south of the Lay Brothers' Reredorter. That drain, too, made use of stone tiles for its base and one of the sides.[57]

The Kitchen

The structural development of the monastic Kitchen was divided by St. John Hope into two main phases: an original room measuring about 7.5 metres by 10 metres attached to the primary Refectory; and an enlarged Kitchen, about

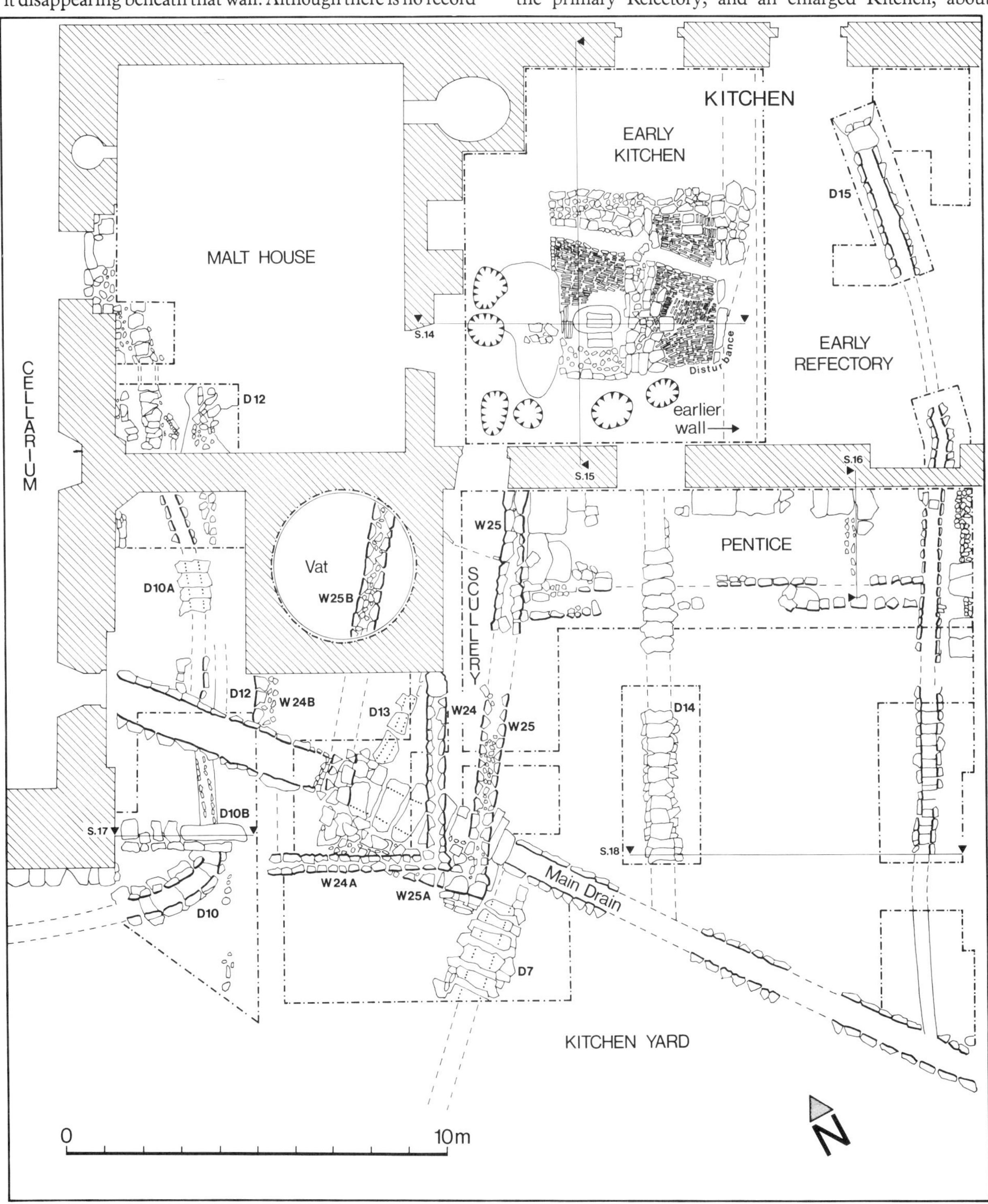

Fig. 16. Plan of Malthouse, Kitchen and Kitchen Yard. For sections see Figs 17, 18.

double this size, which was created when the Refectory was turned at right-angles to the axis of the range.[58] This interpretation was based upon the structural evidence of a demolished north-south wall which had once bisected the area of the present Kitchen: the earliest Kitchen had been confined to the western half, whilst the eastern half had been the west end of the Refectory. This interpretation was confirmed in the 1954 excavations (Fig. 16).

St. John Hope also recorded that traces of the kitchen hearths had been destroyed during the repairs of the 1890s.[59] The remains had not been planned, but he included on his Abbey ground plan the probable siting and orientation of the second-phase hearths, based upon the pattern of vaulting and comparable arrangements at Fountains Abbey. In this respect his interpretation differs significantly from the excavation evidence, which placed all phases of hearth to the west of the original Kitchen-Refectory wall. It should be noted, however, that the ground immediately east of this wall was not excavated, and seems in fact to have been much disturbed in recent times.[60]

Though almost the whole of the primary Kitchen was investigated, the published plan records little other than the sequence of hearths. The section drawings (Fig. 17, S14, S15) provide more general information on the walls and floors. The sequence of structural phases, based upon the drawings and descriptions, is as follows:

Primary Kitchen phase. The foundation trenches for the original walls, including the Kitchen-Refectory partition, were cut into the surface of the natural clays and gravels. Though the drawings do not make it clear, they were undoubtedly also cut through the layer of soil which overlay the boulder clay, and which is best interpreted as the pre-monastic soil horizon. A rectangular trench, measuring 2.2 metres by 3.6 metres was also cut through this soil, and more deeply than the walls into the boulder clay. This was the base for the primary Kitchen hearth, lying slightly south of the centre of the room. The trench was filled with rubble to the surface of the natural clay, and upon this were set the pitched stones of the hearth itself. Around it, a thin layer of mortar represented the flooring. It lay at roughly the same level as both the surface of the hearth stones and the surface of the wall foundations. This structural activity can be assigned to the primary Abbey building phase in the later twelfth century.

Second Kitchen phase. The Kitchen-Refectory partition wall was demolished and the Kitchen was enlarged eastwards. At the same time, the hearth was also extended eastwards, at least as far as the demolished wall. There was, however, no corresponding extension of the deep rubble base. The new hearth incorporated a spine wall which bisected it in a north to south direction; and it was edged on the north by a wall or substantial kerb. It is possible that part of the former Kitchen-Refectory partition was also retained, to support the vaulting. The reconstruction took place when the Refectory was reoriented, in the early thirteenth century.

Third Kitchen phase. A trench aligned north-west to south-east was cut through the northern half of the hearth. Its purpose is unknown. The initial activity of rebuilding was the deposition of a layer of soil upon the phase 1 and 2 floor, in preparation for the construction of a new floor at a higher level. Before the work was completed, an elongated, oval-shaped pit had been cut through this soil and the underlying levels. It is now clear (Chapter 17) that the pit was used for bell founding, an activity that was probably confined to a few days during building operations. There is no reason to suppose that the Kitchen went out of use for more than a week or two. Thereafter, a new hearth was constructed on the surface of the second-phase hearth. It was confined to the south-west quarter of that hearth, and was composed of a set of large stones, dished towards the centre. A layer of sand was used to provide a final levelling above the backfilled bell-founding pit, and a flagged floor was laid above it. The remains of flagging recorded in the north-east corner of the Kitchen (K2) may well have belonged to this phase. These modifications took place in the fifteenth century or later, in view of the date attributed to pottery in the backfill of the bell-founding pit.[61] Unfortunately, this pottery cannot now be identified in the surviving assemblage.

The Kitchen Yard

The most significant structural find in this area was a building which extended southwards from the south-west corner of the Kitchen to the main drain (Fig. 16). It was formed by walls about 0.6 metres wide (W25, W25A, W25B). In the structural sequence it is later than the original Kitchen: the north end of W25 abutted the Kitchen wall. It is equally clear that the building pre-dates the fifteenth century Vat and the room south of the Vat. Internally it measured about 9 metres by 3 metres. At the north end it was linked to the Kitchen by means of a doorway which was cut through the kitchen wall obliquely, and therefore specifically for this purpose. The date of the doorway — late twelfth-century according to St. John Hope — may be the construction date for the excavated building. On the other hand, the entrance may have been re-set in this position in the early thirteenth century, when the Refectory was reoriented.

Functionally, the building was ancillary to the Kitchen. It was probably a scullery. Much of the interior had been destroyed by the later Vat, and the excavation records for the remainder of the building are not comprehensive. Nevertheless, there was some evidence within the floor area for both water supply and waste disposal. Towards the north end of the building two lengths of lead piping, obviously part of a single east-west supply line, emerged from beneath the Vat and W25. The same supply may be represented by the earlier of the two pipes which projected from the *Cellarium* doorway. Both seem from the photographs to have been about one inch in diameter. The piping pre-dated the construction of W25, and could be unrelated. On the other hand, it may well have been designed or modified to provide this structure with water. This suggestion is strengthened by the presence of a small capped drain (D13) which ran south on the axis of the building and discharged into the main drain. Its point of origin could well have been a sink next to, and fed by, the water pipe. Unfortunately the relevant area is beneath the Vat. Elsewhere in the building there were traces of mortar flooring. The stretch of the main drain lying within the structure was capped by large stones.

The location of the Scullery, at the extreme west end of the Kitchen south wall, perhaps indicates a desire on the part of the builders to create the largest possible kitchen yard. The orientation of the Scullery, obliquely to the axis of the Kitchen, was presumably determined by the alignment of the main drain which runs from the *Cellarium* in a south-easterly direction. It was deemed necessary to build the south wall of the Scullery on the south side of the drain, but close to it. The long axis of the building was therefore an approximation to both Kitchen and drain alignments. This does not, of course, explain *why* it was necessary for the structure to encompass

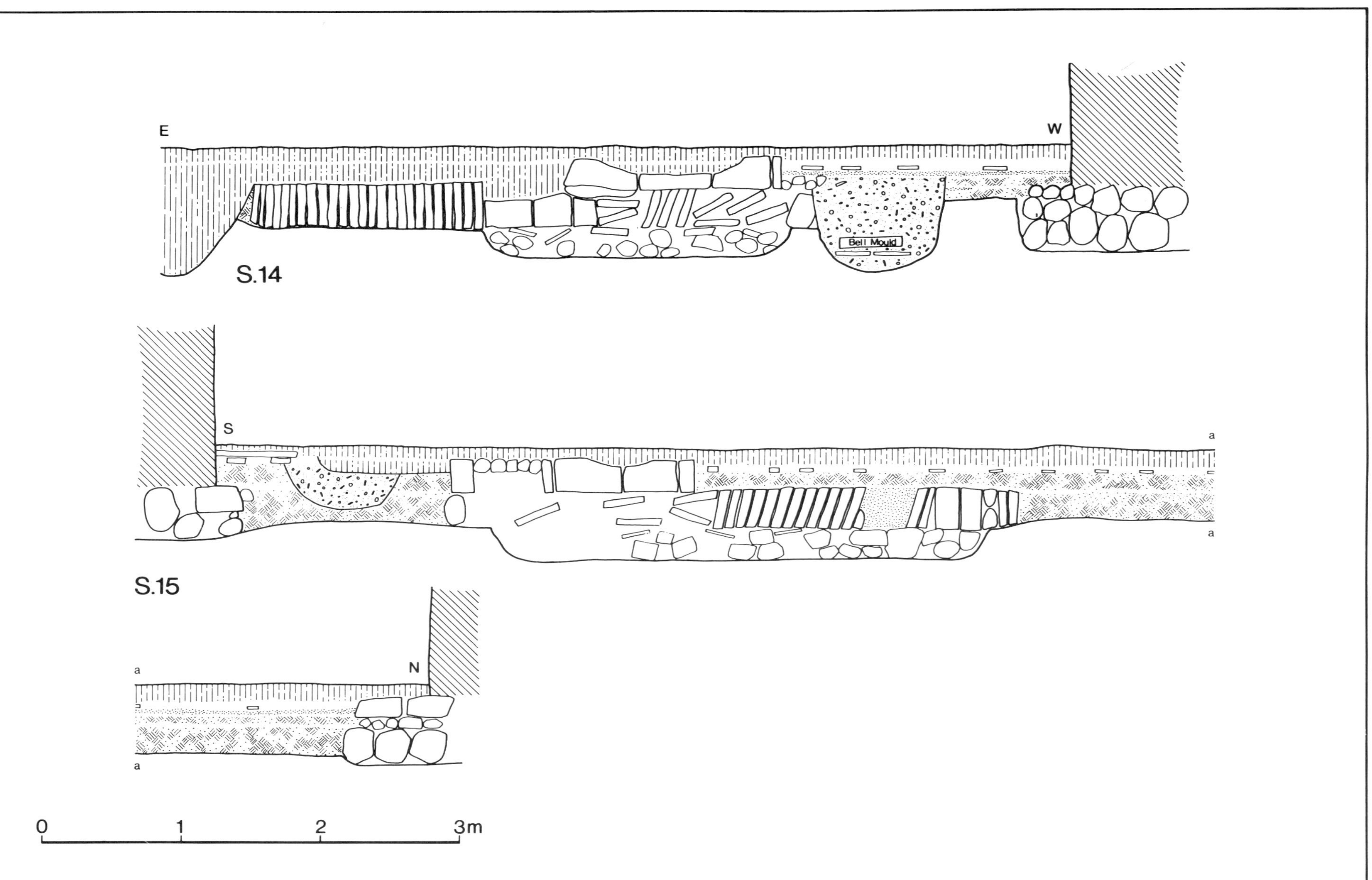

Fig. 17. Kitchen: sections.

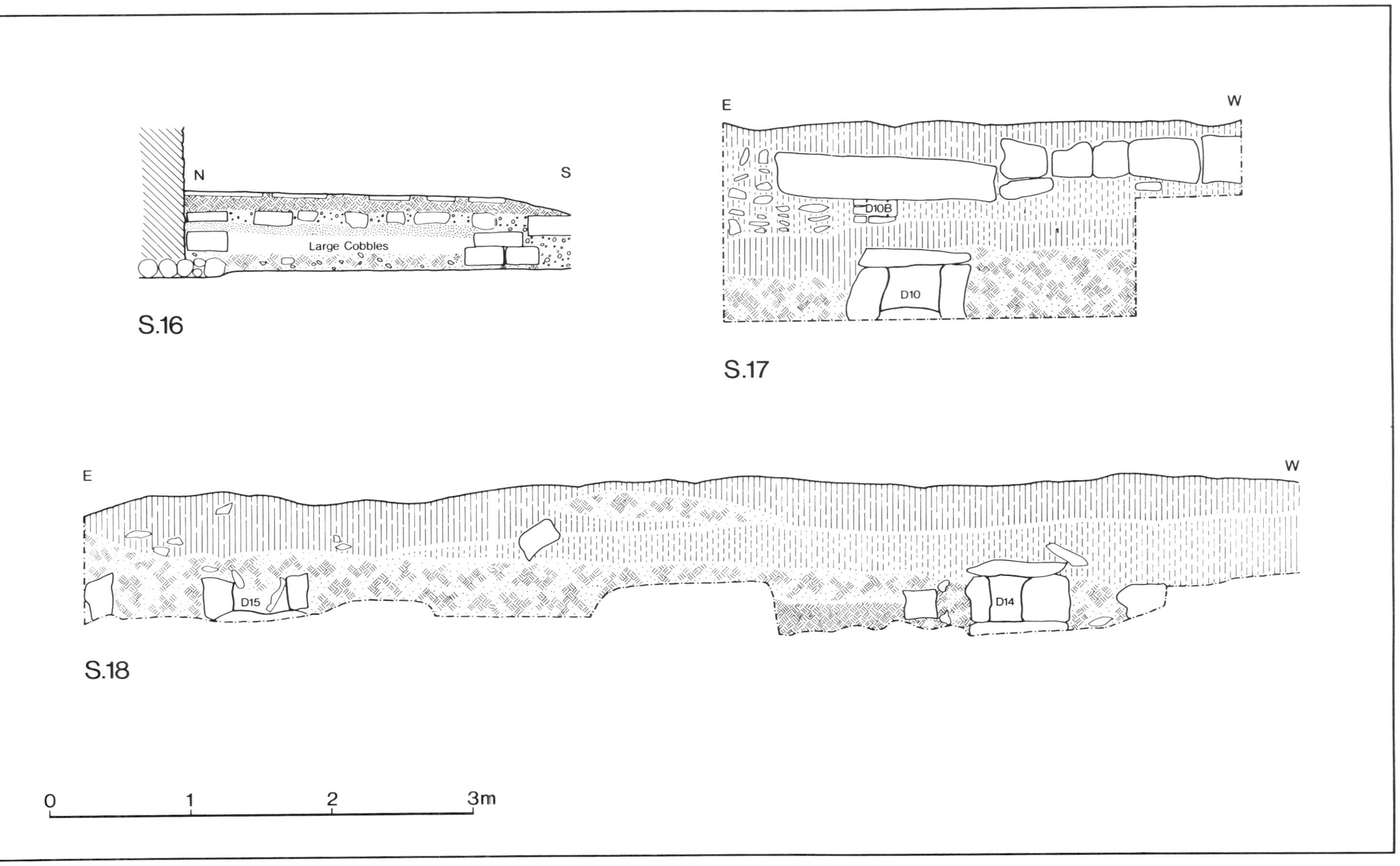

Fig. 18. Kitchen Yard: sections. The spacing of the information shown cn this section does not correspond with that shown on the plan (Fig. 16). They are both reproduced here as originally drawn.

part of the main drain. A possible explanation, but one for which there is no evidence, is that the Scullery was linked to structures still further south.

The south-east corner of the Scullery was provided with an offset buttress foundation. This may have been built because of the proximity of another drain, D7, which ran southwards from the main drain immediately east of the Scullery. It was argued in the earlier excavation report[62] that during the period before the Refectory was re-aligned, the south-easterly line of the main drain ended here and turned sharply southwards, continuing as D7 towards the river. The detailed evidence for this suggestion is put forward in some notes (by C. V. Bellamy) among the archive papers. In the first place, it was found after heavy rainfall that the gradual descent of the drain floor from the north-west ceased at this point, and that the floor gradually rose towards the Refectory. Secondly, a bank of yellow clay which provided an impervious backing to the east side lining of D7 was seen to continue northwards, beneath the floor of the main drain, and to extend north-westwards behind the north lining of the main drain. The contemporaneity of this stretch of the main drain and D7 is further evidenced in their relationships to the Scullery. The side walls of the building were carried over the main drain on arches which were integral to the drain sides. Equally, the south side of the east wall arch was of the same build as the west side lining of D7. The general impression is that the main drain, D7 and the Scullery are all of the same structural phase. We have already noted that the Scullery was not a primary feature, but had been erected in the late twelfth or early thirteenth century. Either the main drain between the *Cellarium* and D7 was not a feature of the primary building phase, or it had been rebuilt when the Scullery had been erected (see Chapter 11).

The remains of the Scullery were overlain by insubstantial wall foundations (W24, 24A, 24B) which formed a room attached to the south wall of the Vat. The room can therefore be dated to the fifteenth century or later, and it may have been constructed after the Dissolution.

The south wall of the Kitchen was fronted by a pentice which extended between the building identified as the Scullery and the north-south Refectory. The pentice was represented on excavation by a series of floors, and was crossed by two Kitchen drains (Fig. 18, S16, S18). The earliest feature was the more easterly drain, D15, which was sealed by the lowest pentice floor. It was traced northwards through the Kitchen to a point about 1.5 metres from the north Kitchen wall, where it terminated in an area of robber disturbance. Near here, a one-inch diameter lead water pipe, with an upward bend, perhaps for a stand-pipe, was found (SF 320). Southwards, D15 ran close to the foundation of the Refectory as far as the main drain. The site notes indicate that its point of outflow into the main drain had been blocked in recent times. The excavators believed the drain to be a primary monastic feature, since it was culverted beneath the south wall of the Kitchen (or, rather, the south wall of the Refectory in the original layout). Yet the wall above the drain had been modified when the Refectory was realigned to form a deep and wide recess;[63] and the culvert as shown on the archive photographs may have belonged to this phase. Furthermore, the line of the drain to the south seems deliberately to avoid the west wall of the second-phase Refectory (Pl. 15). On balance, D15 is likely to have been constructed when the Refectory was reoriented, in the early thirteenth century. The robbed feature at its north end may well have been some kind of water container.

The lowest pentice floor has a *terminus post quem* derived from D15, and another provided by the construction of the Scullery. It was composed of large cobbles. On the west it extended up to the east wall of the Scullery (Pl. 16), and on the south it was furnished with a 'kerb' of dressed stones, probably the base for a timber wall. This floor[64] was cut by a second drain, D14, which again crossed the Kitchen Yard to meet the main drain. The origin of D14 was in the Kitchen: it ran northwards beneath the threshold of the south entrance, where it cut the wall foundation, but was lost once it entered the building, because of later disturbance. The suggestion that D14 belongs much earlier in the sequence,[65] is contradicted by all the available evidence. Above D14 was a new floor (floor B) on a base of sand; and this in turn had been superseded by a third floor of large flags on clay. The sequence of pentice layers is illustrated in Fig. 18, S16.

If D15 is later than the north-south Refectory, as suggested above, then the whole sequence of drains and floors starts after the beginning of the thirteenth century. This first drain was apparently disused when the second floor (B) was laid.[66] The fill of D15, sealed by floor B, contained pottery dated to the fifteenth century.[67] The second and third floors are, therefore, both attributable to the last century of the monastic occupation.

Plate 15. Kitchen Yard: drain (D15) from the south-west.

Plate 16. Kitchen Yard: fragments of the scullery east wall, from the south-west, and the paved pentice floor beyond.

Chapter 8
Structures South of Lay Brothers' Reredorter

When the Abbey grounds were laid out as a public park in the 1890s, the labourers engaged in this work apparently uncovered structural remains to the south and south-west of the Lay Brothers' Reredorter.[68] No records have been found to indicate the precise location and character of these remains, but they may have been associated with the building about 3 metres south of the Reredorter which was investigated in 1961-62.[69] The impetus for this work was in fact provided by attempts to unravel the complexities of the drainage system; in particular, to establish whether a drain uncovered south of the *Cellarium* (D11) was linked to the Reredorter.

The first trenches were dug near the junction of D11 and drain D10 (KY 5b, Fig. 9) and adjacent to the south wall of the Reredorter (5d). Further excavations were based on an area grid numbered LR I to LR X. Not all the grid squares and baulks were fully excavated; nor are all the excavated trenches fully recorded. Plans and sections exist for trenches 5b and 5d, and for areas LR II-IV and X. There is also a section drawing of the west baulk of LR I.

The principal elements of the LR structures were the two drains, D10 and D11, and a building of several phases (Figs 19 and 20). The relationships of these elements are not entirely clear; but the earliest feature in the sequence seems to have been D10, a deep drain which was traced into this area from its junction with the main drain east of the *Cellarium* (Fig. 16). It ran beneath the east walling of the LR building (W20A), and may still have been in use when that wall was constructed: the published photograph[70] seems to show W20A running over the drain capstones, though separated from them by a layer of soil. Drain 10 was not observed south-west of this point, despite attempts to trace it.[71] On the west side of the excavations there was, however, an east-west line of flagstones of more than one phase (Fig. 19; Pl. 17), which could represent the floor of the continuation of D10. The ground between D10 and the flagging was not, apparently, excavated below the paved floor of the building (Fig. 21, S24, S25).

The relationship of D10 and D11 is also uncertain. The lines of the two drains merged just east of the most easterly excavation trench (5b). The excavators investigated the junction by tunnelling beneath the asphalt path. They determined 'that this small structure ran down into the bigger channel and did not cut through it to continue on a south-east line'.[72] Drain 11 may have been a secondary feed into D10: it can be seen on the archive photographs to be structurally later than D10. Alternatively it may have replaced D10, continuing its line north-eastwards to the main drain. The chief obstacle to accepting the first alternative is that D11 is recorded as flowing from west to east, whereas in the Kitchen Yard D10 was recorded as flowing south and west from the main drain. The alignments of the two drains suggest that, if in contemporary use, they both flowed in the same general direction. As to the second alternative, there is no record that D11 cut through the capping or the fill of D10; but it may be significant that to the east of the *Cellarium* immediately south of the main drain, a small drain D10B overlay D10 (Fig. 18, S17). The construction date of drain D10 is unknown, though

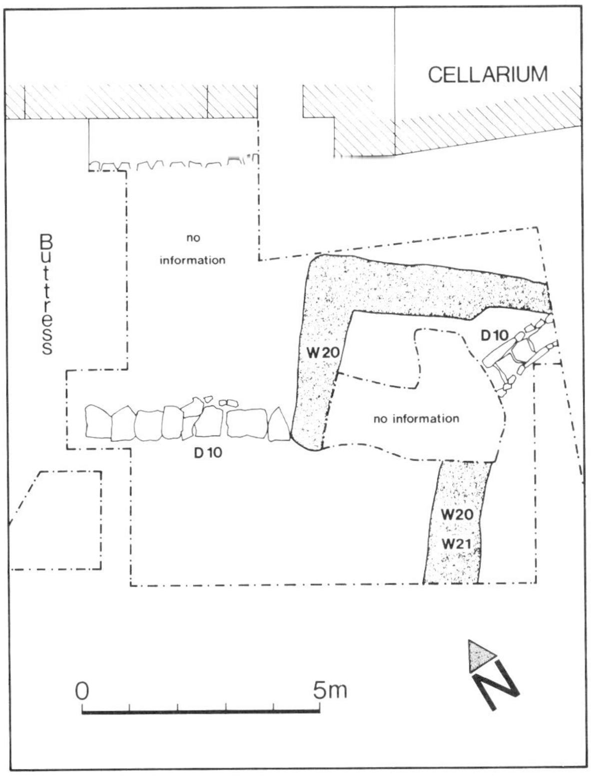

Fig. 19. Structures south of Lay Brothers' Reredorter: plan of earliest remains. For sections see Fig. 21.

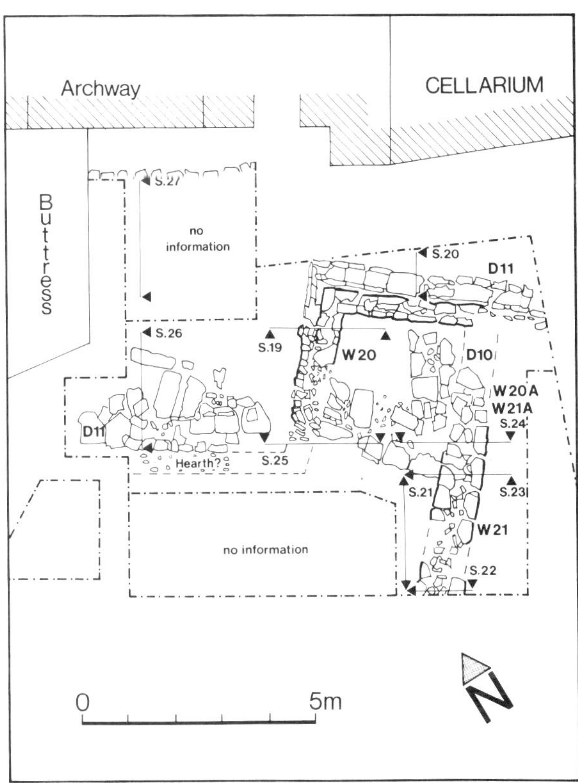

Fig. 20. Structures south of Lay Brothers' Reredorter: plan of later remains. For sections see Fig. 21.

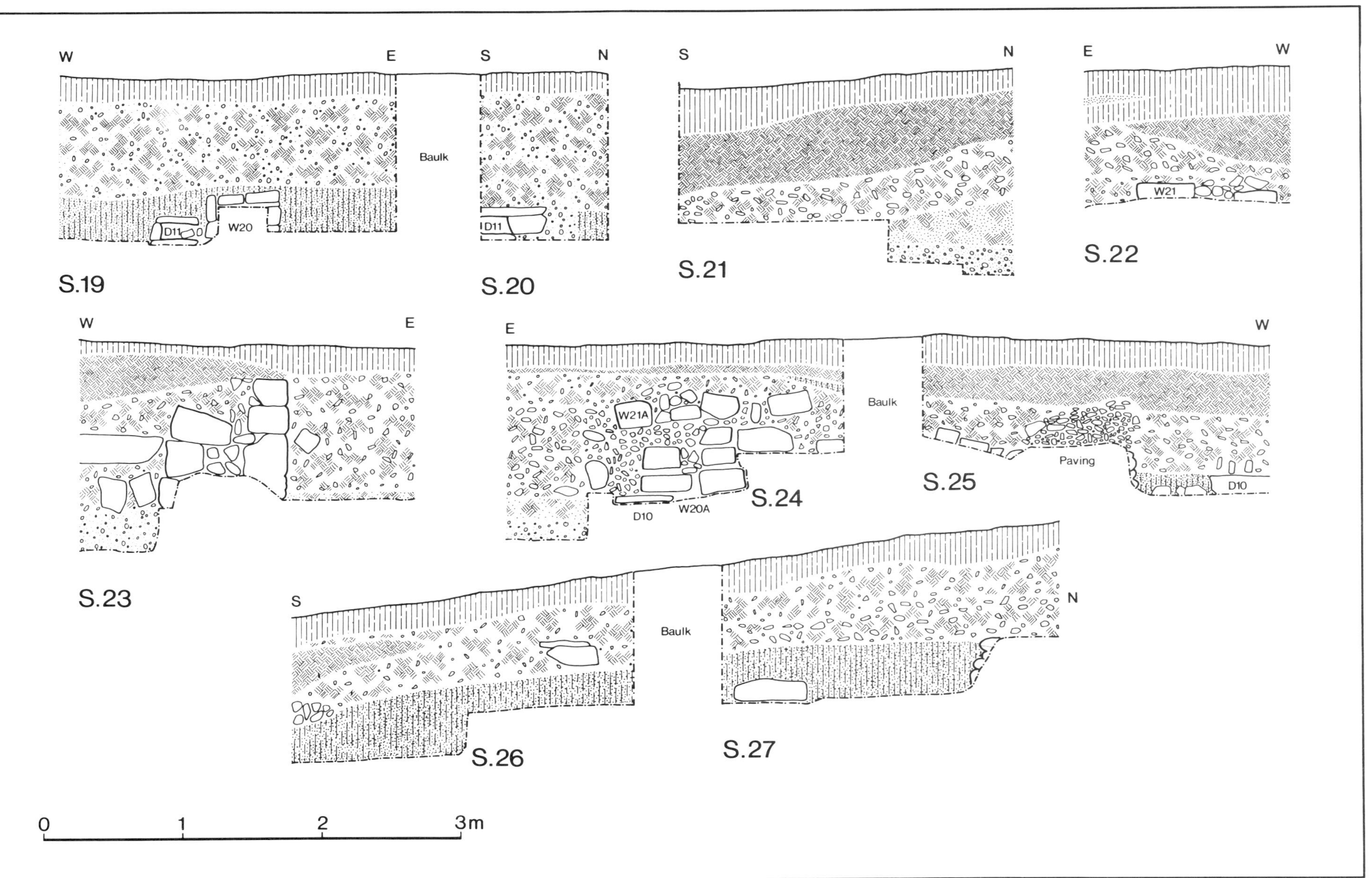

Fig. 21. Structures south of Lay Brothers' Reredorter: sections.

it would seem to have been an early, if not primary Abbey feature, judging by its relationships. Drain 11 is unquestionably associated with the primary building in this area. It ran immediately outside, and depended upon, the north and west walls (W20; Fig. 21, S19, S20). On the west side it could be traced only as far as the east end of the line of flags which has been suggested as the continuation of D10. These flags were, however, overlain in places by a second layer of flags, and by edging stones. Given the available records it is impossible to be precise; but in general terms it seems most probable that D11 followed the same course as that proposed for D10. D11 is recorded as having drained from west to east, and the flags and edging stones in question were set at least 0.3 metres higher than the earlier flags.

The building itself was composed of neatly-constructed walls (W20) about 0.6 metres wide, set on rubble foundations. The north wall foundation was almost completely intact. On the west side it extended as far as the east-west flagging, where its rubble base cut the line of the ?D10 flags. From that point the wall may have turned westwards: there was no sign of its continuation southwards, and a band of rubble seems to have run along the south side of the flagging.

The structure of the east wall is rather more complicated. Its north end had been robbed out, the line preserved internally by the edge of the paved floor. The primary wall over D10 (W20A) was of the same width and character as the north and west walls. It was overlain by an obviously later phase of walling (W21A): the two were separated by a bank of earth and stones, and were on slightly different alignments (Fig. 21, S24).[73] It is clear that W21A was only a short stretch of rebuilt masonry, and that the walling which ran southwards to the edge of the excavations (W21; Fig. 21, S22, S23) was more in line with W20A.[74] W21 was similar to W20 and W20A in alignment and structural characteristics, being neatly faced and set on a small rubble foundation. It has previously been regarded as a 'late monastic' wall, unassociated with W20, on the ground that it was significantly wider than W20;[75] but the archive photographs suggest that it had at some stage been widened by the addition of a new external face; and the archive plans show that this face lay outside the line of the rubble foundation. In view of this, it seems best to regard W21 as, in its original form, a continuation of W20A.

The building (or rather, the corner of the building) thus defined contained areas of paving, not all of which were original to the structure. The recorded areas of flooring seem, largely, to follow the pattern of the baulks between the areas, which were taken down only to this level after the areas between them had been largely completed. In view of this it would be unwise to attempt a detailed interpretation of the paving sequence. The building has previously been given an early and brief life-span, on the basis that it was served by D10 (*sic*), which was an early stretch of the main drain, superseded in the early thirteenth century.[76] Such an interpretation, itself questionable, fails to take account of D11. It seems much more probable that these structures, perhaps associated with the Lay Brothers' Infirmary, were in use during and beyond the thirteenth century.

Fragments of various other structures were found to the north-west of the building, but the records are insufficient to permit much useful discussion. At the north end, trench 5d revealed an area of flooring along the south side of the Reredorter. The flagstones had extended along the front of one of the large archways which opened into the ground floor of the Reredorter. When that archway had been blocked up, the flags immediately against the arcade had been removed. On the south side, about 1.7 metres south of the Reredorter and running parallel to it, was a kerb or wall footing associated with the flags (Fig. 21, S27). The structure may well have been a pentice attached to the Reredorter: St. John Hope[77] records that there was formerly structural evidence for a pentice on the north side of the same building.

Plate 17. Area south of Lay Brothers' Reredorter: general view of structures, from the east.

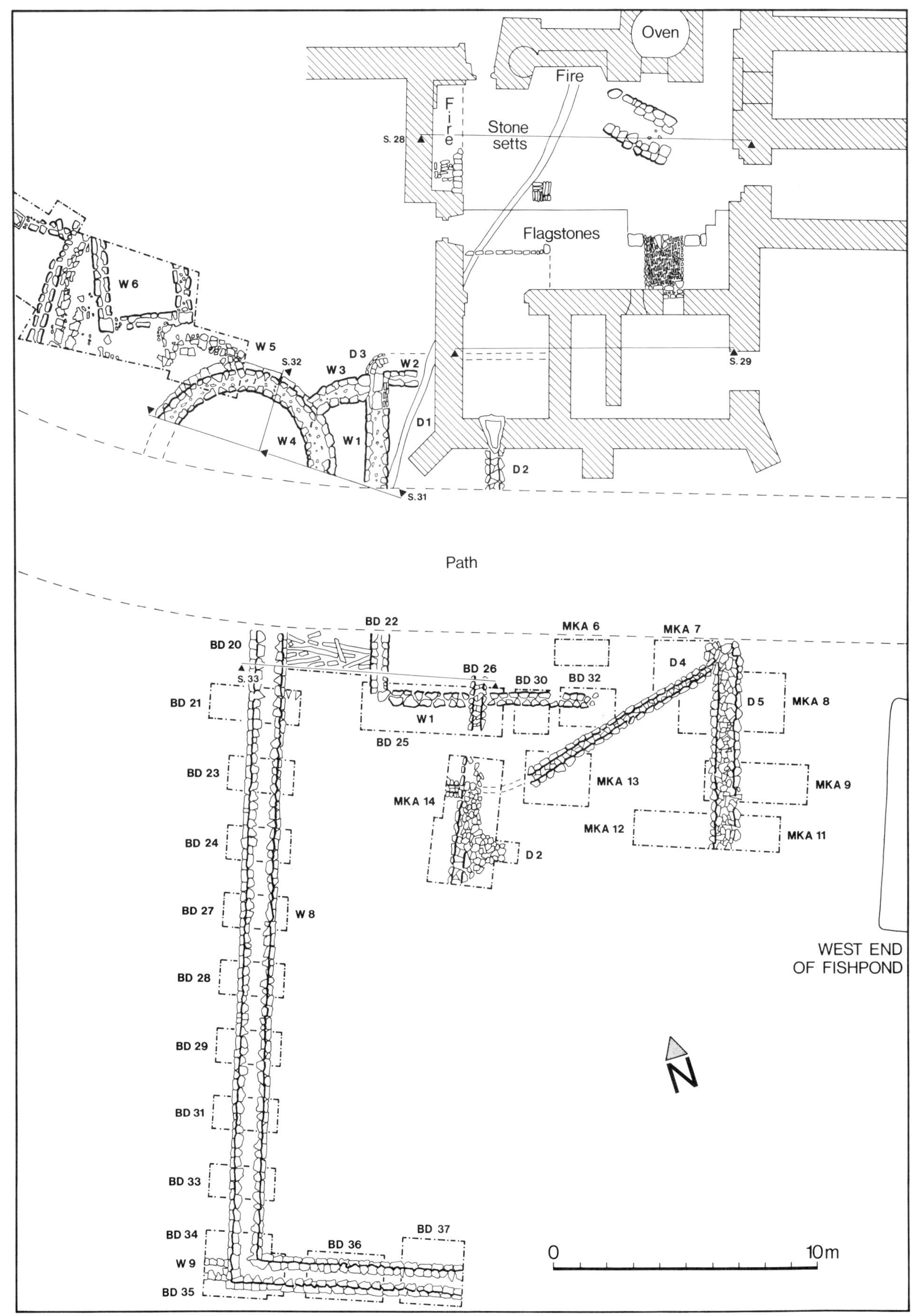

Fig. 22. Plan of Meat Kitchen and structures to the south. For sections see Figs 23-25.

Chapter 9
The Meat Kitchen and Structures to the South

Introduction

When, in the fifteenth century, a Misericord was created on the ground floor of the Refectory building, it was provided with its own kitchen and service facilities. The Meat Kitchen, Scullery and other ancillary rooms were built against the south-east corner of the Misericord, across the south end of the Warming House Courtyard (Fig. 22). Part of the east wall of this block was formed by part of the west wall of the Dorter Range. A pentice fronted the north wall of the Meat Kitchen. It had probably extended some distance northwards from its east end, along the Dorter Range.

Within the Meat Kitchen itself[78] there was a small doorway in the west wall, giving access towards the outbuilding at the south-west corner of the Misericord. North of this was a large fireplace. A second fireplace with a side oven, and a large independent oven were located in the north wall. At the west end of the same wall was a service doorway leading to the Misericord *via* the pentice. Another opening at the east end led to the northern arm of the pentice. On the east side of the room was a doorway into the passage south of the monks' Reredorter. Finally the south wall of the Meat Kitchen contained a wide doorway opening into a room which proved on excavation to have been a scullery. Further east was another doorway, giving access to the room in the south-east corner of the block. A second opening into this room was, according to St. John Hope, an oven entrance: the oven base was seen on the north side of the opening.

Excavations in the Meat Kitchen were undertaken in 1952, 1956 and 1957: they were published in *Report 3*, pp. 37-8, *Report 7*, pp. 29-32 and *Report 8*, pp. 60-2. They seem to have covered the entire floor area of the building, but no detailed, unpublished information is available. To the south-west of the Meat Kitchen a number of trenches were excavated initially to trace the line of the water conduit (the so called 'bath drain') which issued from the Warming House Courtyard cistern. These trenches, labelled BD 20 to BD 37 (Fig. 9), did not achieve their primary objective; but they revealed instead a most important sequence of early levelling layers and enclosures. A second series of trenches, labelled MKA, explored these features further east. The published evidence appears in *Report 7*, pp. 32-4, *Report 8*, pp. 56-60 and *Report 9*, pp. 78-87. Once again, none of the original site records has been found, other than a general plan of the trenches on which Fig. 22 is based.

Phase one: early water courses south of the Meat Kitchen

In the present topography of Kirkstall Park, the surviving southern ranges of the Abbey appear to be sited close to the edge of a river terrace, about 70 metres north of the River Aire itself. It is very probable that the intervening ground was once occupied by earlier or subsidiary water courses, before the river became fixed artificially in its present bed. Some relevant pieces of detailed information were noted in earlier publications.[79] In the first place, two fishponds survived in this low-lying area in the mid-eighteenth century.[80] One of these lay some distance south of the *Cellarium*. The other was further north-east; it lay about 15 metres south of the Abbot's Lodging and the Dorter Range (Fig. 29). Each was rectangular, with its long axis roughly east to west. Both seem to have been about the same width. The pond south of the Abbot's Lodging was by far the longer, extending more than 50 metres.

These ponds may well have marked one or more old river courses. They may, additionally, have been the last survivors of more extensive chains of fishponds. Such an interpretation certainly accords with the general stratigraphic evidence south of the Meat Kitchen, which indicated a substantial depth of tipped clayey soil and rubble (the medieval 'made ground') overlying river silts.

The two key elements of the stratigraphic record are the sections through the circular building, to the south-west of the Meat Kitchen, and through the trench BD 20, about 7 metres further south. The first of these (Fig. 25, S32) revealed that the natural gravels dipped sharply away beneath the northern sector of walling. The building had largely been constructed upon a layer of clay and stones 0.75 metres thick, which overlay river silts. The silts began at a depth about 2 metres below the present turf line. The east-west section of BD 20 (Fig. 26, S33) revealed a similar sequence. The river silts began 2 metres to 3 metres below the modern surface, and were overlain by 'medieval make-up' which varied from 0.45 metres to 0.75 metres in thickness. Trench BD 20 also contained a quantity of preserved timbers: 'lines of oaken stakes were driven into the mud and oaken planks were fixed horizontally by small dowels'.[81] The lines of stakes ran east to west. There were perhaps three or four of them originally, but the surviving records are not sufficiently detailed to be certain of the precise arrangement. The timbers survived only in the silt: higher up, they had rotted away. There is no record of voids in the medieval make-up; but there is, in fact, no detailed record of the make-up at all. It should also be noted that the previously published section drawing[82] is a composite drawing based on two trenches which were not, in fact, in line (BD 20 and BD 25/26; Fig. 22). The extent of timbering shown on the drawing merely indicates the length of trenching to this depth in BD 20.

The available evidence is insufficient to enable a detailed interpretation to be made. In particular, it is not known whether there were different medieval fills to the north and south of the timbering, although there seem to have been large boulders on the north side only.[83] All that can be said with reasonable certainty is that the stakes and planks recorded were in line with the north side of the more easterly of the fishponds shown by Burton.[84] They may represent a jetty, as suggested in the previous report,[85] dating from a time when this course of the river was navigable. Alternatively, the timbers may have been revetting for the side of a fishpond: either a continuation of the one to the east, or a second stew in line with it.

The use of this stretch of fishpond or water course should probably be dated to the late twelfth and early thirteenth

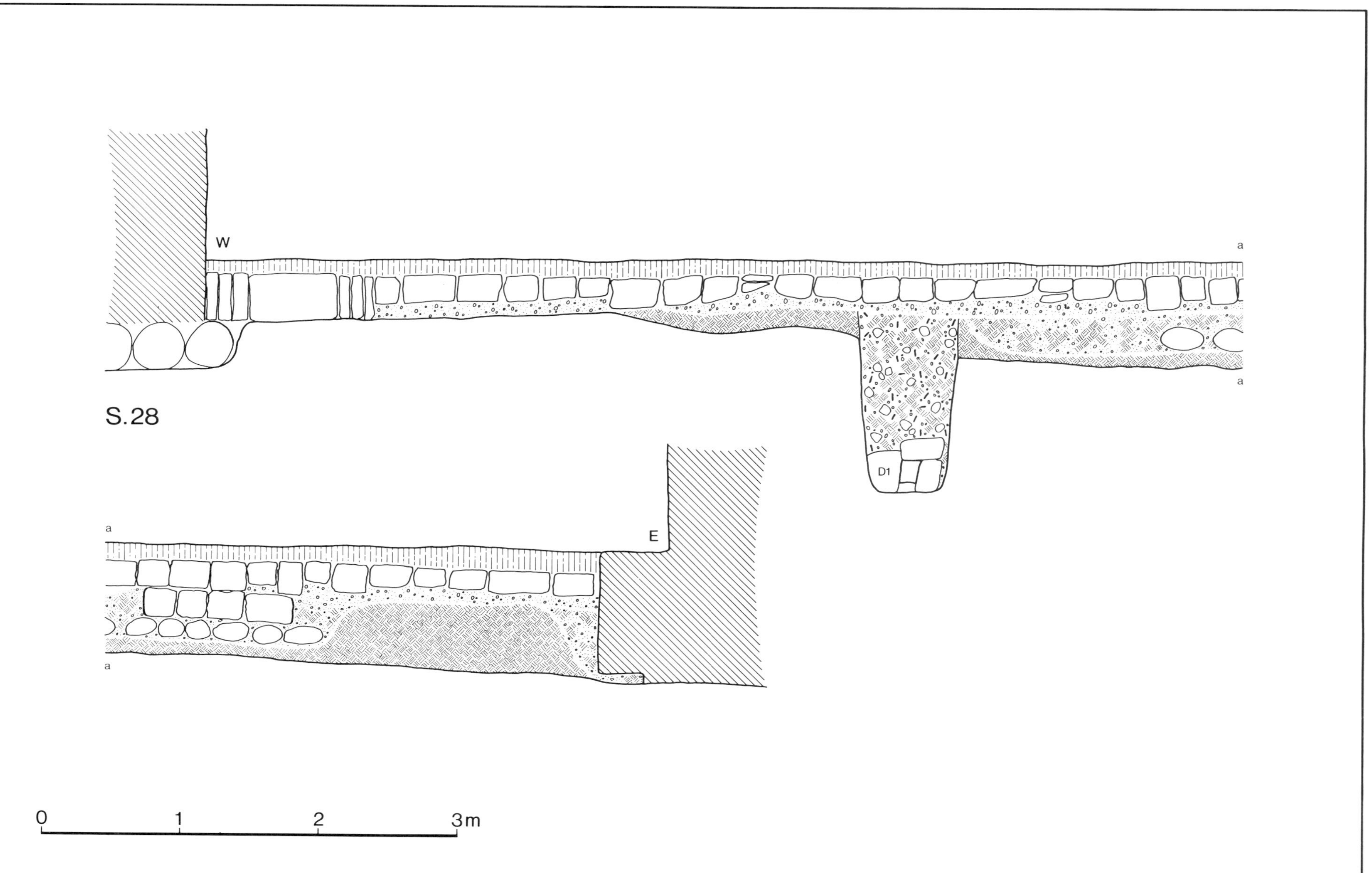

Fig. 23. Meat Kitchen: sections.

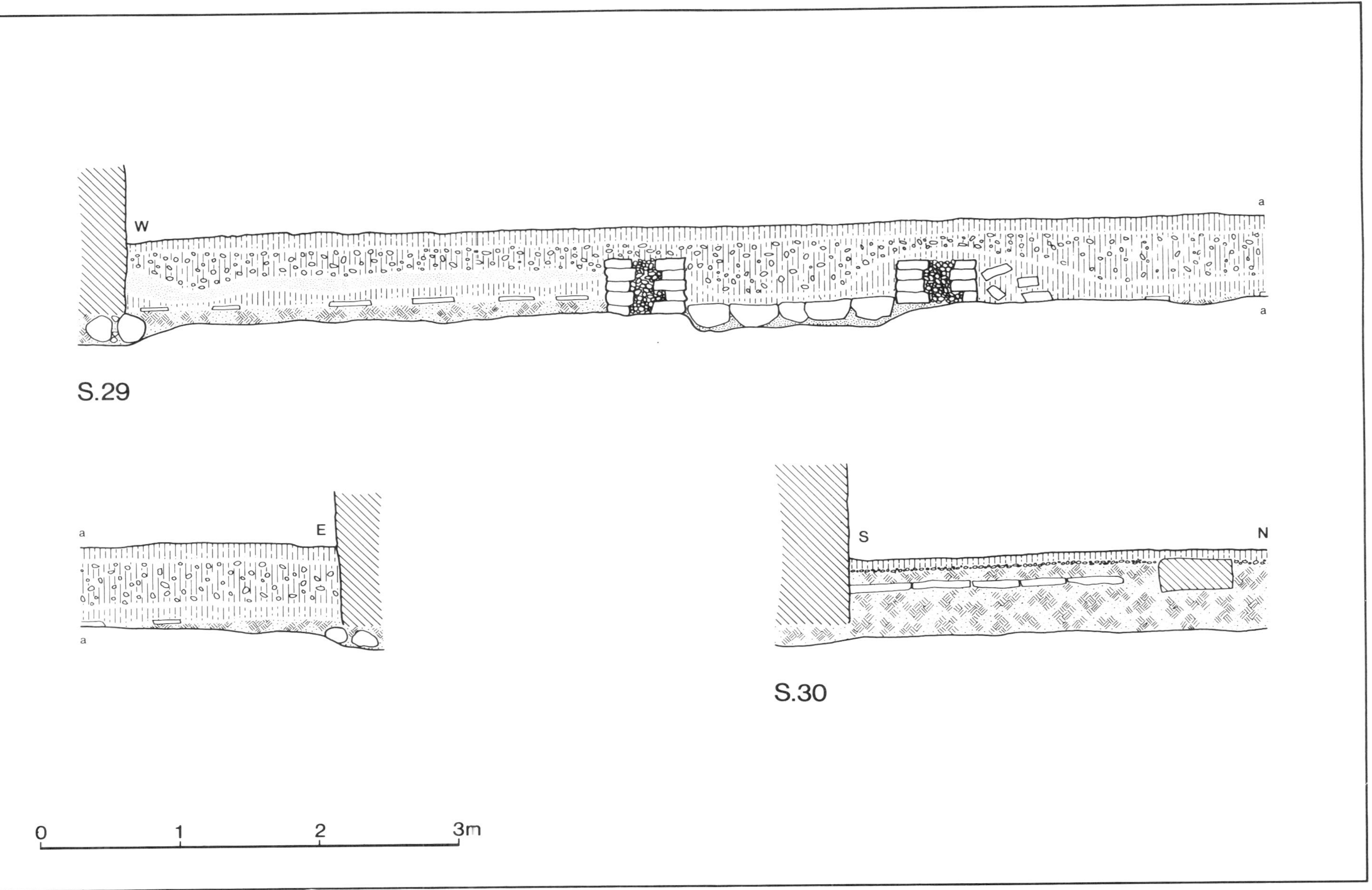

Fig. 24. Meat Kitchen and pentice: sections.

centuries. Three small potsherds were found in the silt around the timbers: two of them were from twelfth-century vessels and the third was an unrecognised type.[86] None of them can now be found. The overlying make-up, which presumably buried the timberwork, contained pottery mainly of the thirteenth or fourteenth centuries. On historical grounds, a major expansion of facilities is more likely to have occurred in the thirteenth rather than the fourteenth century. Some later pieces of pottery from this assemblage [87] may well have been introduced into the make-up when the timbers rotted.

Phase two: enclosures and buildings south of the Meat Kitchen

A series of trenches showed that the make-up layer extended southwards, to a line about 30 metres south of the Meat Kitchen. It was confined there by an east-west wall, which was probably a retaining wall close to the thirteenth-century course of the river.[88] The reclamation work was undertaken in order to extend southwards the Abbey buildings and enclosures. All the structural remains in this area were set into the make-up layer, except for the south side retaining wall (in BD 35 to BD 37), which seems to have been constructed before the tipping was completed.[89] The west end of this wall was apparently bonded into a long wall running northwards (W8), which itself rested upon the make-up layer. These two walls, at least, must therefore have been erected during reclamation. Wall 8 had battered foundations. In BD 20 (Fig. 26, S33) it seems to have had a series of layers on its west side, including a mortar spread, identified as flooring, at the level of the lowest offset foundation course.[90] At such a depth relative to the wall, this mortar is unlikely to have been an internal floor level, and may well have belonged to the sand and mortar spread recorded below the enclosure walls south of the Kitchen Yard (Chapter 10).

On balance, it is probable that these walls formed the south and west sides of an enclosure which fronted the Warming House Courtyard, the Dorter Range, the Abbot's Lodging and possibly the Infirmary complex. The corner of W8 was abutted by another wall, W9, which may have bounded a second enclosure south of the Kitchen Yard and *Cellarium*.

Two buildings can be associated with these enclosures. One of them was circular in plan (W4), with an internal diameter of 5.4 metres. It stood upon the northern edge of the medieval make-up layer (Fig. 25, S31, S32). Its southern half could not be examined since it lay under a park pathway. Nevertheless, it seems fair to assume that on its south side it was abutted by the W8 enclosure wall. Two other linking walls extended from its north and east sides. The former, W5, is described in the chapter which follows (Chapter 10). The latter, W3, linked the circular building to a rectangular one which lay partly beneath the southern end of the Meat Kitchen.

The rectangular structure, like the circular one, had been set upon the surface of the made ground (Fig. 26, S33). Its west wall (W1), traced by trenching to its full extent, was found to be 12 metres long. Only the west end of the north wall (W2) was recovered, but its foundation stones were seen to have been incorporated in the west wall of the Meat Kitchen. Furthermore, a small drain (D3) which ran around the north-west corner of the building, was apparently traced across the northern end of the south-west room in the Meat Kitchen, through the floor make-up.[91] The south wall of this building was also traced by trenches, to a point about 8 metres from the west wall, where the remains ceased abruptly. The foundations were of slight construction,[92] and probably served a timber building. An archive photograph (Pl. 18) shows a padstone at its north-west corner. It may have had dimensions fairly similar to those of the succeeding Meat Kitchen complex.

A short stretch of walling on a north-west to south-east alignment was found beneath the floor of the Meat Kitchen, in the northern end of that building (Fig. 23, S28). It was heavily robbed, and its associations are unknown; but on the basis of alignment it may have been an enclosure wall running between the south-east corner of the (second) Refectory and the room south of the monks' Reredorter.

The remaining feature of this phase was the water conduit (previously described as the 'bath drain' D1), which extended south-west from the cistern in the Warming House Courtyard (Chapter 5). It was traced beneath and beyond the Meat Kitchen (Fig. 23, S28): it passed beneath the north and west walls of the rectangular building described above, where it was seen to have been cut into the make-up layer (Fig. 25, S31). A coin of Richard I (SF 389) was found in its construction trench;[93] but this has no particular significance for dating since the conduit already possesses an early thirteenth-century *terminus post quem*, provided by the date of the cistern. The course of the conduit was lost beneath the park pathway: there was no trace of the feature on its predicted line (in BD 20) on the south side of the path. The suggestion in the earlier report, that 'it had fulfilled its purpose in carrying waste water to the river',[94] makes little sense in view of the fact that it was clearly designed to lead fresh water to a particular place. Moreover, D1 had been cut into the make-up layer which had, presumably, obliterated any natural water course in this location. The conduit probably turned west beneath the path, to serve a building or even a fishpond on the south side of the Kitchen Yard.

It has already been argued that the reclamation of this area took place in the thirteenth century, and that two at least of

Plate 18. South of the Meat Kitchen: the north-west corner padstone (behind trowel) of the pre-Meat Kitchen building (W1-2), from the north-west. The small external drain D3 runs around the corner.

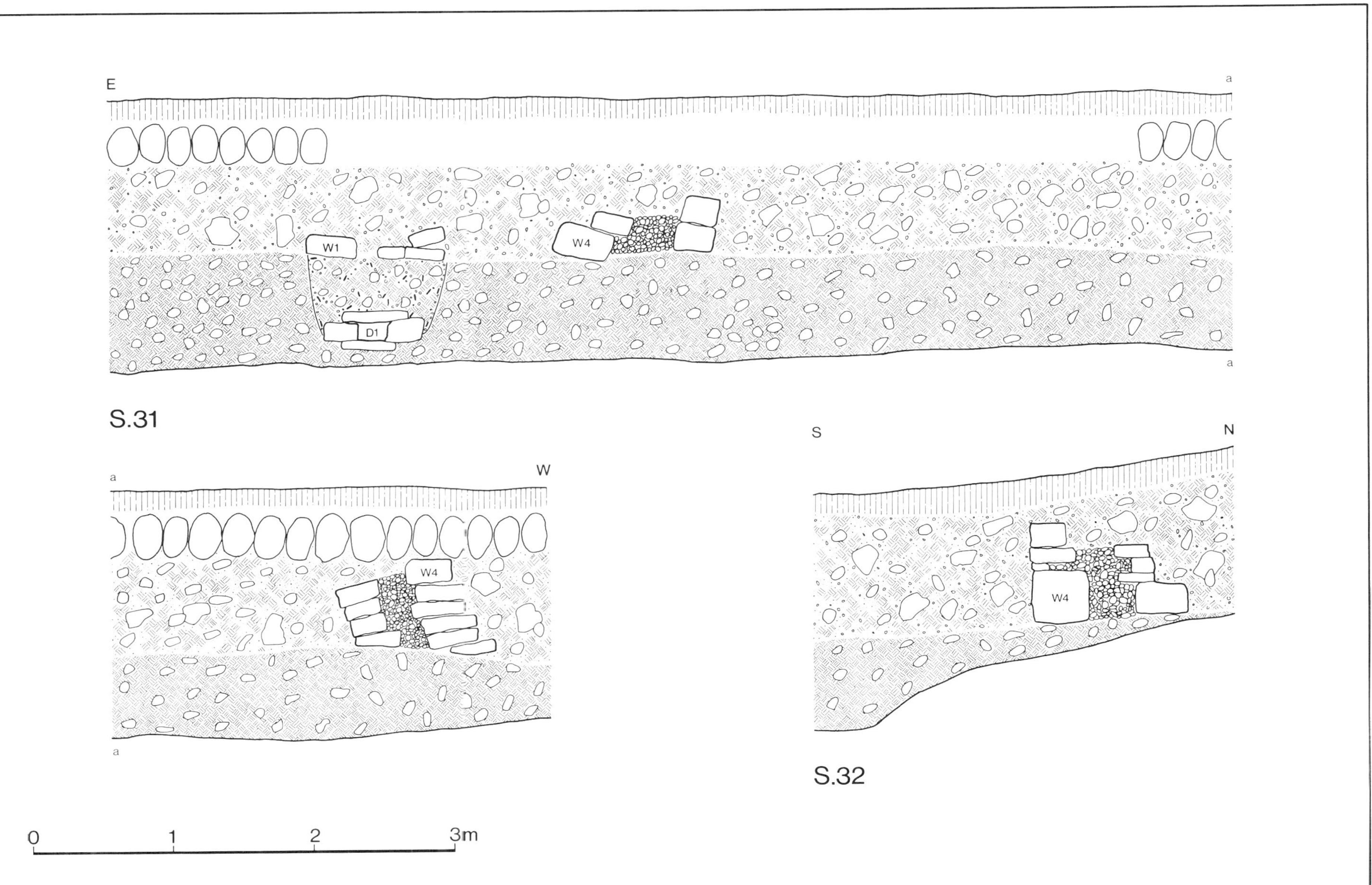

Fig. 25. Structures to south-west of Meat Kitchen: sections.

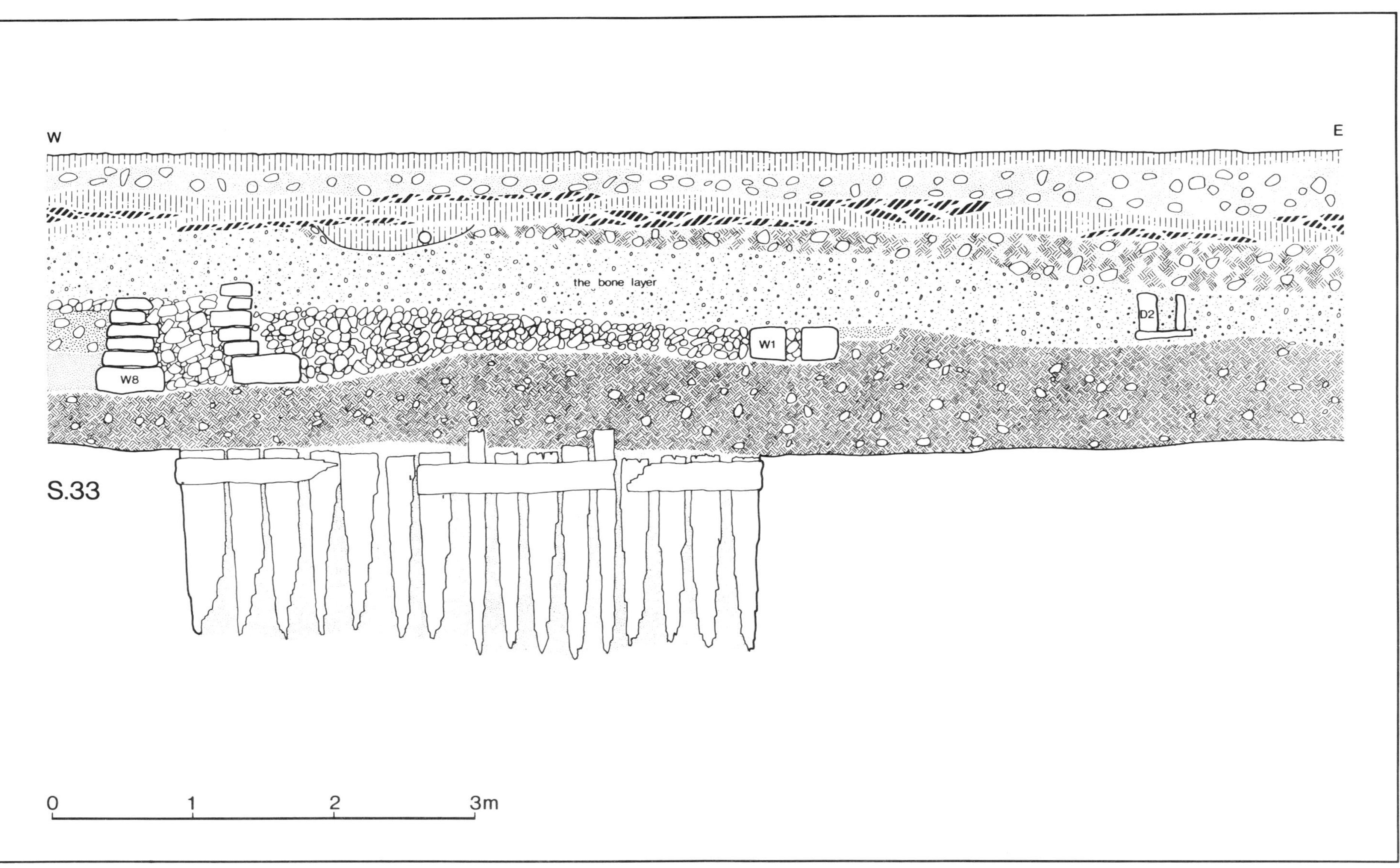

Fig. 26. Structures south of Meat Kitchen: section. The length and spacing of information on this section does not correspond with that shown on the plan (Fig. 22). They are both reproduced here as originally drawn.

the enclosure walls were erected during that operation. The circular and rectangular buildings can probably also be ascribed to that century, to a period of expansion - projected or actual - in the size of the monastic community. The circular building survived substantially into the early eighteenth century, to be recorded on an engraving of the Abbey (Pl. 2). It seems to have had two doorways, and two low openings close to the ground, but otherwise blank walls on its southern aspect. There can be little doubt that it was a dovecote. The proximity of the eastern fishpond suggests that this part of the Abbey site was devoted to domestic food production, and contained, perhaps, vegetable gardens, fruit trees and the like, as well as the dovecote and fishpond.

Phase three: intermediate features

One of the pre-Meat Kitchen features which post-dated phase two was a small drain, D4, described by it excavators as being very similar to the 'bath drain':[95] it, too, may therefore have been a water conduit, supplying the same structure or pond as the Warming House cistern conduit. It ran in an approximately north-east to south-west direction, and rested upon a gritty silt layer containing decayed animal bone (the 'lower bone layer' which marked the beginning of the gradual accumulation of kitchen waste). This conduit seems to have disturbed[96] and therefore to have post-dated the rectangular building attributed to phase two. At the same time it pre-dated the drain D2 running southwards from the Meat Kitchen Scullery.[97]

Westwards, the feature was traced as far as trench MKA 14. To the north-east, it was found in trench MKA 7, where it 'came to the edge of' a wide flagged drain (D5) running from north to south.[98] This drain had a floor of several layers of flags. Some edging stones also survived. Like the conduit, it rested upon the 'lower bone layer' which produced pottery assigned to the late fourteenth or early fifteenth century.[99]

Phase four: the Meat Kitchen and associated features

The entire floor area of the Meat Kitchen was cleared progressively over several years, to reveal a building measuring 10 metres by 12 metres internally, divided into four rooms. The largest unit was the Kitchen itself, which occupied the northern two-thirds of the structure. It was floored for the most part with large stone setts, mainly re-used facing stones and architectural blocks derived from the cloister arcade (Fig. 23, S28). Along the south side of the room, opposite the west doorway, there was a band of flagging instead. It was presumably below this flagging that a Netherlands jetton (SF 403) was found. A hearth formed by vertically-set flags was located at the east end of the flagging, in front of an opening into the south-east corner room. Beyond the hearth was a small area of mortar flooring which abutted the south and east walls of the building. It also extended beneath the hearth, which seems therefore to have been a secondary feature. Another, much smaller hearth was found in the centre of the western half of the room.

The south-west corner room was provided with a wide doorway giving access from the Kitchen. The floor immediately north of the doorway was separated from the rest of the Kitchen by a line of edging stones, described as a worn kerb but possibly the base of a partition, screening this room from the external doorway in the west wall. The room was probably a scullery. It contained the remains of a flagged floor; and set into the south wall at floor level was a stone trough or sink. Presumably the sink was fed by piped water, like the similar troughs in the Guest House Scullery; but no evidence of piping was recorded. The sink discharged into an open, stone-lined drain (D2), which was traced 16 metres southwards, presumably on its course to the river (Fig. 26, S33). On its way, it crossed D4.

The central of the three southern rooms was a narrow space with a floor of carefully laid flagstones, with mortared joints (Fig. 24, S29). It had a narrow doorway at the south end of its east wall, which opened into the south-east room. This last unit again provided evidence of a flagged floor. It had a doorway in its north wall, giving access to the Kitchen, and another in the east wall.

On the north side of the Kitchen the pentice noted by St.John Hope would have provided shelter for food being carried from the Kitchen to the Misericord (Fig. 24, S30). It had a doorway at the west end, leading into the Warming House Courtyard. The cobbled floor sealed Cistercian ware,[100] and a French jetton (SF 402), both of late fifteenth-century date. Such a date would be appropriate for the Meat Kitchen complex as a whole.

A large quantity of animal bones, with soil, stones and sixteenth-century pottery, had been deposited along the west side and to the south of the Meat Kitchen. The bulk of this material, called 'the bone layer' in previous reports, had unquestionably accumulated during the last fifty years or so of monastic occupation: it overlay the foundations of phase-two walls, and had built up against the sides of the Scullery drain D2 (Fig. 26, S33). The use of this area for dumping refuse may, however, pre-date the known Meat Kitchen buildings, since features D4 and D5 overlay the lowest stratum of bone (the 'lower bone layer'). The animals represented included ox, sheep, goat, pig and deer. Fish and fowl were also present. Dr Ryder contributed lengthy and valuable sections on the animal bones to the previous reports.[101] The reader is referred to these for further details (see also Chapter 18).

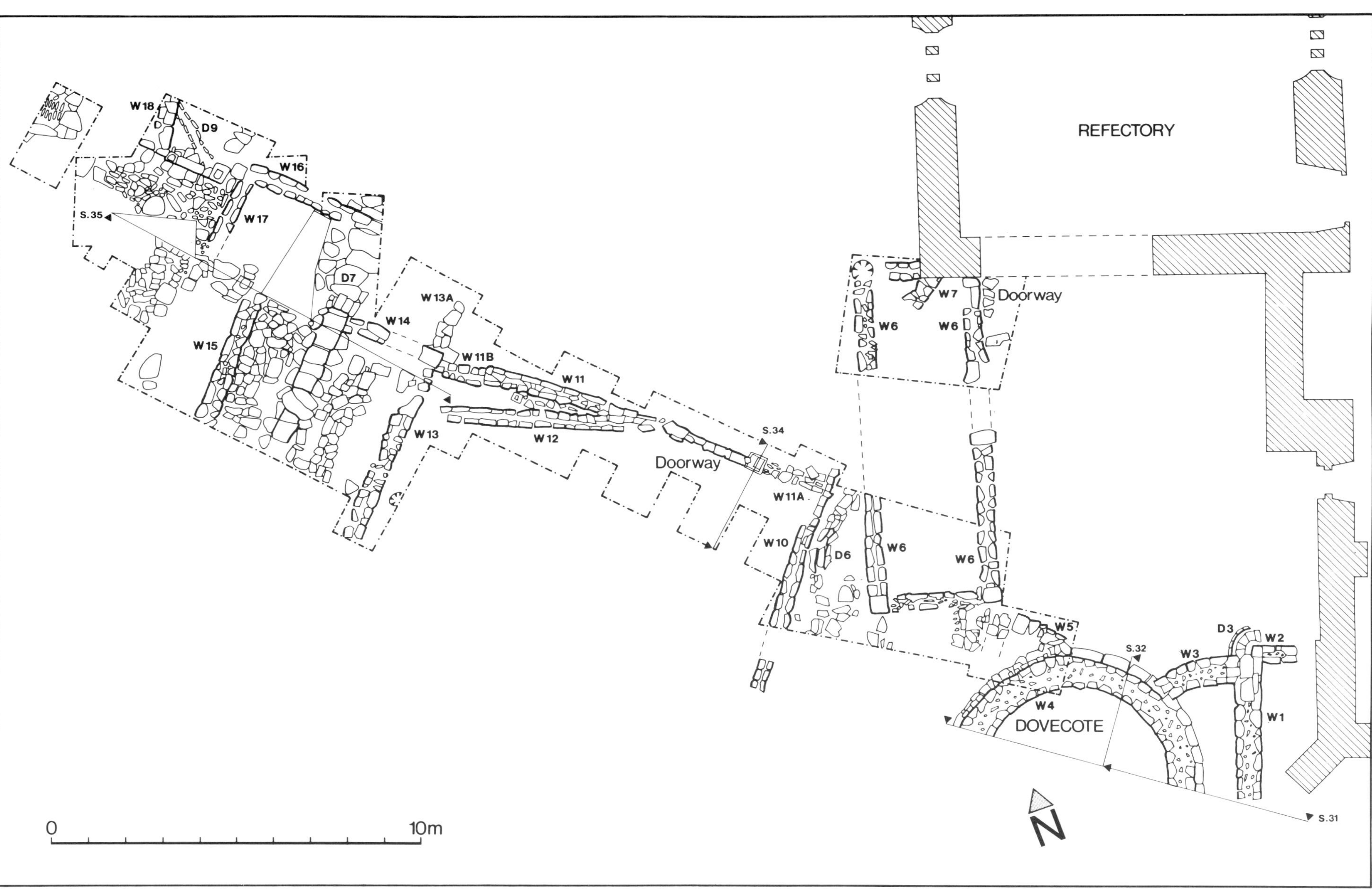

Fig. 27. Plan of structures south of Kitchen Yard. For sections see Figs 25, 28.

Chapter 10
Structures South of the Kitchen Yard

Introduction

A series of buildings and enclosure walls was traced along the south side of the Kitchen Yard and south of the second-phase Refectory. They were investigated over a number of years by means of dispersed trenches, numbered WR 1-14 (Fig. 9). These were followed by a more concentrated group of trenches, WR A to H. Original plans and sections survive for most areas, although the written record is sparse.

The structures are of various phases, but all save the latest follow generally a north-west to south-east alignment, roughly parallel to the main drain and to the buildings south of the Lay Brothers' Reredorter. Indeed, these latter buildings may well have been part of the same series. The orientation of the buildings on the accompanying illustration (Fig. 27) is different from that shown on a previously published plan.[102] The new alignment follows more closely a general plan, made in 1959, which survives in the archives. The remains were originally called the 'Workshop Range', later abandoned in favour of 'South Range'.[103] Only one of the buildings, the late structure attached to the south end of the Refectory, was recorded by St. John Hope.[104]

East end: early phase

The clearest stratigraphical sequence occurs at the east end of this area, where the early phase includes the circular structure, W4, which has been discussed in Chapter 9. The curving wall, W5, running up to W4 from the west, was additional, though it may well have been installed during the same phase of construction. At the west end of W5 was (as is evident on the photographs: Pl. 19) a squared stone, possibly a padstone for a timber; and next to it, another possible stretch of walling running south-westwards. All these remains (again on photographic evidence) underlay the earth and rubble make-up for the building defined by W6.

In a similar stratigraphic relationship to the W6 building was an area of cobbling beyond its south-west corner. It had been laid upon a spread of sand, clay and mortar, which itself lay upon the natural clay and gravels. It incorporated a length of drain, D6, and extended beneath enclosure wall W10. There was no walling directly associated with the paving or drain; but two stretches of wall occur in an equivalent position in the general sequence of strata, and probably belong to the same period of occupation. The first is a short

Plate 19. South of the Kitchen Yard: padstone and fragments of wall to the north-west of the circular building (W4), from the south. The south-east corner padstone of the late medieval building (W6) attached to the south wall of the Refectory intrudes in the top left hand corner.

length of wall (W7) which extended a little way from the south-west corner of the Refectory, in a south-westerly direction. It is recorded as having butted against the Refectory.[105] The second wall (W11) is the long enclosure wall running north-westwards, which also stood directly upon the sand, clay and mortar spread (Fig. 28, S34). It is possible that W7 had once extended up to W11, forming the south-east corner of the Kitchen Yard. Wall 11 was itself composed of three distinct stretches. At the south-east end, W11A was a rough rubble construction, and should probably be dated to the later phase. Immediately north-west of it was a doorway, flanked by squared jamb stones. Sockets cut out of the end threshold stones marked the position of the timber door jambs. Beyond, W11 continued for a distance of 7.5 metres as a neatly-faced wall, set upon the sand and mortar level. At its north-west end there may have been another doorway, later blocked by the rougher walling W11B.

The dating of the first-phase structures is not very precise; but in general they seem to belong to the thirteenth century. This is certainly true of W7 and W5 which butt, respectively, the second Refectory and the circular building; and it is supported by the dating of pottery beneath the cobbled surface to the twelfth and thirteenth centuries.[106]

East end: later phase

The main element of the later phase is the building defined by walls W6. It measured 9 metres by 2.5 metres internally, and was composed of mortar-bonded walls. The south-west and south-east corners were formed by large squared padstones for timber uprights (Pl. 19). Other padstones were found at the north end of the east wall (abutting the Refectory south wall (Pl. 20)) and half-way along that wall. The north-west corner stone had been robbed out. Immediately south of the north-east padstone was an entrance threshold, with remains of flagging both within and without. The flagging had probably extended across the whole floor area, and had been removed in the late nineteenth century. The remains unquestionably marked a timber-framed structure with interrupted sills, extending to two bays in length.

The south-west corner of the building had been cut through the first-phase paving. The paving had been buried by a spread of earth and rubble which extended beneath the floor of the building. On top of the make-up was a second paved floor, which is said to have butted W6.[107] The later paving was also associated with W10, an enclosure wall running southwards. The earlier drain D6 continued in use beneath this paving, though it was re-aligned at the south end where its original course was cut by W10. Wall 11A formed the new junction between W10 and the pre-existing W11; W7 was demolished. Further to the north-west, W11 was at some stage replaced by W12, which followed a more westerly route towards the W13 building. On the archive section drawings both W11 and W12 are shown sitting on the sand and mortar layer, surrounded and overlain by earth and rubble. It is possible that the record has been oversimplified.

The dating of this second phase is even more tenuous than that for the first. The pottery from the make-up layers of the W6 building was described simply as 'mixed'.[108] It is tempting, however, to relate these structures to the reconstruction of the Refectory and the development of the Meat Kitchen complex in the fifteenth century.

West end

The enclosure wall W11-W11B ran up to the east corner of a building defined by walls W13, W14 and W15. The structure was 4.5 metres wide internally, and aligned north-east to south-west; its southerly extent was not determined. The side walls were neatly faced, with rubble cores. The north-east wall W14 unfortunately lay along the boundary of several trenches, and was not fully recorded. The interior was paved with large stones; and in the centre, along the axis of the building, was a line of drain capstones at the same level (Fig. 28, S35). The capstones belonged to D7 (Pl. 21), which extended southwards from and at right-angles to the main

Plate 20. South of the Kitchen Yard: the north end of building W6, from the north-west. The south end wall of the Refectory is on the left.

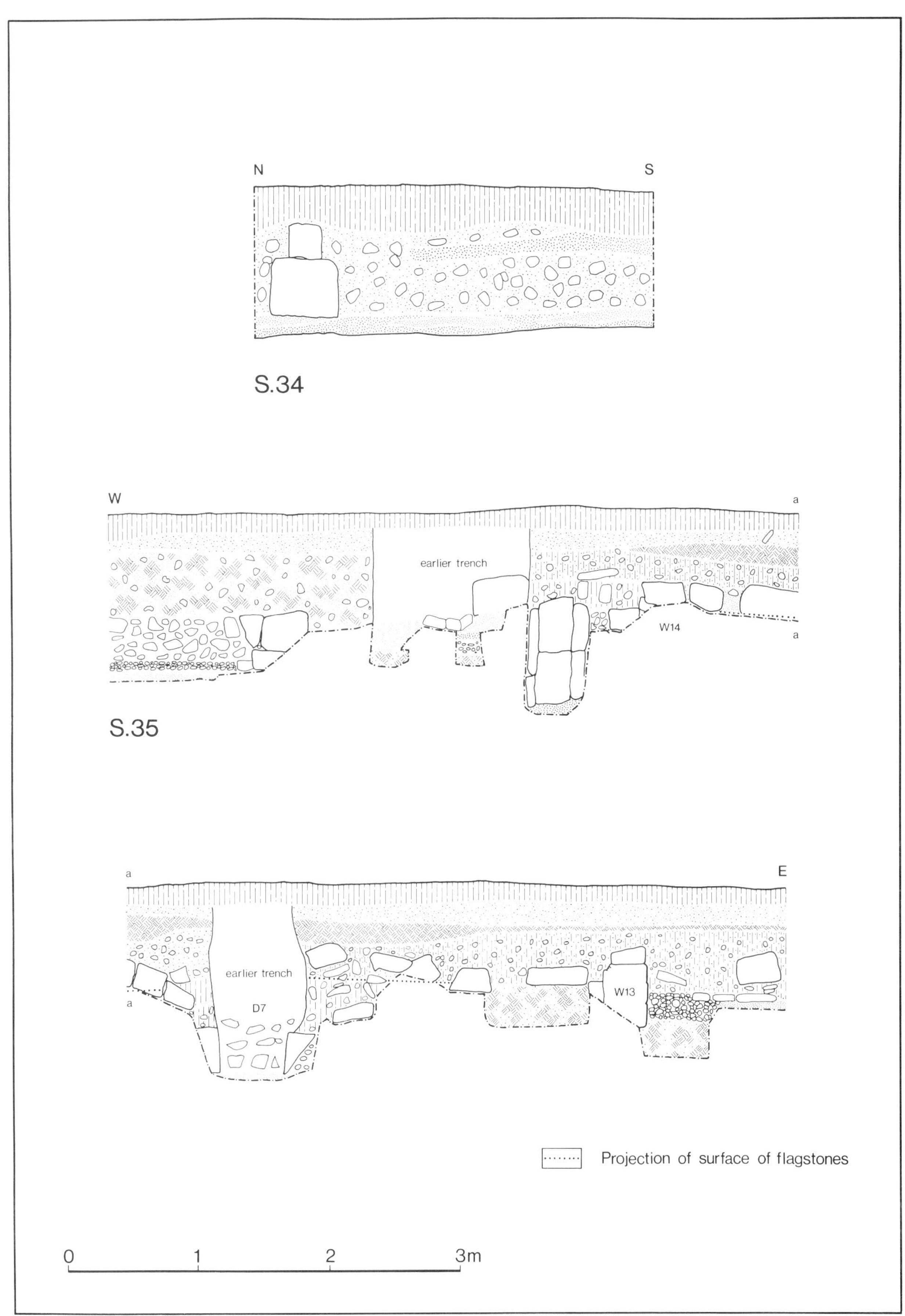

Fig. 28. Structures south of Kitchen Yard: sections.

drain (see Fig. 30). The building was structurally later than the drain, but it seems to have been positioned astride D7, as if the drain served some purpose within it. The earlier suggestion,[109] that this relationship was 'incidental', depends on the unwarranted assumption that D7 was no longer in use when the building was erected.

The remaining structures exposed in this area were more fragmentary, and it is not always possible to distinguish building interiors from exteriors. Some kind of (open?) enclosure to the north of W14 is indicated by the course of walls W13A and W16. From the north-west end of W16, W17 returned south-westwards, as far as a point in line with W14. Two substantial post sockets, at the south-west end of W17 and the north-west end of W14, (Fig. 28, S35), were thought to be post-medieval,[110] though the grounds for this attribution are unknown.

On its north-west side, W17 bounded an extensive area of paving, perhaps the interior of another building. The edge of this paving continued south-westwards beyond W17, but on the same course. It is probable that W17 had once extended much further in this direction. Running north-west from the north-east end of W17 was another wall which contained a doorway, with sockets for timber jambs (Pl. 22), and which had probably extended north-westwards to form the back wall of a hearth discovered in the most westerly trench. The presence of the hearth is further support for the suggestion that the paving represents the floor of a roofed structure. Finally, on the north-east side of the doorway was a wall (W18) running north-eastwards, which accommodated a small drain or water-pipe conduit, D9, within its fabric.

Plate 21. South of the Kitchen Yard: drain D7, from the south.

The dating of these buildings depends entirely upon their relationship to structures in adjacent areas. The drain D7, which preceded the building W13-15 and W16, has been dated *via* the Kitchen Scullery to the late twelfth or early thirteenth century (see Chapter 7 above). At the same time, W11, with a *suggested* thirteenth-century date, appears to have been aligned to W14. The structures are unlikely to have had a domestic function, given their situation; but otherwise their purpose is unknown. It is unfortunate that none of the pottery from this area can now be related to the recorded stratigraphy.

Plate 22. South of the Kitchen Yard: doorway, with socket stones for timber jambs, at the west end of the area, from the south.

Chapter 11
Building Phases South of the Cloister

Most of the excavation areas lay within and to the south of the southern claustral range. As can be seen on Figure 9, the trenches were widely dispersed: for the most part they grew out of attempts to trace various drains and conduits. The discoveries were, therefore, very fragmentary; but they were sufficiently coherent to allow a few, broad structural periods to be defined. These are based, inevitably, upon St. John Hope's phases for the standing buildings. The structures known only from excavation have been attributed to particular phases by means of direct archaeological dating evidence; or indirectly, by their associations with standing buildings which are themselves dated by architectural features.

Period I: the twelfth century (Fig. 29)

The first period is dated to the later twelfth century, and is defined by the primary stone buildings of the Abbey. The *Cellarium* and Dorter Range are both primary; and once erected they underwent few structural modifications. The South Range, containing the Kitchen, Warming House and Refectory was affected by more substantial changes. The original layout, as adduced by St. John Hope and confirmed by excavation, comprised an east to west Refectory with a small Kitchen at one end and a Warming House at the other. Our knowledge of the internal arrangements of these rooms is sparse. The earliest of the excavated kitchen hearths was a small, square setting slightly south of centre in the room. The west wall probably contained the serving hatch which supplied the Lay Brothers' Refectory. An entrance in the north wall gave access from the Cloister, and another in the south wall led to the Kitchen Yard. The wall dividing the Kitchen from the Refectory must have contained a hatch to allow the transfer of food. This may have been a full-height opening at the north end of the wall: otherwise, a blocked window between the Kitchen and Refectory doorways[111] is difficult to explain.

The Refectory was entered by a doorway at the west end of its north wall. The only internal feature attributable to this phase was the void of a water pipe which ran between the south wall and the centre of the room. It may have served a central laver or fountain, similar to the one at Clairvaux which was used for washing drinking vessels.[112] The enlargement in the excavated foundation of the south wall probably marked the site of the *pulpitum*: it does not fit the pattern of arcading, which in the South Range is limited to the upper part of the wall.

The remains of the wall separating the Refectory from the Warming House comprised two areas of rubble foundation with a gap between them. The southern expanse of rubble obviously marked something more than a partition: it may indicate that the fireplace was set in the south-west corner of the room. At the east end of the room, doorways in both the north and south walls allowed passage from the Cloister to the Warming House Courtyard.

The most difficult area of interpretation concerns the primary water supply and drainage systems. The pipe line which ran beneath the Parlour, and which pre-dated the foundations there, may have linked cisterns in the Infirmary Cloister and the main Cloister, in an arrangement similar to that illustrated at Canterbury.[113] The cistern in the main Cloister had the appearance more of a Suspirail, a ground-level structure used to remove sediment and reduce pressure,[114] than of a cistern with a header tank. It seems to have been linked to a deep, circular structure with vertical sides, perhaps a well, located a short distance from the Cloister Lavers. Wells in similar positions are known from Reading and from Lewes.[115] At Durham Abbey, St. John Hope excavated a stone-lined well with a similar diameter to that of the Kirkstall feature. It was again sited near to the Cloister laver, and was adjacent to its supply pipe-line.[116] Hope suggested that the Durham well functioned in a manner similar to that at Canterbury,[117] which provided an emergency supply when the pipes became blocked. Water was drawn from it to the top of a hollow column on the pipe-line, and this gave enough pressure to keep the laver in operation. The surviving wall-lavers at Kirkstall are dated to the thirteenth century. An earlier free-standing laver is, therefore, a possibility.

The problems of interpreting the drainage system centre upon the course of the main drain. Until the end of the 1950s it was assumed that the present course of the main drain, running more or less directly from the twelfth-century *Cellarium* to the twelfth-century monastic Reredorter, was established during the initial building campaign. In following such a route, it would compare well with the earliest arrangements at Waverley Abbey.[118] During the last few years of the Leeds Museum excavations, this assumption was, however, challenged on a number of grounds.

In the first place, the main drain deviates from a straight line where it passes beneath the east and west Refectory walls. It would not have done so before that building was erected in the early thirteenth century; but there was no record in the excavations of rebuilding along this stretch of drain.[119] Therefore, it was suggested that the stretch beneath the Refectory had not been installed during the twelfth century. Secondly, an alternative course for the main drain was found in the Kitchen Yard, in the substantial drain (D7) which runs southwards. Various pieces of evidence were adduced to support the idea that D7 and the main drain on its west side were built at one time (see Chapter 7, p.28). Another southward-running drain, D10, was proposed as an even earlier main drain course.[120] Finally, if the 'main drain' did not originally cross the Kitchen Yard, it could not have flushed the monks' Reredorter. The so-called bath drain (D1), from the Warming House Courtyard cistern, was proposed as the source of water to flush the Reredorter in the earliest phase.[121]

These arguments and others[122] are ingenious rather than convincing. The principal objection is that the Warming House Courtyard drain D1 was certainly installed no earlier than the early thirteenth century; and in any case it passed unequivocally beneath the main drain and on to the south. Therefore, the monks' Reredorter has no known independent source of flushing water. Secondly, the surviving records of the Refectory excavation provide no details on the main drain;

nor whether evidence of rebuilding was found, or even sought. Thirdly, drains D7 and D10 are not incompatible with a fully functioning main drain. They could well have been alternative courses which were used during periods of maintenance or rebuilding. The channel which runs south from the main drain sluice box near the Guest House[123] presumably had this kind of function. Fourthly, the main drain lining was rebuilt almost completely in the late nineteenth century, when it was re-employed for drainage purposes. In the Kitchen Yard only the lowest course of side stones seems to be original. Arguments about the dating of various stretches of drain cannot, therefore, be solved easily, by looking for breaks in the masonry bonding. There is, however, one piece of evidence which suggests that the stretch of drain within and around the Refectory was rebuilt when the Refectory was itself reconstructed: it is a distinct change in the alignment of the main drain beneath the Meat Kitchen north wall. This may reflect an alteration from a direct line between *Cellarium* and Reredorter, to a course which would allow the drain to pass at right-angles beneath the Refectory walls.

In general, we may conclude that, at the very least, the case for a multiple drainage system in the first phase is not proven. Furthermore, on the ground of building efficiency, we may ask why the monks would *not* have used the simplest and most obvious method of flushing the monks' Reredorter: by using the water which had already flushed the Lay Brothers' Reredorter.

Two other features shown on Figure 29 are the rubble-filled trenches on the east side of the *Cellarium* and on the west side of the Dorter Range. Their possible functions have already been discussed (Chapter 5, p.14), and their similarity to wall foundations has been noted. If they do represent walls rather than drains, then they must belong to a structural phase which preceded the building of the southern claustral range, though they may have been contemporary with the *Cellarium* and Dorter ranges. The last feature of this phase is the timberwork south-west of the monks' Reredorter, which presumably revetted a water course or fishpond. If the latter, then it must have served the Infirmary, since, in Cistercian houses, the consumption of fish was confined to the sick bretheren until the thirteenth century.[124]

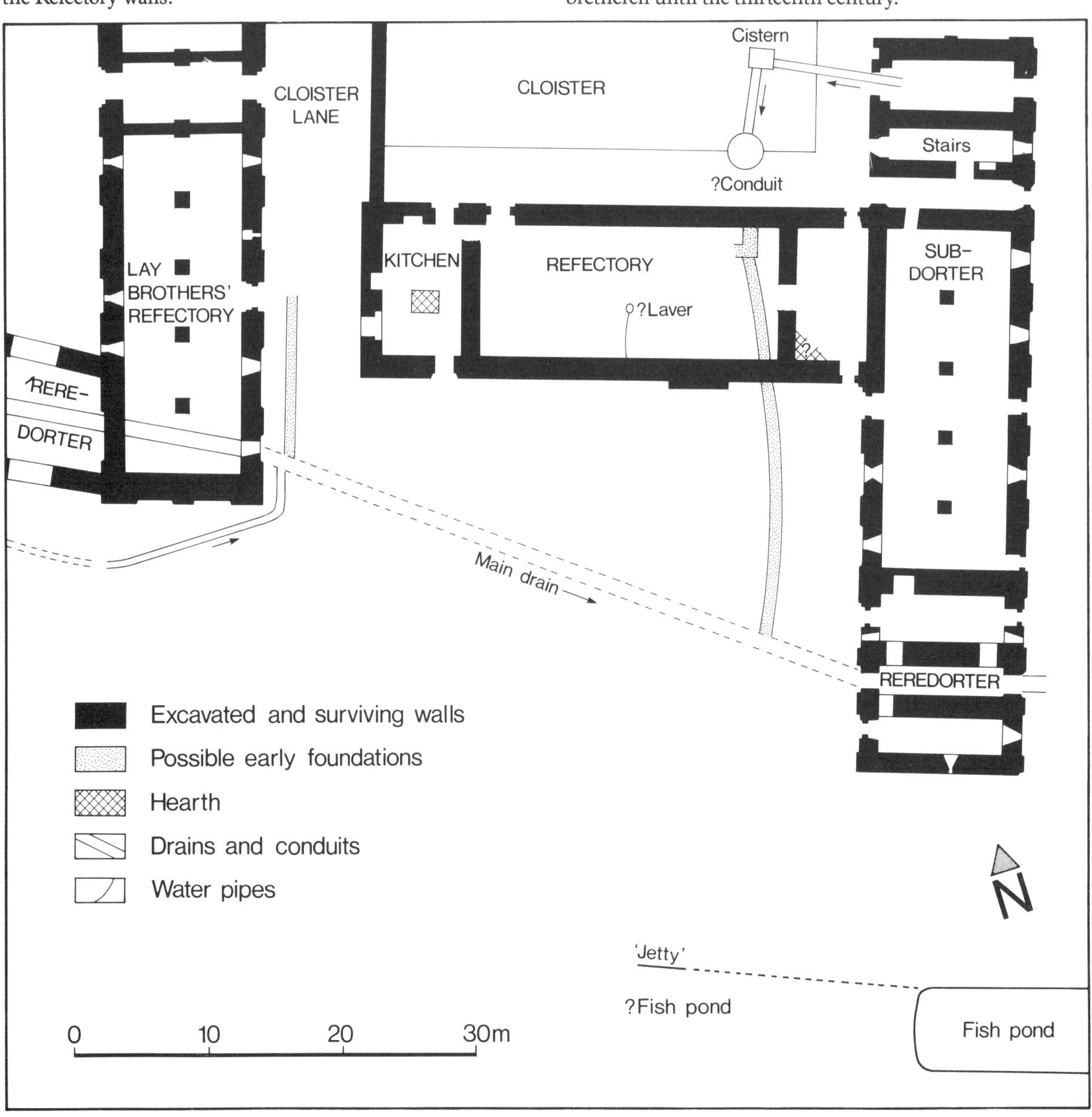

Fig. 29. Buildings south of the Cloister: first-phase plan.

Period II: the thirteenth and fourteenth centuries (Fig. 30)

The second structural period begins with the reorientation of the Refectory and the consequent enlargement of the Kitchen and the Warming House. The Kitchen was furnished with a bigger hearth, presumably signifying a greater number of monks or lay bretheren. It was also given a drain which may have begun at a water source. The main cleansing facilities were, however, provided in a separate scullery, which projected southwards from the south-west corner of the Kitchen. The Scullery contained another drain, which presumably served a sink in the northern half of the room. A water pipe which may have provided the building with a tap ran beneath the floor, and was probably linked to the piping found beneath the entrance to the Lay Brothers' Refectory in the *Cellarium*. Just outside that entrance, the pipe must have been carried over drain D10A, which probably disposed of the surface water in the Cloister Lane.

The Refectory contained another stretch of water pipe, in its north-west corner, close to the newly-inserted entrance. This probably served a wall laver used for washing the

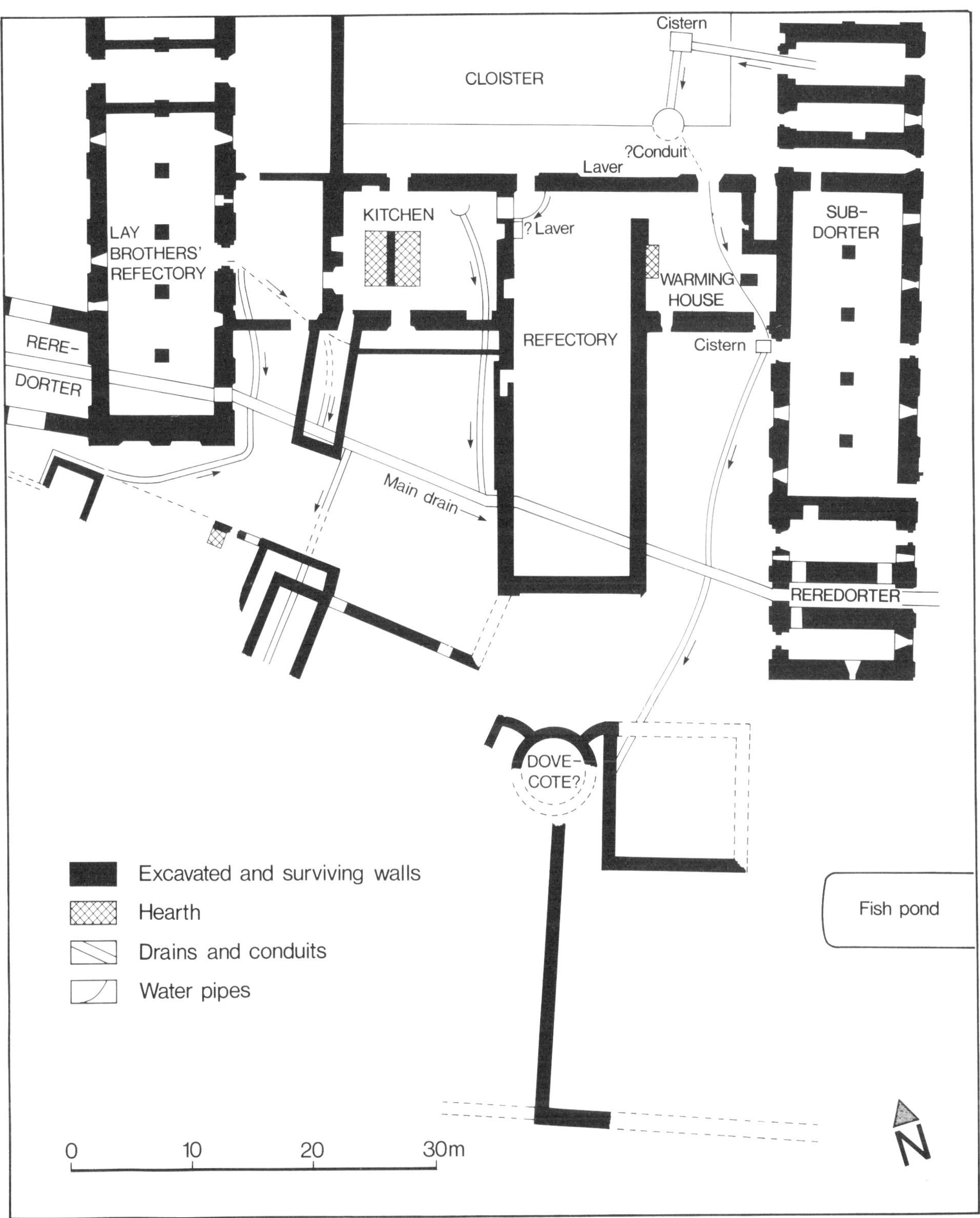

Fig. 30. Buildings south of the Cloister: second-phase plan.

drinking vessels after meals: a laver in this position, and probably for this purpose, is found at Waverley;[125] and at Kirkstall, the cupboard[126] set in the wall to the south of the laver position may have been used to store the vessels after cleansing. A new *pulpitum* was built into the west wall.

The Warming House was enlarged and provided with a new fireplace on the west side; on the east, a new flight of Dorter stairs was inserted. A lead water pipe was installed in a trench which ran from the north Warming House doorway to a cistern just outside the twelfth-century south entrance. It presumably gained water either from the wall-mounted lavers which were now installed, or from the cistern which fed those lavers. The Warming House Courtyard cistern was similar in form, and perhaps therefore in function, to the one in the Cloister. Both seem, from the surviving evidence, to have been subterranean chambers; but it is conceivable that each had a superstructure supporting a header tank, and that the pipes turned vertically upwards, one to supply a tank and the other to carry water away. The stone-lined conduit (D1) running south from the cistern may once have contained a pipe, as did a similar one at Durham.[127] Its destination is unknown, but it may have supplied a fishpond if not a building.

The southern stretch of the conduit (D1) ran through an area of 'made ground' which had been used to fill up the length of water course or fishpond immediately south of the Refectory and Warming House Courtyard. Later in construction than the conduit, but assigned to this phase, were two buildings set on the surface of the 'made ground'. One of these, circular in plan, was almost certainly a dovecote. The other was a timber-framed building, possibly square in plan. It function is unknown, save that it lies within an area which seems otherwise to have been devoted to domestic food production.

The area was divided by stone walls into at least two major enclosures. The north side of the more westerly of these enclosures was bounded by walls which ran parallel to the main drain, and which marked also the south side of the Kitchen Yard. The eastern half of this boundary was composed of a simple enclosure wall, with at least one doorway in it. The western half comprised a series of building and enclosure walls which seem to have run beyond the south

Fig. 31. Buildings south of the Cloister: third-phase plan.

end of the *Cellarium* and along the south side of the Lay Brothers' Reredorter. Some of these buildings may have been associated with the Lay Brothers' Infirmary, which was probably attached to the Reredorter as at Waverley[128] and at Fountains.[129]

Period III: the fifteenth century (Fig. 31)

The principal building alterations of this period resulted from two major changes in monastic life in the later Middle Ages. The first was the disappearance of the lay brothers, who at the end of the twelfth century had probably been much more numerous than monks. The creation of a Malthouse between the Kitchen and the *Cellarium* probably signifies formally the disuse of the Lay Brothers' Refectory. The construction of a vat on its south side must also have involved the destruction of the Kitchen Scullery. At the same time, the Cloister Lane to the north was abolished by the removal of its east side wall. If the buildings south of the Lay Brothers' Reredorter were also part of their facilities, these too may have been demolished.

The second change was the greater toleration of meat eating, which in the late fifteenth century led to the horizontal division of the Refectory block. The Kitchen, with a smaller hearth, now served a Refectory on the first floor; and at ground level a new meat refectory, or Misericord, was served by a new Meat Kitchen built against its south-east corner. The floor of the Misericord included inlaid mosaic tiles derived from an earlier floor. East of the Refectory block, the Warming House was modified. A new hearth and floor were installed, and beneath the floor a drain ran from the lavers to the Warming House Courtyard. It had probably extended as far as the main drain, like the similar one at Waverley.[130] The Dorter stairs were modified to allow access from the Warming House, and the space beneath the staircase was partitioned off.

The Meat Kitchen was built across the southern end of the Warming House Courtyard. Besides the Kitchen proper, it contained three rooms, one a Scullery and another probably for storage. The Scullery sink was presumably fed by piped water, but there is no record of a pipe. The drain ran south, across the sites of the Period II buildings and enclosures. A new building was erected at the south-west corner of the Refectory. Its alignment and entrance position indicate that it was associated with the Meat Kitchen. It was a timber-framed structure, erected upon a levelling layer which incorporated the demolished remains of the earlier walls. To the west, the enclosure walls were modified; but it is not certain how many of the structures south of the Malthouse were retained.

Chapter 12
The Abbot's Lodging

In the thirteenth century the abbot of Kirkstall was provided with his own suite of rooms, separate from the monks' dormitory. These lodgings survive substantially today, as an impressive example of a first-floor hall with solar above and undercroft below.[131] In 1956 the ground floor was almost totally excavated, in areas number I-IV (Fig. 32).[132] The unpublished drawings and notes have survived.

The excavations unfortunately produced no evidence of flooring in the undercroft. In fact, they revealed only two features of monastic date. The first of these was a short stretch of the main drain which lay beneath the east end of the undercroft, and which had been blocked and filled with soil. It was part of the thirteenth-century course of the drain, which had run below the east wall of the Abbot's Lodging and under the Chapel-Kitchen block of the Infirmary. When the Visiting Abbots' Lodging was erected in the fourteenth century, the drain was diverted to serve this new building; and the change of direction was accompanied by the blocking of a one metre stretch of the old drain immediately to the east.

To the east of the blocking, the old course of the drain recommenced at a square, cistern-like feature of uncertain date. A medieval 'drain' ran up to this feature from the south-west, where it entered the undercroft beneath the threshold of the south entrance. Though described as a soakaway drain in the previous report,[133] it comprised a triangular setting of stone tiles, with the apex at the bottom, in a narrow trench. It is much more likely to have been a water pipe conduit, discharging into the west end of the shortened drain. If so, it should probably be dated to the fourteenth century.

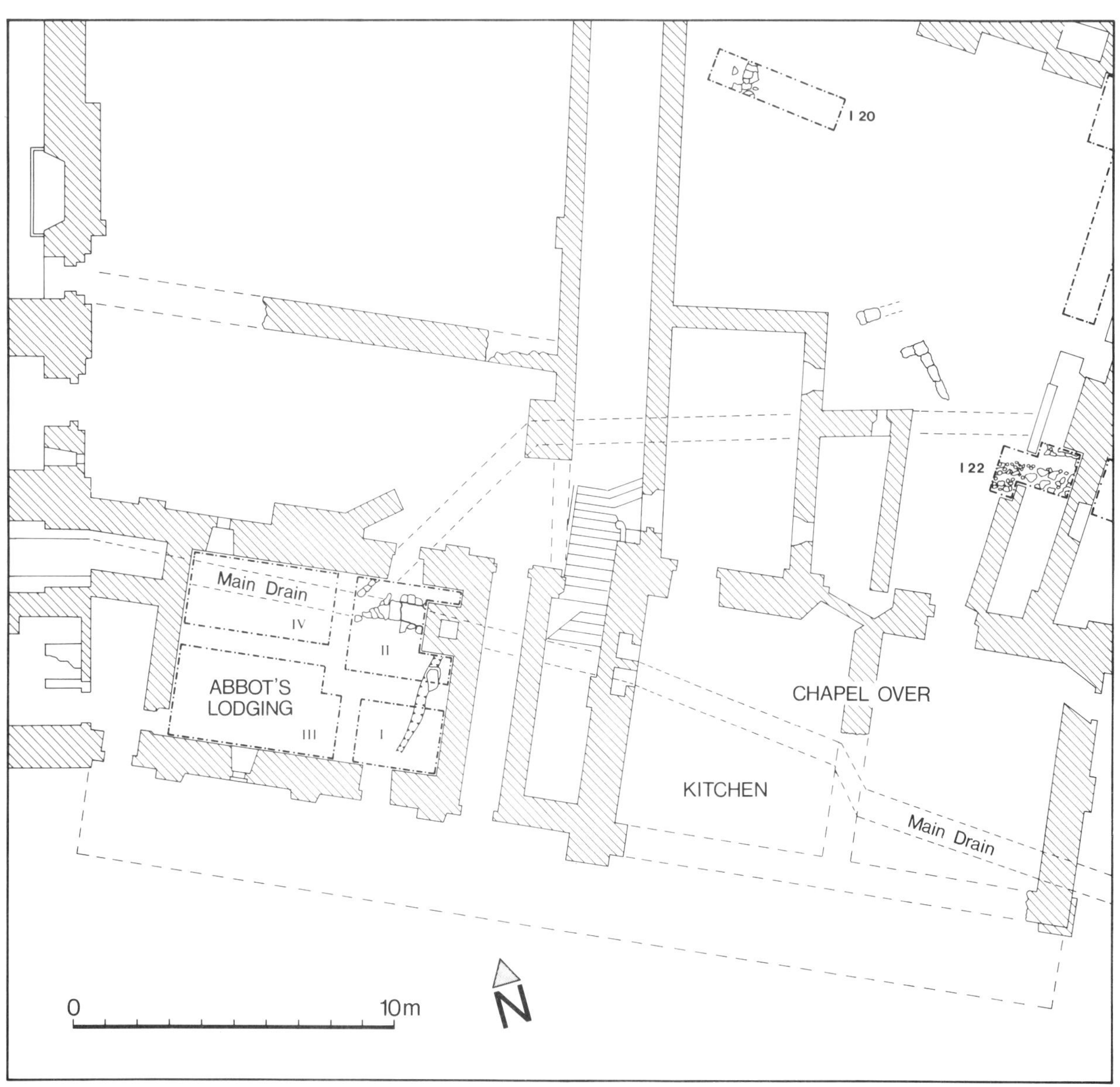

Fig. 32. Plan of the Abbot's Lodging.

Chapter 13
The Infirmary

The Infirmary, the dwelling of sick and elderly monks, lay on the east side of the Dorter Range. Its principal component was an aisled hall, aligned east-west (strictly north-east to south-west). It measured about 25 metres by 14 metres internally and was connected to the Cloister by a corridor, via the sub-Dorter passage. On the south side of the hall was a two-storey block, aligned north to south and identified by St. John Hope as the Visiting Abbots' Lodging. The south end of this was attached to another two-storey building, oriented east-west and identified as the Chapel and Kitchen of the Infirmary.[134]

The history of the buildings seen and described by St. John Hope can be summarised briefly. He ascribed to the early thirteenth-century Infirmary the main structure of the hall, though he believed that it contained only a single aisle, the south aisle, at that period, with timber posts rather than stone pillars forming the arcade. He also attributed to that period the Chapel-Kitchen block, lying about 16 metres to the south and presumably attached to the hall by means of a corridor. In the fourteenth century the hall was substantially rebuilt: the south aisle posts were replaced by stone pillars, a new north arcade was erected, and the east wall was largely rebuilt. On the east side, the Visiting Abbots' Lodging was erected between the hall and the Chapel-Kitchen block. 'There are reasons for supposing that it replaced an earlier structure of wood'[135] according to St. John Hope, though he does not in fact give those reasons.

In the fifteenth century a number of cubicles were created in the hall, to provide accommodation for inmates at a time when there was greater emphasis upon privacy and comfort. The arcades were walled up, and St. John Hope believed that additional apartments were created at first-floor level, over the aisle chambers. Among other changes, the east end of the south wall was taken down and rebuilt immediately south of its original course. A new Kitchen and Scullery were attached to the east end of the north wall.

In the 1959 season parts of the aisled hall were excavated in the hope of recovering closely dateable pottery (Fig. 33).[136] Trenches were sited in the east end of the hall (I 1-I 6), and in the Kitchen Yard (I KY1-I KY4) and Scullery (I S1-I S4) attached to the east end of its north wall. Work then progressed westwards along the interior of the south aisle (I 7-I 14), and revealed a stretch of wall foundation belonging to a previously unknown and earlier building. The investigation of this new building was resumed in 1964:[137] trenches I 14/64, I 15/64 and I 16-I 24 were dug in the Infirmary, the Infirmary Court, and the Visiting Abbots' Lodging, in order to trace the course of its foundations. Original plans, section drawings and notes are available for both years. They vary greatly in the amount of detail which they show. On the previously published plan, the composition of the early building foundations appears to change considerably from one stretch to another.[138] It seems, however, from the site plans that some at least of these differences are due to uneven recording; and for this reason the foundation stones and patches of cobbles have been re-drawn for the accompanying illustration (Fig. 33).

The excavations have in fact added little directly to our knowledge of the buildings described by St. John Hope. In the area of the north Kitchen Yard, a posthole was discovered on the line of the pentice wall. In the south aisle of the hall, the remains of a flagstone floor were discovered in the east end bay, and the line of the thirteenth-century south wall, demolished and replaced in the fifteenth century, was confirmed (Fig. 34, S37; Fig. 35, S38.). The flags rested upon a packing of broken stone tiles, which itself lay upon 'layer 1', described below. They evidently marked a late floor, since they were bounded on the north side by the fifteenth-century blocking wall in the south arcade. A spread of mortar beneath the wall may well have indicated an earlier floor. On the south the flagging was limited by the foundations of the thirteenth-century south wall. At their east end, these foundations were bonded into those of the east wall. The lowest course of south wall foundation rested upon a footing of rubble stones packed vertically in a trench. This form of construction extended westwards as far as the junction with the west wall of the Visiting Abbots' Lodging, whence it was replaced by horizontal rubble. It may have been an earlier

Plate 23. General view of the Infirmary area, from the north-east.

foundation, reused when the hall was constructed. The western part of the dismantled wall had been replaced by a stone platform, measuring 3.5 metres by 1.5 metres (Fig. 35, S38). It had a flagged surface, and must have been erected in the fifteenth century. Its purpose is unknown.

The two key strata found in all excavated trenches were layers 1 and 2. The first of these, encountered beneath the topsoil, was a band of clay containing small cobbles. Layer 2 was described as charcoal-flecked brown clay, and it separated layer 1 from the natural clays and gravels.[139] Layer 2 was about 0.3 metres thick in the area of the south aisle; but to the north it gradually thinned out, and was absent entirely from the north aisle (Fig. 35, S38).

The excavators believed it to have been material deliberately dumped on the site when the thirteenth-century hall was erected, to level up the pre-existing slope of the ground towards the river.[140] Whereas the natural gravels were clearly cut by the hall foundation trenches, there were no such trenches visible at the level of the brown clay. Layer 2 contained sherds which were said to date to the early thirteenth century, and layer 1 contained what was described a 'late monastic pottery'.[141] In the south aisle the patches of flagging already described sealed both layers. Once again, layer 2 incorporated pottery attributable to the early thirteenth century or later, as well as a coin of King John (1199-1216; SF 389); whereas layer 1 included Cistercian ware.

The four westerly trenches in the south aisle encountered

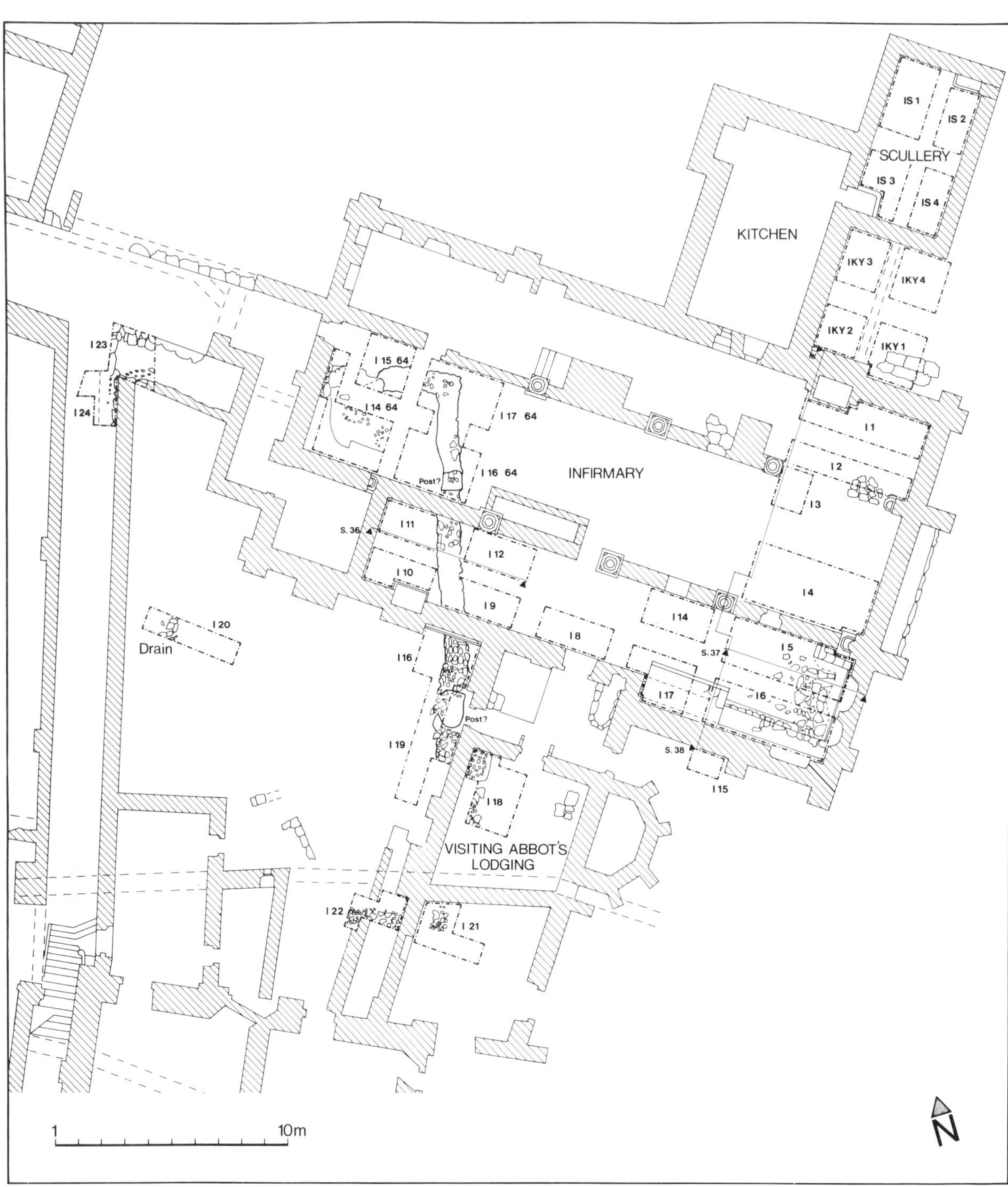

Fig. 33. Plan of the Infirmary. For sections see Figs 34, 35.

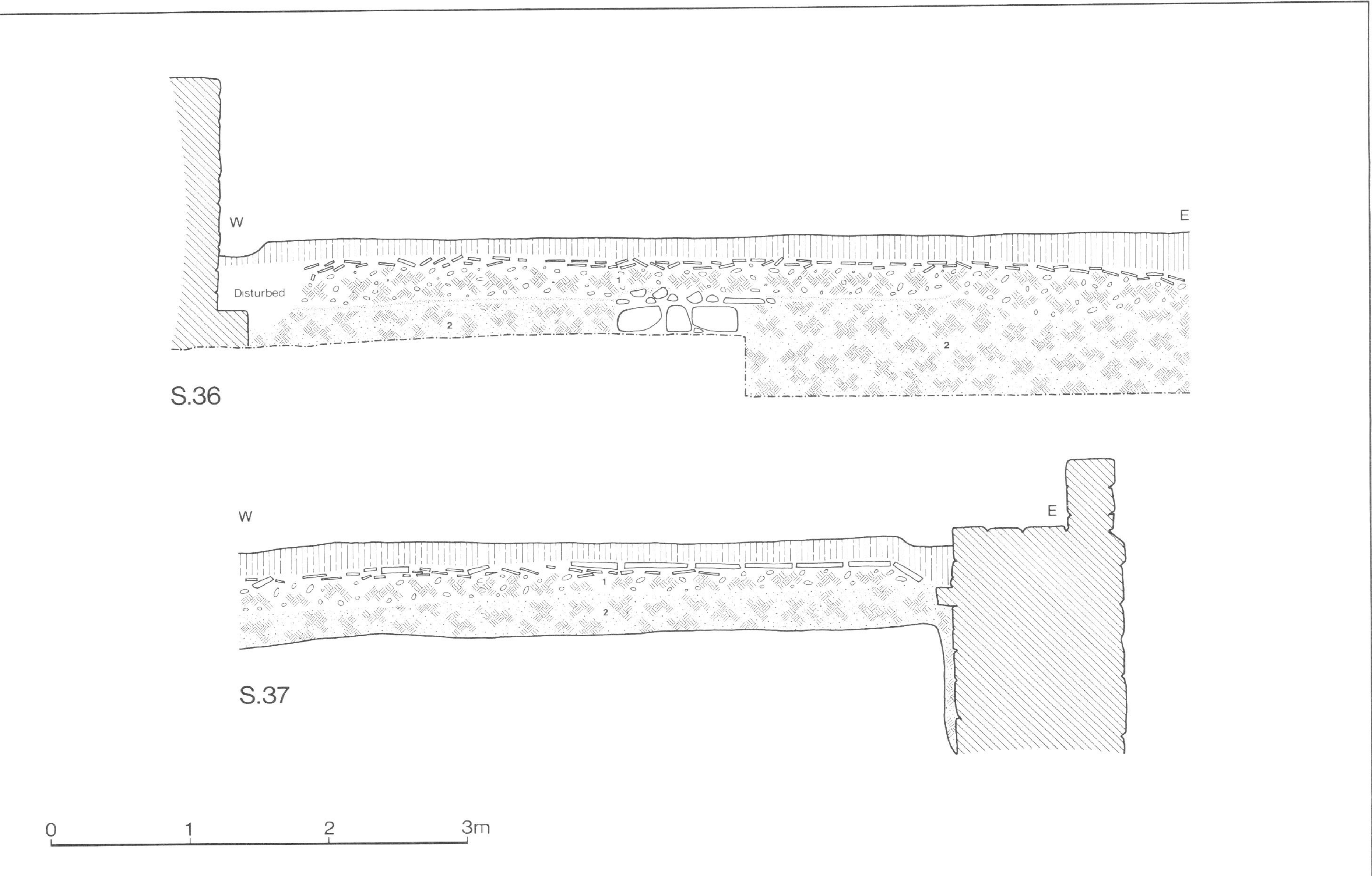

Fig. 34. The Infirmary: sections.

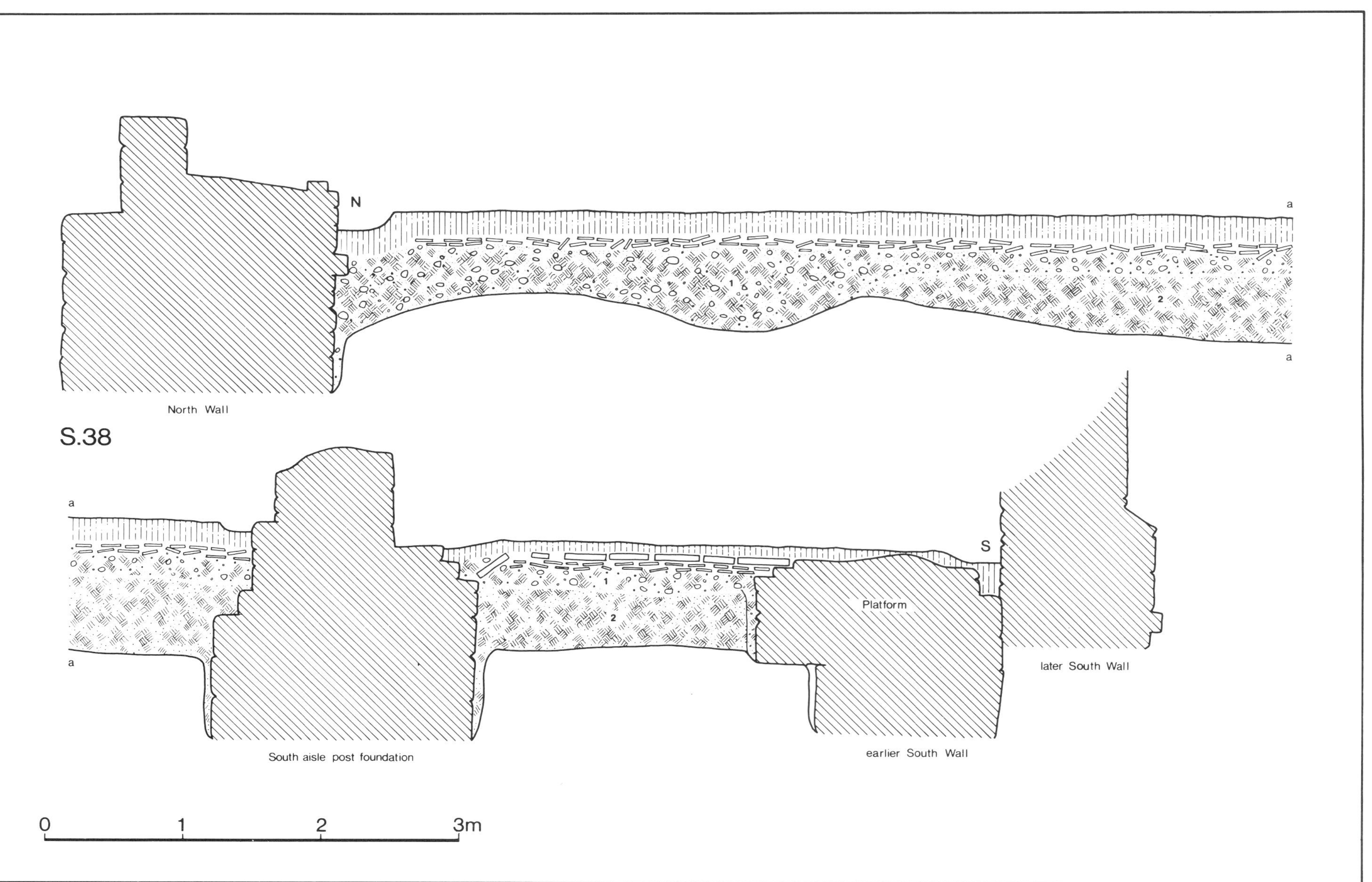

Fig. 35. The Infirmary: section.

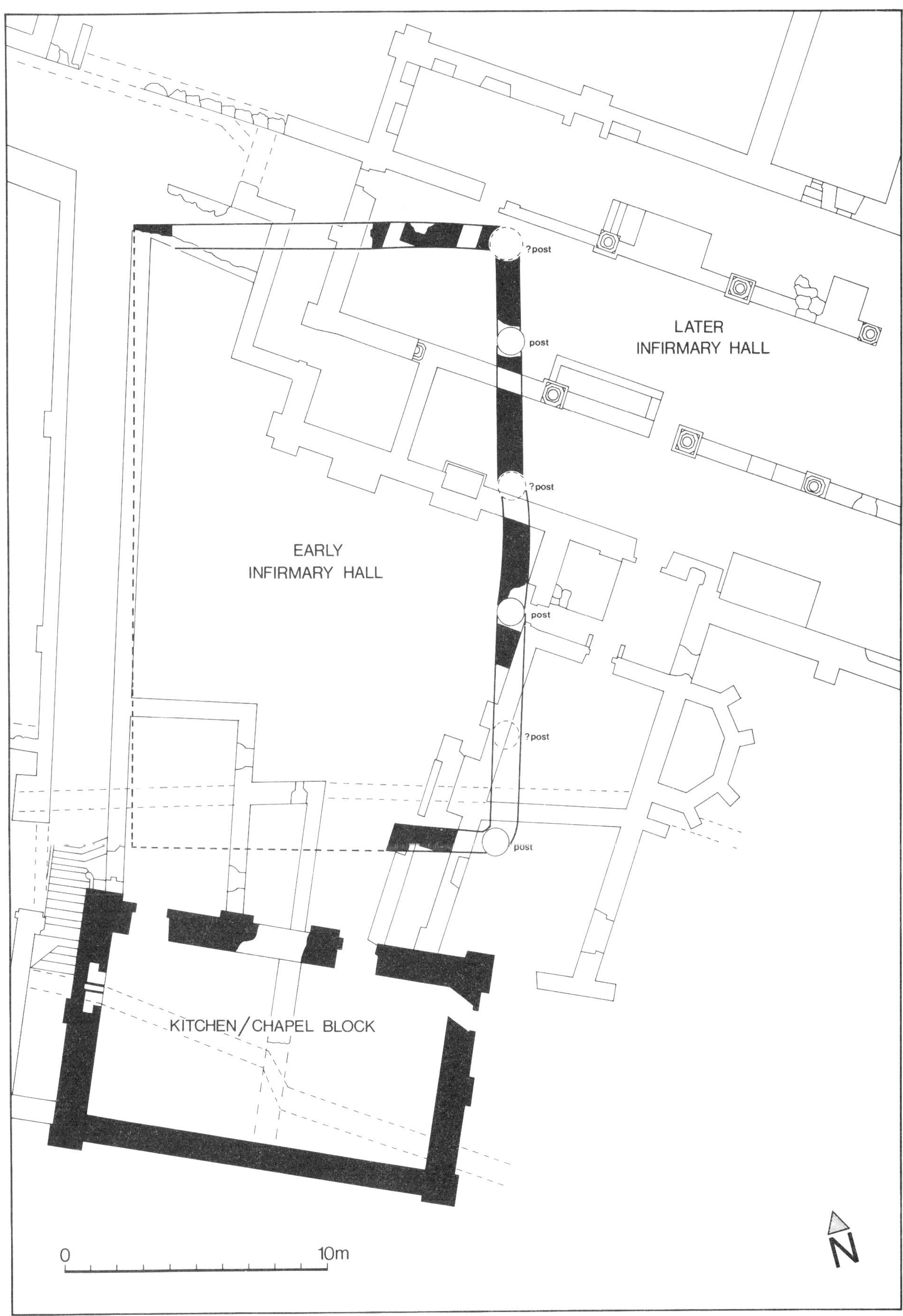

Fig. 36. First-phase plan of the Infirmary.

the pitched rubble foundation of an unknown building which predated the Infirmary hall. The base of the foundation sat upon the surface of natural clay (Fig. 34, S36). The rubble was surrounded by brown clay similar to layer 2, but, on the original drawing, the topmost stones protruded into layer 1 above. On both sides of the foundation, the surface of the brown clay was covered by spreads of mortar.

These relationships present certain difficulties for the published interpretation of layers 1 and 2. In particular, the brown clay surrounding the early foundation should not be part of layer 2, *if* layer 2 represents material dumped on the site when the present Infirmary hall was being constructed: for it is impossible to believe that the floor make-up associated with the early building foundations would have been removed entirely and then replaced by layer 2. The solution adopted by the excavators was to regard the brown clay around the early foundations as a separate layer: layer 2a. Yet there is nothing in the original records to support this differentiation. The division between 2 and 2a marked on the published section drawing[142] does not appear on the original (see Fig. 34, S36). On the site drawings, it seems much more likely that the early foundation was trenched into layer 2; and that this layer was in fact the pre-existing soil layer. The absence of layer 2 in the north aisle of the Infirmary would then be attributable to later disturbance, a suggestion much more in keeping with the soil divisions marked on the relevant section (Fig. 35, S38).[143] The finds from the brown clay outside (to the east of) the early building could then be regarded as material deposited in the soil during the life of that building. Their status as dating evidence for the construction of the Infirmary hall would be unaffected. It is significant that no artefacts were recovered from layer 2 within the area of the early building, where it would presumably have been sealed by flooring.

During the 1964 season further stretches of the early building foundations were uncovered by means of trenching. They all had the same general characteristics: pitched rubble of varying sizes trenched through layer 2 to the natural clay beneath. As such they invite comparison with the foundations of the subsidiary aisled hall, the West Hall, in the Abbey Guest House, excavated by the Archaeology Unit in recent years. There, too, the pitched rubble foundations were cut through the old soil layer (brown clayey loam) to the surface of natural. The building had been mainly a timber structure, based upon principal posts set in the outer walls opposite the pairs of aisle posts. The principals had been set upon large blocks on discrete, shallow foundations of small stones. Between these, deeper stretches of foundation marked lengths of stone walling which screened the building, but which had no part to play in supporting the superstructure.

The comparison can be taken further. The early building beneath the Infirmary was undoubtedly an aisled structure: its width, 14 metres internally, is identical to that of the Infirmary hall itself. There were, moreover, certain irregularities in the foundations which may have marked the positions of principal posts. One such place was in I 16/64 (see Fig. 33), where a depression in a patch of rubble was first thought to indicate a post position.[144] This interpretation was then abandoned, and the rubble, shallower than that of the adjacent stretches of foundation, was identified as an entrance blocking.[145] The original suggestion can, however, be reinstated, since the post footings of the Guest House timber hall had similar characteristics. Another irregularity occurred in I 16, where the foundation seems to have been enlarged; and a third possible place was in I 21, where a discrete patch of stones was uncovered on the line of the foundation. In some section drawings, layer 2 appears to overlap the top of the foundations;[146] but a similar phenomenon was observed in excavating the Guest House timber hall, and is thought to have been due to the use of clayey soil to level the tops of the rubble foundations for the lowest horizontal courses.

An interpretation of the general characteristics of the early Infirmary building is given in Fig. 36. There is little doubt that it was, in fact, an earlier hall, a timber structure with screen walls, which was replaced at some stage by the east-west stone-built hall. St John Hope dated the latter hall to the early thirteenth century, to the same period as the southern Chapel-Kitchen block which has a lancet window.[147] The first half of the thirteenth century was, indeed, a significant period for Cistercian infirmaries generally. The one at Waverley, which is the earliest stone infirmary apart from Rievaulx, was built around 1200. The surviving structures at Fountains, Meaux and Louth Park were all begun in the 1220s.[148] These must all have been preceded by twelfth-century infirmaries, which were presumably built of timber.[149]

The discovery of the north-south hall at Kirkstall would now, however, allow the east-west hall to be dated somewhat later than the early thirteenth century, without the need to find, in consequence, a new function for the Chapel-Kitchen block. If the interpretation of layer 2 is correct, then it would seem that debris associated with the occupation of the early Infirmary Hall was accumulating in the first half of the thirteenth century; but not, apparently, in the twelfth century (Chapter 14, p. 110). The Chapel-Kitchen block could have been erected in association with this early hall. The rebuilding and realignment of the hall could have taken place in the mid- or later thirteenth century, or even in the fourteenth century, on the basis of the *terminus post quem* provided by the finds beneath it, in layer 2. An early thirteenth-century date was accepted for the pottery because that was the dating attributed to the building by St. John Hope; but the pottery could well have been deposited later. Furthermore, the hall could have been repositioned specifically in order to enlarge the Infirmary Court, and thereby to allow it to encompass the Visiting Abbots' Lodging.

PART TWO

The Finds

An examination of the original site records, the published annual reports and the objects themselves shows that for some categories of finds, such as tiles, little of what was actually excavated has survived. The difficulty that this has created for assessing the pottery and small finds is discussed separately below (pp. 60, 120). Few of the excavation codes are shown on the detailed archaeological plans (Figs 6-36). For ease of location, therefore, all general area codes for finds mentioned in this report are indicated on Figure 37, while the detailed breakdown of specific codes within more general areas is shown on Figure 9. It has not been possible to locate some codes; but these relate to material which is not published in this report. A full list of finds is deposited with the site archive.

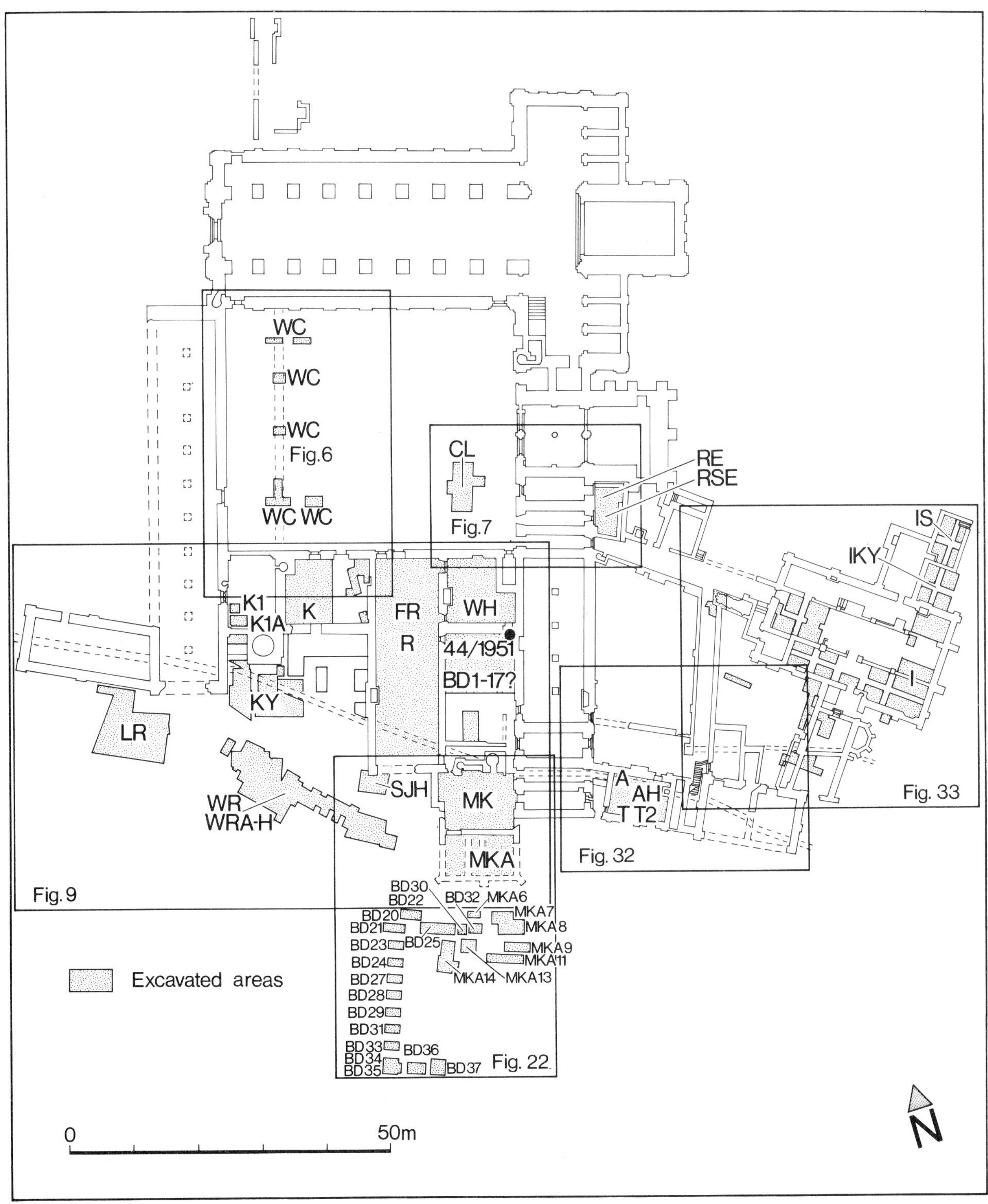

Fig. 37. Location of codes for all finds mentioned in this report. Details of their location are given in Table 1.

Chapter 14
The Pottery

by Stephen Moorhouse and A. M. Slowikowski

This report is divided into a number of sections. For ease of reference to any part an index is provided:

Table 1. The description of site codes located on Fig. 37.

Site code	Description	Site code	Description
44/1951	Warming House cistern	LRX	South of Lay Brothers' Reredorter
A	Abbot's Lodging	MK	Meat Kitchen
AH	Abbot's Lodging	MKA 1-5	Meat Kitchen service rooms
BD 1-17	? Warming House courtyard	MKA 6-14	South of Meat Kitchen
BD 20-32	Medieval 'made ground'	R	Refectory
CL	Cloister	RE	East Room
FR	Refectory (early Frater)	RSE	East Room
I	Infirmary	SJH 1	Range south of Kitchen Yard
IKY	Infirmary Kitchen Yard	T1, T2	Abbot's Lodging
IS	Infirmary Scullery	WC	Cloister Wall
K	Kitchen	WH	Warming House
KY	Kitchen Yard	WR	Range south of Kitchen Yard
K1, K1A	Malthouse	WRA-H	Range south of Kitchen Yard
LR	South of Lay Brothers' Reredorter		

Introduction

The excavations carried out for Leeds City Council between 1950 and 1964 had produced a large collection of pottery covering the lifespan of the Abbey. A section on the pottery was included in each annual report by Mrs Jean Le Patourel, while the final report summarised knowledge of medieval pottery as it was in the mid-1960s. In the light of new information revealed during excavations of the Guest House, it was decided to re-examine the pottery, and carry out a full quantitative analysis. This had not been done during the original post-excavation work because single groups of material had been excavated over a number of seasons and had been published piecemeal. An example is the large and important group from the Warming House cistern.

The pottery sections in the annual reports were models for their time and introduced ideas which did not achieve general currency for many years. For example, reference is made to the number of vessels represented in the Meat Kitchen and the Cloister cistern groups, rather than to the number of sherds.[150] Sherds from the same vessel but from different areas are noted.[151] Methods of construction are also occasionally noted, for example the separately-applied base found in the Kitchen.[152] A jar of Pimply ware (Type 1) from the Refectory (no. 54) is said to have been made by a left-handed potter working a clockwise wheel.[153]

Most of the pottery was housed in Leeds City Museum, arranged by date in boxes and by type within the boxes. A selection of material from the excavations formed part of the Yorkshire and Humberside School Museums Service mobile collection. All the pottery was brought together for re-examination, but it soon became clear that some of it was missing. The site records indicated that more pottery was excavated from certain areas, such as the Warming House, than survived in the collection. This was also apparent from the number of pieces now missing which were either illustrated or mentioned in the published reports. A number of vessels had glue on their edges for pieces that could not be found, such as Fig. 39, no. 1 from the pre-Cloister cistern group. There is an extensive card index of the material in the museum collection, but the individual cards give only a very brief description of the pottery, repeat the excavation codes marked on the pottery, and are of no help in locating the material.

An attempt was, however, made to reconstitute the groups. In some cases it was no longer possible to read the codes marked on the pottery, and in other cases the code could no longer be related to the site. The main difficulty was that codes created during the excavation, though marked on the finds, were not transferred consistently to the drawn plans, sections and written descriptions of those areas. In most cases layers on sections were not originally numbered, and arbitrary numbers or letters were introduced for the purpose of the report. It cannot be assumed that the higher the number in an area, the earlier the deposit, because context numbers were given to parts of trenches. In the absence of site records for some areas (see Appendix A), much of the surviving material cannot even be assigned to particular trenches.

This report therefore concentrates on those groups which can be authenticated from the site records. They are located in Fig. 38. When the re-grouping of the material had been completed a new type series was created in the light of new pottery types found in the Guest House. The different types were worked out principally by examination of the fabric, although differences in form, decoration and methods of manufacture were also taken into consideration. Each type was allocated a common name, where one did not already

Table 2. Details of the pottery groups published here. For their location see Fig. 38.

Group number	Location of groups		Illustration number	Archaeological evidence		Date (pp.110-11)
	Area	Sequence		Text	Principal Plans	
1	Cloister cistern	Pre-Cloister cistern	1-6	p.9	Figs 7-8	1152-late 12C
		Cloister cistern levelling layer	7-14	p.9	Figs 7-8	late medieval
		Fill of cistern	15-38	p.9	Figs 7-8	mid 16C
		Topsoil	39-46	p.9	Figs 7-8	—
2	Refectory	Make-up of first Refectory	47	p.19	Figs 13-15	1152 — early 13C
		Primary features	48-53	p.19	Figs 13-15	1152 — early 13C
		Make-up of second Refectory	54-87	p.21	Figs 13-15	early 13C
		Setting of slabs	88-89	p.21	Figs 13-15	early 13C
		Topsoil	90-110	p.22	Figs 13-15	early 13C — 1539
3	Infirmary	Layer 2	111-138	p.52	Figs 33-36	1152 — late 13C
		Layer 1	139-162	p.52	Figs 33-36	late 13C — 1539
		Topsoil	163-170	p.52	Figs 33-36	late 13C — 1539
4	Warming House	Layer 9	171-172	p.15	Figs 10-11	? 1152 — late 12C
		Layer 8	173-177	p.15	Figs 10-11	13C
		Layer 7	178-180	p.15	Figs 10-11	13C
		Layer 5	181-184	p.15	Figs 10-11	13C
		Layer 4	185	p.17	Figs 10-11	early 15C
		Layer 2	186-7	p.17	Figs 10-11	early 15C
5	Warming House cistern	Fill	188-228	p.17	Fig. 10	early 15C
6	Made ground S. of Meat Kitchen	Fill	229-246	p.36	Figs 22,26	? 13C

exist, based where possible on fabric or form descriptions, rather than date or source.

New types have been recognised since the original reports were written. Kirkstall Abbey B has been renamed Northern Gritty ware (Type 7 in this report); and late medieval versions of it have been defined: Late Medieval Gritty ware (Type 23) and Rawmarsh type ware (Type 19). Kirkstall A has been subdivided into Reduced Humber ware (Type 16), Oxidized Humber ware (Type 15) and Late Medieval Smooth ware (Type 30).

Selection for illustration was based on differences in shape, size, decoration, manufacturing techniques and evidence of use. Some of the pottery had already been illustrated in the original reports. This was, however, re-drawn both because new information had been gained since the first publication and also for consistency of style. Most of the information has been presented in tabular form, with the illustrated pottery being described by a combination of the Pottery Type Definitions and the Pottery Information Table (Table 8). The sorting, drawing, preparation of draft type definitions and compilation of all quantitative information was carried out in about 200 man hours.

The groups described in this report have been presented in chronological order. The dating of them is mainly on typological grounds, but as a collection they span the life of the Abbey and provide an important series of associated types for the area west of Leeds. To avoid duplication, the unassociated and unstratified material has been omitted from this report and will be assessed along with the unstratified material from current excavations on the site of the Abbey Guest House. The pottery and archive are deposited with Leeds City Museum.

References throughout this pottery report are kept to a minimum. The current knowledge of medieval pottery in West Yorkshire is to be discussed by the writers in a forthcoming publication which will contain reports on a number of medieval sites excavated by the West Yorkshire MCC Archaeology Unit. The pottery types defined and

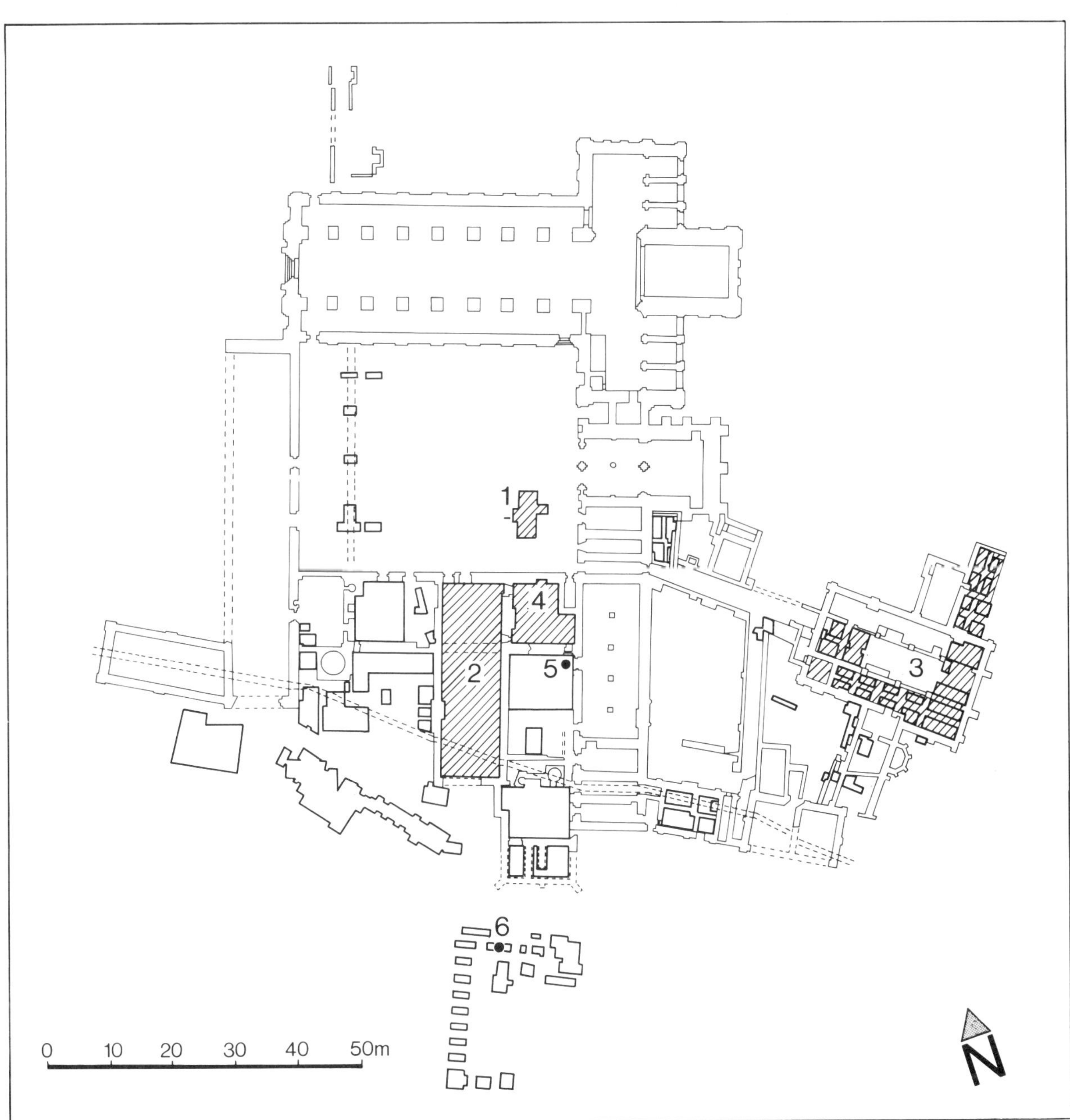

Fig. 38. Location of published pottery groups.

discussed in this report will be fully documented there.

Definitions of terms

Tradition. A collection of pottery with a range of general characteristics identified with a geographical area, e.g. Gritty wares of the north of England.
Regional style. A more closely defined collection of pottery within a tradition, probably typical of the products of a single potter or kiln group, e.g. Stepped jug ware.
Bowl. A vessel whose base diameter is greater than its height and whose rim diameter is greater than that of the base.
Jar. A vessel whose height is greater than the diameter of its base and where the rim diameter is no greater than that of the base. This term has been used in preference to the term 'cooking pot' as it does not imply a specific use.

Location of pottery groups (Fig. 38; Table 2)

This report presents a series of groups of pottery from the 1950-64 excavations. The six groups whose authenticity could be confirmed from surviving site records are located on Fig. 38. The much larger quantity of material whose original association could not be confirmed, together with the unstratified material, is reserved for the report on current excavations (1979 onwards) on the Guest House.

Pottery type definitions

Much of the local pottery from the site falls into a few types, and individual descriptions would be repetitive. The material is described by a composite type definition, covering all the vessels of that particular type on the site. A standard arrangement has been adopted, following that devised in the Sandal Castle report and to be followed in subsequent reports on medieval pottery produced by the Archaeology Unit. The defined type is given a common name based, wherever possible, on descriptive elements of the pottery rather than date or source. The range of forms is described, with reference to illustrated vessels as examples. Glaze and methods of manufacture are mentioned where diagnostic of the type. The range of decoration is described separately, with reference to the illustrated examples. Finally, all vessels of that type illustrated on Figs 39-56 are listed. Vessels with unique or unusual forms and features are noted in the type definitions. The types are arranged in chronological order as they appear in the sequence of groups.

Type 1
Common name: Pimply ware.
Hard, gritty fabric, usually oxidised when it is a white-buff colour.
Forms: Mainly jars and bowls, usually small and thin-walled, although larger jars do occur (no. 54). Jugs are also present, but not as frequent. All vessels have slightly sagging bases and are unglazed.
Decoration: Jars and bowls are plain. Jug no. 39 is decorated with rouletting beneath the rim and jug no. 48 is thumbed at the base of the strap handle. There is one sherd from an unrecognised vessel (no. 4) which is decorated with an applied thumbed strip. These vertical thumbed strips have been found on twelfth- and thirteenth-century pottery from other sites in the modern county. They occur on large vessels and served not only as decoration, but also as an aid to handling.
Illustrations: 2-4, 7, 39, 47-51, 54-71, 90-92.

Type 2
Common name: York type ware.
Hard, gritty, pale orange-pink in colour, oxidised.
Forms: Only one example is present, a small jar with everted rim.
Decoration: None
Illustration: 72.

Type 3
Common name: Hillam type ware.
Hard gritty, buff-pink in colour, oxidised.
Forms: Only one example is present, a jug with square rim and straight sides.
Decoration: None
Illustration: 1.

Type 4
Common name: Developed Stamford ware.
Hard, very fine, smooth fabric, white in colour, oxidised.
Forms: Only one example is present, a possible jug, whose sherds were found both among the Refectory material and in the collection excavated from the Guest House in 1981 (see Table 10, no. 73).
Decoration: This vessel has a thick green external glaze and applied combed strip decoration.
Illustration: 73.

Type 5
Common name: South-west Midlands Coarse ware.
Soft, extremely gritty fabric, partially reduced, varying in colour from buff-orange through red-brown to light grey. These vessels appear to be hand made and finished on a wheel. This type is common all over the south-west Midlands, and at Dudley Castle it has been found in fourteenth-century contexts.[154]
Forms: Only jars and bowls are present, with either upright or everted rims.
Decoration: Usually plain and unglazed.
Illustrations: 53, 74.

Type 6
Common name: Tripod Pitchers.
Fairly soft, very sandy, partially reduced fabric, pale orange where oxidised and grey where reduced.
Forms: These vessels have the typical rounded shape of pitchers throughout the south-west Midlands, with sloping strap handles. They had three small feet, although no bases have been found at Kirkstall Abbey.
Decoration: Usually green-glazed externally. The most common decoration is a combed pattern on the body (no. 52), but notched decoration on the handle is known (no. 89), as is a 'twisted rope' inlaid into the handle (no. 52).
Illustrations: 52, 89.

Type 7
Common name: Northern Gritty ware.
Fairly hard, gritty fabric. Usually oxidised when it is orange-brown in colour, sometimes with a grey core, although partially reduced or completely reduced examples occur, when they are light grey in colour.

Forms: A wide variety of forms occurs, including jars, bowls, pipkins, jugs, curfews, urinals, chalices, lids, dripping pans and industrial vessels. Although the rims of jars vary, they tend to be rounded and the bodies vary from rounded (no. 189) to barrel shaped (no. 190) to sagging bellied (no. 188) with slightly sagging bases. They vary in size. Bowls also vary in size from the very small (no. 202) to the large (no. 6). They occur in both rounded (no. 196) and straight-sided forms (no. 195). Jugs also vary in size and shape, and their handles are most often strap, applied to the body and thumbed; jug no. 206 is unusual in that it has a twisted rope handle, with a single thumbing at its base. Although jars, bowls and jugs predominate, other forms occur. Curfews (nos 145 and 177), urinals (no. 237), lids (nos 95, 122 and 236), pipkins (no. 218), a lid or chalice (no. 15) and dripping pans (no. 124 and 238) are also present. Two vessels with possible industrial uses were found (nos 88 and 80). Only the lower parts of these vessels survive, but they appear to be straight sided, roughly manufactured and the bases are very thick, up to 2cm. at the base angle. There are also two unrecognisable forms, no. 184 and no. 123, the latter being a possible jug form, with the addition of many holes bored through the body before firing, possibly for use as a strainer.

Decoration: Jars are always plain and bowls are only rarely decorated. Bowls nos 198 and 6 are grittier than usual and have applied thumbed strips. Thumbing along the edges of the handle, and impressed decoration along the rim are found on bowl no. 75. All other bowls are plain. Decoration is more common on the jugs, which are patchily glazed, usually on the upper parts of their bodies, either green or brown. It includes wavy lines (no. 166), random semi-circular stamps (no. 77), applied impressed strips (no. 40), applied plain strips (no. 115), combed decoration (no. 172) and randomly applied pellets (no. 178). Decoration sometimes also occurs on other vessels. Curfew no. 177 and unrecognisable form no. 184 have thumbed decoration along their rims. One variant of this type has a very distinctive use of white clay. This only occurs on jugs and is usually seen as applied and impressed circular pads or strips of white clay (nos 132, 214-18). Rarely, white clay in the form of a slip is used as an over-all cover, as on pipkin no. 218.
Illustrations: 5-6, 8, 15, 40, 75-80, 88, 93-96, 111-24, 132, 139-45, 163-67, 171-79, 181-86, 188-218.

Type 8
Common name: Orange Gritty ware.
Soft, very gritty, orange-pink fabric, usually oxidised, sometimes with a light grey or creamy yellow core.
Forms: Jugs and bowls predominate. Some vessels have wide handles springing straight from the rim. Handles are strap and jug rims vary from the upright (no. 82) to the everted (no. 81). This could be a softer, underfired version of Northern Gritty ware (Type 7) but it has been classified as a separate type because it has occurred so frequently both on the Abbey site and at the Guest House, and could well have been deliberately underfired. This could be the type that is referred to in the published reports as an underfired version of 'the familiar Kirkstall gritted ware'.
Decoration: This is restricted to jugs and consists of applied and impressed white clay or horizontal incised lines, and patchy green or brown glaze on the exterior, upper part of the body.
Illustrations: 81-82, 126-31, 146, 168.

Type 9
Common name: 'Stepped Jug' ware.
Fairly hard, gritty fabric, usually white but sometimes pale pink in colour, oxidised.
Forms: All examples of this type are jugs. Few sherds were found and it was impossible to illustrate a full profile, but at Sandal Castle, where full profiles were obtained, this type was characterised by either a barrel shape with a ridge around the base of the neck or a ridge around the middle of the body, giving the vessel a 'stepped' appearance.[155]
Decoration: At Kirkstall Abbey this consisted of impressed decoration running vertically down the body of the jug.
Illustration: 133.

Type 10
Common name: Unidentified non-local wares.
Fairly soft to hard, fine sandy fabrics of as yet unrecognised type from a variety of probably non-local sources.
Forms: All are single jugs, of varying sizes, shapes and decoration.
Decoration: Includes applied pellets (no. 41), horizontal incised lines (no. 137) and applied twisted strips with comb impressions (no. 135).
Illustrations: 9, 16, 41, 83-85, 97-99, 135-37, 147, 187.

Type 11
Common name: Fine sandy ware.
Hard, sandy fabric, fairly smooth and fine. Orange in colour when oxidised and light grey when reduced.
Forms: This is one of the unrecognised non-local sandy types (Type 10), but has been allocated a separate number because several examples have been found, not only at Kirkstall, both in the Abbey and the Guest House, but also at Elland Hall. All vessels are jugs, of various shapes and sizes, with strap handles thumbed at their bases.
Decoration: A tubular spouted jug (no. 134) is decorated with applied stamped pads of white clay. Stabbing occurs on a handle from a jug (no. 221), and around the base angle (no. 100).
Illustrations: 86, 100, 134, 219-21.

Type 12
Common name: Pink fine ware.
Hard, fine, sandy fabric fairly smooth, oxidised, pink in colour. This type originates probably in the south-eastern Midlands.
Forms: Jugs, although among the unassociated material there is an unrecognised form with a bowl-like rim.
Decoration: Interior is glazed a mottled green-yellow colour, exterior is glazed a patchy light yellow colour.
Illustration: 242

Type 13
Common name: Rouen ware.
Hard, very smooth, fine white fabric, oxidised.
Forms: Only one jug was found.
Decoration: A clear glaze over brown panels with pellets of white clay, separated by strips of rouletted white clay.
Illustration: 42.

Type 14
Common name: South-western French Polychrome ware.
Fairly soft, very smooth, fine grey-white oxidised fabric.
Forms: Jugs sometimes with moulded faces at their rims.

Decoration: Glazed green internally, and painted various colours externally.
Illustration: 148.

Type 15
Common name: Oxidised Humber ware.
Fairly hard, smooth sandy fabric. Light orange-brown in colour, oxidised.
Forms: Jugs and jars occur.
Decoration: Vessels often have a patchy green glaze externally, with runs towards the base, indicating that the vessel was fired in an upright position.
Illustration: 17, 180.

Type 16
Common name: Reduced Humber ware.
Hard, sandy fabric, reduced and grey throughout, slightly coarser than Oxidised Humber ware (Type 15).
Forms: Mainly jugs.
Decoration: External green glaze.
Illustration: 18.

Type 17
Common name: Skipton on Swale jugs.
Fairly hard to hard, smooth sandy, oxidised, orange brown fabric.
Forms: All are drinking jugs, small and cylindrical in shape, flat-based and without pouring lips. Rod handles are attached to the body by applying and pressing with the thumb at any angle, leaving the mark of the thumb nail running along the length of the impression at the base of the handle. Throwing lines are often very pronounced on the interior, and the exterior has been smoothed over.
Decoration: Unglazed and undecorated.
Illustrations: 10, 222-25.

Type 18
Common name: York White ware.
Fairly hard, smooth, sandy fabric. Always oxidised, it is a creamy white colour, sometimes with a pink core.
Forms: Jugs with thumbed bases and sometimes tubular spouts. Lobed cups and seal jugs also occur; the latter are very rare and occur only amongst the unassociated material. There is one very small bowl (no. 149), and a fragment of a possible lid (unillustrated).
Decoration: Jugs have a green-yellow glaze and lobed cups have a mottled green glaze. Decoration on jugs includes impressed applied strips and random impressions.
Illustrations: 11-13, 43-44, 101, 138, 149-52, 169, 226.

Type 19
Common name: Rawmarsh type ware.
Hard to very hard, gritty fabric with frequent black inclusions (iron-ore) giving a speckled appearance. Colours range from buff to red-brown when oxidised and purple-grey when reduced.
Forms: Mainly jugs and cisterns. Cisterns occur with two and three handles.
Decoration: Glazed orange-brown to purple-brown, often mottled when oxidised, and dark purple when reduced.
Illustrations: 19-21.

Type 20
Common name: Tudor Green type ware.
Fairly hard, fine, smooth white fabric, oxidised.
Forms: Jugs and lobed cups, although the latter only occur among the unasssociated material.
Decoration: A thick, even bright green glaze.
Illustration: 22.

Type 21
Common name: White-slipped Humber ware.
Hard, sandy, fairly smooth fabric. Oxidised to a red-brown colour, with an overall white slip beneath the glaze.
Forms: Only one fragment of a lobed cup was found.
Decoration: A clear glaze with the addition of copper to give a speckled green appearance.
Illustration: 102.

Type 22
Common name: Baildon ware.
Hard, sandy, smooth fabric. Oxidised internally, orange-brown in colour, reduced externally, grey in colour.
Forms: Only one jug was found.
Decoration: Incised wavy lines on the shoulder and a thick green glaze.
Illustration: 23.

Type 23
Common name: Late Medieval Gritty ware.
Hard, fairly rough gritty fabric, both reduced and oxidised examples occur. Colours when oxidised range from orange to brown, when reduced, light to dark grey. This appears to be one of the late medieval developments of the Northern Gritty ware (Type 7) tradition.
Forms: Not a common type at Kirkstall; on other sites jars, jugs and cisterns are found, but only one was found at Kirkstall.
Decoration: Purple glaze on reduced examples and brownish green on oxidised examples.
Illustration: 245.

Type 24
Common name: Cistercian ware.
Hard, fine, smooth fabric, brick-red to purple in colour.
Forms: Mainly cups of various types. There are concentric grooves on all the bases where the vessel has been removed from the wheel with a loop of wire, and patches of sand on which the vessel rested.
Decoration: All vessels have a thick brown to black glaze, internally and externally, often gathering in the base angle where the vessel rested at a tilt. There is some applied decoration in white clay (no. 25).
Illustrations: 24-8, 103-07, 153-57.

Type 25
Common name: Reversed Cisterian ware.
Hard, fine, sandy fabric, creamy-white, always oxidised. Sometimes highly fired to give an almost vitrified, light grey appearance to the fabric.
Forms: Few fragments were found, but forms are presumably similar to those of Cistercian ware (Type 24).
Illustration: 25.

Type 26
Common name: Yellow ware.
Fairly hard, white fairly smooth fabric, oxidised.
Forms: Bowls are the most common form.

Decoration: Number 160 has a 'V' shaped roulette design along the top of the rim and no. 161 has an impressed decorated rim. A thick clear glaze gives a bright yellow appearance to the vessels.
Illustrations: 160-62.

Type 27
Common name: Vitrified Earthenware.
Very hard, almost stoneware fabric. Brick-red to purple in colour when underfired, but more usually chocolate brown. Similar in appearance to Cistercian ware (Type 24) but the forms are totally different.
Forms: Jars and cisterns.
Decoration: Number 158 has cut outs in the rim. Glaze is purple-brown in colour, thick on the exterior and thinner on the interior.
Illustrations: 158-59.

Type 28
Common name: Brick-red Sandy ware.
Hard, fairly fine, sandy fabric, oxidised, brick-red in colour.
Forms: Three-handled cisterns.
Decoration: Glazed externally, green-brown to purple. Decorative strengthening around the neck in the form of an applied thumbed strip.
Illustration: 30.

Type 29
Common name: Midland Purple type ware.
Very hard, gritty and rough fabric. Reduced, grey-purple in colour. A similar type can be found all over the Midlands, although it is less gritty than the Northern equivalents.
Forms: Small jugs and jars.
Decoration: None, except for a purple glaze occasionally, on the upper parts of their bodies.
Illustrations: 108-09.

Type 30
Common name: Late Medieval Smooth ware.
Hard, very smooth, although can have an uneven surface due to grits showing through, or small pits where they have fallen out. Both oxidised and reduced examples occur, red-brown when oxidised and grey when reduced, sometimes both on the same vessel.
Forms: The majority of vessels are round-rimmed jugs with strap handles. Other vessels include urinals, cisterns and jars, although not all forms are found among the associated groups.
Decoration: Stabbing on the handles.
Illustrations: 14, 31-33, 110.

Type 31
Common name: Late Medieval Oxidised Sandy ware.
Fairly soft to hard, smooth, sandy fabric. Grey in colour where reduced, particularly under the glaze, and light orange where oxidised.
Forms: Majority appear to be handled jars.
Decoration: Incised horizontal lines as decoration on the shoulder.
Illustration: 170.

Type 32
Common name: Martincamp flask (Type 1).
Very hard, smooth stoneware, oxidised, buff-pink in colour.
Forms: Flat sided flasks, with tall narrow necks applied to bodies that have been separately thrown. No complete profiles were found.
Decoration: None.
Illustration: 35.

Type 33
Common name: Langerwehe stoneware.
Very hard, smooth stoneware with glossy brown exterior and dull grey-brown interior.
Forms: Most appear to be small jugs, but no complete profiles were found.
Decoration: None.
Illustrations: 36-37, 228.

Type 34
Common name: Siegburg stoneware.
Very hard, smooth stoneware, brown-grey in colour.
Forms: Tall jugs with flared necks.
Decoration: External grey glaze.
Illustrations: 34, 227.

Type 35
Common name: Raeren stoneware.
Very hard, smooth stoneware, with shiny grey or brown exteriors and dull grey-brown interiors.
Forms: Small drinking jugs, hand-thrown without the use of a template. Characterised by a vertical neck, round body with pronounced throwing lines, internally and externally, and a frilled base.
Decoration: None.
Illustrations: 38, 45-46.

Type 36
Common name: Crucibles.
Hard, fairly gritty, reduced fabric, grey in colour. Occasional light orange oxidised patches.
Forms: Small round-based vessels with pouring lips.
Decoration: None.
Illustration: 87.

Pottery quantification (Tables 3-7)

The method of quantification is based on the minimum number of vessels, a technique which is described elsewhere. Its advantage is that it identifies sherds from the same vessel, which can sometimes be widely scattered across a site. It also allows a wide range of questions to be considered which are not possible using other methods of quantification (see pp. 102-07 below).

The material is quantified by group, and presented chronologically within each group, pottery types down the left-hand side and the stratified sequence across the top. For each type, the number of vessels, the sherds representing them and the proportion of those vessels against the total number of vessels in the group is given. Percentages have been rounded up or down to the nearest whole number. Thus in Table 3, the Cloister cistern group, Pimply wares in the pre-Cloister cistern deposit are represented by nine sherds representing nine vessels which account for 75% of the vessels in that deposit. The total for vessels and sherds is given at the bottom of each column.

Table 3. Pottery quantification from the Cloister cistern group.

Type		Pre-Cloister cistern		Cloister cistern levelling layer		Fill of Cloister cistern	
Type number	Common name						
1	Pimply	9:9	75%	1:6	10%		
2	York type						
3	Hillam type	1:13	8%				
4	Developed Stamford						
5	South-west Midlands						
6	Tripod pitchers						
7	Northern Gritty	2:45	17%	1:2	10%	1:1	3%
8	Orange Gritty						
9	'Stepped jug'						
10	Unidentified non-local			1:1	10%	1:1	3%
11	Fine Sandy						
12	Pink Fine						
13	Rouen						
14	South-western French Polychrome						
15	Oxidized Humber					3:3	9%
16	Reduced Humber					1:1	3%
17	Skipton on Swale			1:4	10%		
18	York White			3:7	30%		
19	Rawmarsh type					3:11	9%
20	Tudor Green type					1:1	3%
21	White-slipped Humber						
22	Baildon					1:2	3%
23	Late Medieval Gritty						
24	Cistercian					5:8	16%
25	Reversed Cistercian					1:1	3%
26	Yellow						
27	Vitrified Earthenware						
28	Brick Red Sandy					2:3	6%
29	Midland Purple type						
30	Late Medieval Smooth			3:4	30%	9:?	28%
31	Late Medieval Oxidized Sandy						
32	Martincamp					1:1	3%
33	Langerwehe					2:2	6%
34	Siegburg					1:1	3%
35	Raeren						
36	Crucibles						
	Post-medieval						
	TOTAL:	12:67		10.24		32:36+	

Table 4. Pottery quantification from the Refectory.

		Phase 1			Phase 2		Phase 2 or 3	
Type								
Type number	Common name	Floor make-up in first Refectory	Primary features		Make-up layers for construction of second Refectory		Setting of slabs	
1	Pimply	1:28	4:181	57%	39:154	63%	3:8	60%
2	York type				1:2	2%		
3	Hillam type							
4	Developed Stamford				1:7	2%		
5	South-west Midlands		1:23	14%	1:4	2%		
6	Tripod pitchers		1:70	14%			1:1	20%
7	Northern Gritty				12:27	19%	1:5	20%
8	Orange Gritty				2:4	3%		
9	'Stepped jug'							
10	Unidentified non-local		1:1	14%	3:3	5%		
11	Fine Sandy				2:2	3%		
12	Pink Fine							
13	Rouen							
14	South-western French Polychrome							
15	Oxidized Humber							
16	Reduced Humber							
17	Skipton on Swale							
18	York White							
19	Rawmarsh type							
20	Tudor Green type							
21	White-slipped Humber							
22	Baildon							
23	Late Medieval Gritty							
24	Cistercian							
25	Reversed Cistercian							
26	Yellow							
27	Vitrified Earthenware							
28	Brick Red Sandy							
29	Midland Purple type							
30	Late Medieval Smooth							
31	Late Medieval Oxidized Sandy							
32	Martincamp							
33	Langerwehe							
34	Siegburg							
35	Raeren							
36	Crucibles				1:1	2%		
	Post-medieval							
	TOTAL:	1:28	7:275		62:204		5:14	

Table 5. Pottery quantification from the Infirmary.

Type number	Common name	Infirmary Layer 2 (Phase 1)		Infirmary Layer 1 (Phase 2)	
1	Pimply			3:3	2%
2	York type				
3	Hillam type				
4	Developed Stamford				
5	South-west Midlands				
6	Tripod pitchers				
7	Northern Gritty	51:70	42%	59:110	44%
8	Orange Gritty	59:183	49%	6:8	5%
9	'Stepped jug'	1:1	1%		
10	Unidentified non-local	5:49	4%	2:8	2%
11	Fine Sandy	1:19	1%		
12	Pink Fine				
13	Rouen				
14	South-western French Polychrome			1:2	1%
15	Oxidized Humber				
16	Reduced Humber				
17	Skipton on Swale			1:2	1%
18	York White	4:4	3%	9:29	7%
19	Rawmarsh type			4:17	3%
20	Tudor Green type				
21	White-slipped Humber				
22	Baildon				
23	Late Medieval Gritty				
24	Cistercian			19:34	14%
25	Reversed Cistercian				
26	Yellow			3:14	2%
27	Vitrified Earthenware			19:34	14%
28	Brick Red Sandy				
29	Midland Purple type				
30	Late Medieval Smooth			7:7	5%
31	Late Medieval Oxidized Sandy				
32	Martincamp				
33	Langerwehe				
34	Siegburg				
35	Raeren				
36	Crucibles				
	TOTAL:	121:326		133:268	

Table 6. Pottery quantification from the Warming House.

Type											
Type number	Common name	WH 9	WH 8	WH 7		WH 6		WH 5	WH 4	WH 2	
1	Pimply										
2	York type										
3	Hillam type										
4	Developed Stamford										
5	South-west Midlands										
6	Tripod pitchers										
7	Northern Gritty	3:5	5:66	2:8	40%	1:1	50%	4:21	1:2	1:1	50%
8	Orange Gritty										
9	'Stepped jug'										
10	Unidentified non-local									1:1	50%
11	Fine Sandy										
12	Pink Fine										
13	Rouen										
14	South-western French Polychrome										
15	Oxidized Humber			1:1	20%						
16	Reduced Humber										
17	Skipton on Swale										
18	York White										
19	Rawmarsh type										
20	Tudor Green type										
21	White-slipped Humber										
22	Baildon										
23	Late Medieval Gritty										
24	Cistercian										
25	Reversed Cistercian										
26	Yellow										
27	Vitrified Earthenware										
28	Brick Red Sandy										
29	Midland Purple type										
30	Late Medieval Smooth			2:5	40%	1:2	50%				
31	Late Medieval Oxidized Sandy										
32	Martincamp										
33	Langerwehe										
34	Siegburg										
35	Raeren										
36	Crucibles										
	Post-medieval										
	TOTAL:	3:5	5:66	5:14		2:3		4:21	1:2	2:2	

Table 7. Pottery quantification from the Warming House cistern and from the medieval made ground south of the Meat Kitchen.

Type		WH Courtyard cistern		Medieval made ground south of the Meat Kitchen	
Type number	Common name				
1	Pimply	2:2	4%	8:8	5%
2	York type				
3	Hillam type			1:1	1%
4	Developed Stamford				
5	South-west Midlands				
6	Tripod pitchers				
7	Northern Gritty	38:284	73%	108:109	69%
8	Orange Gritty				
9	'Stepped jug'				
10	Unidentified non-local	1:15	2%	1:1	1%
11	Fine Sandy	3:30	6%	1:1	1%
12	Pink Fine			1:2	1%
13	Rouen				
14	South-western French Polychrome				
15	Oxidized Humber			13:13	8%
16	Reduced Humber				
17	Skipton on Swale	4:6	8%	9:11	6%
18	York White	1:1	2%	5:5	3%
19	Rawmarsh type			1:49	1%
20	Tudor Green type				
21	White-slipped Humber				
22	Baildon				
23	Late Medieval Gritty			1:1	1%
24	Cistercian				
25	Reversed Cistercian				
26	Yellow				
27	Vitrified Earthenware				
28	Brick Red Sandy				
29	Midland Purple type				
30	Late Medieval Smooth			7:10	4%
31	Late Medieval Oxidized Sandy				
32	Martincamp				
33	Langerwehe	1:1	2%		
34	Siegburg	2:2	4%		
35	Raeren				
36	Crucibles				
	Post-medieval			1:1	1%
	TOTAL:	52:341		157:212	

Pottery Information Table (Table 8)

Table 8 provides a range of information for the vessels illustrated in Figs 39-56. The common name is given in column 4 and the reader is referred to the appropriate type definition in column 3. An asterisk against the illustration number in column 1 shows that the vessel is individually mentioned in the type definition. Column 5 gives the number of sherds from each context; for example in no. 6, thirty-six sherds come from CL III 3 and seven from CL III 2. The form of the vessel, where known, is given in column 6.

The initials in column 7 refer to the various forms of use evident on the pottery, and the presence of the potter's finger prints:

F Finger and thumb print
H Hole
R Residue
S Sooting
W Wear marks

These are discussed in more detail on pp. 99-102. Column 2 notes whether the vessel has been illustrated in the previous annual reports.

Table 8. Pottery Information Table.

1	2	3	4	5	6	7
Illust. number	Thoresby illust. number	Type number	Common name	Context and number of sherds	Form	Evidence of use and finger-prints
CLOISTER						
Pre-Cloister cistern						
1	1954 fig. 24, no. 2	3	Hillam type	3-CLI 3; 1-CL 3; 3-CL 3 S Ext.; 6- unmarked	Jug	
2*		1	Pimply	1-CLI 3	–	
3		1	Pimply	1-CL 3 S Ext.	–	
4*		1	Pimply	1-CLII 3	–	
5		7	Northern Gritty	2-CL 2 S Ext.	–	
6*	1953 fig. 18, no. 1	7	Northern Gritty	36-CLIII 3; 7-CLIII 2	Bowl	
Cloister cistern levelling layer						
7		1	Pimply	4-CLI 2A; 1-CLI +; 1-CL S Ext.	Bowl	
8		7	Northern Gritty	1-CD 2;1- unmarked	Jug	
9		10	Unidentified non-local	1-CLII 2A	Jug	S
10		17	Skipton on Swale	2-CLII 2A; 1-CD 2 T; 1-CLI 2A	Jug	
11		18	York White	2-CLII 2A	Jug	
12		18	York White	1-CLII 2A; 1-CL +; 1- unmarked	Jug	
13		18	York White	2-CLII 2A	–	W
14		30	Late Medieval Smooth	1-CLI 2A	–	
Fill of Cloister cistern						
15*		7	Northern Gritty	1-CLII N Ext.	Chalice/lid	
16		10	Unidentified non-local	1-CLII 5	Jug	
17		15	Oxidized Humber	1-CLII 5	Jug	
18		16	Reduced Humber	1-CLII 5	Jug	
19		19	Rawmarsh type	9-CLII 5	Jug/cistern	
20		19	Rawmarsh type	1-CLII 5	–	
21		19	Rawmarsh type	1-CLII 1	Cistern	
22		20	Tudor Green type	1-CLII 5	Jug	
23	1960-64 fig. 17, no. 19	22	Baildon	1-CLII 5; 1-CLII +	Jug	
24		24	Cistercian	1-CLII 5	Cup	
25		24	Cistercian	1-CLII 5	Cup	
26		24	Cistercian	1-CLII 5	Cup	
27		24	Cistercian	1-CLII 5	Cup	
28		24	Cistercian	4-CLII 5	Cup	
29		25	Reversed Cistercian	1-CLII 5	Cup	F
30	1953 fig. 18, no. 6	28	Brick Red Sandy	2-CLII 2	Cistern	
31		30	Late Medieval Smooth	2-CLII 6	–	
32		30	Late Medieval Smooth	3-CLII 1A	–	R (White)
33		30	Late Medieval Smooth	1-CLI 1A	Urinal	
34		34	Siegburg	1-CLII 5	Jug	
35		32	Martincamp	1-CL 2	Type 1 flask	
36		33	Langerwehe	1-CLII 6	Jug	
37		33	Langerwehe	1-CLII 5	Jug	
38		35	Raeren	1-CLII 1	Jug	
Topsoil						
39	1953 fig. 18, no. 4	1	Pimply	1-CLI +	Jug	
40*		7	Northern Gritty	1-CD +	Jug	
41*		10	Unidentified non-local	1-CLII 1	Jug	
42	1950 fig. 4, no. 5	13	Rouen	2-50/5; 1-52/50; 1-CD + 52/13; 1-CD +; 1-unmarked	Jug	
43		18	York White	1-CL 8 Ext.	Jug	
44		18	York White	1-CLIV 1	Spouted Jug	
45		35	Raeren	2-CD +	Jug	
46		35	Raeren	1-CL 2	Jug	

Table 8. Pottery Information Table. Continued

Illust. number	Thoresby illust. number	Type number	Common name	Context and number of sherds	Form	Evidence of use and finger-prints
1	2	3	4	5	6	7
REFECTORY						
Make-up for first Refectory and primary features Phase 1						
47		1	Pimply	13-R2 3; 8-R2+3 2; 1-R4 2; 1-R4 3A; 1-R5 3; 1-R5 4; 1-R5 5; 2-unmarked	Jar	
48		1	Pimply	1-R2 2; 3-R4 2; 1-R4 3A; 18-R5 2; 2-R5 2A; 3-R5 3; 4-R5 5; 74-R5 12; 1-R5 +; 44- unmarked	Jug	
49	1955 fig. 10, no. 7	1	Pimply	1-R5 2; 3-R5 12; 1-FRI 2E; 1- unmarked	Jar	
50	1955 fig. 10, no. 6	1	Pimply	3-R5 12; 1-R7 9; 1-R7 +; 1 unmarked	Jar	
51		1	Pimply	1-R4 2; 1-R4 3A; 14-R5 12; 2- unmarked	Jar	S
52*	1955 fig. 10, no. 11	6	Tripod pitcher	1-R4 2; 1-R5 1; 1-R5 2; 11-R5 3; 50-R5 12; 6-unmarked	Tripod pitcher	
53		5	South-west Midlands	2-R4 2; 8-R5 2; 4-R5 3; 4-R5 5; 3-R5 12; 2- unmarked	Jar	
Make-up for second Refectory Phase 2						
54*		1	Pimply	59- unmarked	Jar	
55		1	Pimply	3-R5 3; 1-R5 4; 1-R5; 1-R7 9	Jar	
56	1955 fig. 10, no. 5	1	Pimply	1-R7 + 8 2	Jar	
57		1	Pimply	1-R4 3A	Jar	
58		1	Pimply	1-R3 6; 1-R4 2; 1-R5 2A; 1-unmarked	Jug	
59		1	Pimply	2-R5 2A	Jug	
60		1	Pimply	1-R6 1 2A	Jug	
61		1	Pimply	1-R4 2	Jug	
62		1	Pimply	3-R5 2; 1-R5 2A; 12-R5 3; 9-R5 12	—	S
63		1	Pimply	3-R4 2; 1-R4 3; 1-R48 3	—	
64		1	Pimply	1-R5 2B; 1-R5 7; 1-R5 9; 1-unmarked	—	
65		1	Pimply	2-R5 2; 1-R + SW; 4- unmarked	—	S
66		1	Pimply	3-R4 2	—	
67		1	Pimply	1-R7 2	—	
68		1	Pimply	11-R4 3A	—	S
69		1	Pimply	1-R7 2	—	
70		1	Pimply	1-R5 2	—	
71		1	Pimply	1-R4 2	—	S
72	1955 fig. 10, no. 3	2	York type	2-R4 2	Jar	S
73	1960-64 fig. 16, no. 1	4	Developed Stamford	5-R4 2; 1-KA81 E1/2 307; 1-KA81 E1 307	Jug	
74		5	South-west Midlands	3-R 3; 1-R +	Bowl	
75*	1955 fig. 10, no. 10	7	Northern Gritty	2-R4 2; 1-R8 SW 3	Handled jar	S
76		7	Northern Gritty	2-R5 2A; 2-R5 +; 1-R7N9; 1-R8 +	Jug	
77*		7	Northern Gritty	1-R2.4 Bk	Jug	
78		7	Northern Gritty	4-R8 SW 3; 1-R8 +	Jug/Jar	
79		7	Northern Gritty	1-R7 9	—	
80*		7	Northern Gritty	1-R4 2	Industrial vessel	
81*		8	Orange Gritty	1-R4 2; 2-R5 2	Jug	
82*		8	Orange Gritty	1-RE 2	Jug	
83		10	Unidentified non-local	1-R7 2	Jug	
84		10	Unidentified non-local	1-RSE Panel	Jug	
85		10	Unidentified non-local	1-R4 2	Jug	
86		11	Fine Sandy	1-R7 N9	Jug	
87		36	Crucible	1-R4-5 2	Crucible	

Table 8. Pottery Information Table. Continued

1	2	3	4	5	6	7
Illust. number	Thoresby illust. number	Type number	Common name	Context and number of sherds	Form	Evidence of use and finger-prints
Setting of slabs						
88*		7	Northern Gritty	1-R4 3; 1-R5 9; 3-R7N12	Industrial Vessel?	
89*		6	Tripod Pitcher	1-R5 9	Tripod pitcher	
Topsoil and disturbance						
90		1	Pimply	1-R7 +; 2 unmarked	Jug	
91	1955 fig. 10, no. 4	1	Pimply	1-R5 +	Bowl	
92		1	Pimply	1-R7 +	—	
93		7	Northern Gritty	1-R + SW	Jar	
94		7	Northern Gritty	1-R2 +	Jug	
95*	1960-4 fig. 16, no. 12	7	Northern Gritty	2-R2 2; 5-unmarked	Lid	
96		7	Northern Gritty	1-R6ST	Jug	
97		10	Unidentified non-local	6-FRI 3; 2-FRI 3B; 1- unmarked	Jug	
98		10	Unidentified non-local	1-RSW +	Jug	
99		10	Unidentified non-local	1-R + SW; 2- unmarked	Jug	
100*		11	Fine Sandy	1-R8N3	Jug	
101	1953 fig. 18, no. 7	18	York White	1-FRII 1A; 19-FRII +	Lobed cup	
102		21	White-slipped Humber	1-FRI +	Lobed cup	
103		24	Cistercian	2-FR +	Cup	
104		24	Cistercian	1-R8 +; 2- unmarked	Cup	
105		24	Cistercian	1-R6 +	Cup	
106		24	Cistercian	1-R8 +	Cup	
107		24	Cistercian	1-R8 +	Cup	
108		29	Midland Purple type	4-FRI 3; 1-FRI 3A	Jug	
109		29	Midland Purple type	1-R4 +	Jug	
110		30	Late Medieval Smooth	1-R8 + SW	Jug	
INFIRMARY						
Layer 2 (Phase 1)						
111		7	Northern Gritty	1-I4 10	Jar	
112		7	Northern Gritty	1-I16 2	Bowl	
113		7	Northern Gritty	4-I5 2	Jug	
114		7	Northern Gritty	1-I6 2	Jug	
115		7	Northern Gritty	1-I6 2	Jug	
116		7	Northern Gritty	1-I12 2A	Jug	
117		7	Northern Gritty	3-I3 2	Jug	
118*		7	Northern Gritty	1-I8 2	Jug	
119		7	Northern Gritty	1-I15 2	Jug	
120		7	Northern Gritty	1-I5 2	—	
121		7	Northern Gritty	1-I9 2	—	
122*		7	Northern Gritty	1-I15 2B	Lid	
123*		7	Northern Gritty	1-I15 2B		H (before firing)
124*		7	Northern Gritty	3-I9 2	Dripping pan	
125		8	Orange Gritty	1-I2 +; 1-I5 2; 3-I9 1; 11-I9 2; 1-I12 1; 4-I12 2; 6-I12 2A; 1-I14 2; 1-I15 1A; 4-I16 1	Jar	
126		8	Orange Gritty	5-I15 1A; 7-I15 2	Jar	
127		8	Orange Gritty	1-I12 2	Jar	
128		8	Orange Gritty	1-I4 2; 1-I12 2; 1-I14 1A	—	
129		8	Orange Gritty	5-I9 2; 5-I12 1; 1-I15 2	Jug	
130		8	Orange Gritty	1-I3 2; 1-I8 +; 2-I8 1; 4-I8 2; 2-I9 2; 3-I12+; 4-I12 2; 4- unmarked	Jug	
131		8	Orange Gritty	4-I5 2; 3-unmarked	Jug	

Table 8. Pottery Information Table. Continued

1 Illust. number	2 Thoresby illust. number	3 Type number	4 Common name	5 Context and number of sherds	6 Form	7 Evidence of use and finger-prints
132*	1959 fig. 31, no. 10	7	Northern Gritty	2-I7 1; 1-I8 1; 6-I8 2; 2-I9 1; 21-I9 2; 2-I12 1; 6-I12 2; 2-I12 2A; 9-I16 1	Jug	
133		9	'Stepped jug'	1-I15 2B	Jug	
134*	1959 fig. 31, no. 12	11	Fine Sandy	1-I5 2; 2-I6 1; 2-I8 2; 3-I12 1; 7-I12 2; 1-I16 2; 1-I16/17 1; 2-WRE 2	Spouted Jug	
135*		10	Unidentified non-local	1-I14 2; 1-I5 2	Jug	
136		10	Unidentified non-local	1-I12 2	Jug	
137*		10	Unidentified non-local	1-I 10; 1-I3 1;1-I3 2; 8-I4 2	Jug	
138		18	York White	1-I5 2	Jug	
Layer 1 (Phase 2)						
139		7	Northern Gritty	1-I3 1; 1-I8 +; 1-unmarked	—	
140		7	Northern Gritty	1-I 7 1	Jug	
141		7	Northern Gritty	1-I21 1	Jug	
142	1960-4 fig. 17, no. 20	7	Northern Gritty	1-1252; 2-1254; 1-1255; 2-1256; 2-1257; 1-I14 1; 2-120 1; 1-BD 25; 1-BD23 5; 12- unmarked	Jug	R (White)
143		7	Northern Gritty	1-I15 1A	Jug	
144		7	Northern Gritty	1-I17 1	Jug	
145*		7	Northern Gritty	2-I15 1A	Curfew	S
146		8	Orange Gritty	1-I7 1A; 1-I9 1	Jug	
147		10	Unidentified non-local	1-I5 1; 2-I14 1; 1-I18 1; 11-I18 +; 2-I121 1	Jug	
148	1959 fig. 31, no. 11	14	South-western French Polychrome	1-I8 1; 1-I14 1	Jug	
149*		18	York White	1-I21 1	Bowl	
150		18	York White	3-14 1A; 1-I14 N. Baulk 1A; 4-I19 1	Jug	
151		18	York White	1-I15 1A	Jug	
152		18	York White	8-I21 +	Jug	
153		24	Cistercian	1-I2 1	Cup	
154		24	Cistercian	1-I21 1	Cup	
155		24	Cistercian	5-I5 1	Cup	
156		24	Cistercian	1-I2 1; 2-I2 +; 1-I3 1; 3-LR4 2	Cup	
157		24	Cistercian	1-I15 1	Cup	
158*		27	Vitrified Earthenware	2-I1 1	Jar?	
159		27	Vitrified Earthenware	10-I1 1; 2-I2 +; 5-I15 +; 1-LR3 1	Cistern	
160*		26	Yellow	1-I14 1; 4-I15 1; 1-I15 +; 5-unmarked	Bowl	
161		26	Yellow	2-I 15 1	—	
162		26	Yellow	1-I10 1	Bowl	
Topsoil						
163		7	Northern Gritty	1-I22 +	Jar	
164		7	Northern Gritty	1-I21 +	Bowl	
165		7	Northern Gritty	16-I15 +	Jug	
166*		7	Northern Gritty	1-I15 +	Jug	
167		7	Northern Gritty	1-I +	Jug	
168		8	Orange Gritty	1-I16 +	Jug	
169		18	York White	1-I21 +	Jug	
170		31	Late Medieval Oxidized Sandy	1-I15 +; 66-unmarked	Handled Jar	

Table 8. Pottery Information Table. Continued

1 Illlust. number	2 Thoresby illust. number	3 Type number	4 Common name	5 Context and number of sherds	6 Form	7 Evidence of use and finger-prints
WARMING HOUSE						
Layer 9						
171		7	Northern Gritty	1-WH 9	Jug	
172*	1952 fig. 13, no. 11	7	Northern Gritty	2-WH 9; 1-WH 6	Jug	
Layer 8						
173		7	Northern Gritty	18-WH 8	Jar	
174	1952 fig. 13, no. 7	7	Northern Gritty	16-WH 8	Bowl	
175		7	Northern Gritty	1-WH 8	Bowl	
176		7	Northern Gritty	2-WH 8; 1-WH 7; 24- unmarked	Bowl	
177*	1952 fig. 12, no. 1	7	Northern Gritty	1-WH 8; 1-52/1; 2-LRI 3	Curfew	S
Layer 7						
178*	1952 fig. 13, no. 8	7	Northern Gritty	6-WH 7; 1- unmarked	Jug	
179		7	Northern Gritty	1-WH 7	Jug	
180		15	Oxidized Humber	1-WH 7	Jug	
Layer 5						
181		7	Northern Gritty	1-WH 5	Bowl	S
182		7	Northern Gritty	1-WH 5	Jug	
183		7	Northern Gritty	7-WH 5; 4-WH 7; 1-BDIII 1; 1-CD +; 1- unmarked	Jug	
184*		7	Northern Gritty	1-WH 5; 1-WH +; 3- unmarked	—	S
Layer 4						
185		7	Northern Gritty	1-WH (Sand); 1-CI	—	S
Layer 2						
186		7	Northern Gritty	1-WH 2	Jug	
187		10	Unidentified non-local	1-WH 2	Jug	
WARMING HOUSE COURTYARD CISTERN: FILL						
188*	1951 fig 8, no. 12	7	Northern Gritty	6-44/1951; 5- unmarked	Jar	
189*		7	Northern Gritty	15-44/1951; 5- unmarked	Jar	H (after firing)
190*	1951 fig 8, no. 19	7	Northern Gritty	3-44/1951; 1- unmarked	Jar	
191		7	Northern Gritty	1-44/1951	Jar	
192		7	Northern Gritty	1-44/1951	Jar	
193		7	Northern Gritty	1-44/1951	Jar	
194		7	Northern Gritty	2-44/1951	Jar	
195*	1956 fig. 13, no. 8; 1957 fig 17, no.2	7	Northern Gritty	3-44/1951; 1-MKII 6; 1-MKA 6; 6- unmarked	Bowl	
196*	1951 fig. 8, no. 11	7	Northern Gritty	11- unmarked (possibly WH Cistern)	Bowl	
197		7	Northern Gritty	1-44/1951; 1- unmarked	Bowl	
198*		7	Northern Gritty	3-44/1951; 2- unmarked	Bowl	
199		7	Northern Gritty	2-44/1951; 1-KY8 2; 2-KY8 3; 1- unmarked	Bowl	
200		7	Northern Gritty	3-44/1951	Bowl	
201	1951 fig 8, no. 14	7	Northern Gritty	1-44/1951; 1- unmarked	Bowl	
202*		7	Northern Gritty	1-44/1951	Bowl	
203	1951 fig 6, no. 4	7	Northern Gritty	1-44/1951	Bowl	S
204		7	Northern Gritty	6-44/1951; 16- unmarked	Jug	
205	1951 fig 9, no. 22	7	Northern Gritty	1-44/1951; 14- unmarked	Jug	
206*	1951 fig 9, no. 21	7	Northern Gritty	44/1951	Jug	
207		7	Northern Gritty	1-44/1951	Jug	
208		7	Northern Gritty	1-44/1951	Jug	
209		7	Northern Gritty	1-44/1951	Jug	
210		7	Northern Gritty	1-44/1951	Jug	
211		7	Northern Gritty	1-44/1951	Jug	

Table 8. Pottery Information Table. Continued

1 Illust. number	2 Thoresby illust. number	3 Type number	4 Common name	5 Context and number of sherds	6 Form	7 Evidence of use and finger-prints
212		7	Northern Gritty	1-44/1951	Jug	
213*	1951 fig 7, no. 9	7	Northern Gritty	67- unmarked (NE corner of Courtyard)	Jug	
214*	1951 fig 9, no. 23	7	Northern Gritty	5-44/1951; 7- unmarked	Jug	F (unclear)
215*	1951 fig 7, no. 10; 1960-64 fig. 16, no. 7	7	Northern Gritty	58-44/1951; 1-BD12	Jug	
216*		7	Northern Gritty	1-44/1951; 4- unmarked	Jug	
217*		7	Northern Gritty	5-44/1951; 2- unmarked	Jug	
218*	1958 fig 8, no. 15	7	Northern Gritty	1-44/1951	Pipkin	S
219	1951 fig 9, no. 25	11	Fine Sandy	15-44/1951; 13-AB +	Jug	W
220*		11	Fine Sandy	1-44/1951	Jug	
221		11	Fine Sandy	1-44/1951	Jug	
222		17	Skipton on Swale	2-44/1951	Jug	
223		17	Skipton on Swale	2-44/1951	Jug	R (White)
224		17	Skipton on Swale	1-44/1951	Jug	
225		17	Skipton on Swale	1-44/1951	Jug	
226		18	York White	1-44/1951	Jug	W
227		34	Siegburg	1-44/1951	Jug	
228		33	Langerwehe	1-44/1951	Jug	
MEDIEVAL 'MADE GROUND' SOUTH OF THE MEAT KITCHEN						
229		1	Pimply	1-BD21 12	Jar	
230		3	Hillam type	1-BD20 9	Jar	
231		7	Northern Gritty	1-BD21 5	Bowl	
232		7	Northern Gritty	1-BD21 11	Jug	
233		7	Northern Gritty	1-BD21 11	Jug	S
234		7	Northern Gritty	1-BD21 11	Jug	
235		7	Northern Gritty	1-BD21 5	Jug	
236*		7	Northern Gritty	1-BD20 7	Lid	
237*	1957 fig. 17, no. 5	7	Northern Gritty	1-BD21 5; 2-BD23 5	Urinal	R (red)
238*		7	Northern Gritty	1-BD21 12	Dripping pan	S
239		7	Northern Gritty	1-BD21 11		
240		10	Unidentified non-local	1-BD21 7	Jug	
241		11	Fine Sandy	1-BD21 5	Jug	
242		12	Pink Fine	1-BD21 4; 1-BD21 5	Jug	
243		18	York White	1-BD23 5	Jug	
244		19	Rawmarsh type	4-BD21 5; 2-BDXIII +: 1-BDXI; 1-LR5 2; 2-LR3 1; 5-LR4 2; 1-WRA/B 1; 1-WRD 2; 32- unmarked	Cistern	
245		23	Late Medieval Gritty	1-BD20 7	Jar	
246			Industrial	1-BD21 4	Bowl	

The drawings (Figs 39-56)

An attempt has been made to illustrate the full range of vessels for each pottery type. The pottery has been drawn at a quarter of the actual size. Blacked-in sections indicate wheel-thrown vessels, while hatched sections indicate hand-made vessels. All applied features, such as handles, spouts and decoration, are also shown with their sections hatched. The pie diagram at the base of each drawing indicates the proportion of the vessel present, not its full reconstruction. Where all the sherds present have been drawn the pie diagram has been omitted. Wherever possible sherds have been drawn in what would have been their true position. Where there is no evidence for a handle, even on a jug, one has not been reconstructed.

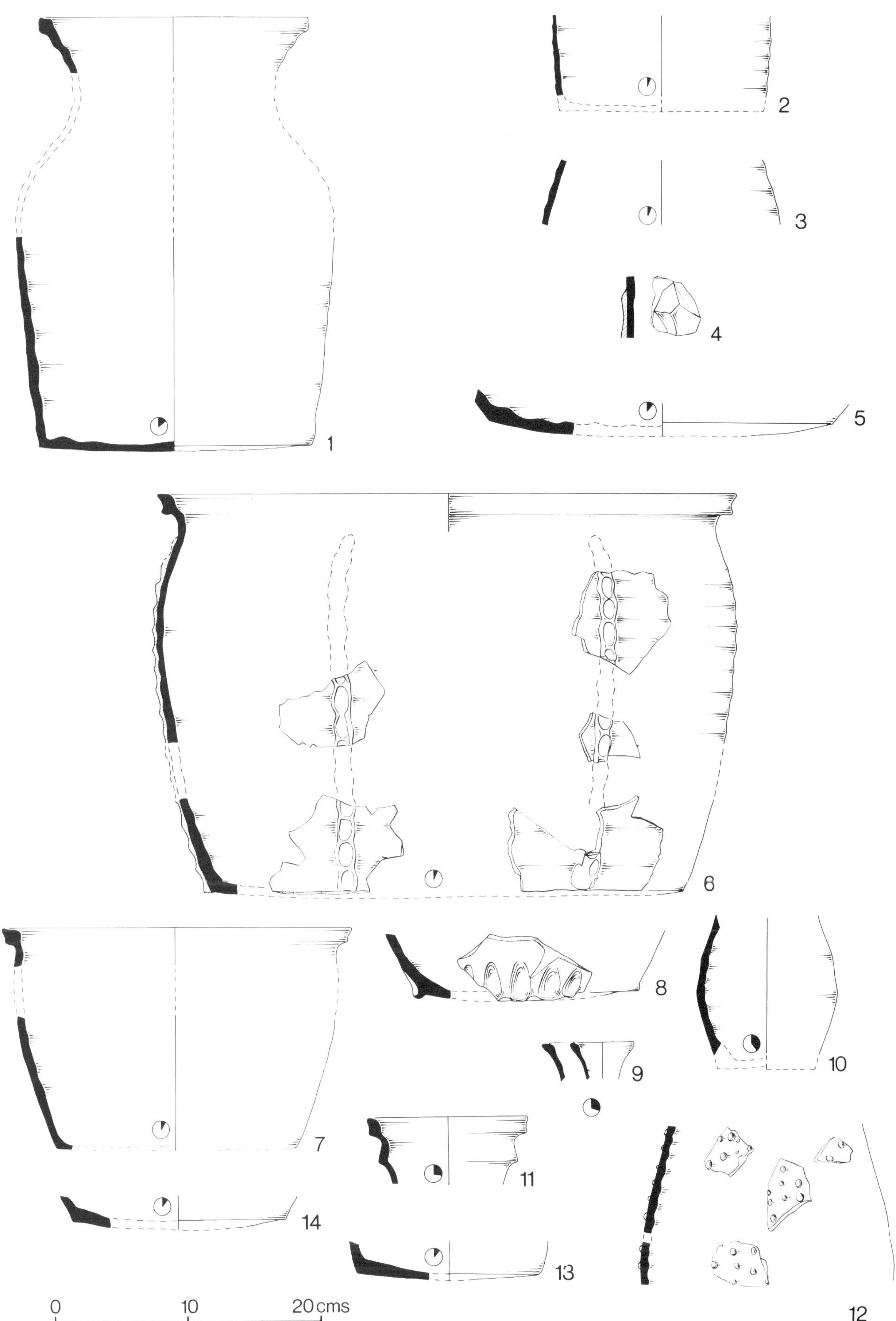

Fig. 39. Pottery: nos 1-6, pre-Cloister cistern; nos 7-14, Cloister cistern levelling layer.

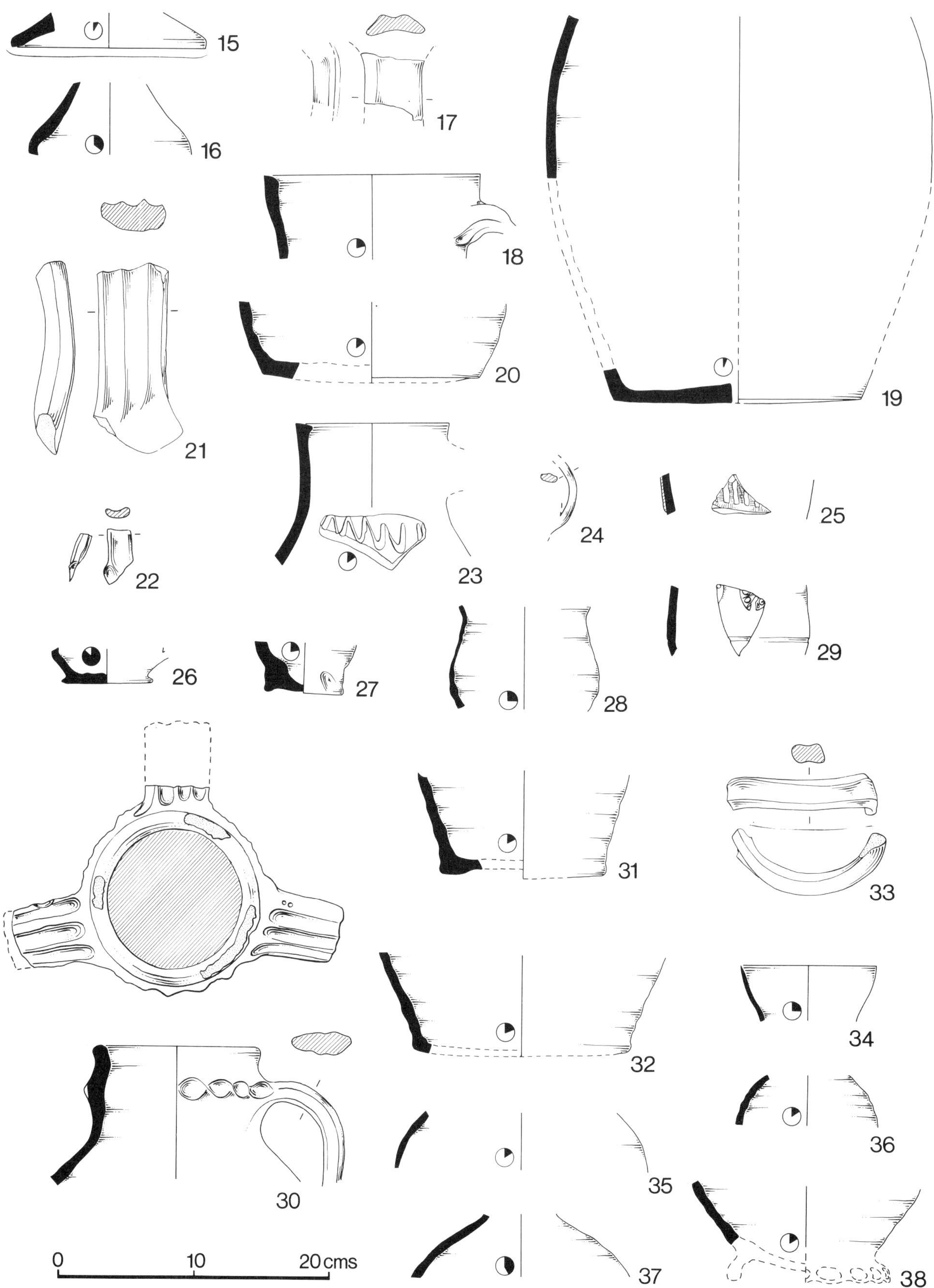

Fig. 40. Pottery: nos 15-38, fill of Cloister cistern.

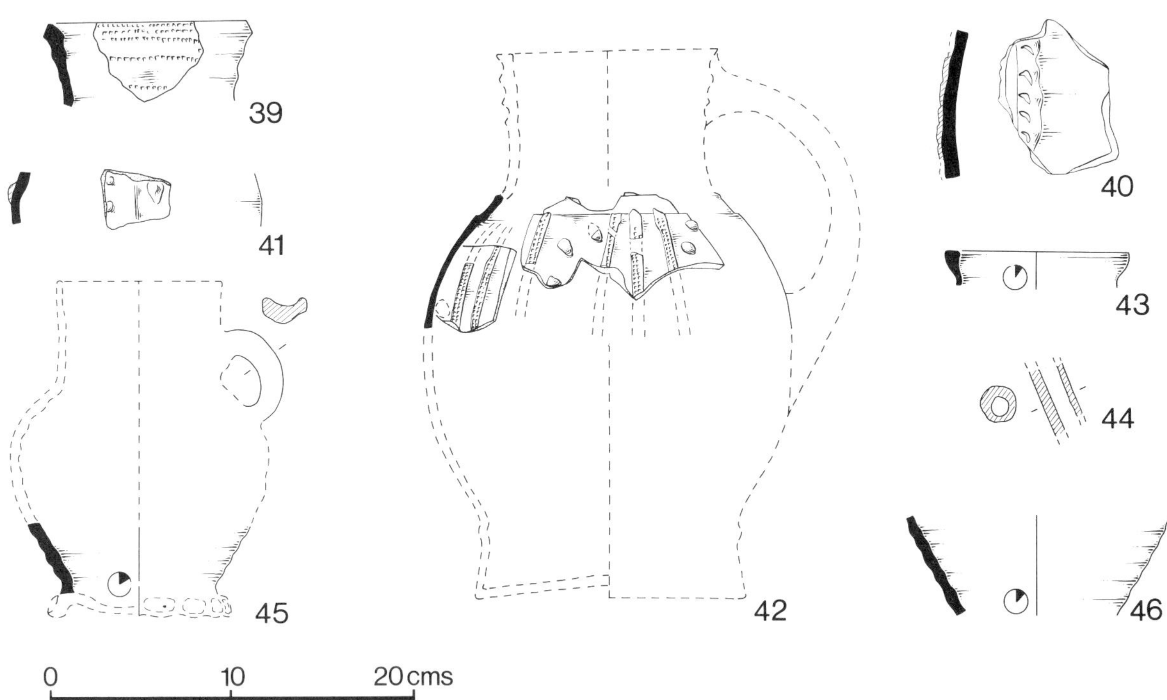

Fig. 41. Pottery: nos 39-46, Cloister cistern topsoil.

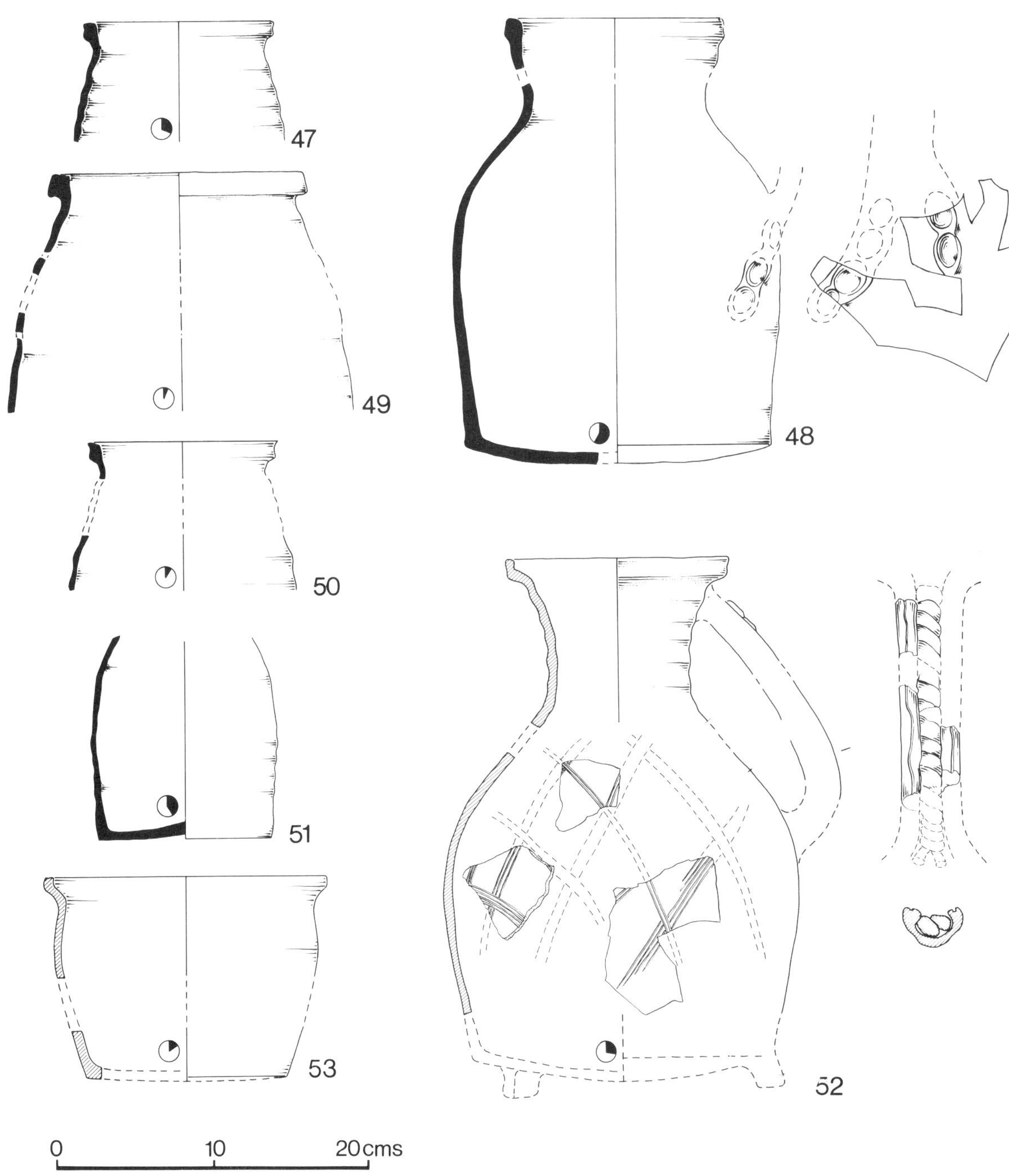

Fig. 42. Pottery. Refectory, Phase 1: no. 47, make-up of first Refectory; nos 48-53, external features.

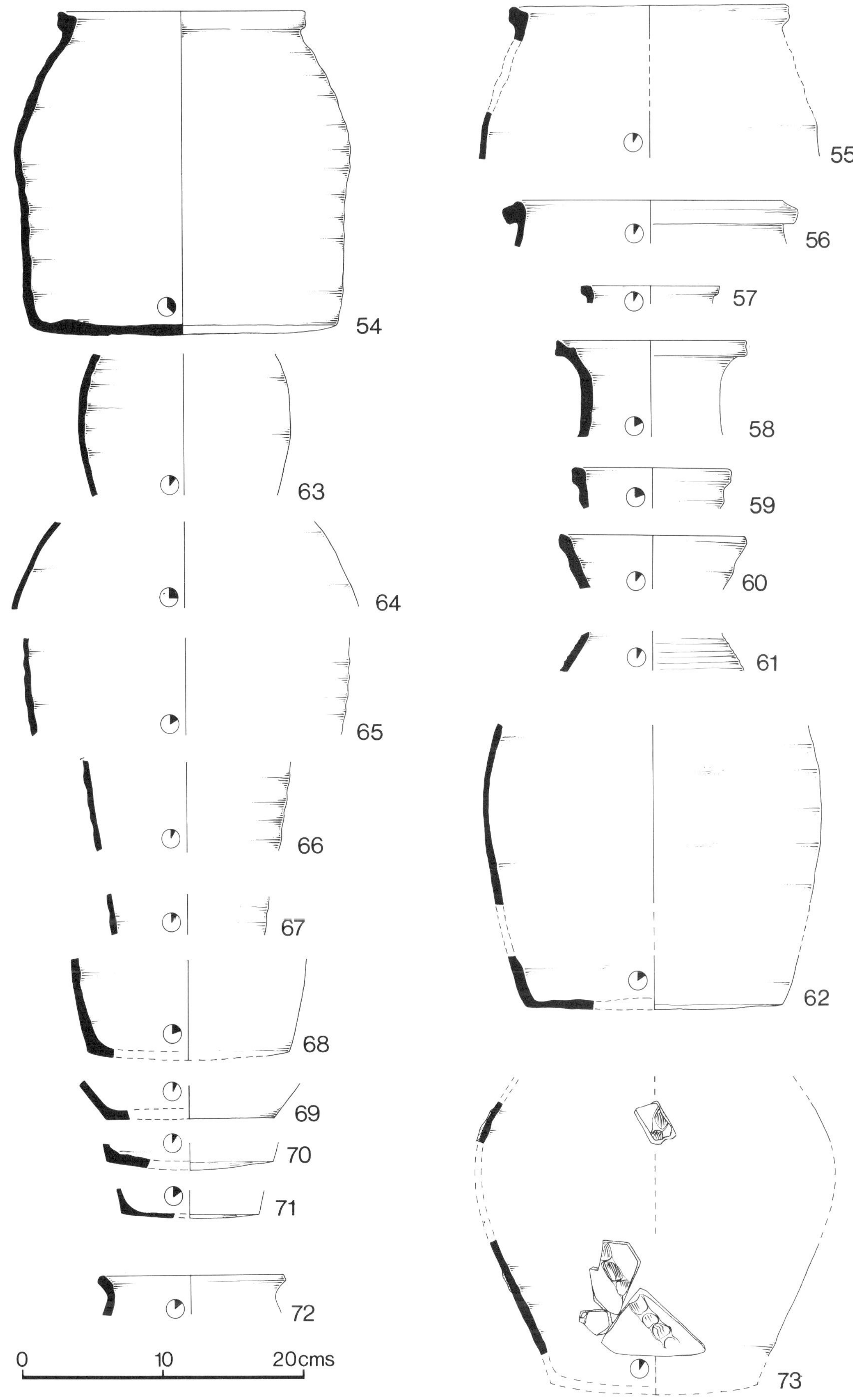

Fig. 43. Pottery. Refectory, Phase 2: nos 54-73, make-up of second Refectory.

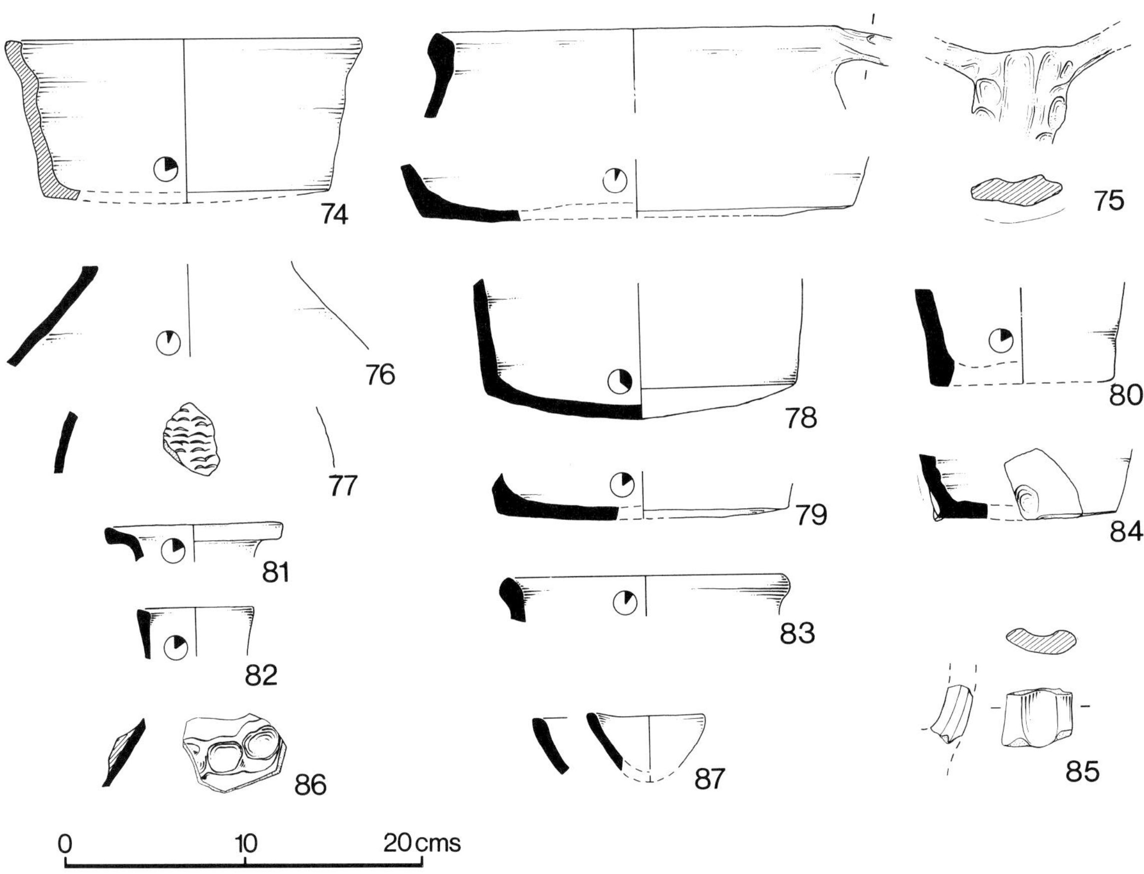

Fig. 44. Pottery. Refectory, Phase 2: nos 74-87, make-up of second Refectory.

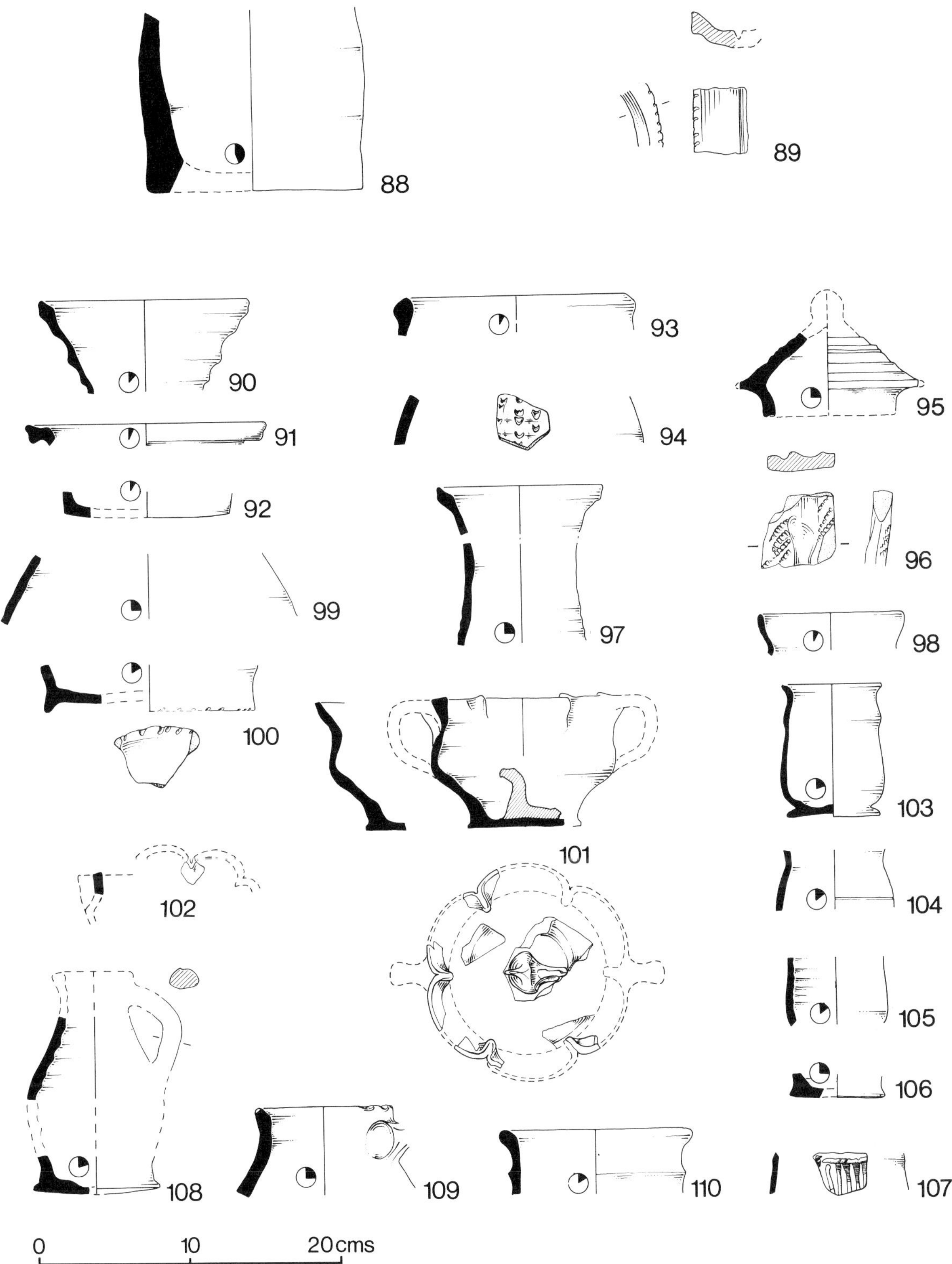

Fig. 45. Pottery. Refectory, Phase 2 or 3: nos 88-89, setting of slabs; nos 90-110, topsoil.

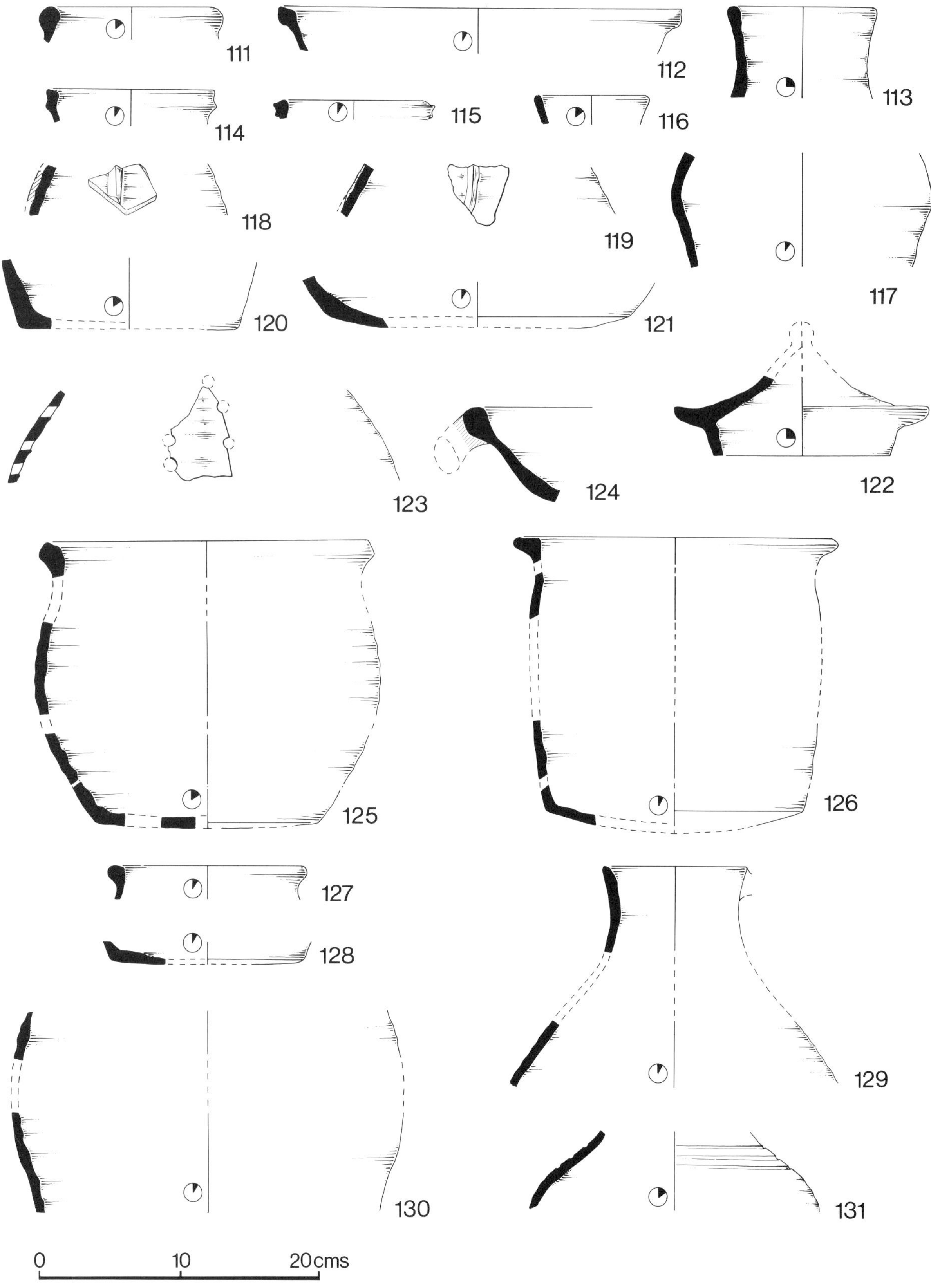

Fig. 46. Pottery. Infirmary: nos 111-131, Layer 2.

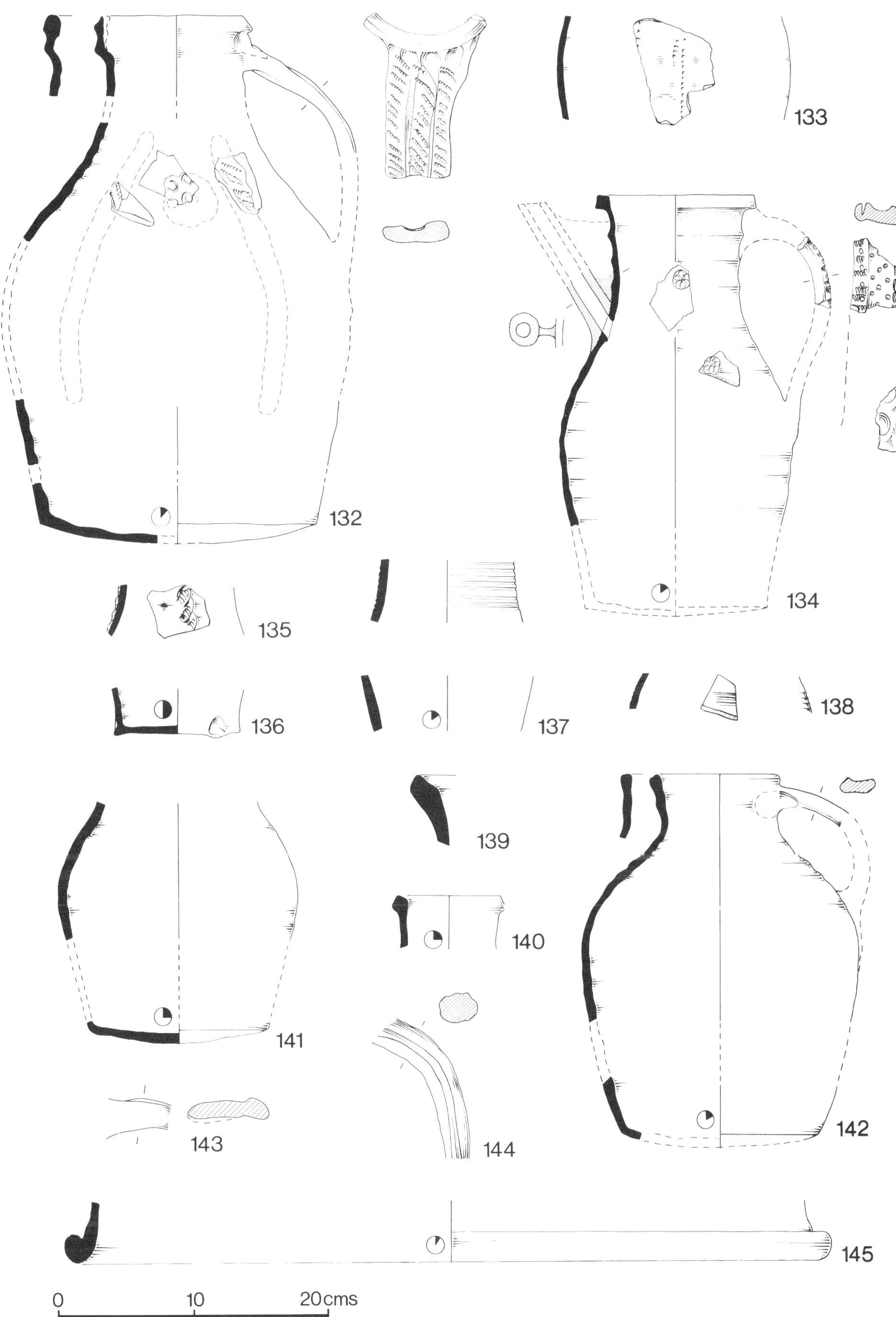

Fig. 47. Pottery. Infirmary: nos 132-138, Layer 2; nos 139-145, Layer 1.

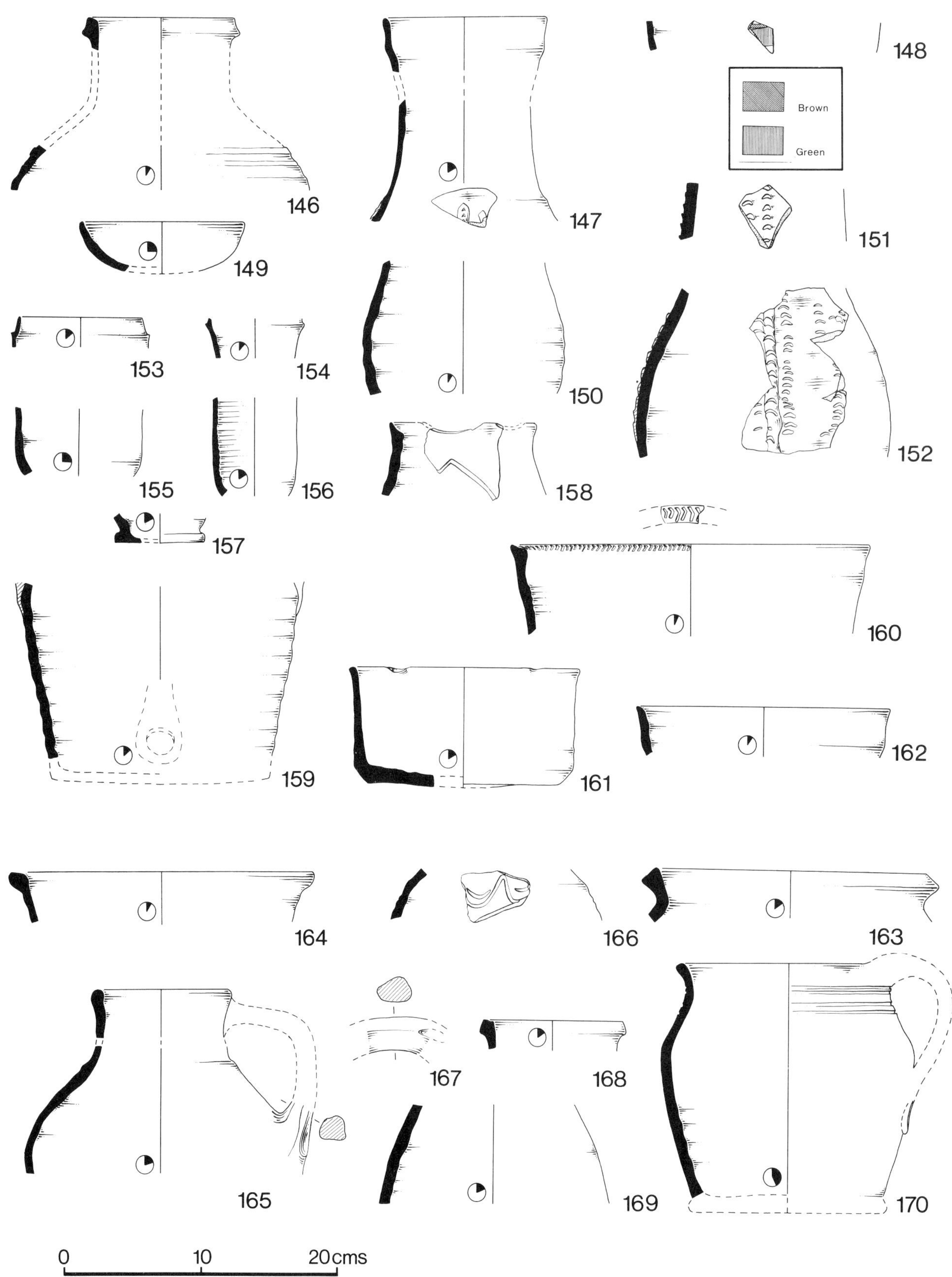

Fig. 48. Pottery. Infirmary: nos 146-163, Layer 1; nos 164-170, topsoil.

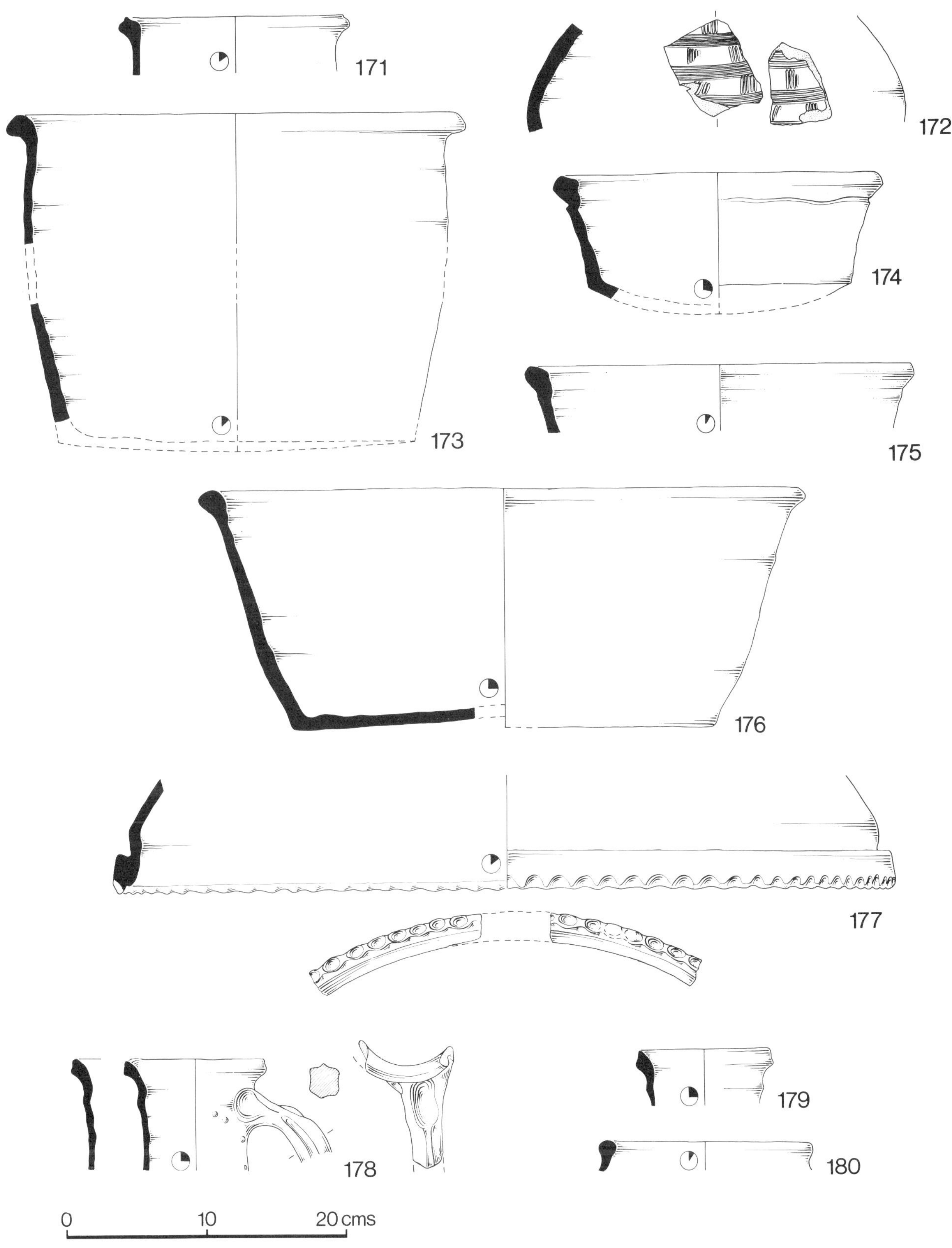

Fig. 49. Pottery. Warming House: nos 171-172, layer 9; nos 173-177, layer 8; nos 178-180, layer 7.

181
182
185
186
183
184
187
0
10
20cms

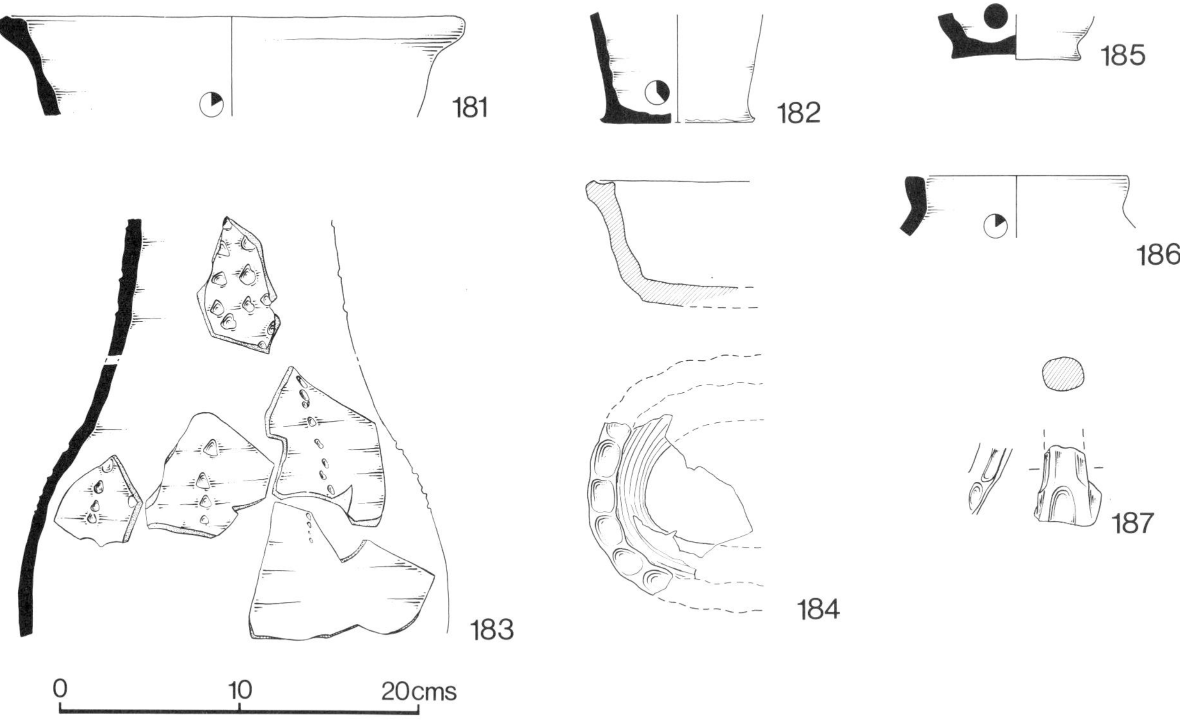

Fig. 50. Pottery. Warming House: nos 181-184, layer 5; no. 185, layer 4; nos 186-187, layer 2.

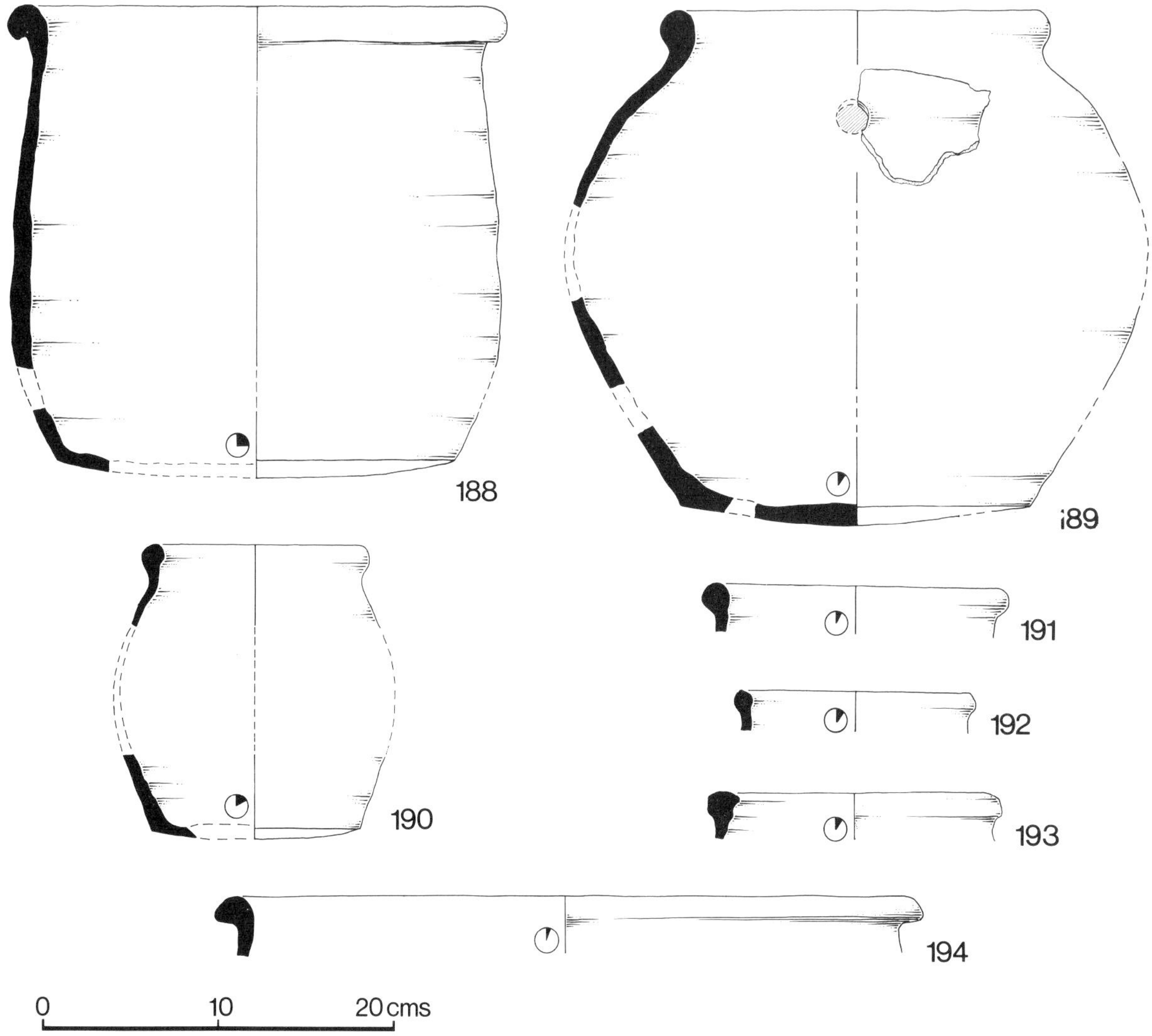

188
189
190
191
192
193
194
0
10
20cms

Fig. 51. Pottery: nos 188-194, fill of Warming House Courtyard cistern.

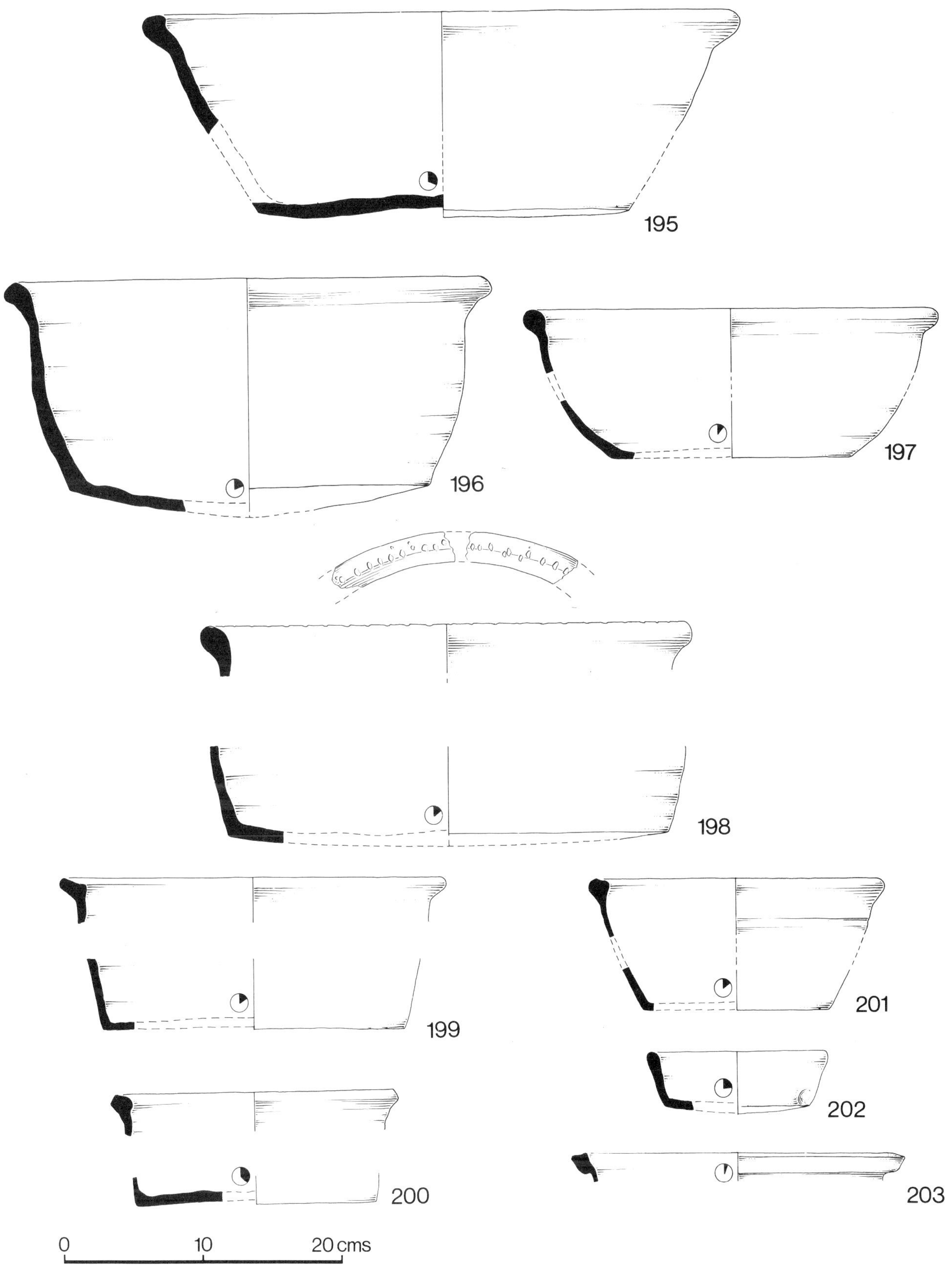

Fig. 52. Pottery: nos 195-203, fill of Warming House Courtyard cistern.

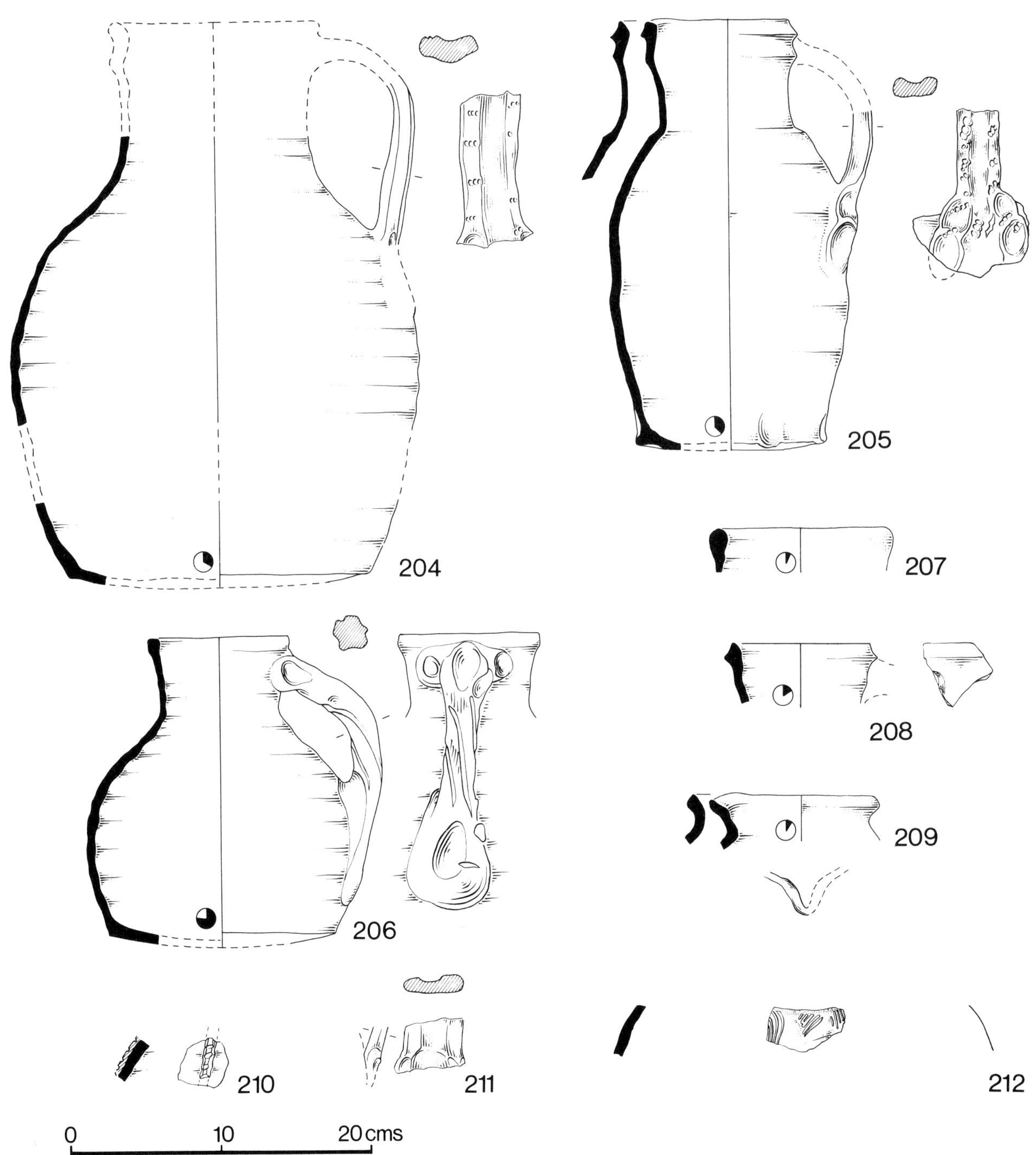

Fig. 53. Pottery: nos 204-212, fill of Warming House Courtyard cistern.

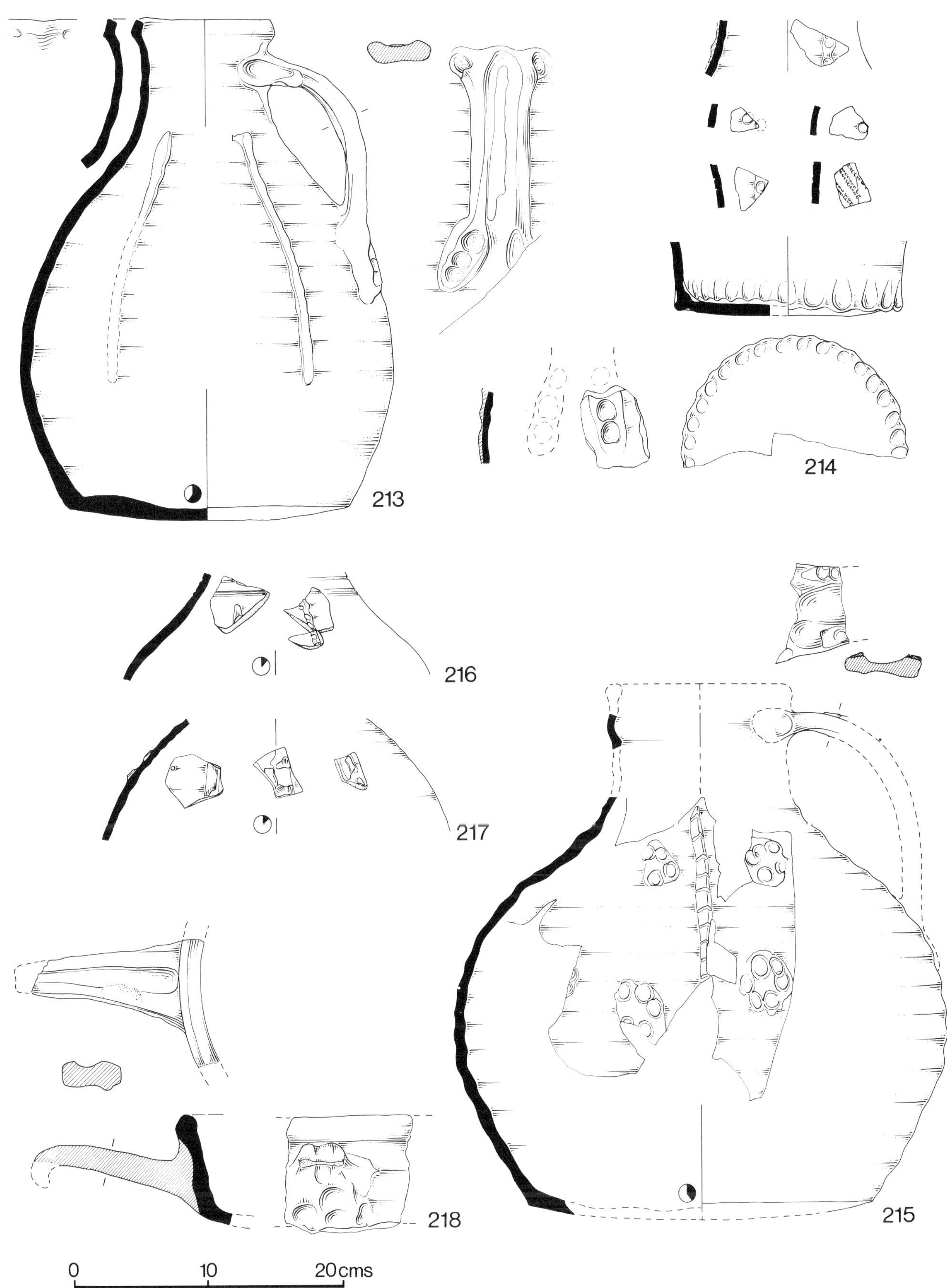

Fig. 54. Pottery: nos 213-218, fill of Warming House Courtyard cistern.

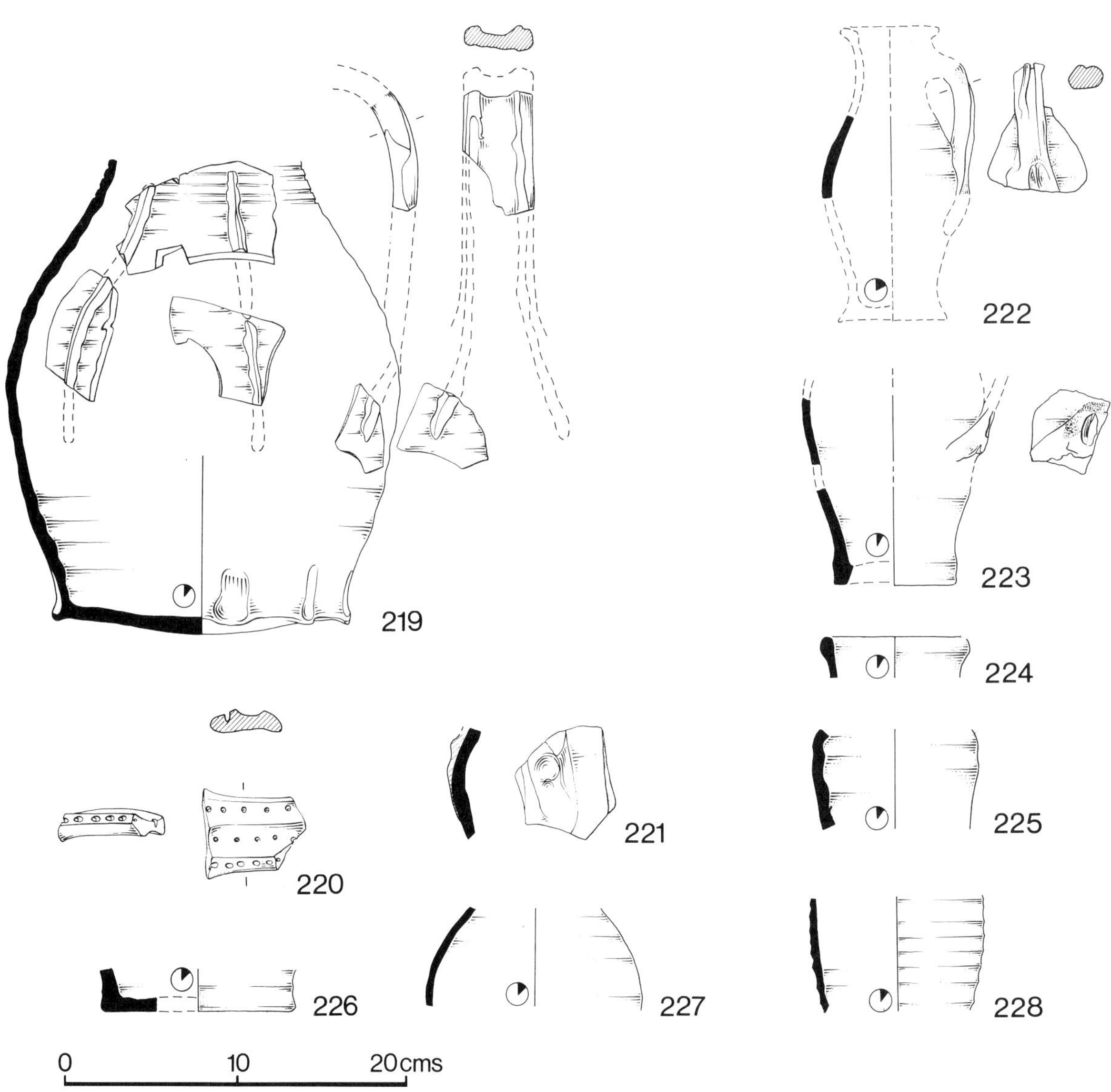

Fig. 55. Pottery: nos 219-228, fill of Warming House Courtyard cistern.

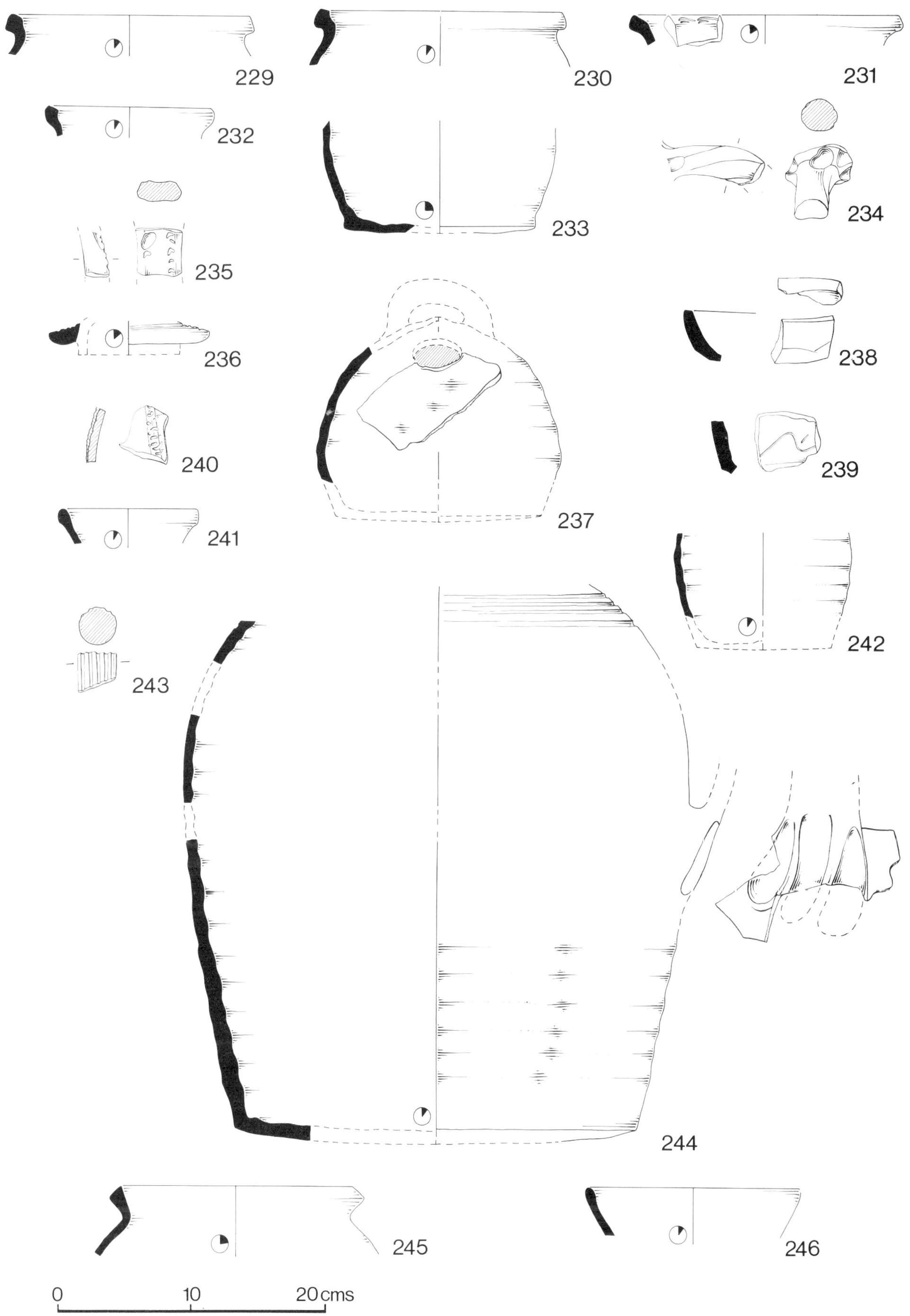

Fig. 56. Pottery: nos 229-246, medieval 'made-ground' south of the Meat Kitchen.

Vessels with sherds from more than one deposit (Tables 9-14)

Recent work has shown that vessels from intensively occupied sites have sherds which are often scattered across a large area.[156] Kirkstall is no exception with some vessels having sherds from the main Abbey buildings and others from current excavations on the Guest House. The significance of this is discussed below (pp. 102-07). All vessels with sherds from more than one deposit are listed below by group. Illustrated vessels are given first, then unillustrated ones. Each table covers one group with contexts arranged across the table in numerical order of area and then context number; they are not arranged chronologically. Column 4 gives the figure number on which the distribution of the sherds is illustrated on Figs 58-62.

Table 9. Vessels with dispersed sherds from the Cloister cistern group.

1	2	3	4	Pre-Cloister cistern				Cloister cistern levelling layer		Unstratified				
Illustration No.	Type No.	Form	Distribution	CL I 3	CL III 3	CL 3	CL 3 S. Ext.	CL I 2A	CL II 2A	CL III 2	CL S. Ext.	CD 2T	CL I+	Unstrat.
1	3	Jug		3		1	3							6
6	7	Bowl			36					7				
7	1	Bowl						4			1		1	
10	17	Jug						1	2			1		

Table 10. Vessels with dispersed sherds from the Refectory.

1	2	3	4	Phase 1			Phase 2													Phase 3	Guest House	Unstratified								
Illust. no.	Type no.	Form	Distribution	R2 3	R5 4	R5 12	R4 2	R5 2	R5 2a	R5 2b	R4 3	R4 B 3	R4 3a	R5 3	R8 SW 3	R5 5	R7 9	R7 N 9	R7 N 12	R5 9	KA 81 307	R5 1	R2 2	R2+3 2	FR 1 2E	R3 6	R5 7	R5 11	R+	Unstrat.
47	1	Jar		13	1		1						1	1		1								8						2
48	1	Jug				74	3	18	2				1	3		4							1							44
49	1	Jar				3		1																	1					1
50	1	Jar				3											1												1	1
51	1	Jar				14	1						1																	2
52	6	Tripod Pitcher				50	1	1						11								1								6
53	5	Jar				3	2	8						4		4														2
55	1	Jar		1										3		1	1													
58	1	Jug					1		1																	1				1
62	1	Jar				9		3	1					12																2
63	1	Jar					3				1	1																		
64	1	Jar								1										1							1			1
73	4	Jug	Fig. 62				5														2									
75	7	Handled bowl					2								1															
76	7	Jug							2									1											3	
81	8	Jug					1	2																						
88	7	Industrial vessel								1									3	1										
—	36	Crucible								1									1	1								2		
—	1	Vessel					2					2																		
—	1	Jar					3					2	1																	
—	1	Jar					1			1		2	15																	
—	1	Vessel					1		1											1				1				2		

Table 11. Vessels with dispersed sherds from the Infirmary.

1	2	3	4	Layer 2 (Phase 1)										Layer 1 (Phase 2)																												
Illust. no.	Type no.	Form	Distribution	I 3 2	I 4 2	I 5 2	I 8 2	I 9 2	I 12 2	I 12 2a	I 14 2	I 15 2	I 16 2	I 1 1	I 2 1	I 3 1	I 4 1	I 5 1	I 6 1	I 7 1	I 7 1a	I 8 1	I 9 1	I 12 1	I 14 1	I 14 1a	I 15 1	I 15 1a	I 16 1	I 16/17 1	I 17 1	I 18 1	I 19 1	I 20 1	I 21 1	I+	WRE 2	BD 2 5	BD 23 5	LR 4 2	LR 3 1	Unstrat.
125	8	Jar	Fig. 60			1		11	4	6	1												3	1				1	4							1						
126	8	Jar										7																5														
128	8	—			1				1																	1																
129	8	Jug						5				1												1																		
130	8	Jug		1			4	2	4													2														4						4
132	7	Jug	Fig. 60				6	21	6	2										2		1	2	2					9													
134	11	Spouted jug	Figs. 60, 62			1	2	5	7				1						2				3							1							2					
135	10	Jug				1					1																															
137	10	Jug		1	8											1																				1						
142	7	Jug																							1									2			1	1				12
146	8	Jug																			1		1																			
147	10	Jug																1							2							1			2	11						
148	14	Jug																				1			1																	
150	18	Jug																								4							4									
156	24	Cup													1	1																				1				3		
159	27	Cistern												10																						6					1	
—	31	Jar															1										4															5
—	7	Jug																										16			1											1

Table 12. Vessels with dispersed sherds from the Warming House.

1	2	3	4													
Illust. no.	Type no.	Form	Distribution	WH 9	WH 8	WH 7	WH 6	WH 5	WH 4 (sand)	WH +	52/1	LR I 3	BD III I	CD +	CI	Unstrat.
172	7	Jug		2			1									
175	7	Curfew			1						1	1				
176	7	Bowl			2	1										24
183	7	Jug				4		7					1	1		1
184	7	—						1		1						3
185	7	—							1						1	
—	7	Jug				9		8								

Table 13. Vessels with dispersed sherds from the Warming House cistern.

1	2	3	4								
Illust. no.	Type no.	Form	Distribution	44/1951	MK II 6	MKA 6	KY8 2	KY8 3	BD 12	AB +	Unstrat.
195	7	Bowl	Fig. 61	3	1	1					6
199	7	Bowl	Fig. 61	2			1	2			1
215	7	Jug	Fig. 61	58					1		
219	11	Jug	Fig. 61	15						13	

Table 14. Vessels with dispersed sherds from the medieval made ground south of the Meat Kitchen.

1	2	3	4											
Illust. no.	Type no.	Form	Distribution	BD 21 4	BD 21 5	BD 23 5	BD X1 1	BD X111 +	LR 3 1	LR 4 2	LR 5 2	WR A/B 1	WRD 2	Unstrat.
237	7	Urinal			1	2								
242	12	Jug		1	1									
244*	19	Cistern	Fig. 58		4		1	2	2	5	1	1	1	32

Methods of manufacture

An attempt was made to examine techniques of manufacture that might help in distinguishing characteristics peculiar to a particular pottery tradition. Not all forms of each type are ever found on one site, but as more pottery is examined from sites in West Yorkshire, a picture of characteristic potting techniques will be built up.

The majority of vessels of all types are wheel-thrown with particularly pronounced throwing lines on the interiors of Skipton on Swale jugs (Type 17). The exceptions are the Type 6 tripod pitchers and the unrecognised form (no. 184) of Northern Gritty ware (Type 7), which are hand-made; and all forms of South-west Midlands Coarse ware (Type 5), which are hand-made but possibly finished on a wheel; and a jug (no. 240) of unrecognised type from the medieval 'made ground' south of the Meat Kitchen, which is coil made. The earlier vessels of Pimply ware (Type 1), York type ware (Type 2), Hillam type ware (Type 3) and Developed Stamford ware (Type 4) are extremely well made with thin, even walls; while vessels of Late Medieval Smooth ware (Type 30), the most common type during the later medieval period on the site, tend to be rougher with several wasters and flawed vessels (unillustrated). It has been suggested that these flawed vessels are evidence for a possible kiln on the site of the Abbey.[157] One jug rim with glaze running over the fracture has already been illustrated.[158] No other evidence for a kiln was, however, found, and these wasters either reached the Abbey in the packing material of a consignment of pots or as seconds, sold cheaply. Most of the domestic pottery would have come from local manufacturers.

Pouring lips are always formed by hand, usually pinched, and it is sometimes possible to identify which hand a potter used. Jug no. 209 of Northern Gritty ware (Type 7) has a lip formed with the right hand. A jar of Pimply ware (Type 1), from the foundation trench of the east wall of the Refectory (no. 54), was said to have been made by a left-handed potter working a clock-wise wheel. The vessel was restored soon after its recovery and the internal surface is now mostly covered with plaster, making it difficult to determine the direction of throwing. The pinched lip of jug no. 21, Northern Gritty ware (Type 7), was formed with the right hand; whereas there are small depressions on either side of the pouring lip of jug no. 213 of Northern Gritty ware (Type 7), indicating that it was formed with both hands, pulled rather than pinched.

Tubular spouts of Fine Sandy ware (Type 11) and York White ware (Type 18) were formed by applying a roll of clay to the shoulder of the jug and then pushing a rod down the centre and through the wall of the vessel. The clay pushed aside by the rod can still be seen on the internal shoulder wall of jug no. 134 of Fine Sandy ware (Type 11). There is strengthening at the neck of a cistern of Brick-Red Sandy ware (Type 28; no. 30) in the form of a thumbed strip which is also a decorative feature.

Handles of all types are applied and smoothed down at the top and bottom. The handles of the Skipton on Swale jugs (Type 17) have been pressed down at the bottom of the handle with the thumb at a slant, leaving the mark of the fingernail running down the centre of the impression. A pipkin of Northern Gritty ware (Type 7; no. 218) has a handle with several very pronounced thumb marks beneath it. Handles vary in shape, most commonly strap, although Northern Gritty ware (Type 7) handles are both strap and rod, while Skipton on Swale jugs (Type 17) have only rod handles. The handles of the handled bowls of Northern Gritty ware (Type 7) and Late Medieval Oxidised Sandy ware (Type 31) spring directly from the rims. Northern Gritty ware (Type 7), Midland Purple type ware (Type 29) and Late Medieval Smooth ware (Type 30) have their bodies pushed into the handle from inside.

The majority of bases tend to sag slightly, although all vessels of Skipton on Swale jugs (Type 17) have flat bases, and there is a number of slightly concave bases among vessels of Pimply ware (Type 1), Northern Gritty ware (Type 7) and Late Medieval Smooth ware (Type 30). These are not necessarily deliberately made, and could have been produced by stacking one vessel on top of another in the kiln. Several examples have thumbing around the base: Northern Gritty ware (Type 7) nos 8, 205 and 214; and Unidentified non-local wares (Type 10) no. 84; as well as York White ware (Type 18) and Orange Gritty ware (Type 8) among the unassociated material. A jug of Northern Gritty ware (Type 7; no. 214) has thumbing beneath the base as well as above the base. There are concentric grooves on the bases of Cistercian ware (Type 24) cups, where the vessels have been removed from the wheel with a loop of wire; this is the only type where this occurs.

Pimply ware (Type 1), Hillam type ware (Type 3) and Martincamp flasks (Type 33) are always unglazed. All other types are glazed, usually with a clear glaze, although White-slipped Humber ware (Type 21) has the addition of copper to the glaze giving it a speckled green appearance. Vessels are rarely glazed all over, usually only the upper part is covered. The exceptions to this are Cistercian ware (Type 24), Reversed Cistercian ware (Type 25), Yellow ware (Type 26) and sometimes Vitrified Earthenware (Type 28).

White clay is used decoratively on some Northern Gritty ware (Type 7) jugs in the form of applied and stamped strips or pads; and a slip of white clay occurs as an internal overall cover on a pipkin (no. 218) of the same type. White slip also occurs on vessels of White-slipped Humber ware (Type 21), where it is found patchily beneath the glaze. Cistercian ware (Type 24) cups occasionally have white slip decoration trailed over them or pads of white clay applied to the body.

Earlier types, Pimply ware (Type 1), York type ware (Type 2), Hillam type ware (Type 3) and Developed Stamford ware (Type 4) tend to be oxidised throughout. Other types vary from the totally reduced to the totally oxidised, with both reduced and oxidised areas often occurring on the same vessel. On vessels of Baildon ware (Type 22) and Late Medieval Oxidised Sandy ware (Type 31) oxidation has occurred except where the glaze has prevented it. There is evidence that vessels have been fired upside down with scars and reduced circles left on bases where the upper pot has been sealed to the lower by running glaze. This has happened on vessels of Late Medieval Smooth ware (Type 30) where the reduced circles are always of jugs, even though cisterns were also present. They were probably stacked differently because of their weight. Vessels of Northern Gritty ware (Type 7) were occasionally reduced internally, indicating that they were stacked in such a way as to exclude all oxygen from the interior of the vessel. Jugs of Oxidised Humber ware (Type 15) have been fired in an upright position, and the glaze has run down the pot towards the base. Cups of Cistercian ware (Type 24) rested on sand (some still adheres to the bottom of some bases) propped up by a bob of clay or a broken sherd, and the glaze has run into part of the base angle where the pot was tilted.

Fingerprints
The pottery was examined for potters' fingerprints whilst being sorted. A few were found although none was clear enough to take impressions, because of the grittiness of most fabrics. Those found on illustrated vessels have all been noted in column 7 of Table 8.

Evidence for use

Medieval pottery displays a variety of evidence for its many uses. This ranges from wear marks to sooting characteristics. Those looked for on the Kirkstall material include wear marks, suspension marks, sooting, residues, secondary holes and unusual primary holes.

Sooting (Fig. 57, Table 15)
All rim, base and body sherds were examined for sooting. A variety of sooting types was found (Table 15), although not all vessels could be assigned to the sooting types because of their fragmentary nature. More vessels with sooting may have been excavated but, because their significance was not recognised, the sooting was probably lost in washing. Sooting is found mainly on the early vessels (Pimply and Northern Gritty wares), suggesting that the late medieval jar form, which is rare, was used for storage.

Without analysis it is uncertain which type of fuel was used, although, from the sooting that survives, the use of charcoal seems unlikely: charcoal does not throw up a flame, and sooting usually ends on a sharply defined line, which is missing on the Kirkstall vessels.

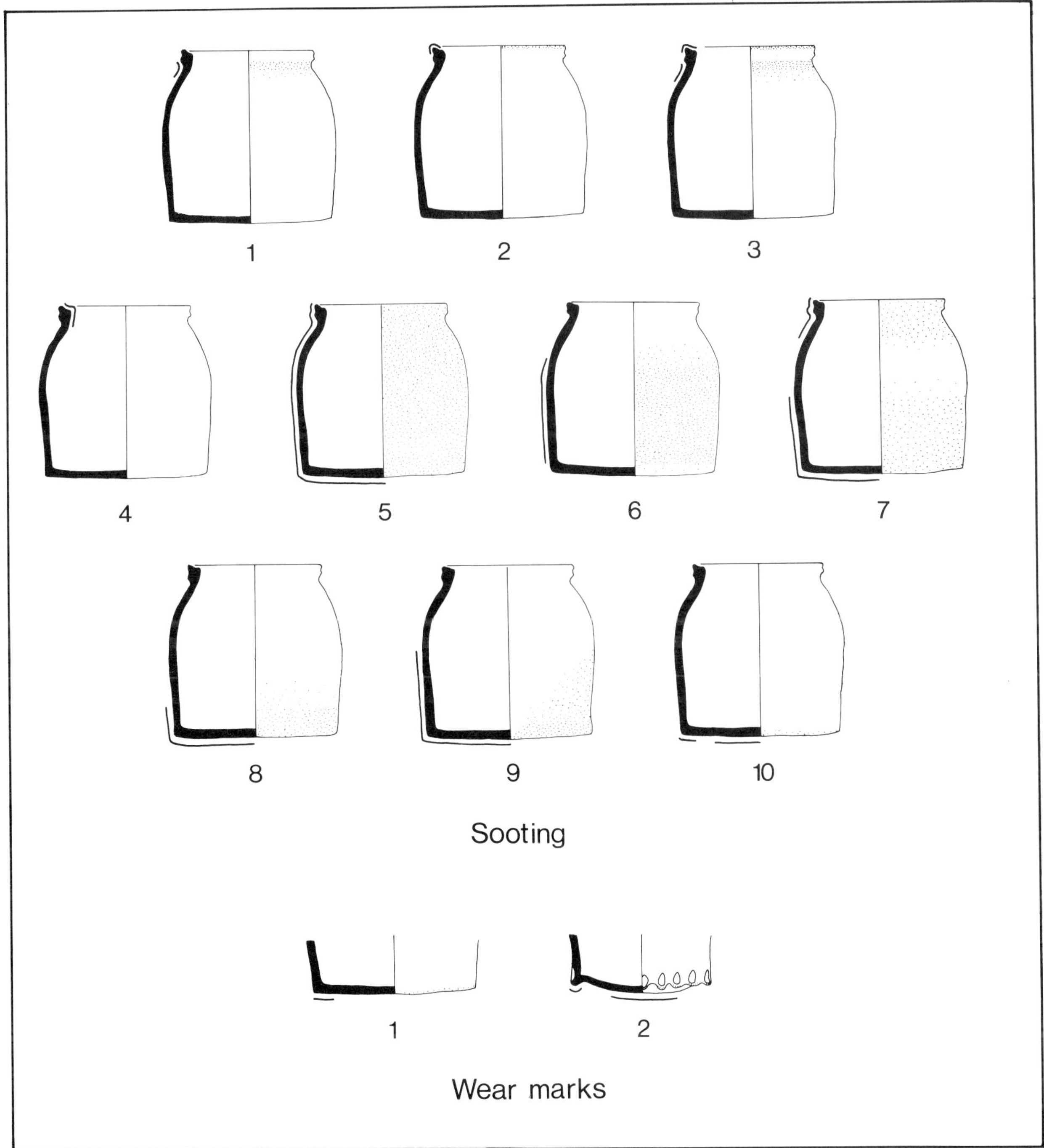

Fig. 57. Sooting and wear mark characteristics present on the published pottery.

Table 15. Sooting characteristics present on the published pottery. Bold numbers are illustration numbers of vessels on Figs 39-56. Others refer to unillustrated vessels.

	Pimply			York	Northern Gritty					Unidentified
Sooting type on Fig. 57	Jar	Bowl	Vess.	Jar	Jar	Bowl	Jug	Pipkin	Vess.	Jug
1	+1	203								
2										9
3								218		
4				72						
5	+2					181			184	
6			65							
7	62									
8	51 68 71								185	
9							233			
10					75					

There is documentary evidence for the use of 'double boilers', smaller vessels resting on the rims of, or suspended in water held in larger vessels.[159] This is a possible explanation for sooting Types 1, 2 and 3. The patchy sooting to one side of the vessel indicated in Type 9 was formed by placing the pot against the fire, not directly over it. Either the pot was used only once or the same side was placed against the fire every time. The use of a lid or covering can be suggested for sooting Type 1 and possibly 6. The lids or coverings of the early medieval period were probably of material softer than the vessel, possibly parchment or linen, because no wear marks were found on the rims of those vessels. A few pottery lids in Northern Gritty ware were found (nos 95, 122, 236). The clean ring found on sooting Type 10 could have been caused by resting the vessel on a trivet. This is not a common sooting type, although examples have been found elsewhere in the county.

Wear marks (Fig. 57, Table 16)

Few wear marks were identified but these were clearly distinguishable from general abrasion. The nature of the wear marks was very limited (Table 16). Only three worn vessels were found among the associated groups, and although several more were found among the unassociated material, they did not differ widely. The majority of wear marks occurred on late medieval vessels, and nearly always on the base. Wear marks on four late medieval rims were noted among the unassociated material (two jugs of Late Medieval Smooth ware (Type 30), one of Midland Purple type ware (Type 29) and one Late Medieval Smooth ware (Type 30) cistern), suggesting the use of lids of a material harder than the pot. No pottery lids of the late medieval period, other than those in Cistercian ware, were found.

Table 16. Wear marks present on the published pottery. Numbers are the pottery illustration numbers.

Wear mark type on Fig. 57	York White		Fine Sandy
	Jug	Vess.	Jug
1	226	13	
2			219

Wear marks in general, whether on the rim or the base, suggest long use, especially on the late medieval vessels, which tend to be harder fired. The pottery shows a distinct dearth of wear marks, contrary to what one would expect from such a large quantity of vessels. This suggests that breakages were frequent, and only rarely were vessels used long enough to show wear.

Residues (Table 17)

Four examples of residues were found, and examined visually (Table 17). All were found inside the bases of a variety of vessels. They were not restricted to any particular type or

Table 17. Residues found on the published pottery.

Illust. no.	Type no.	Common name	Form	Residue	
				Position	Colour
32	30	Late Medieval Smooth	—	inside base	white
142	7	Northern Gritty	Jug	inside base	white
223	15	Oxidized Humber	Jug	inside base	white
237	7	Northern Gritty	Urinal	inside base	red

Table 18. Forms represented in each pottery type; numbers refer to vessels.

Type number	Common name	Jar	Jug	Bowl	Tripod pitcher	Curfew	Dripping pan	Strainer	Lid	Urinal	Flask	Cistern	Lobed cup	Cup	Unidentified vessel
1	Pimply	36	11	2											57
2	York type	1													
3	Hillam type	1	1												
4	Developed Stamford		1												
5	South-west Midlands	4													
6	Tripod pitchers				3										
7	Northern Gritty	18	150	23		1	3	1	2	1					149
8	Orange Gritty	5	20	14											25
9	'Stepped jug'		1												
10	Unidentified non-local		18												
11	Fine Sandy		6												
12	Pink Fine		1												
13	Rouen		1												
14	South-western French Polychrome		2												
15	Oxidized Humber	1	14												
16	Reduced Humber														2
17	Skipton on Swale		17												
18	York White		20	1					1				1		8
19	Rawmarsh type		2									8			15
20	Tudor Green type		1												
21	White-slipped Humber												1		
22	Baildon		1												
23	Late Medieval Gritty	1													
24	Cistercian													43	15
25	Reversed Cisterian													1	
26	Yellow			3											1
27	Vitrified Earthenware	1										1			2
28	Brick Red Sandy											1			3
29	Midland Purple type		2												
30	Late Medieval Smooth	1	16									1			31
31	Late Medieval Oxidized Sandy	1													
32	Martincamp										3				
33	Langerwehe		3												
34	Siegburg		3												
35	Raeren		3												

Table 19. Forms present in individual groups, with forms and groups arranged in chronological order; the numbers refer to vessels; topsoil and unstratified material has been omitted.

	Jar	Jug	Bowl	Tripod pitcher	Curfew	Dripping pan	Strainer	Lid	Urinal	Flask	Cistern	Cup
Pre-Cloister cistern	9	2										
Cloister cistern levelling layer	1	7										
Refectory Phase 1	5	1		1								
Refectory Phase 2	13	18		1								
Warming House Layer 9		1	1									
Warming House Layer 8			2		1							
Warming House Layer 7	1	1										
Warming House Layer 5			3									
Warming House Layer 4		1										
Warming House Layer 2		1										
Warming House cistern	8	30	18			1						
Infirmary Layer 2	6		18	30	1	1	1					
South of Meat Kitchen	16	114				1		1	1			
Fill of Cloister cistern	1	8								1	5	4
Infirmary Layer 1	4	2	5								5	19

form. All had a powdery appearance, three of them being an off-white colour, the fourth being red-brown. This last example is unusual in that it was found inside a urinal: white is the more usual colour associated with uric acid. The pot appears to have been used for something other than the collection of urine.

Forms present (Tables 18, 19)

Pottery was one of the many materials used for containers during the Middle Ages. Wood, leather, pewter, precious metals and glass were common, all of which rarely survive in archaeological deposits because they deteriorate, are burnt or are re-cycled. Some forms of containers were peculiar to certain materials, through tradition, cost or fashion. Drinking bowls and cups were not found in the potter's repertoire until the fifteenth century, but were made by wood turners. Variations in eating habits, and in social and economic conditions meant that the forms in which pottery was made changed throughout the Middle Ages. These changes are reflected in the series of groups from Kirkstall.

The two tables present the information in different ways. In both cases the forms are listed chronologically from left to right as they appear in the sequence of groups, and the quantification gives the number of vessels. Table 18 shows the forms set against the types in chronological order downwards, and includes unstratified pottery; while Table 19 gives the same information against a composite chronological sequence within all of the six stratified groups.

Site distribution of the pottery (Figs 58-62)

Recent work has demonstrated that the spatial distribution of pottery on a site can provide a unique source of information for interpreting stratigraphy, relationships and the uses of areas or buildings. The most productive source of information comes from the distribution of sherds from the same vessel, dispersed for various reasons and often a number of times after the pieces have been initially discarded. This type of evidence has been particularly helpful at Kirkstall in complementing and often amplifying the archaeological evidence. In arguing that the dispersal of pottery around a site is evidence for the movement of soil, mostly through building work, it might seem contradictory to suggest that the distribution of forms may help understand the uses of areas where they are found. Surprisingly this is possible, as is shown below (Fig. 63) with the distribution of the pottery dripping pans from the site.

Many vessels from groups published here, from the unpublished material and from current work on the Guest House have sherds with a localised horizontal distribution. Most pots are represented by a small number of sherds from no more than two contexts. The remaining parts of these vessels clearly lie outside the areas of the site which were excavated. Most of the sherds are small, suggesting that they had been disturbed on more than one occasion, an assumption supported by their sometimes wide distribution (Fig. 62). A number of vessels have sherds scattered across a restricted part of the site: two are illustrated on Fig. 58. The possible reasons for such a distribution are numerous, and are discussed below (pp. 106-07).

An examination of Tables 10 and 11 shows that many vessels from the Refectory and the Infirmary had sherds scattered widely within their respective areas of excavation. Analysis of the location of each sherd from the vessels shows that there were different causes behind the scatters within each area. For example, the archaeological evidence suggests that the make-up layers within the second Refectory were all contemporary; and this is supported by the distribution of sherds throughout the various trenches excavated, and from the stratified deposits within them (Table 10). The date of the pottery is no later than the early thirteenth century, indicating a construction date for the existing Refectory building.

Similarly, the spatial distribution of the pottery from the Infirmary helps to complement and extend the archaeological evidence for the sequence of buildings there. Two distinct horizons were noted throughout the series of excavated trenches. In the structural interpretation (pp. 52-56), Layer 2 is seen to represent the original ground surface, into which the stone-pitched foundations for a timber-framed aisled building were cut. Layer 1 is associated

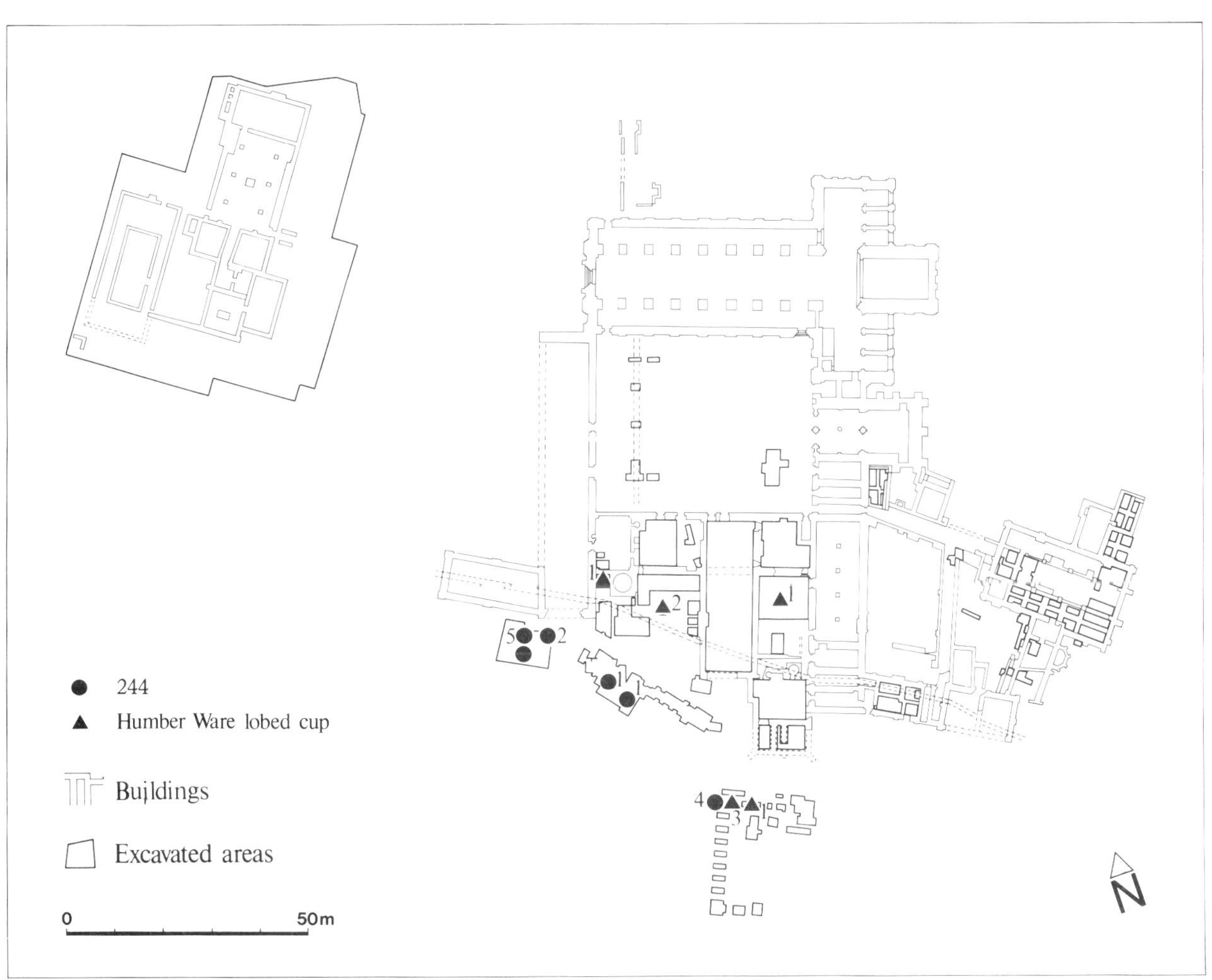

Fig. 58. Distribution of sherds from two pottery vessels, showing the often localised distribution through the disposal of rubbish.

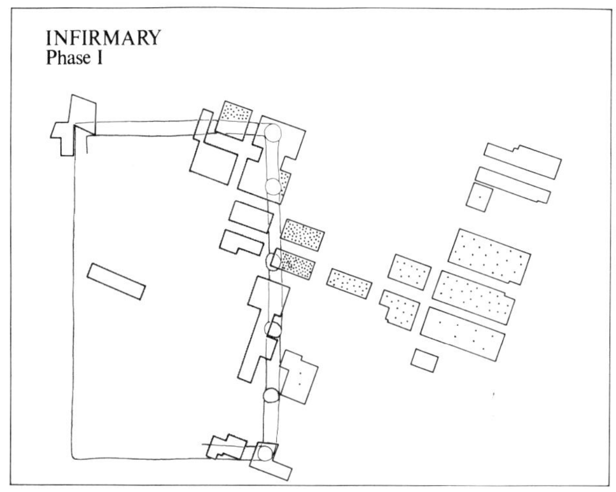

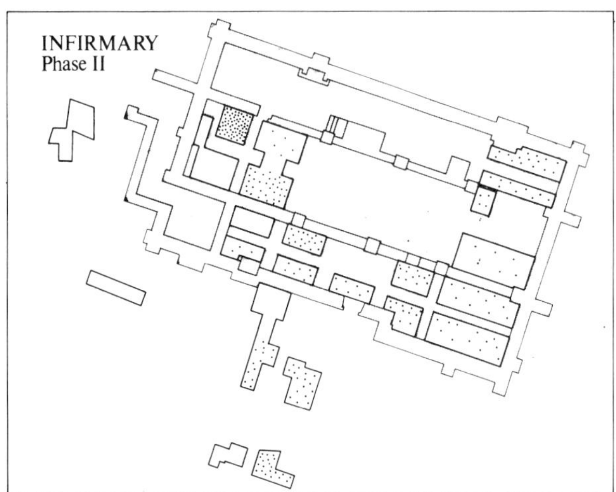

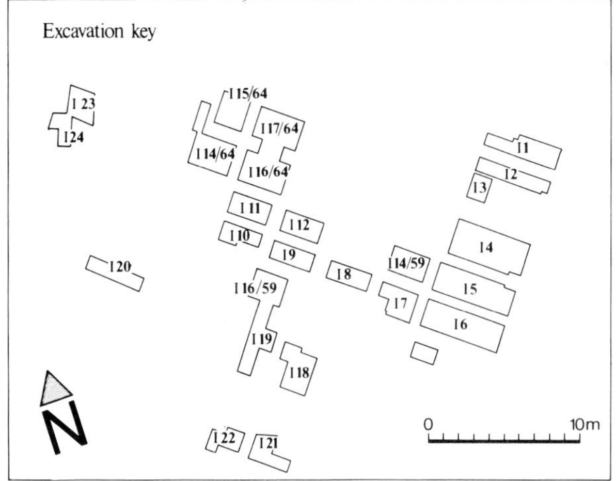

Fig. 59. Distribution of pottery sherds from the two phases (Layers 1 and 2) of the Infirmary. Each dot represents a sherd. For the archaeological evidence for the two phases, see Figs 33, 36. The distribution of material from Phase 1 (Layer 2) suggests three possibilities: the pottery scatter respects the timber building, indicating that it was deposited while the building was in use; concentrations of pottery around the walls suggest an eaves gulley; and the pottery scatter eastwards suggests associated horticultural activity.

with the construction and use of the existing stone building. The first-phase timber structure was laid out on a different alignment from the later stone Infirmary. The distribution of all pottery sherds from Layer 2 (Fig. 59, Phase 1) shows a concentration outside the eastern wall of the early timber building. This suggests that the internal surface was either kept clean of rubbish or that it was sealed by flooring. It seems likely that the material from Layer 2 was discarded after the building had been erected, and probably during its use; otherwise, there would have been an even distribution of pottery throughout all excavated areas, rather than one which respected the wall of the building.

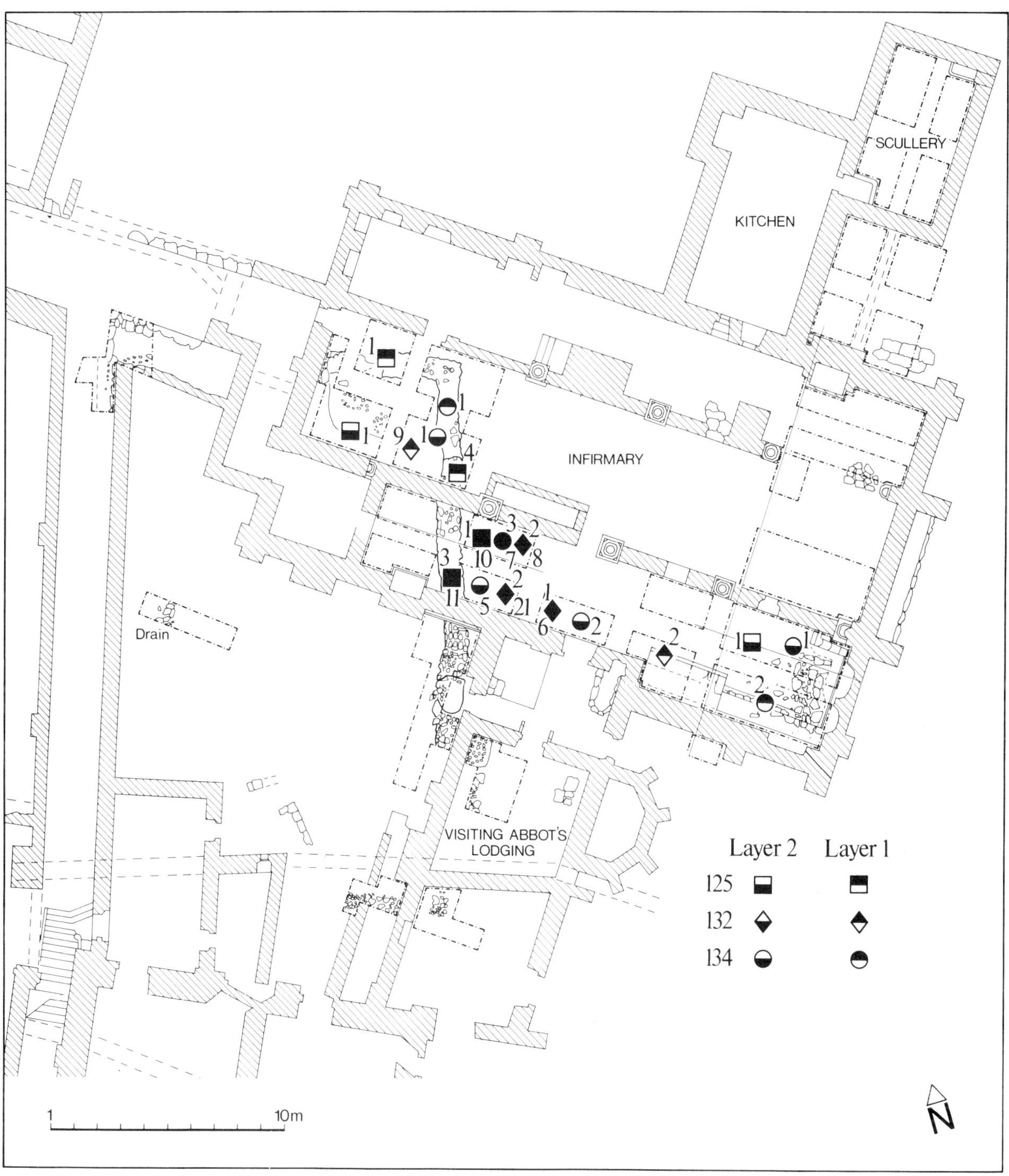

Fig. 60. Distribution of sherds from three Phase 1 vessels between the two phases of the Infirmary. The maximum amount of upward movement into Phase 2 has occurred where later disturbance of the earlier deposits has taken place, such as the insertion of the walls and aisle pillars for the stone Infirmary.

The vertical distribution between the two layers is also of interest. Not surprisingly the distribution of sherds from all Layer 1 vessels is restricted to the second phase (Table 11). Those from the primary phase Layer 2 are mixed between the two horizons. Figure 60 shows the distribution of three vessels, with the numbers of sherds that come from each layer. The stone Infirmary was modified throughout its life, most significantly in the division of the aisles into separate cubicles. This was achieved by the insertion of stone walls between the existing aisle pillars. These alterations probably explain the disturbances and the upwards movement of material from the earlier deposits. It is particularly noticeable in I 12 where all three vessels, along with others which are not plotted (Table 11), have sherds from both layers.

Where a group can be shown to be homogeneous, then sherds from the vessels within the group when found elsewhere on the site can provide relative dating. Such an instance occurs with the Warming House cistern group, dated to shortly after 1420. Of the forty-seven vessels present, only four had sherds from outside the group, whose distributions are shown on Fig. 61. Three of the vessels (nos 195, 199, 219) have sherds which come from stratified deposits. Unfortunately they are of little use, as the areas from which they come are poorly documented.

A number of vessels have sherds with a much wider distribution than the immediate area of excavation (Fig. 62). Indeed, two of them have sherds from current excavations on the Guest House, as well as from the excavations carried out within the main range. The Developed Stamford ware pitcher (no. 73) has sherds from the two sites that actually join. The other vessel, a Humber ware lobed cup, will be published with the Guest House material. Both vessels are very distinctive, and the material from both the 1950-1964 work and the current excavations was being processed together at the time they were recognised. It is very probable that other vessels have sherds with a similar wide distribution pattern, which will only become apparent when all the material from the current excavations has been examined.

The reasons why pottery might be dispersed around a site are too numerous to allow any one cause to be suggested for an

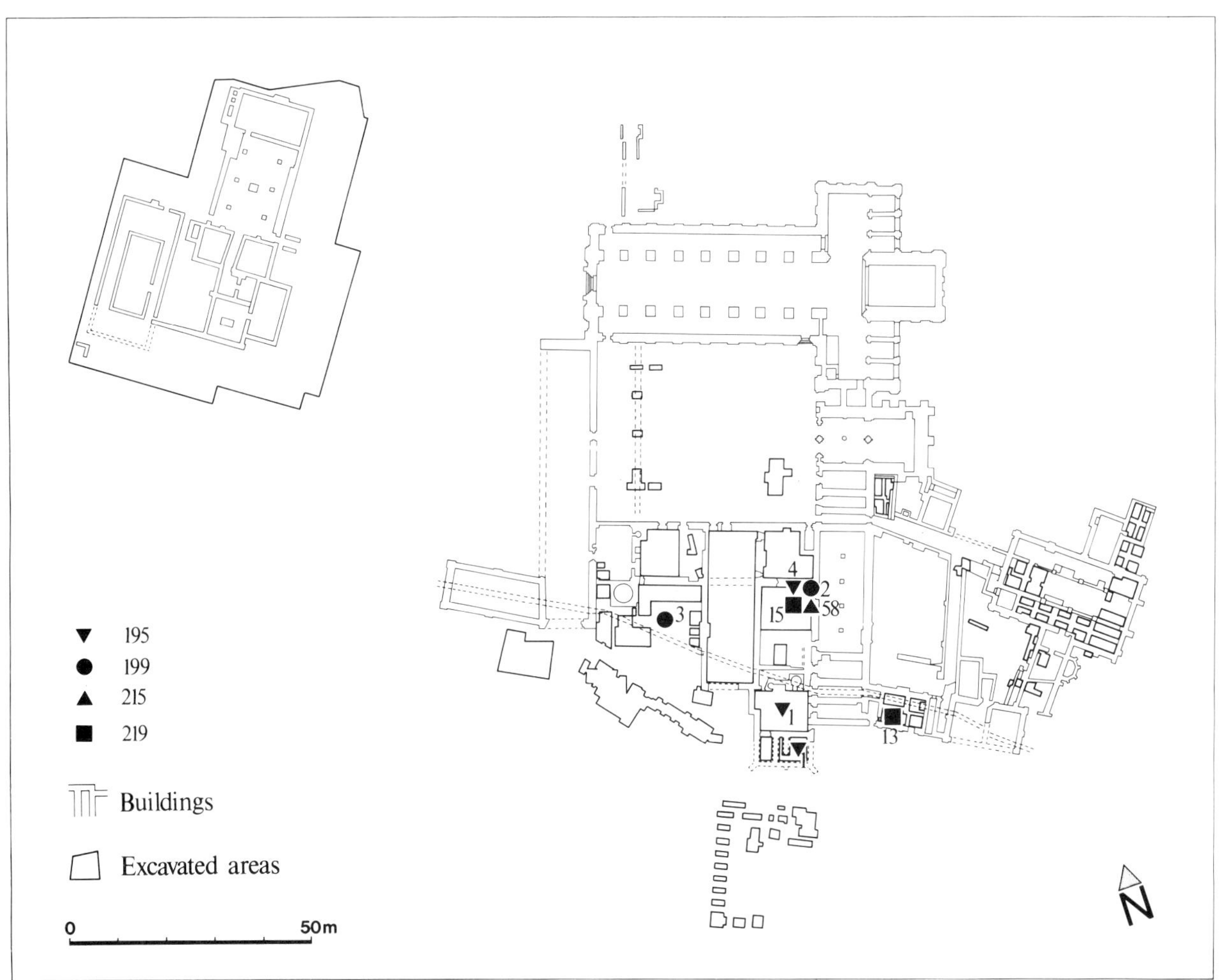

Fig. 61. Limited distribution of sherds from vessels in the Warming House cistern group, from four out of forty vessels.

individual vessel without good evidence. Small abraded sherds could have been moved more than once, making it dangerous to draw conclusions simply from the find spot of sherds during excavation. The six published groups form a small part of a much larger collection of material to be included in the report on the Guest House excavations. These excavations have also produced an extensive collection of well-stratified pottery. The significance of the distribution of sherds from vessels published here may become clearer when work on all this pottery has been completed. Yet it is already clear that the spatial analysis of sherds from a site which has been trenched sporadically can be a rewarding exercise.

Forms (Fig. 63)
The distribution of particular ceramic forms can also be revealing. It could be argued, with some justification, that because sherds are disturbed both vertically and horizontally, then it is of little value for determining where the vessel was used. That pottery can be used for such purposes has been demonstrated at Sandal Castle, where, amongst numerous examples, the purpose of a hearth in the bailey and the location of an alchemical workshop were indicated by the distribution of industrial ceramic forms.[160] Similarly, at Higher Land, Gargrave (North Yorkshire), the position of a dairy was suggested by the concentration in one deposit of all the pottery bowls from one particular phase.[161]

Similar evidence exists amongst the Kirkstall Abbey material. The distribution of ceramic dripping pans from all the material (including the unstratified material not included here) coincides precisely with the areas of the site where they would have been used (Fig. 63). Dripping pans are long, narrow shallow-sided trays with handles on one of the long sides. They were used beneath the spit against the fire to collect the juices from the cooking meat; hence the long side without handles is usually sooted from contact with the hot embers. At Kirkstall they are found on the yard surface immediately south of the principal Kitchen, outside the Meat Kitchen and in the Infirmary (which had its own kitchens attached to the north side of the hall).

Non-local pottery (Fig. 64)

The excavations produced a surprisingly high proportion (3.25%) of non-locally made pottery (Fig. 64). The current excavations on the Abbey Guest House have produced an even larger proportion of non-local material. The types which one would not expect to be found at the Abbey include South-west Midlands coarse ware (Type 5), Tripod Pitchers (Type 6), and Unidentified non-local jugs (Type 10). Many more examples of Type 10 exist in the non-associated or unstratified material from the 1950-1964 excavations, which is not reported here; and they are common among the material from the Guest House excavations.

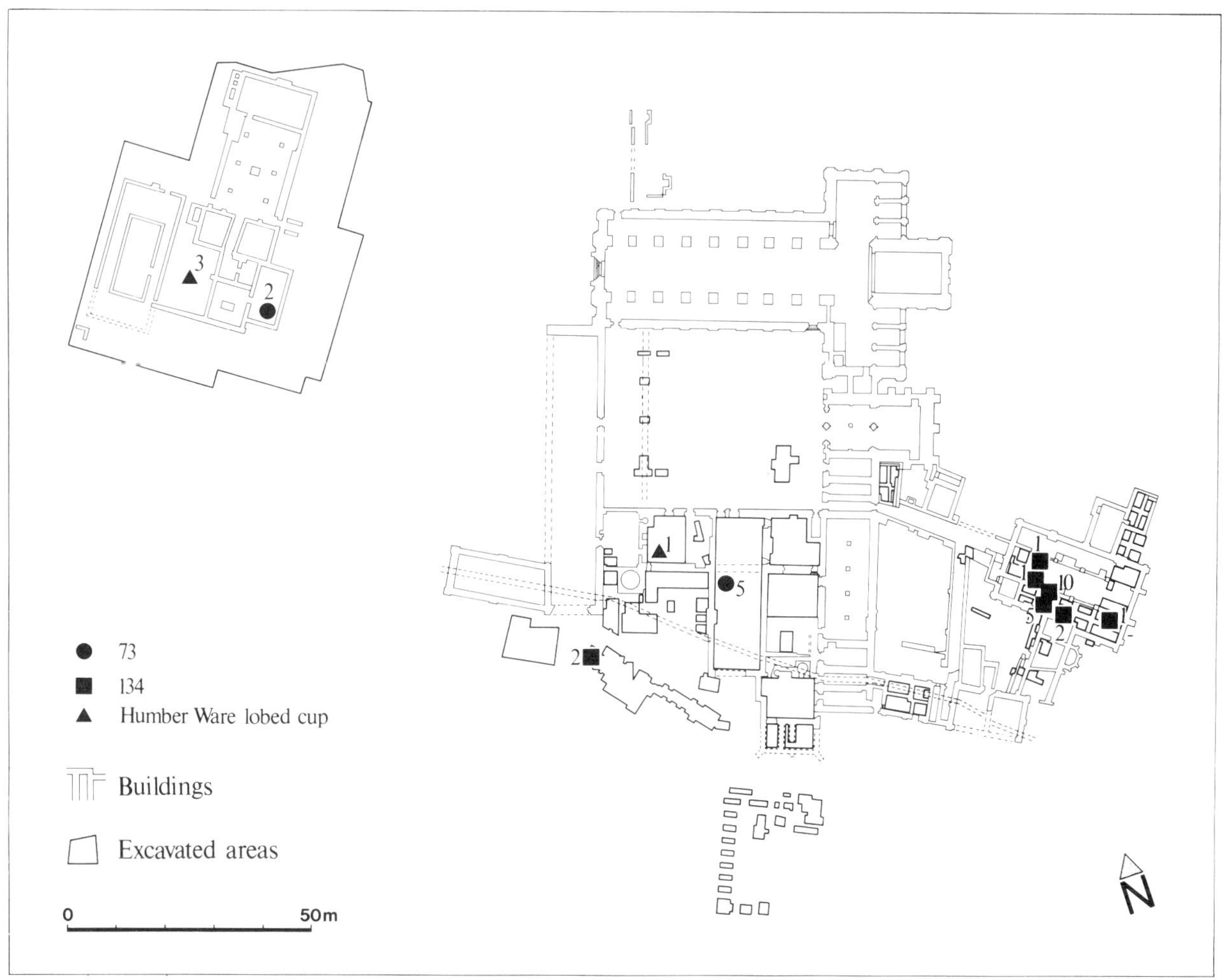

Fig. 62. Widespread distribution of sherds from three pottery vessels, showing dispersal of material around the site, probably disturbed and moved on more than one occasion through building work.

There are a number of possible explanations for the presence of this material on the site. Perhaps the most obvious cause is estate management: monastic and other officers would need to travel between granges and other holdings on administrative business, to hold manor courts or simply to collect rents. This may have been one factor in the presence of some of the pottery, but the sources for the majority of the vessels lie well beyond the boundaries of the Abbey's estate. In fact little appears to have reached Kirkstall from the areas covered by its more distant holdings.

The high proportion from the Guest House is probably explained by visiting households bringing with them pottery as a part of their baggage, either as containers or for use whilst travelling. The purchase of pottery vessels whilst travelling is well documented. Some of it would be discarded on route, but other vessels are likely to have been retained until the end of the journey. The incidence of non-local pottery from monastic guest houses varies from site to site across the country. No appreciable increase was noted at Elstow Priory (Bedfordshire),[162] and no non-local material was recorded in recent excavations of the guest house at Buckfast Abbey (Devon).[163]

The non-local material from the Guest House at Kirkstall Abbey may be the result of special circumstances. Although isolated, the Abbey lay on an important cross-Pennine route during the Middle Ages, a route which connected the centres of two adjoining major estates of the Lacy family: Clitheroe and Pontefract.[164] The Abbey lay 1½ miles from the point at which the route crossed the River Aire. Excavations of the Guest House have shown that whilst the rest of the Abbey was contracting during the fifteenth century, the Guest House was being re-modelled and expanded. This suggests that the Guest House may have been run as a separate concern, or even leased out during the later Middle Ages. The importance of trans-Pennine trade during the Middle Ages is well documented. It may be through Kirkstall's position on this important route that some, if not most of the non-local pottery reached the Abbey, brought there in the baggage of visiting households from other parts of the country, which used the Guest House as we would use a motel today. The high proportion of vessels (Types 5 and 6, and possibly some of Type 10) from the south-western Midlands is probably explained by the very large estates held by the Lacy family in that region. The Lacys founded Kirkstall and the site lay within the extensive honour of Pontefract, also part of Lacy domain. It is therefore not unlikely that generations of the family used the Abbey as a resting place on their numerous inter-estate journeys, and that some if not most of the pottery of south-west Midlands origin reached the Abbey by this means. This suggested manorial link is strengthened by the fact that tripod pitchers of south-west Midlands origin have been found at Castle Hill, Almondbury and at *Hillam Burchard*, both of which formed estate centres for their respective parts of the honour of Pontefract during the twelfth and early thirteenth centuries.[165]

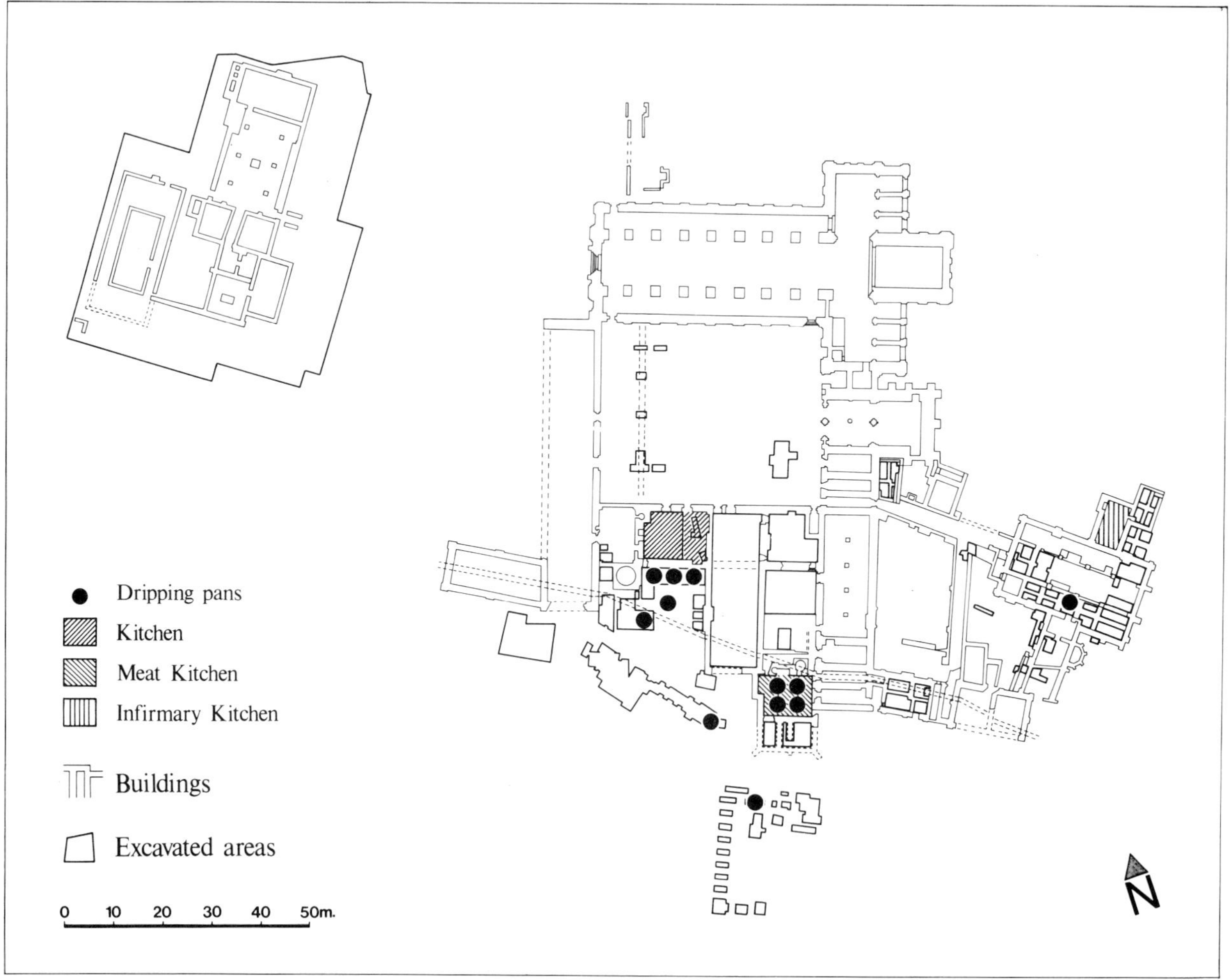

Fig. 63. Distribution of pottery dripping pans from the excavations at Kirkstall Abbey, 1950-1964. They are all found close to where they are likely to have been used.

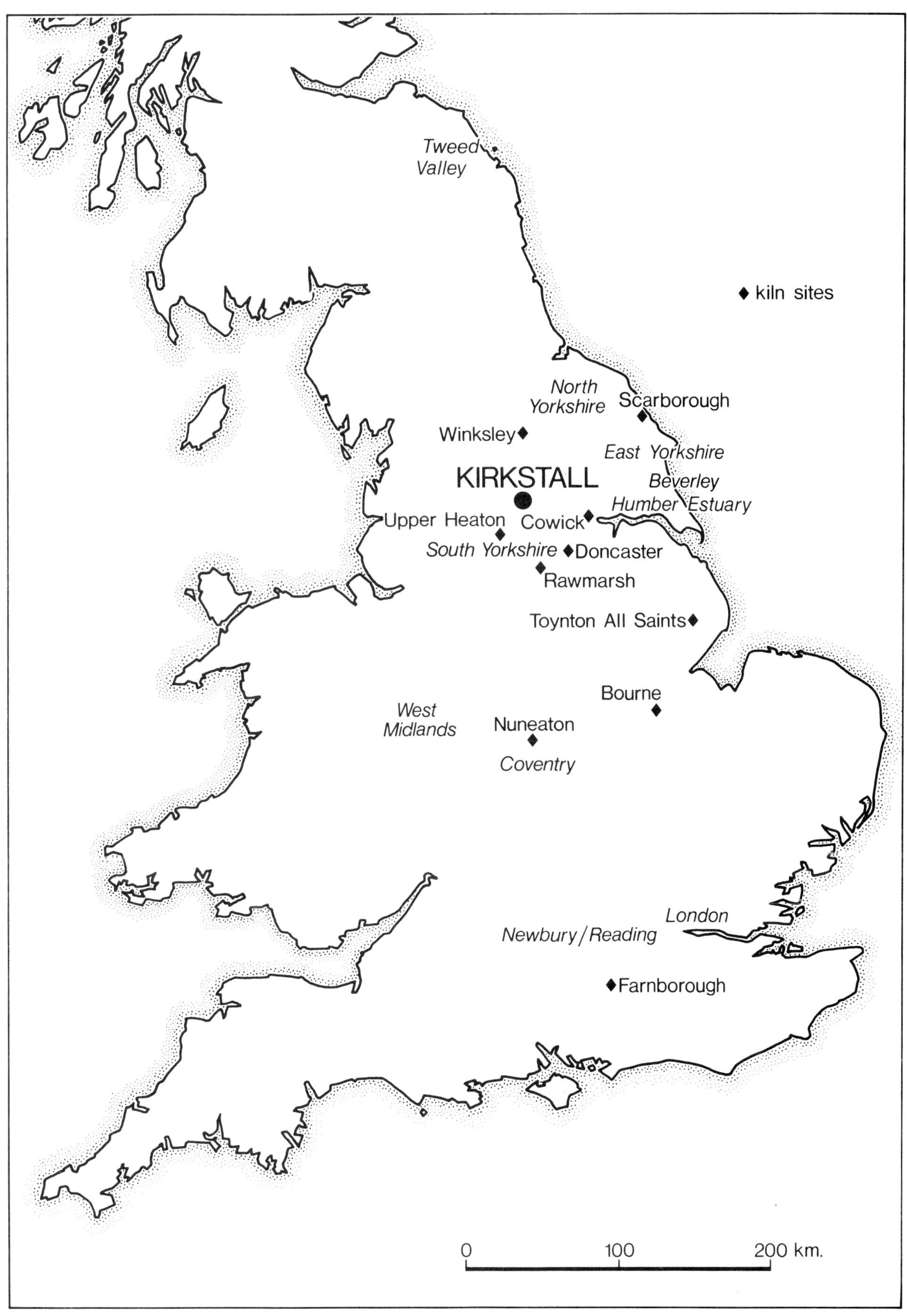

Fig. 64. Sources of the non-local pottery found during excavations at Kirkstall Abbey, 1950-1985. Other non-local types have been found, but their sources are as yet uncertain.

Dating of the pottery groups

The six groups have been selected for publication for a number of reasons: their contents have not been published previously as a group; they constitute all the stratified material from the excavations that can be confirmed from the surviving records; and the groups can be independently dated, either by non-ceramic contents or by their archaeological association. As such they are of considerable importance in understanding the development of medieval pottery in this part of the Aire valley. A summary discussion of some of the pottery types in the published material is found below. The significance of the pottery collection from the Kirkstall Abbey excavations is to form part of a discussion of the development of medieval pottery within West Yorkshire, to be published elsewhere (see p. 61).

Cloister cistern sequence (Table 3; Figs 39-41, nos 1-46)
The archaeological evidence for this sequence suggests that the Cloister cistern belongs to the primary twelfth-century construction work (pp. 9-11). The construction of the cistern cut through a metal-working site. As this is unlikely to have been in operation in the Cloister garth once the buildings had been erected, then it should belong either to the Abbey construction period or to pre-Abbey occupation. The Abbey was founded in1152, but construction work continued into the late twelfth century; Abbot Alexander, who died in 1182, is accredited with most of the building work. It seems likely, therefore, that the material associated with the metal-working (Fig. 39, nos 1-6) dates to no later than the late twelfth century, but could belong to earlier in the century. The levelling layer (2A) which post-dates the construction of the cistern could have been deposited at any time after the mid-twelfth century; but it seems, from its ceramic contents (Fig. 39, nos 7-14) to belong to the later Middle Ages. The cistern is likely to have remained in use throughout the life of the Abbey, and to have gone out of use at the Dissolution. The latest material in its fill (Fig. 40, nos 15-38) is consistent with a mid-sixteenth century date.

Refectory (Table 4; Figs 42-45, nos 47-110)
The earliest group of pottery from this area is associated with the construction of the primary, east-west Refectory (Table 4; Fig. 42, no. 47). This must belong to a period after the foundation of the site and before the construction of the second, north-south Refectory, which occurred during the early thirteenth century (pp. 20-21). The group dates therefore to the second half of the twelfth century, with an emphasis on the third quarter. The associated material (Table 4; Fig. 42, nos 48-53) to the south of the first Refectory could have been deposited at any time during the use of this building; but it was sealed by the construction of the second Refectory. The date range is thus from 1152 to the early thirteenth century, when the latter building was erected.

The majority of the stratified pottery came from the construction and levelling deposits associated with the building of the north-south Refectory (Table 4; Figs 43-44, nos 54-87). The make-up levels contained two coins of about 1220, and the pottery group is in keeping with an early thirteenth century date. A small group of pottery (Table 4; Fig. 45, nos 88-89) was associated with a small group of set stones which, archaeologically, could only be assigned generally to Phase 2 or 3 (p. 21). The four vessels present are typologically early and, if they are not residual, suggest that the stone setting is contemporary with the construction of the second Refectory. The unstratified pottery (Table 4; Fig. 45, nos 90-110) contains a mixture of twelfth through to sixteenth century material. It is probably derived from the use of the second Refectory up to the Dissolution.

Infirmary (Table 5; Figs 46-48, nos 111-70)
A reassessment of the archaeological evidence had suggested the existence of two superimposed structures: the first, of timber, was probably the original Infirmary (Layer 2); and the second, the surviving structure of stone (Layer 1), was the Infirmary in use until the sixteenth century (pp. 55-56). Each phase had a large quantity of pottery associated with it.

The dating of the first group (Table 5; Figs 46-47, nos 111-38) is determined by the date when the stone Infirmary was constructed. It seems likely that this took place no earlier than late thirteenth century (see below). If the timber structure is the primary Infirmary, then it is interesting to note that the material associated with it contains none of the white Pimply wares (Table 5). Generally in the region these are superseded about 1200 by the Gritty wares, which remain in use until they are in turn superseded by the late medieval wares in the fifteenth century. The white Pimply wares are associated with all authenticated primary-phase deposits across the site. In the current excavations of the Guest House they are restricted to the pre-Guest House deposits: the Guest House complex was erected during the early thirteenth century. Their absence from a large group associated with the timber building beneath the existing Infirmary may, therefore, be significant. The general outline dates for the deposit are 1152 to the thirteenth century. However, if the absence of Pimply wares is genuine and reflects the period of use and not an accident of deposition, then this timber Infirmary hall may not have been built until the early thirteenth century. An even earlier Infirmary building may lie elsewhere.

The distribution of these sherds from this group gives it an added importance. Plotting their distribution (Fig. 59, Phase 1) shows that most of the pottery is concentrated to the east of the building and not within it, suggesting that the floor area was covered while in use. It also suggests that the pottery was deposited while the building was in use and not during its construction. Thirdly, and perhaps more significantly, it has been argued that the layer into which the foundations for the timber structure were dug was the pre-Abbey soil horizon (p. 56). The pottery from the use of the building was found within the soil and not lying upon it. As the contemporary external area to the east of the early timber building was not cobbled or otherwise surfaced, and the surviving records describe humic soil conditions, it seems that it may have been used for gardens. The heavier concentration of pottery against the building might suggest a loose accumulation of sherds beneath the eaves, along which the rain water could run.

The pottery from Layer 1 associated with the stone Infirmary spans the Middle Ages. There was at least one major alteration to the stone building, the walling-in between the aisle posts to form separate cubicles. The archaeological evidence for this is not clear in the surviving records. The presence of sherds from typologically early vessels, the remainder of which were found in Layer 1 (p. 106; Fig. 60) shows that the construction of the stone building and its subsequent modification disturbed earlier material. As these alterations cannot now be distinguished archaeologically, the extreme dates for the group are late thirteenth century to the Dissolution.

Warming House (Table 6; Figs 49-50, nos 171-87)
The material from the Warming House provides a stratified sequence from the earliest phases of the Abbey buildings to the Dissolution. The archaeological sequence is illustrated in Fig. 11, S 6 and described on pp. 14-17. The earliest material, from layer 8, comes from beneath the Warming House, probably from the old ground surface. The absence of Pimply wares, present in other early groups, suggests that material was not being deposited in the area until later in the twelfth century. However, as the Warming House forms part of the original stone complex built during the second half of the twelfth century, the absence of even residual Pimply ware is surprising. Apart from a coin from the third phase of the Warming House (see below), the only dating evidence for the sequence is by the association of features found inside the building with features of adjoining structures. Thus, only a general dating for the various phases can be given. Layer 7 relates to the first or early second phase flooring. The second phase flooring (layer 5), dating generally to the thirteenth century, lies over the make-up layer 6. The third phase make-up levels (layers 2, 4) lying beneath the stone-flagged floor contained a coin of about 1420 (p. 146). The combined evidence for the rebuilds of phase 3 suggests a fifteenth century date. The dates for the sequence of layers are summarised in Table 2.

Warming House cistern (Table 7; Figs 51-54, nos 188-229)
The Warming House cistern contained a large collection of pottery deposited when the cistern went out of use. The substantial parts surviving from a number of vessels suggest that the group is a contemporary one. The dating of the fill rests on the date of the pottery and on a coin of about 1420 found with the pottery towards the bottom of the cistern. The fill was covered by the floor level of the lean-to pentice against the southern wall of the Warming House. However, this could not be dated independently. The fill of the cistern was excavated on more than one occasion (p. 14). Assuming that the coin was undisturbed in the fill, and not redeposited in the soil after the first attempt at excavation, then the group must date to after about 1420.

This group provides an important link in the development of late medieval pottery in the region. Gritty wares were introduced about 1200 and appear to have continued into the later Middle Ages. Until now, this hypothesis has lacked supporting evidence: it has been based upon an absence of other common local types between the Pimply wares of the twelfth century and the late medieval types introduced sometime during the fifteenth century. The cistern group, however, demonstrates clearly that the Gritty wares continued well into the fifteenth century. The presence of the two stoneware vessels from Siegburg (Fig. 55, no. 227) and Langerwehe (Fig. 55, no. 228) is in keeping with deposition around the middle of the fifteenth century.

Made ground south of the Meat Kitchen
(Table 7; Fig. 56, nos 230-47)
Excavations south of the Meat Kitchen revealed a series of large vertical stakes running in line east-west, with a deep silty deposit to the south. This was originally interpreted as a jetty, but it is equally likely to have been the northern revetment to one of the fishponds known to lie south of the main complex (pp. 33-36). The material published here (Fig. 56, nos 230-47) comes from the make-up deposit to the south of the stakes.

Most of the material from the fill comprises single sherds from vessels (Table 7), and is likely all to be residual. The date of deposition should be after the date of the latest pottery present, which appears to be fifteenth century (Table 7, Type 30). This, however, creates some problems for dating the buildings which seal the deposit. It is probable that the area was reclaimed in order to expand the conventual buildings southwards. The development of these structures and enclosures has been discussed elsewhere (pp. 47-48). Although there is no specific evidence for their date of erection, a thirteenth rather than fourteenth century date is the more likely, since in the following century the development of monastic houses in general was either static or in decline. Although there is no evidence in the site records, it is possible that more than one deposit was encountered during excavation. Alternatively later intrusive material may have become mixed through the voids left by the rotting timbers of the revetment.

Concordance of published material 1950-64 and 1986 (Table 20)

Table 20 gives a concordance between the pottery illustrated in the original annual reports and the current publication of the material. The material is listed by the year, the figure and the illustration number of the original report (column 1). The context given in column 2 is that used in this report, and not the description given in the original report. Where illustrated here, the new number shown on Figs 39-56 is given (column 3). The original and re-defined common names are given in column 4 and the form in column 5. In the previous reports some vessels were published from other sites for comparative purposes (as in 1951), while in a few instances parts of the same vessel were published on more than one occasion (e.g. Table 8, no. 196.)

Table 20. Concordance of pottery published in the annual reports between 1950 and 1964 and that published in the present volume.

1			2	3	4		5
Interim Report			Context	New illust. no.	Type		Form
Year	Fig.	Illust.			Original	Re-defined	
1950	4	1	Kitchen Yard		Hard, even grey ware fifteenth century	Late Medieval Smooth	Cistern
1950	4	2 }	" "		"	"	Cistern
1950	4	3 }					
1950	4	4	" "		"	"	Jug
1950	4	5	Kitchen Yard, Cloister and Warming House	42	Early fourteenth-century imported French ware	Rouen	Jug
1950	4	6	Kitchen Yard		Smooth even red ware sixteenth century	missing	
1950	4	7	Kitchen Yard		"	missing	
1951	6	1	Foundation trench of east wall of Refectory	54	Hard, gritty late twelfth century	Pimply	Jar
1951	6	2	Almondbury		Hard, gritty late twelfth century	Pimply	Jar
1951	6	3	Ilkley		Hard, gritty late twelfth century	Pimply	Jar
1951	6	4	Warming House cistern fill	203	Hard, gritty late twelfth century	Pimply	Jar
1951	6	5	Ilkley		"	"	Jar
1951	6	6	Almondbury		"	"	Jar
1951	6	7	Almondbury		"	"	Jar
1951	6	8	Almondbury		"	"	Jar
1951	7	9	Warming House cistern fill	213	Hard, gritty, grey ware	Northern Gritty	Jug
1951	7	10	"	215	"	"	Jug
1951	8	11	"	196	"	"	Bowl
1951	8	12	"	188	"	"	Jar
1951	8	13	"		"	"	Jar
1951	8	14	"	202	Smoother, red ware with little grit	"	Bowl
1951	8	15	"	218	Coarse grey ware	"	Pipkin
1951	8	16	"		Red gritty ware	"	Bowl
1951	8	17	"		"	"	Bowl
1951	8	18	"		Hard, coarse grey ware	"	Jar
1951	8	19	"	190	'Usual gritty ware'	"	Jar
1951	8	20	"		Hard, light grey ware similar to twelfth-century cooking pots	Pimply	Jar
1951	9	21	"	206	Gritty, grey ware	Northern Gritty	Jug
1951	9	22	"	205	Gritty, grey ware	"	Jug
1951	9	23	Warming House cistern fill	214	Gritty, grey ware	"	Jug
1951	9	24	Courtyard — u/s		Smooth, purple grey ware	missing	Jug
1951	9	25	Warming House cistern fill	219	"	Fine Sandy	Jug
1952	12	1	Warming House	177	Hard, gritty base	Northern Gritty	Curfew
1952	12	2	Warming House Courtyard		Twelfth-century Gritty	Pimply	Jar
1952	12	3	Warming House Courtyard		Twelfth-century Gritty	missing	Jar
1952	12	4	Warming House Courtyard		Twelfth-century Gritty	Pimply	Jar
1952	12	5	Warming House Courtyard		Transition from twelfth century to Gritty ware	Northern Gritty	Jar
1952	13	6	Warming House — below mortar floor		Hard, gritty ware	Northern Gritty	Bowl
1952	13	7	Warming House — below mortar floor	174	Coarse grey ware	Northern Gritty	Bowl

Table 20. Concordance of pottery published in the annual reports between 1950 and 1964 and that published in the present volume. Continued

1			2	3	4		5
Interim Report			Context	New illust. no.	Type		Form
Year	Fig.	Illust.			Original	Re-defined	
1956	13	5	SW of Meat Kitchen		Smooth, buff York type	York White	Jug
1956	13	6	Abbot's Lodgings		Grey, gritty ware	Northern Gritty	Jug
1956	13	7	Warming House cistern, Meat Kitchen and Meat Kitchen Annexe	195	Grey, gritty ware	Northern Gritty	Bowl
1956	13	8	Meat Kitchen		Grey, gritty ware	Northern Gritty	Bowl
1956	13	9	SW of Meat Kitchen		Pinkish, gritty ware	Northern Gritty	Condiment
1957	17	1	West of circular building		Hard, gritty ware	Northern Gritty	Bowl
1957	17	2	Warming House cistern, Meat Kitchen and Meat Kitchen Annexe	195	Gritty ware	Northern Gritty	Bowl
1957	17	3	West of circular building		Very hard, gritty ware	missing	Jar
1957	17	4	Bone layer above timber revetment		Reversed Cistercian	Reversed Cistercian	Cup
1957	17	5	Bone layer above timber revetment	237	Pink, gritty fabric	Northern Gritty	Urinal
1958	25	1	Structures south of Meat Kitchen		Kirkstall B	Skipton on Swale	Jug
1958	25	2	Structures south of Meat Kitchen		Kirkstall B	missing	Jug
1958	25	3	Structures south of Meat Kitchen		French Polychrome	South-western French Polychrome	Jug
1958	25	4	Structures south of Meat Kitchen		Kirkstall B	missing	Jug
1959	31	1	'Other parts of the Abbey'		Gritty ware	Northern Gritty	Base
1959	31	2	'Other parts of the Abbey'		Gritty ware	Northern Gritty	Base
1959	31	3	Infirmary Layer 2		Soft, pink, gritty ware	Orange Gritty	Jug
1959	31	4	Infirmary Layer 2		Very hard, gritty ware	Northern Gritty	Jug
1959	31	5	Infirmary		Hard, gritty ware	missing	Jug
1959	31	6	Omitted in pottery descriptions				Jar
1959	31	7	—	—	—	—	Tile
1959	31	8	Infirmary Layer 2		Fine, slightly sandy, buff work	missing	Jug
1959	31	9	Infirmary Layer 2		Slightly gritty, pink ware	Northern Gritty	Jug
1959	31	9a	"		"	"	Jug
1959	31	9b	"		"	"	Jug
1959	31	10	Infirmary	132	"	"	Jug
1959	31	10a	Infirmary	132	"	"	Jug
1959	31	11	Infirmary Layer 1	148	Polychrome	South-western French Polychrome	Jug
1959	31	12	Range south of Kitchen Yard and Infirmary Layer 2	134	Sandy northern type	Fine Sandy	Jug
1959	31	13	South of Refectory and Meat Kitchen		Twelfth-century Gritty	missing	
1959	31	14	South of Refectory and Meat Kitchen		Gritty ware	Northern Gritty	Bowl
1959	31	15	Infirmary Layer 1		Hard, gritty ware	Northern Gritty	Dripping pan
1959	31	16	Infirmary Layer 2	134	Sandy, northern type	Fine Sandy	Jug
1959	31	17	South of Refectory and Meat Kitchen		Gritty, grey ware	Northern Gritty	
1959	31	18	Not noted		Hard, gritty ware	missing	
1959	31	19	South of Refectory and Meat Kitchen		Hard, smooth, grey ware	Late Medieval Smooth	Jug

Table 20. Concordance of pottery published in the annual reports between 1950 and 1964 and that published in the present volume. Continued

Interim Report (1)			Context (2)	New illust. no. (3)	Type (4)		Form (5)
Year	Fig.	Illust.			Original	Re-defined	
1960-4	16	1	Refectory	73	Stamford	Developed Stamford	Jug
1960-4	16	2			Scarborough		Jug
1960-4	16	3	Kitchen Yard		South Yorkshire Lightly Gritted ware	South Yorkshire Lightly Gritted ware	Jug
1960-4	16	4	Kitchen Yard		Similar to South Yorkshire Lightly Gritted ware	Northern Gritty	Jug
1960-4	16	5	Meat Kitchen		Reduced Humber	Smooth Humber	Jug
1960-4	16	6	Bath Drain		East Pennine Gritty	Northern Gritty	Jug
1960-4	16	7	Warming House cistern and Bath Drain	215	East Pennine Gritty	Northern Gritty	Jug
1960-4	16	8	South of Lay Brothers' Reredorter		East Pennine Gritty	Northern Gritty	Jug
1960-4	16	9	"		"	"	Jug
1960-4	16	10	Kitchen Yard		York area	York White	Jug
1960-4	16	11	Kitchen Yard		South Yorkshire Gritty	South Yorkshire Lightly Gritted	Jug
1960-4	16	12	Refectory	95	East Pennine Gritty ware	Northern Gritty	Lid
1960-4	16	13	Kitchen		Probably sixteenth century	Northern Gritty	Lid
1960-4	16	14	Infirmary Layer 2	122	East Pennine Gritty ware	Northern Gritty	Lid
1960-4	16	15a	Kitchen Yard		Not described	Northern Gritty	Dripping pan
1960-4	16	15b	"		"	"	Dripping pan
1960-4	16	15c	"		"	"	Dripping pan
1960-4	17	16	Meat Kitchen		Soft fabric. Import	missing	Jug
1960-4	17	17	—	—	—	—	Tile
1960-4	17	18	South of Lay Brothers' Reredorter		Late Humber ware	Late Medieval Smooth	Jug
1960-4	17	19	Cloister	23	Early sixteenth century Baildon Kiln 2	Baildon	Jug
1960-4	17	20	Infirmary	142	Late East Pennine Gritty ware	Northern Gritty	Jug
1960-4	17	21	Kitchen Yard		Late East Pennine Gritty ware	Late Medieval Gritty	Jug
1960-4	17	22	Drain in range south of Kitchen Yard		Fifteenth-century very hard-fired work	Vitrified Earthenware	Cistern
1960-4	17	23	Kitchen Yard		Hard ware with purplish fracture	Midland Purple type	Jug
1960-4	17	24	Kitchen Yard		Humber ware	Reduced Humber	Jug
1960-4	17	25	Kitchen Yard		East Pennine Gritty ware	Rawmarsh type	Cistern
1960-4	17	26	Range south of Kitchen Yard		Reduced Humber ware	Reduced Humber ware	Jug
1960-4	17	27	Kitchen Yard		East Pennine Gritty ware	Orange Gritty	Bowl
1960-4	17	28	Range south of Kitchen Yard		East Pennine Gritty ware	Late Medieval Gritty	Jar
1960-4	17	29	Range south of Kitchen Yard		East Pennine Gritty ware	Late Medieval Gritty	Jar
1960-4	17	30	Kitchen Yard		Humber ware	Oxidized Humber ware	Bowl
1960-4	17	31	Range south of Kitchen Yard		Cream ware	Yellow	Chafing dish
1960-4	17	32	Range south of Kitchen Yard		Cistercian	Cistercian	Flask
1960-4	17	33	Refectory		Cistercian	Cistercian	Cup

Table 20. Concordance of pottery published in the annual reports between 1950 and 1964 and that published in the present volume.

1			2	3	4		5
Interim Report			Context	New illust. no.	Type		Form
Year	Fig.	Illust.			Original	Re-defined	
1952	13	8	Warming House — below mortar floor	178	Grey, gritty ware	Northern Gritty	Jug
1952	13	9	Warming House		Grey, gritty ware	missing	Jug
1952	13	10	Warming House		Hard, gritty ware	Northern Gritty	Jug
1952	13	11	Warming House — below mortar floor	172	Coarse, gritty ware	Northern Gritty	Jug
1952	13	12	Warming House		Grey, gritty ware	Northern Gritty	Jug
1952	13	13	Kitchen Yard, Cloister and Warming House	42	Fourteenth-century French	Rouen	Jug
1952	13	14	Warming House	184	Fifteenth-sixteenth century gritty purple-grey	Northern Gritty	Bowl
1952	13	15	Warming House		Fifteenth-sixteenth century gritty purple-grey	Northern Gritty	Bowl
1952	13	16	Under cobbled floor outside Meat Kitchen		Cistercian	Cistercian	Cup
1953	18	1	Pre-Cloister cistern	6	Twelfth-century, pink gritty ware	Pimply	Bowl
1953	18	2	Cloister		Twelfth century	Pimply	Jar
1953	18	3	Sub-Dorter		Not described	Northern Gritty	Bowl
1953	18	4	Cloister cistern topsoil	39	Not described	Pimply	Jug
1953	18	5	Cloister cistern fill		Grey, gritty ware	Late Medieval Smooth	Cistern
1953	18	6	Cloister cistern fill	30	Red, gritty ware	Brick Red Sandy	Cistern
1953	18	7	Refectory	101	Smooth, cream ware paralleled at York	York type	Lobed cup
1953	18	8	Cloister cistern fill		Cistercian	Cistercian	Base
1953	18	9	Cloister cistern fill		Cistercian	Cistercian	Base
1954	24	1	Kitchen — u/s		Twelfth-century Gritty	Pimply	Jar
1954	24	2	Pre-Cloister cistern	1	Twelfth-century Gritty	Hillam type	Jug
1954	24	3	Kitchen — u/s		Twelfth-century Gritty	Pimply	Jar
1954	24	4	Kitchen		Soft gritty	Northern Gritty	Pipkin
1954	24	5	Cloister		Medium hard, grey sandy ware	South-west Midlands	Bowl
1954	24	6	Kitchen		Hard, gritty, grey ware	Late Medieval Smooth	Cistern
1954	24	7	Kitchen		Resembling modern 'flower pot'	Skipton on Swale	Jug
1955	10	1	Bath Drain		Twelfth-century Gritty	Pimply	Jar
1955	10	2	Not described		Twelfth-century Gritty	Pimply	Jar
1955	10	3	Refectory	72	Twelfth-century Gritty	Early York type	Jar
1955	10	4	Refectory	91	Twelfth-century Gritty	Pimply	Jar
1955	10	5	Refectory	56	Twelfth-century Gritty	Pimply	Jar
1955	10	6	Refectory	50	Twelfth-century Gritty	Pimply	Jar
1955	10	7	Refectory	49	Twelfth-century Gritty	Pimply	Jar
1955	10	8	Refectory		Twelfth-century Gritty	Pimply	Jar
1955	10	9	Refectory		Twelfth-century Gritty	Pimply	Jar
1955	10	10	Refectory	75	Resembling twelfth-century Gritty	Northern Gritty	Jar
1955	10	11	Refectory	52	Bowl with elaborate rim treatment	Tripod Pitcher	Pitcher
1955	10	12	Construction trench of Bath Drain		Gritty ware	Northern Gritty	Jar
1956	13	1	SW of Meat Kitchen		Gritty, grey ware	Late Medieval Smooth	Jug
1956	13	2	SW of Meat Kitchen		Gritty, grey ware	Late Medieval Smooth	Jug
1956	13	3	SW of Meat Kitchen		Smooth, buff York type	York White	Jug
1956	13	4	Below floor in Meat Kitchen		Smooth, buff York type	York White	Jug

Table 20. Concordance of pottery published in the annual reports between 1950 and 1964 and that published in the present volume. Continued

1			2	3	4		5
Interim Report			Context	New illust. no.	Type		Form
Year	Fig.	Illust.			Original	Re-defined	
1960-4	17	34	Kitchen Yard		Cistercian	Cistercian	Lid
1960-4	17	35	Kitchen Yard		Cistercian	Cistercian	Cup
1960-4	17	36	Range south of Kitchen Yard		Cream ware	Yellow ware	Chafing dish
1960-4	18	1	Kitchen Yard		Italian maiolica	Italian maiolica	Jug
1960-4	18	2			French maiolica	French maiolica	
1960-4	18	3a	Cloister		Type I imported flask	Martincamp	Flask
1960-4	18	3b	Bath Drain		Type I imported flask	Martincamp	Flask
1960-4	18	3c	Bath Drain		Type I imported flask	Martincamp	Flask
1960-4	18	3d	Unstrat.		Type I imported flask	Martincamp	Flask
1960-4	18	4e	Bath Drain		Type II stoneware	Martincamp	Flask
1960-4	18	4f	Unstrat.		Type II stoneware	Martincamp	Flask
1960-4	18	3g	Bath Drain		Type II stoneware	Martincamp	Flask

Chapter 15
The Ceramic Roof Fittings

by Stephen Moorhouse

There is little roofing material amongst the surviving pottery. This is in contrast to the amount which can usually be expected from a monastic site; and, indeed, it conflicts with statements made in a number of the original published reports as to the quantities found in some areas.[166] Most of the flat roofing tiles have probably been lost since excavation; and it is likely that the finials and ventilator hood have survived because they were thought to be parts of pottery vessels: they were found in the boxes of pottery. All variations in form and decoration have been illustrated, including all pieces of ornamental roof furniture. Unfortunately, few of the pieces are marked, and of those which can be located, most are from topsoil.

More complete examples of most of the tile types illustrated here are represented among material from the current excavations on the Guest House. The tiles from the Abbey as a whole will be discussed more fully in the Guest House publication.

Flat roof tiles (Fig. 65, nos 1-6)

The few groups of flat roofing tile which have survived come from mainly three areas: the Kitchen Yard; the range south of the Kichen Yard (only WR9), and the Infirmary Layer 2. The surviving pieces appear to be parts of large collections which have not survived; and the only remaining pieces from the Infirmary are small fragments which were extracted from the boxes of pottery. Despite such an unrepresentative collection from the Infirmary, the sample does suggest that the roof of the first phase timber Infirmary hall was covered in pottery tiles.

The fabric of most of the tiles is uniformly a lightly gritted fine sandy fabric, with a texture varying with the degree of firing, and ranging in colour from a light buff to a hard reduced dark grey. The majority of the tiles are smooth textured, low fired with soapy surfaces, and light pink cores with buff surfaces; some have a light grey core. A few are more highly fired and have a harsh texture, with much darker surfaces and core. All pieces are unglazed and, with very little variation, average 15mm. in thickness.

As so little of the tile survives, no statistical work has been attempted. A large quantity of tiles has come from current excavations on the Guest House, where a variety of near complete tiles has been recovered. The types of tiles, their sizes and the positions and type of hanger (nail-hole, nib or a combination of both) will be discussed when that material is published, along with the collection published here. As applied nibs can often be off-centre, no attempt has been made here to reconstruct complete tiles. Most assemblages of medieval ceramic roof tiles produce an animal paw print. Kirkstall is no exception (Fig. 65, no. 6). Unfortunately the impression is too blurred to identify the animal.

Gutter tile (Fig. 65, no. 7)

Gutter tiles are distinguished from plain ridge tiles in that the smooth surface (the open side) is on the concave part of the tile, which, like the Kirkstall tile, is invariably glazed. They were used either along the eaves to collect water draining from the roof, or in the angle where two roof lines met. The fabric of no. 7 is identical to the oxidised ridge tiles, covered with a glossy mottled green glaze on the concave surface.

Ridge tiles (Fig. 65, nos 8-9)

Few pieces of ridge tile are present in the collection. The only two pieces with crests are illustrated (nos 8-9). The fabric is different from that of the flat roof tiles, probably reflecting manufacture by different people: ridge tiles and roof furniture were made by potters, and flat roof tiles made by tilers. The fabric is harsher, containing more sand and irregularly shaped white calcitic pieces of varying size. All pieces are highly fired with dark grey core and margins and dull pink surfaces. The upper surfaces are covered in a dull mottled green decayed glaze. The sides of the tiles average 20mm. in thickness. Both pieces conform to the low-thumbed crest profile typical of applied ridge crests found in Yorkshire.[167] The profile of no. 8 may be much larger, for some ridge tiles from current excavations on the Guest House have projecting semi-circular crests at least 40mm. high.

Hip tile (Fig. 65, no. 10)

Only one hip tile was present in the collection. Insufficient survived to give its length. The fabric is similar to that of the flat roof tiles, fully oxidised with a pink core and darker surfaces. Significantly the tile was found in the area of the circular structure interpreted as a dovecote south of the Meat Kitchen (Figs 22, 27). It seems likely that the tile may have come from the conical roof.

Finials (Fig. 65, nos 11-13)

Fragments of three separate finials have survived, all of which are illustrated:

No. 11. Lower part from a faceted plate finial in a very smooth lightly sanded fabric, reduced to light grey in the upper fracture and brick red in the lower part where it joins the top of the ridge tile. Covered all over in a glossy shiny olive green glaze. The sequence of manufacture appears to have been as follows: a flat slab of clay was applied to the top of the ridge tile; a semi-circular hole of about 11cm. diameter was then cut out; the outer profile was cut into a series of (?) eight facets; the edges were then chamfered with a knife and the two junctions smoothed all round on to the top of the tile. Unmarked.

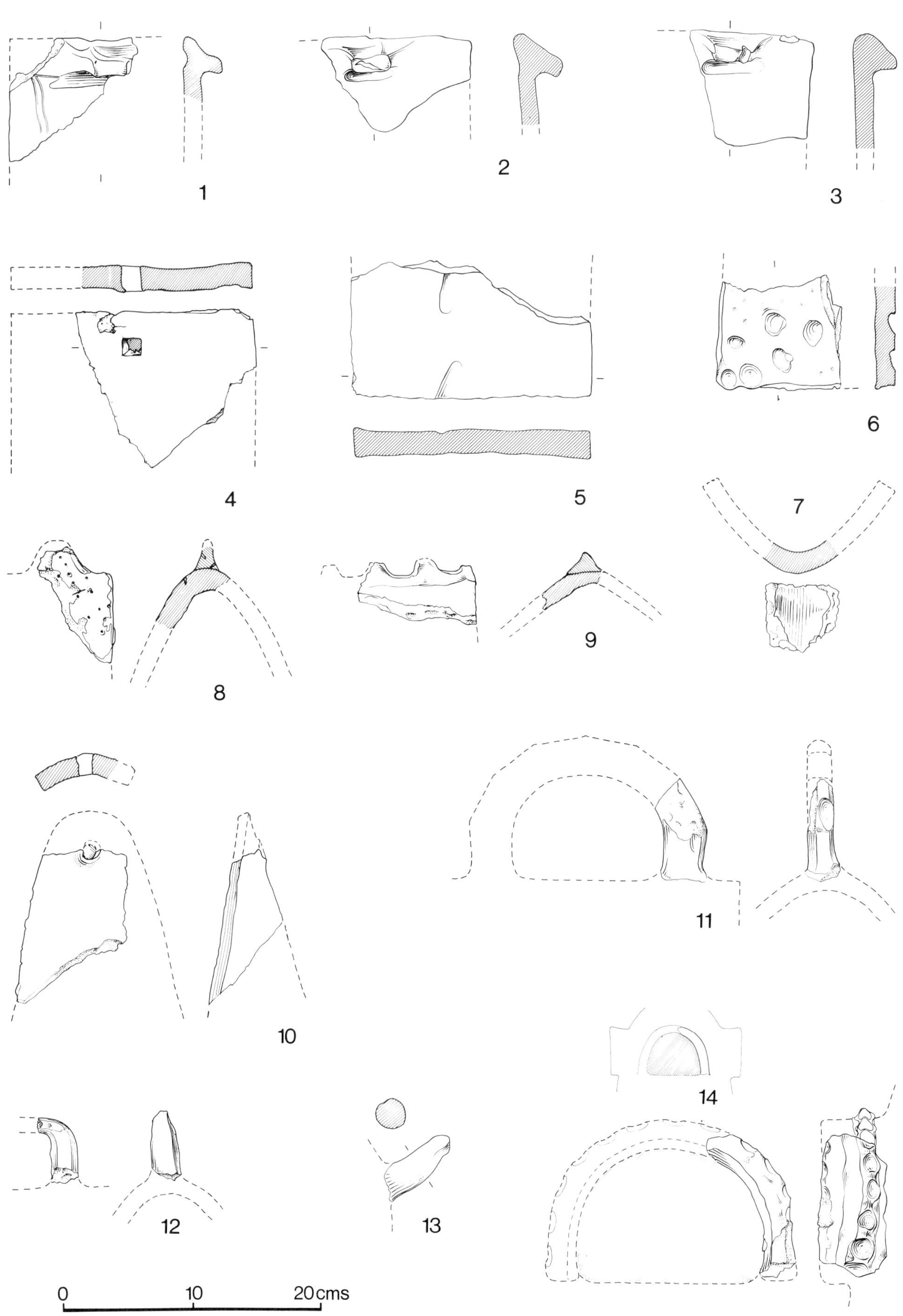

Fig. 65. Ceramic roofing materials.

No. 12. Arm or body from a finial crest in a coarse sandy fabric, the core totally reduced to a dark grey and covered all over in a glossy olive green glaze; the glaze concentration shows that the piece was fired inverted to the position as drawn. Hand moulded, the piece was smoothed on to the body of the ridge tile. The form is uncertain but similar pieces occur on more complete tiles found at Sandal Castle (West Yorkshire), where they appear to form part of a debased animal frieze along the ridge crest.[168] Infirmary I 21, topsoil.

No. 13. Single sherd in the same fabric as the flat roof tiles, with soapy texture, blue grey core with dull pink surfaces and covered in a patchy watery lime green glaze. The coarse nature of the fabric, and the size and crudeness of the piece suggests that it does not come from a pottery vessel. A more likely suggestion is that it forms one of a number of horns projecting from the body of a globular finial. A variety of forms is known from the south of England.[169] Not marked.

Ventilator (Fig. 65, no. 14)

No. 14. Single sherd forming the larger part of a canopy hood surrounding an opening in the side of a ventilator. The fabric is sandy, fully oxidised to a bright brick red and covered externally with a glossy orange coloured glaze with green mottling. Sufficient survives to show the form of the opening and the depth of its surrounding hood, while the small scale reconstruction suggests the form of the complete ventilator. The fabric and glaz indicate that this piece may not be a local product. A number of pottery ventilators are known from the historic county of Yorkshire and the Kirkstall example is a useful addition to these.[170] Not marked.

Chapter 16
The Small Finds

by Holly B. Duncan and Stephen A. Moorhouse
contributions by: Dr L. A. S. Butler, Dr J. Blair,
Dr I. H. and Mrs A. Goodall, Dr J. Henderson, Dr G. F. Hornung

Introduction

The original published reports indicate that a substantial number of finds was recovered. However, only a small percentage now survives. Some of the survivors are either unmarked or from contexts which cannot be confirmed from the surviving site records, and a few have site codes which cannot be identified. Furthermore, several boxes of small finds were stolen from the Archaeology Unit's offices in Leeds, though about half of them were later recovered by the police, and they had all, fortunately, been recorded and drawn previously. In essence, very few of the surviving objects can be confidently assigned to stratified, pre-Dissolution deposits. Nevertheless, some general comments can be made concerning the finds as a whole.

Kirkstall was the centre of a large and prosperous agricultural estate. Its tenants and residents, monks as well as lay brothers, formed a community which to a certain extent was self-sufficient. A range of activities was carried out by the inhabitants of the Abbey, as is evidenced by the variety of tools recovered. For certain purposes, however, craftsmen were employed on a short-term basis to practise their specialised skills. An example of this is illustrated by the remains of bell casting (p. 150). The surviving finds from the 1950-1964 excavations can be roughly grouped into five categories — craft equipment, domestic utensils, building fittings, personal accoutrements and coinage.

Craft equipment

The craft equipment is represented by various tools. While these serve to indicate the types of activities being carried out at the Abbey, they offer little in the way of dating evidence. In fact many of these implements have altered little in form from Roman times to the present.

Woodworking is represented by an axe (SF 24) and a carpenter's bit (SF 28). The form of the axe is derived from a well known Viking type, the 'bearded axe' and can be paralleled on the Bayeux Tapestry and at Deganwy Castle.[171] It was most likely used for lopping and felling trees. Throughout the medieval period iron was a valuable material and steel was even more highly prized.[172] The axe from Kirkstall, like many of the cutting tools of this period, had a piece of steel 'shut' or welded onto its edge. Normally, the socket on this type of axe was formed by folding the tail of the axe over and welding it against one side to form a loop. A well defined ridge in front of the point of junction served to protect this weak point.[173] The Kirkstall axe, however, was evidently repaired in antiquity and the point of junction occurs on one side of the socket. A third implement, a file (SF 23) may also be associated with woodworking as it was commonly used for sharpening saws.[174]

The broad bladed chisel or drove (SF 25) was used by masons to smooth-dress plane surfaces. The use of chisels not only for carving but also for dressing stone was apparently introduced in the later twelfth century.[175] Both the chisel and the lead plumb bob (SF 231) indicate building activity at the Abbey. The presence of a shears' blade (SF 20) and a spindle whorl (SF 409) may indicate the production of textiles, although shears had many other uses, for example the cutting of parchment. Awls, such as SF 21 and SF 22, were used in leather working to pierce holes.[176]

As mentioned previously iron was a valuable and expensive material. For this reason implements such as spades and shovels were made of wood and provided with an iron shoe. Two very fragmentary portions of spade shoes (SFs 29, 30) were recovered from the excavations, suggesting agricultural activity, perhaps in this case in the Abbey garden.

Domestic utensils

Domestic activities, such as the preparation and consumption of food are indicated by bronze vessel fragments (SFs 189-91), sherds of glass bowls and flasks (SFs 377, 383, 387), and the pewter spoon bowl (SF 233). The whittle-tang knife (SF 18) had many domestic uses, one of which may have been as an eating utensil. The small perforated whetstone (SF 411) would have been hung from a man's or woman's girdle and was used to sharpen knife blades.

Building fittings

The third category, building fittings, comprises a range of objects from door furniture, to roofing materials, to water pipes. Five keys were recovered from the excavations, but only three are classifiable. Small find 3 is an uncommon type[177] although it does occur sporadically throughout the medieval period and is therefore not easily dated. Small finds 4 and 5 are both of Type VII B,[178] which was a very common form of key. The shape of the bow is frequently used as a criterion for dating and it appears that SF 5, at least, dates to the fourteenth or fifteenth century.

A considerable amount of iron was used in medieval buildings not only for accessories, for example furniture, but also for constructional purposes.[179] The door furniture recovered from the Abbey included pivots (SF 11-13) strap hinges (SFs 6-10), a portion of a barrel padlock (SF 1) and two door studs (SFs 15, 16).

Nails were used in great quantities in medieval buildings, and the types of nail were known by a variety of names depending upon the purpose for which they were used, their shape and price.[180] Ordinary nails were referred to as plank or board nails, while clout nails, a common type, were used to attach patches of iron and were usually associated with repairing carts or ploughs.[181] Roofing nails, for fastening down lead sheets like those from Kirkstall (see below), were presumably made with broad flat heads. A large number of nails were found during the excavations and, although many survive only as shanks or in a very poor state of preservation, it is evident that the commonest form had a rectangular head and shank. The second commonest form had a flat rounded head and a rectangular shank. These were probably general purpose nails. Many of the complete nails are clenched, and the width of the timber can be determined. Medieval door nails frequently had a decorative coating of tin. The three examples of lead-headed nails from the Abbey (SFs 145, 146, 155) may also have been ornamental in character.

Little can be said of the window glass due to its fragmentary condition and poor state of preservation. From the end of Roman Britain until possibly as late as the 1220s, the production of glass for either vessels or windows was not practised on a commercial basis in Britain.[182] It appears however, that by the end of the twelfth century the glazing of church windows was not uncommon.[183] Indeed much of the growth of the glazing industry of medieval England may have been due to ecclesiastical patronage.

There are four basic categories of window glass from the Abbey: translucent colourless, green, blue and painted glass. In addition numerous fragments were either partially or totally devitrified and few if any comments can be made about them. The majority of the fragments are from potash-based window glass, although three sherds of cobalt blue (SF 350) have a suggested soda-lime-silica composition. No complete quarrels survive nor can the majority of pieces be dated. The three fragments of blue glass mentioned above can be paralleled at York and have a suggested date in the twelfth century. Most of the painted glass appears to have had a translucent colourless ground while the paint is consistently of a reddish brown colour. The majority of the fragments of painted glass date to the fourteenth century. None of these appears to have depicted human figures. It is noteworthy that the statutes of the Cistercian order prohibited the use of pictorial glass in their own churches,[184] a restriction which was relaxed during the thirteenth century.

Several pieces of lead window came (SF 234-45) were recovered from the excavations. Many of these have been flattened or twisted, distorting the original cross section. Most fragments, however, appear to have had H-shaped cross sections. The internal width of the few measurable pieces (13 out of 27) varies from 2.5mm. to 4.2mm., whereas the thickness of the glass sherds varies from 0.9mm. to 5mm., the majority centring around 2.1mm. to 3.8mm.

Numerous pieces of lead come from roof fittings of various types. Most are probably portions of lead guttering, flashings or perforated covers to fall-pipes (Figs 71, 73), and not part of the roof covering itself. Two groups stand out. A number of small rectangular sheets of roughly uniform size, *c.* 100mm.×50mm., have two perforations for nails in one end, while the opposite end is folded over (Fig. 72). Reuse is suggested by some which have three or four nail holes. Impressions around most of the holes suggest that the nails had large square heads up to 30mm. square. A small group of lead-covered iron nails survive (SFs 306, 307.1). A nail has been driven through one end of a strip of lead sheet, and the other end has been bent over the nail head, completely covering it. These were non-corrosive covers to protect the iron nail head, which would quickly rust if left on the roof, exposed to the weather.

Several other fragments of lead sheet and strips were recovered from the excavations: many of them were probably offcuts and scrap destined to be melted down and reused. Lead had many uses during the medieval period ranging from roofing material, window came, piping, gutters, spouts and caulking to pilgrims badges and decorative bosses for windows.

Eight portions of lead pipe, varying between three-quarters of an inch and 2 inches in internal diameter, remain from the excavations. Of these only four lengths can be roughly provenanced: three lengths of 2 inch (50mm.) diameter pipe from the Warming House (SFs 322, 323, 326) and one length of 1 inch (25mm.) diameter pipe from the Kitchen area (SF 320). The plumbing system of Kirkstall Abbey is discussed in detail elsewhere in this report (Chapter 11). In addition to the lead pipe, portions of three bronze tap handles were recovered. Two tap handles were found in the Refectory: one is a complete solid handle with leaf and ball terminal, while the other is the lower portion of a hollow handle (SFs 187.1, 187.2). On solid tap handles the water exited from a hole in the base of the key. Hollow tap handles worked as spouts, the water flowing from the upper end of the handle. A hollow tap handle very similar in form to the Kirkstall example was found at Lewes in Sussex.[185] The third handle, found in the Kitchen Yard, is the upper portion of a solid tap handle (SF 188). This terminates in a zoomorphic head with a ball enclosed in its jaw. A similar zoomorphic terminal was found on a hollow tap from Kilburn Priory and it has a suggested date in the twelfth or thirteenth century.[186] Both the solid tap handles were previously examined by Professor Zarnecki who was of the opinion that they dated to the twelfth century.[187]

Personal accoutrements

The objects which fall into the fourth category, personal accoutrements, include belt and strap fittings, jewellery and toilet implements. The former are fairly common finds on medieval sites. These fittings may have come from men's or women's girdles, shoes or harness fittings.[188] Iron buckles, such as SFs 57-59, are, of necessity, of a more utilitarian design and are virtually undateable. Bronze buckles are most often cast and can vary from simple forms to those elaborately decorated. The one surviving example from the 1963-64 excavations appears to be a portion of a 'spectacle' buckle (SF 172). Somewhat similar buckles of this type have been dated to the fourteenth and fifteenth centuries.[189]

Belts and straps were frequently decorated with small copper alloy mounts in the form of studs, rosettes, or bars.[190] Two examples of the latter type (SF 176) were found in the Meat Kitchen and can be paralleled at York.[191] The decorated bronze stud (SF 179) may also have served as a strap mount. In addition to serving as a decoration, these mounts may also have strengthened the strap.[192]

Three pins were recovered from the excavations (SFs 181-83), only one of which was provenanced. Small find number 182 was made from an oval-sectioned wire which was tightly coiled to form the head. This was the normal type of medieval pin. The second pin, SF 181, has a damaged hexagonal head and is rare and, as yet, undateable. The third pin (SF 183) with a looped-over head, may in fact be from a brooch or a buckle.

Two provenanced implements were found (SFs 184, 185): one from the Infirmary and the second from the buildings south of the Kitchen Yard. These may be ear scoops or unguent spoons. They were sometimes combined with tweezers or manicure sets.[193]

The horseshoe (SF 61) and prick spur (SF 63) illustrate one of the principal methods of transport. Although only a portion of the horseshoe survives, the form of its edge and nail holes suggest a date after the twelfth century. Spurs were introduced into England by the Vikings and, if complete, these can be roughly dated. Unfortunately, the example from the Abbey is poorly preserved and the diagnostic features, the points and the terminal, do not survive.

Coins

Several coins were recovered from the excavations, the identifications of which were initially published in the Thoresby Society *Reports*. Although a number of these coins are presently unaccounted for they have been included here. Six of the eighteen coins date from the late twelfth to mid-thirteenth centuries, while only one dates to the fourteenth century. These coins may have come to the Abbey as revenues from their sizeable holdings of land, from trade of agricultural produce or as donations. The remainder of the coins and jettons date to the fifteenth and sixteenth centuries and over half of these originated on the Continent, either in the Low Countries or in France. Perhaps some of these Continental coins reached the Abbey precinct by way of the adjoining Guest House, whose visitors were often persons of high status and wealth.

Layout of the catalogue

The small finds have been catalogued according to material and within each category the finds are further subdivided by function. As no small finds recording system had been used during the excavations, a separate numbering sequence has been imposed on all the surviving finds. The index below gives the sequence of materials and their inclusive numbers:

Iron objects	1-171
Copper alloy objects	172-228
Lead and lead alloy objects	229-330
Bone objects	331-333
Glass	334-388
Coins	389-407
Stone objects	408-417
Mortar	418
Plaster	419

Illustrated finds are indicated by an asterisk to the left of the catalogue number. In all cases, the original description of finds spot is given. Some of the objects were X-rayed before drawing. The plate and object number follow the description. The plates are housed with the site archive. The location of the site and layer codes can be found on Figs 9 and 37. Finally, the context groupings of the small finds are given in Appendix C.

Iron objects

Lock and door furniture

***1/1958** Possible end plate from a barrel padlock: flat circular disc, diameter 50mm. Structures south of Kitchen Yard, WR 10, topsoil. *Fig.* 66.

2/1958 Key handle (badly damaged) with rectangular sectioned shaft, length 60mm., and a portion of a circular bow. X-ray plate 49, no. 25. Drain D1, MKA 7 6.

3/1956 Possible key handle, with tubular shaft, collar and a lozenge-shaped bow; the bit has broken off; total length 82.2mm. Drain D1, BD VIII, topsoil.

***4/US** Key with symmetrical ward cuts and step, length 130mm. X-ray plate 42, no. 1. No provenance. *Fig.* 66.

5/US Key with oval bow and broken bit, length 155mm. No provenance. No longer extant.

6/1960 Fragment of a possible strap hinge, length 105mm., tapering in width from 30 to 20mm. A circular perforation survives near the wider end. X-ray plate 47, no. 19. Kitchen Yard, KY 23, topsoil.

7/US Pinned strap hinge, length 70mm., (?) post-medieval. Bent at right angles and tapering toward one end where the remains of a perforation survive. X-ray plate 42, no. 3. No provenance.

8/1959 Strap hinge fragment, 20 by 45mm. Infirmary, I 5 2. No longer extant.

***9/US** Fragment of a strap hinge, length 70mm., width tapering from 35 to 22mm., with two perforations near one end. X-ray plate 42, no. 1a. No provenance. *Fig.* 66.

10/1958 Portion of a strap hinge, badly damaged. No original edges survive. Portions of two rectangular perforations (3mm. by 4mm.) occur along one edge. Rectangular in section, sub-rectangular in plan. Length 80.4mm., width 32.7mm. Structures south of the Kitchen Yard, WR 10, topsoil.

***11/US** Hinge pivot, roughly L-shaped with bend in stem. Sub-rectangular in section. Length 56mm., height 24.6mm. No provenance. *Fig.* 66.

***12/US** L-shaped hinge pivot, sub-rectangular in section. Length 71.7mm., height 37.8mm. No provenance. *Fig.* 66.

***13/US** Pivot, probably from a door, roughly L-shaped. One end is encased in lead for insertion into masonry. Length 138mm., height 34.7mm. Kitchen Yard/Structures south of the Kitchen Yard. *Fig.* 66.

14/US Damaged L-shaped hinge pivot of tapering thickness, rectangular in section. Length 90.7mm., height 22.3mm. No provenance.

***15/1962** Complete heavy door stud, corroded beneath head, with irregular shaped head, *c.* 70mm. by 65mm. The head was originally of pyramid form. The clenched end of the shaft suggests that the door was 80mm. in thickness. X-ray plate 46, no. 18. Structures south of the Lay Brothers' Reredorter, LR II 1. *Fig.* 66.

***16/US** Head of a large door stud of rectangular plan, originally the head was a pyramid but is now

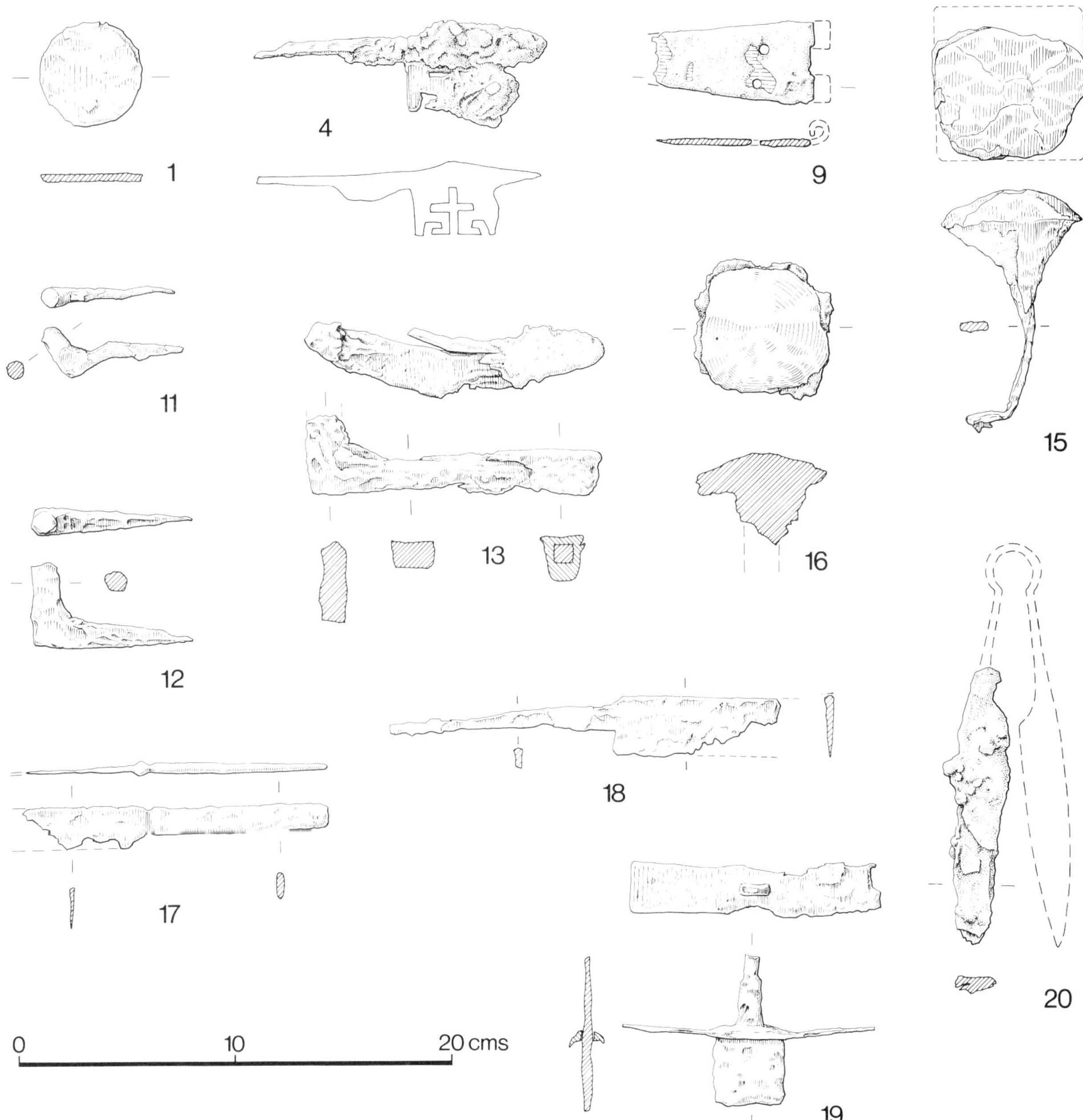

Fig. 66. Ironwork.

domed. A small portion of a rectangular sectioned shank survives. Originally of similar size to no. 15. Present length 41.5mm. No provenance. *Fig*. 66.

Knives, dagger, shears blade

***17/1953** Portion of a knife with a solid rectangular handle. Length 140mm. Post-medieval. Refectory, FRI, topsoil. X-ray plate 42. no. 2. No longer extant. *Fig*. 66.

***18/US** Whittle tang knife with straight backed blade, length 185mm. X-ray plate 42, no. 5. No provenance. *Fig*. 66.

***19/US** Part of a small sword or large dagger, with tang forged in through guard. Height 62mm. No provenance. *Fig*. 66.

***20/1960** Single shears blade, length 130mm. X-ray plate 42, no. 4. Kitchen Yard, KY4 2A. *Fig*. 66.

Tools

***21/1952** Awl, rectangular in section, length 90mm. Warming House, WH 3. *Fig*. 67.

***22/US** Awl, sub-rectangular in section. Length 85mm. No provenance. *Fig*. 67.

***23/1958** File, triangular in section, Length 108mm. Structures south of Kitchen Yard, WR 11, topsoil. *Fig*. 67.

***24/1959** Derivative bearded axehead, with wrap-round haft and steel forged on to edge of blade, repaired in antiquity; length 190mm., width of blade 139mm. Structures south of Kitchen Yard, WR 14. *Fig*. 67.

***25/US** Drove with square-sectioned shaft (*c*. 10.5 by 10.5mm.) and splayed, sub-rectangular blade of triangular section. Length 120mm. No provenance. *Fig*. 67.

26/US Portion of a badly damaged drove/chisel (?), consisting of a rectangular sectioned shaft gradually widening to a blade of rectangular plan and section. Present length 93mm., width of blade 28mm. X-ray plate no. 44, no. 12. No provenance.

***27/1958** Fragment of a small (?) chisel, consisting of a short rectangular shaft and an expanded rectangular head, wedge-shaped in section. Length 33.5mm. Drain Dl, MKA 7 5. *Fig*. 67.

***28/US** Carpenter's bit with triangular point and rounded shaft. Length 90mm. No provenance. *Fig*. 67.

***29/US** Portion of a spade shoe consisting of a rectangular sectioned rod, the upper section of which has been splayed and curved round to form a partial socket, U-shaped in section. The socketed portion of the shoe has a rectangular perforation or nail hole to fix it to the spade blade. Length 108.5mm. No provenance. *Fig*. 67.

30/1962 Portion of a spade shoe (see no. 27). Length 113.8mm. Structures south of Lay Brothers' Reredorter, LR III 2.

Structural objects and miscellaneous fittings

***31/US** Masonry cramp, rectangular in section. Length 110mm. No provenance. *Fig*. 67.

32/US U-shaped staple of rectangular section. Height 53mm. No provenance.

33/1957 Ring/staple, loop diameter 50mm., shaft length 30mm. X-ray plate 43, no. 8. Meat Kitchen: rooms at south end, MKA.

34/1960 Three hooks, lengths 40mm., 50mm., 60mm. Kitchen Yard, KY 8 2. No longer extant.

35/1963-64 Rod of circular section, one end bent into hook. Opposite end missing. Latch lifter (?), length 160mm., diameter c. 8mm. Structures south of Kitchen Yard, WRB 3.

36/1960 Portion of an oval link, 33 by 56mm. of rectangular cross-section. Kitchen Yard, KY 8 1.

***37/1958** Annular washer, external diameter 52mm., internal diameter 25mm. Structures south of Kitchen Yard, WR 13, topsoil. *Fig*. 67.

38/US Annular washer, external diameter 50mm., with irregular off-centred hole, 12 by 15mm. No provenance.

39/1959 Collar, diameter 45mm. Infirmary, I 16 1. No longer extant.

***40/US** Rectangular collar, width 45mm. No provenance. *Fig*. 67.

***41/1959** Sub-rectangular collar, with tapering ends. Rectangular in section, 40 by 50mm. Infirmary, I 14 1A. *Fig*. 67.

***42/US** Incomplete collar, rectangular in plan and section. The centre of the front face widens abruptly and contains the remains of a circular perforation. External dimensions 40.7mm by 39.9mm. No provenance. *Fig*. 67.

***43/1954** Wedge of tapering thickness, 30 by 53mm. Kitchen, topsoil. *Fig*. 67

***44/1958** Wedge of tapering thickness, 29 by 58mm. Structures south of Kitchen Yard, WR 10, topsoil. *Fig*. 67.

***45/US** Clench bolt, length 55mm. No provenance. *Fig*. 67.

46/1958 Possible clench bolt, in poor condition, rectangular head and rectangular sectioned shank. Length 58.6mm. Structures south of Kitchen Yard, WR 11/12 baulk, topsoil.

47/1958 Strip, width 10mm., length 135mm. Structures south of Kitchen Yard, WR 9, topsoil.

48/1959 Flat strip, tapering toward one end. Rectangular section. Length 76mm. Structures south of Kitchen Yard, WR 14, topsoil.

49/1957 Badly corroded rectangular sectioned strip, bent. Width 29.4mm., length 69mm. Badly damaged strip of rectangular section. Length 54.7mm., width 22mm. Drain Dl, MKA 7 6.

50/1958 Portion of a strip of rectangular plan and section. One end is slightly slanted, the opposite end is broken. Width 9mm., length

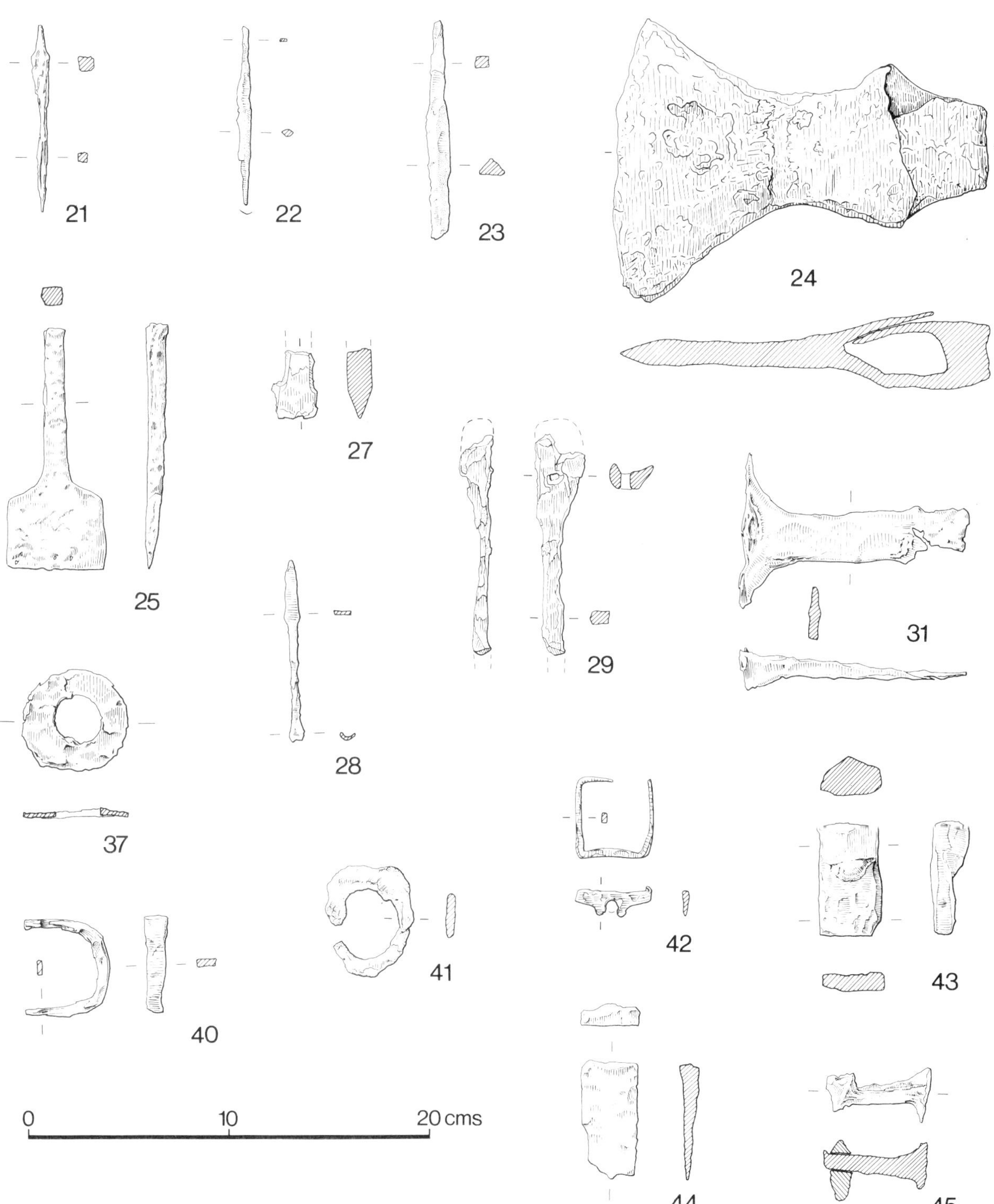

Fig. 67. Ironwork.

49mm. Structures south of Kitchen Yard, WR 10/11 1.

51/1954 Rod of circular section, diameter 12mm., length 51.3mm. Kitchen, topsoil.

52/1962 Rod of rounded square section, diameter 12.5mm., length 189mm. Structures south of Lay Brothers' Reredorter, LR II 1.

53/1963-64 Curved rod of circular section, diameter 5mm., length 240mm., possibly a bucket handle. X-ray plate 48, no. 21. Structures south of the Kitchen Yard, WRB 3.

54/US Rod of rounded section (13.6 by 12.8mm.), tapering to a flat, rectangular sectioned head. The opposite end is broken off. Length 137.5mm. X-ray plate 48, no. 23. No provenance.

55/1958 Tapering rod of rectangular section. The rod tapers to a damaged point at one end. The opposite end is sharply tapered, forming a short stretch of a rectangular sectioned shaft before the break. Length 88.3mm. X-ray plate 49, no. 24. Structures south of Kitchen Yard, WR 10/11 1.

56/1959 Portion of a sheet of iron, curved and badly damaged. Rectangular in section. No original edges survive. Thickness 3.3mm. Length c. 78mm. Structures south of Kitchen Yard, WR 14, topsoil.

Buckles

***57/1958** Fragment of a rectangular buckle frame of rectangular cross section. Length 60mm. Structures south of Kitchen Yard, WR 9, topsoil. *Fig*. 68.

***58/1964** Two joining fragments of a circular buckle with a cross bar, diameter 45mm. Post-medieval. Infirmary, I 16 1. *Fig*. 68.

***59/1958** Possible corner fragment of a rectangular buckle frame of rectangular cross-section. Structures south of the Kitchen Yard, WR 9 3. *Fig*. 68.

Horseshoes and spur

60/1958 Portion of a horseshoe with plain edge, width 20mm., and four rectangular nail holes surviving; post-medieval. X-ray plate 45, no. 14. Drain Dl, MKA 7 2.

***61/US** Portion of a horseshoe with plain edge, width 35mm., and three rectangular nail holes surviving. X-ray plate 48, no. 22. No provenance. *Fig. 68.*

62/1960-63 Portion of a modern horseshoe, recangular in section and varying in width and thickness. Two rectangular nail holes, *c*. 6mm. by 2.5mm., survive near the broken end. Length 96.5mm. X-ray plate 43, no. 7. Kitchen Yard, KY 4-8 baulk 1 A.

***63/US** Damaged and incomplete prick-spur retaining a small portion of the point (form unidentifiable) and part of one arm. The terminals do not survive. No provenance. *Fig*. 68.

Nails

***64/1954** *1 Nail, head incomplete, square sectioned shank, length 73mm. *Fig*. 68.

*2 Nail, square slightly domed head, rectangular sectioned shank, length 60mm. *Fig*. 68.

Nail head incomplete, rectangular sectioned shank, length 56mm.

Nail, rectangular head and shank. Length 55mm.

*3 Nail, square head and rectangular sectioned shank, length 50mm. *Fig*. 68.

*4 Nail, (offset) head, bent rectangular sectioned shank, length 42mm. *Fig*. 68.

*5 Nail, rectangular head and shank, length 35mm. *Fig*. 68.

*6 Nail, incomplete head, damaged rectangular sectioned shank, length 40mm. *Fig*. 68.

7 Nail shank, rectangular section, length 48mm.

All Kitchen, topsoil.

65/1963 Nail shank, rectangular section, length 75mm. Nail shank, rectangular section, length 32mm. Both Malt House, K 1B, topsoil.

66/1963 Nail shank heavily corroded and bent at right angles, rectangular section. Length *c*. 65mm. Malt House K 1 Bl.

67/1963 Nail, head incomplete, rectangular sectioned shank, length 46.5mm. Kitchen, K 2 1.

68/1960-63 Two badly corroded nails, lengths 40mm., 45mm. Kitchen Yard. No longer extant.

69/1960-63 Nail, slightly domed rectangular head, rectangular sectioned shank. Length 65mm. Nail, head incomplete, rectangular sectioned shank, length 85mm.

Both Kitchen Yard, KY 4 2.

70/1960-63 Two nail shanks very corroded, rectangular section, lengths 32.3mm., 57mm. Both Kitchen Yard, KY 4 2A.

71/1960-63 Nail, incomplete head, rectangular sectioned shank, length 53mm.

Nail, rectangular head, rectangular sectioned, length 56mm.

Two nail shanks, rectangular sectioned, lengths 43.7mm., 24.5mm

All Kitchen Yard, KY 4-8 baulk 1A.

72/1960-63 Two nails, badly damaged heads (incomplete), shanks rectangular sectioned. Both Kitchen Yard, KY 8.

73/1960-63 Three nails, heads damaged, rectangular sectioned shaft, length 46mm., 50mm., 44mm.

Two nail shanks, rectangular sectioned, lengths 39mm., 64mm.

All Kitchen Yard, KY 8, topsoil.

***74/1960-63** *1 Nail, square head, rectangular shank, length 67mm. *Fig*. 68.

*2 Nail, large flat rounded head, rectangular shank, length 27mm. *Fig*. 68.

3 Nail, incomplete oval head and

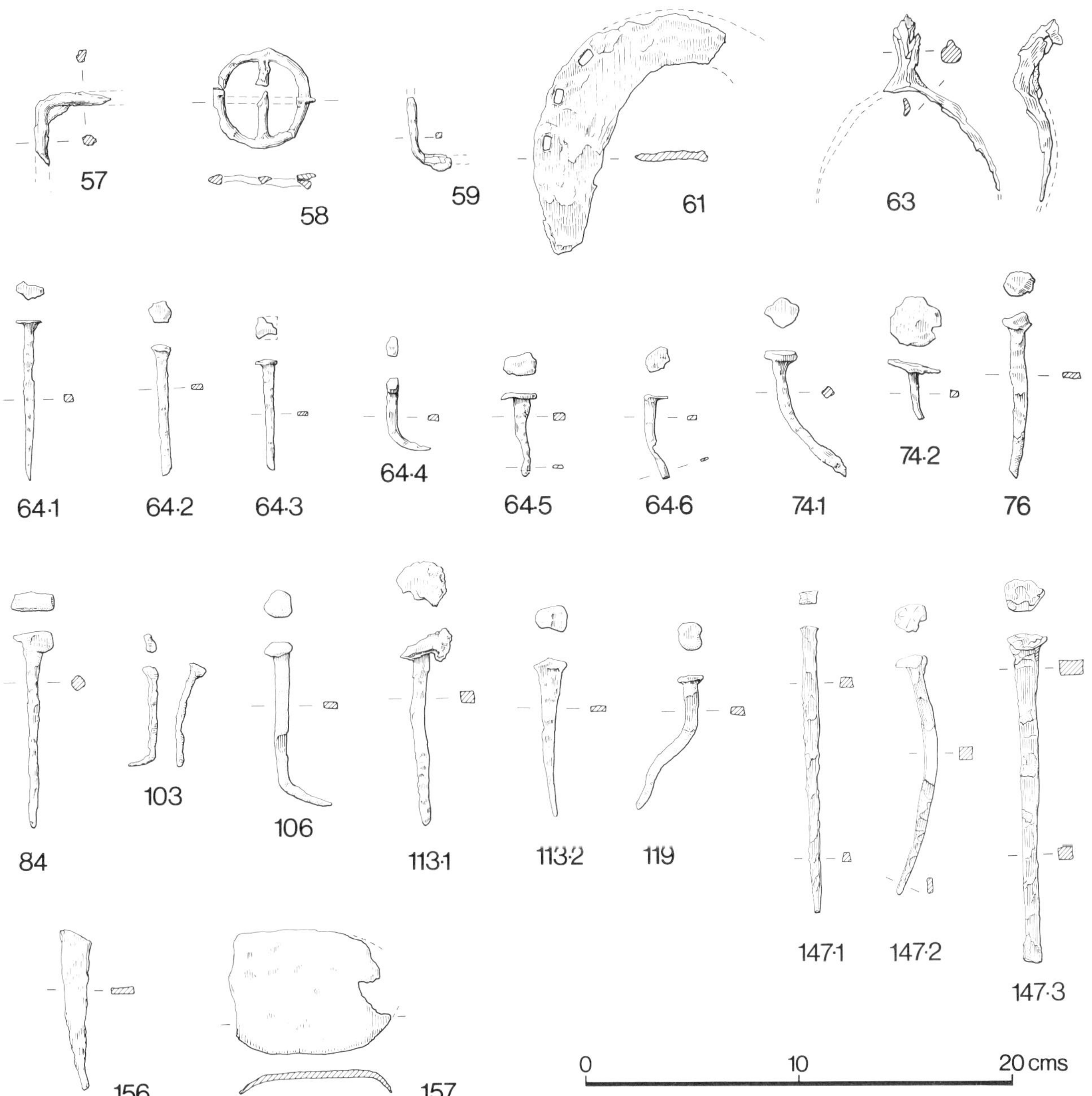

Fig. 68. Ironwork.

rectangular shank, length 56mm.
4-8 Five nail shanks all of rectangular section, lengths vary between 30mm. and 70mm.
All Kitchen Yard, KY 8 1.

75/1960-63 ?Nail, shank badly corroded and damaged, rectangular in section, length 90mm. Kitchen Yard, KY 8 2.

***76/1960-63** *1 Nail, incomplete rounded head, rectangular shank, length 74mm. *Fig.* 68.
2-3 Two nail shanks, both rectangular sectioned, lengths 25mm., 50mm.
All Kitchen Yard KY 8 2.

77/1960-63 Nail, rounded head, rectangular sectioned shank, length 25.8mm.
Nail, rectangular head and shank, length 45mm.
Four nail shanks, rectangular section, lengths from 37.5mm. to 64.8mm.
Kitchen Yard KY 8 2A.

78/1960-63 Badly corroded nail with round head, rectangular (?) shank, length 40mm.
Badly corroded nail with rectangular head and shank, length 56mm.
Nail, round head, rectangular sectioned shank, length 50mm.
L-shaped nail, rectangular sectioned shank, length 33mm.
Three fragments nail shanks, lengths 22mm., 28mm., 30mm. Rectangular in section.
All Kitchen Yard, KY 8 2A.

79/1960-63 Nail shank, rectangular section, length 44.8mm.
Kitchen Yard, KY 10.

80/1960-63 Nail, square head, rectangular section shank, length 46mm.
Nail shank, rectangular section, length 45mm.
Both Kitchen Yard, KY 10 1.

81/1961 Nail, rounded head, rectangular sectioned shank, length 55mm.
Nail shank, square section, length 35.5mm.
Both Kitchen Yard, KY 10 1.

82/1960-63 Nail fragment, rounded head and rectangular shank, length 21.5mm. Kitchen Yard, KY 10 1.

83/1960-63 Nail, incomplete head, shank rectangular in section and bent at right angles, length 78mm.
Nail, badly corroded, head rectangular, shank rectangular, length 59mm.
Nail, sub-rectangular head, rectangular sectioned shank, length 57mm.
Nail, oval head and rectangular sectioned shank, length 83mm.
Nail, rectangular head and shank, badly corroded, length 16mm.
Nail, head rectangular, rectangular shank, length 45mm.
Nail, rectangular head, rectangular shank, length 33.4mm.
Nail, rectangular head and shank, length 25mm.
Nail, incomplete head, rectangular shank, length 27mm.
Eleven fragments of nail shanks, all rectangular, lengths between 19mm. and 42mm.
All Kitchen Yard, KY 10 B13.

***84/1962** Nail, rectangular head and shank, length 87mm.
Structures south of Lay Brothers' Reredorter, LR VI 2. *Fig.* 68.

85/1958 Nail, round slightly domed head, and rectangular sectioned shank, length 30mm.
Drain Dl, MKA 7 5.

86/1958 Four nails, rectangular heads and shanks, lengths between 29mm. and 76mm.
Three nails, incomplete heads and rectangular shanks, lengths 61.5mm., 48mm., 39mm.
Nail, round head, rectangular shank, length 34mm.
Portions of two nail shanks, rectangular sectioned, lengths 68mm., 29mm.
Drain Dl, MKA 7 6.

87/1958 Nail, rectangular head, square shank, length 45mm.
Drain Dl, MKA 8 6.

88/1956 Nail, square head, rectangular shank, length 35mm.
Drain Dl, BD XI.

89/1956 Nail, sub-rectangular head, rectangular shank, length 50mm.
Drain Dl, BD XI, topsoil.

90/1956 Nail, round head, rectangular shank, length 54mm.
Nail, incomplete head, rectangular shank, length 60mm.
Both Drain Dl, BD XI 1.

91/1956 Nail square head, rectangular shank, length 49mm.
Drain Dl, BD XII 1.

92/1958 Nail, head incomplete, shank rectangular, badly corroded, length 50mm.
(?) Nail shank, rectangular section, length 26mm.
Both structures south of Kitchen Yard WR.

93/1958 Nail, incomplete round head, rectangular shank, length 25mm.
Nail shank fragment, rectangular shank, very corroded, length 34mm.
Nail shank, rectangular section, length 25mm.
All structures south of kitchen Yard, WR 8, topsoil.

94/1958 (?) Nail, with broken rectangular head, rectangular section, length 45mm.
Fragment of a nail shank, rectangular section, length 26mm.
Structures south of Kitchen Yard, WR 9, topsoil.

95/1958 Nail, rectangular head and shank, length 55mm.
Structures south of Kitchen Yard, WR 9 1.

96/1958 Nail very badly corroded, head rectangular,

shank rectangular in section, length 44mm.
Nail, incomplete, sub-rectangular head, length 13mm.
Nail shank, incomplete rectangular section, length 21mm.
All structures south of Kitchen Yard, WR 9 2.

97/1958 Two (?) nail shanks, badly corroded, rectangular section, lengths 53mm., 56mm. Both structures south of Kitchen Yard, WR 9 3.

98/1958 Nail, shank badly corroded, square section, length 42mm.
Structures south of Kitchen Yard, WR 9 5.

99/1958 Nail, square head, rectangular section, length 28.6mm.
Three nail shanks, all rectangular section, lengths 23mm., 40mm., 55mm.
All structures south of Kitchen Yard, WR Baulk 9/10, topsoil.

100/1958 Nail shank, rectangular section, length 33mm. Structures south of Kitchen Yard, WR Baulk 9/10 1.

101/1958 Two nails, both with incomplete (round) heads, rectangular shanks, lengths 45mm., 58.8mm.
Two nail shanks, rectangular sectioned, length 27mm., 41mm.
All structures south of Kitchen Yard, WR 10, topsoil.

102/1958 Nail, rectangular head, and shank of rectangular section, length 70.5mm.
Nail, oval head, rectangular sectioned shank, one end curled over, length 40mm.
Nail shank, rectangular section, length 34mm.
All structures south of Kitchen Yard, WR 9 Extension East 1.

***103/1958** Two nails, heads incomplete, rectangular sectioned shanks, lengths 50mm., 52mm. Both structures south of Kitchen Yard, WR 10 1A *Fig*. 68.

104/1958 Nail shank(?), rectangular section, head and point missing, bent at right angles, length 44.5mm. Structures south of Kitchen Yard, WR 10 A1.

105/1958 Nail, rounded head, rectangular sectioned shank, length 74.8mm.
Nail head covered in corrosion, rectangular sectioned shank, length 59mm.
Nail, head damaged, rectangular sectioned shank, length 43mm.
Three nail shanks, rectangular sectioned, lengths 41mm., 64mm., 45mm.
All structures south of Kitchen Yard, WR 11, topsoil.

***106/1958** *Nail, rounded head, rectangular shank, length 90mm. *Fig*. 68.
Two nails, (?) rectangular heads, lengths 29mm., 40mm.
Three nail shanks, all of rectangular section, lengths 61mm., 43mm., 37mm.
Nail, very corroded head, rectangular shank, length *c*. 80mm.
All structures south of Kitchen Yard, WR 11 A, topsoil.

107/1958 Two nails, rectangular heads and rectangular sectioned shanks, lengths 29.5mm., 52mm.
Nail, shank rectangular, length 30mm.
All structures south of Kitchen Yard, WR 11 A 1.

108/1958 Three nails, rectangular heads and shanks, lengths 56mm., 31mm., 36mm.
Nail, L-shaped with rectangular shank, length 35mm.
Portions of nine nail shanks of rectangular section, lengths between 29mm., and 77mm.
All structures south of Kitchen Yard, WR 12 1 A.

109/1958 (?) Nail, with damaged, incomplete head and rectangular sectioned shank, bent at right angles, length 45mm.
Nail, round head, square sectioned shank, point missing, length 26mm.
Nail shank, bent, rectangular in section, point wedge shaped, length 36mm.
All structures south of Kitchen Yard, WR 12/13 baulk, topsoil.

110/1958 (?) Nail shank badly corroded, length 68mm.
Nail, shank rectangular section, length 51.6mm.
Nail, round head, rectangular sectioned shank, length *c*. 55mm.
Nail, head incomplete, rectangular sectioned shank, length 28.4mm.
All structures south of Kitchen Yard, WR 12/13 baulk 1.

111/1958 Four nails, incomplete rectangular heads, rectangular sectioned shanks, length between 27.4 and 65mm.
Nail shank, rectangular section, length 55mm.
All structures south of Kitchen Yard, WR 13, topsoil.

112/1958 Nail, large flat octagonal head, shank rectangular section, length 38mm.
Nail, round head, rectangular shank, length 37.6mm.
Nail, rectangular head and shank, length 38mm.
Three nail shanks, rectangular section, lengths 36.4mm., 31mm., 49mm.
All structures south of Kitchen Yard, WR 13 1B.

***113/1959**
- *1 Nail, damaged rounded head, square shank, length 88mm. *Fig*. 68.
- *2 Nail, damaged rounded head, rectangular shank, length 72mm. *Fig*. 68.
- 3-5 Three nail shanks, rectangular sectioned, lengths 70mm., 55mm., 45mm.
- 6-7 Two nails, corroded, with sub-rectangular heads, rectangular shanks, lengths 45mm., 45mm.
- 8 Nail, damaged oval head and bent rectangular shank, length *c*. 38mm.
- 9-10 Portions of two damaged shanks of

rectangular section, lengths 38mm., 24mm.
All structures south of Kitchen Yard, WR 13 A, topsoil.

114/1959 Nail, subrectangular head, rectangular shank, length 45mm.
Nail, incomplete corroded head, rectangular shank, length 30mm.
Both structures south of Kitchen Yard, WR 13A, topsoil.

115/1959 Two nails, heads incomplete, rectangular sectioned shanks, lengths 39mm, and 56.3mm.
Seven (?) nail shanks, lengths between 30mm., and 39.4mm.
Nail, shank rectangular sectioned with end curled over, length 35mm.
Nail, rectangular head and shank, very badly corroded, bent at right angle, length 55mm.
All structures south of Kitchen Yard, WR 13A 1.

116/1959 Nail, rectangular head and shank, length 51.8mm.
Nail, shank very badly corroded, rectangular in section, length 50.5mm.
Both structures south of Kitchen Yard, WR 14, topsoil.

117/1959 Nail, square head, damaged rectangular (?) shank, length 24mm.
Two fragments (?) nail shanks, badly damaged rectangular sections, lengths 64mm., 77mm.
All structures south of Kitchen Yard, WR 14, topsoil.

118/1959 Nail, round, slightly domed head, rectangular shank, length 39mm.
Nail, round head, rectangular shank, length 45mm.
Nail, L-shaped, rectangular shank, length 55mm.
Nail, L-shaped, rectangular shank, length 41mm.
Nail, L-shaped, rectangular shank, length 36mm.
Two fragments nail shank, both rectangular, lengths 35mm., 40mm.
Nail, badly corroded, rounded head, square shank, length 29mm.
All structures south of Kitchen Yard, WR 14, topsoil.

***119/1959** *1 Nail, rounded head, rectangular shank, length 70mm. *Fig.* 68.
2 Nail, badly corroded, incomplete rectangular head, length 47mm.
3 Nail, rectangular head and shank, length 28mm.
4 Nail, badly corroded head, unidentifiable, rectangular shank, length *c.* 35mm.
5-7 Three fragments nail shanks, all rectangular, lengths 27mm., 44mm., 40mm.
All structures south of Kitchen Yard, WR 14 2.

120/1959 Nail, rounded head, rectangular shank, length 38.8mm.
Nail, square head, rectangular shank, length 23.7mm.
Nail, rectangular head and shank, length 34.5mm.
Nail, shank rectangular section, length 43mm.
All structures south of Kitchen Yard, WR 14 2.

121/1959 Nail, sub-rectangular head, rectangular shank, length 16mm.
Four nail shank fragments, all rectangular section, lengths between 23mm. and 80mm.
All Infirmary, I 5, topsoil.

122/1959 Two (?) nail shanks, both rectangular section, lengths 24.6mm., 32.4mm. Both Infirmary, I 5 2.

123/1959 Nail, damaged round head, rectangular sectioned shank, length 31.7mm. Infirmary, I 7 1.

124/1959 (?) Nail, square head and square sectioned shank, very badly corroded, length 50mm.
Seventeen nail shank fragments, all badly corroded, all of square or rectangular section, lengths between 20mm, and 36mm.
All Infirmary, I 8 2.

125/1959 Five (?) nail shanks, all of rectangular section, very badly corroded, lengths between 20mm., and 50mm. All Infirmary, I 9 1.

126/1959 Four badly corroded (?) nail shanks all rectangular section, lengths between 30 and 47mm. All Infirmary, I 10 1.

127/1959 Nine (?) nail shank fragments, lengths between 25.7mm., and 41.2mm. All of rectangular section. All Infirmary. I 9 2.

128/1959 Nail, round head, length 30mm. Infirmary, I 11 1. No longer extant.

129/1964 Two rectangular headed nails with rectangular shanks, points missing, lengths 39mm., and 37mm.
Nail shank, rectangular in section, length 32.3mm.
All Infirmary, I 14, north baulk IA.

130/1964 Two L-shaped (offset-rectangular head) nails, rectangular shanks, lengths 54.5mm. and 22.4mm.
Two nails, round flat heads, rectangular sectioned shanks, points missing, lengths 15mm., 30mm.
Seven fragments of nail shanks, all of rectangular section, lengths from 22.6mm to 55.7mm.
All Infirmary, I 15 1.

131/1964 Two nail shanks, badly corroded, rectangular section, lengths all *c.* 39mm. and 40mm.
Rectangular headed nail with rectangular sectioned shank, length 38.2mm.
All Infirmary, I 15 2.

132/1964 Nail, round head, square sectioned shank, point missing, length 35.6mm.
Nail shank, square section, point missing, length 43mm.
Both Infirmary, I 16 1.

133/1964 Three nails, all with rectangular heads and rectangular sectioned shanks, lengths between 26.8mm. and 56mm.
Two nail shanks, rectangular sections, points missing, lengths 43mm. and 41mm.
All Infirmary, I 16 2.

134/1964 Three (?) nail shanks, heavily corroded, all of rectangular section, lengths 28.7mm., 20.4mm., 50mm. All Infirmary, I 16 2.

135/1964 Square headed nail, badly corroded, rectangular sectioned shank, length 50mm.
Nail shank of square section, length 52.7mm.
Both Infirmary, I 16/17 baulk 1.

136/1964 Nail, round head, rectangular sectioned shank, length 45mm. Infirmary, I 17 1.

137/1964 Nail shank, rectangular section, badly corroded, length 37mm. Infirmary, I 17 1.

138/1964 Nail, rectangular head and square sectioned shank very heavily corroded, length 40mm. Infirmary, I 18 1.

139/1964 Nail shank, rectangular sectioned rounded point, length 37.3mm. Infirmary, I 20 1.

140/1964 Two nails, heads damaged and badly corroded, shanks rectangular sectioned, lengths 23mm., 30mm.
Nut, square 16mm., by 16mm., with circular hole diameter 6mm. Modern.
All Infirmary, I 24, topsoil.

141/1960 Nail, flat roughly triangular shaped head and rectangular sectioned shank. Point missing, length 57.3mm.
Nail, rectangular off-set head (L-shaped) and rectangular sectioned shank, length 36mm.
Both Kitchen Yard, KY 9 2A.

142/1960 Nail, flat rectangular head (?), with portion of rectangular sectioned shank, length 25mm.
Nail, square headed with square sectioned shank. Point missing, length 49.4mm.
Portions of five nail shanks, all of rectangular section, badly damaged, lengths between 34mm. and 47.8mm.
All Kitchen Yard, KY 6 6.

143/1958 Four nails, all with flat, rectangular heads and rectangular sectioned shanks, lengths between 38.8mm. and 54mm.
Nail, incomplete rounded head with rectangular sectioned shank, length 62mm.
Nail, incomplete rectangular head and rectangular sectioned shank, length 59.4mm.
Portion of six nail shanks, all rectangular in section, lengths between 35mm, and 57mm.
All structures south of Kitchen Yard, WR 11 B1.

144/1960-63 Four nails, all with damaged and incomplete heads and rectangular sectioned shanks, lengths between 47mm. and 74mm.
Nail head, flat and sub-rectangular in shape.
Nail, rectangular head and rectangular sectioned shank. Point missing, length 26mm.
Portions of six nail shanks all of rectangular section, lengths between 26mm. and 59mm.
All Kitchen Yard, KY 10 1A.

145/1951 Roughly oval leaded nail head and very small portion of rectangular sectioned shank. Nail head 20.4mm. by 21mm. No provenance.

146/US Nail with rounded, leaded head and rectangular sectioned shank, point missing, length 28.7mm., head 23mm., by 22mm. No provenance.

***147/US** Three wall nails (?); flat rectangular heads and rectangular sectioned shanks, tapering to wedge shaped points, lengths 115mm., 153mm., 132mm. No provenance. *Fig.* 68.

148/1958 Nail shank, bent at right angles, rectangular section, length *c.* 54. 8mm. Structures south of Kitchen Yard, WR 10A 1.

149/1958 Portions of two nail shanks, rectangular sections, lengths 37.2mm., 21.2mm. Structures south of Kitchen Yard, WR.

150/1958 Nail, rounded head, rectangular sectioned shank, length 19mm.
Portions of two rectangular sectioned shanks, lengths, 40.6mm., 47mm.
All structures south of Kitchen Yard, WR 9 extension east 1.

151/1959 Nail, rectangular head and shank, length 24.5mm.
Portions of four nail shanks, all rectangular sectioned, lengths between 19.8mm. and 25mm.
All Infirmary I 9 2.

152/1964 Nail, incomplete head, rectangular sectioned shank, point missing, length 33mm. Infirmary I 16 1.

153/1958 Badly damaged and corroded nail, head incomplete, shank rectangular sectioned, length *c.* 85mm. Structures south of Kitchen Yard, WR 10A 1.

154/1959 Nail, damaged rectangular head and rectangular sectioned shank, point missing, length 27mm. Structures south of Kitchen Yard, WR 14, topsoil.

155/1958 Nail, square head and bent, rectangular sectioned shank, length 46.5mm.
Nail, incomplete, head with leaded upper surface and square sectioned shank, length 18mm.
Both structures south of Kitchen Yard, WR 10/11 1.

Miscellaneous iron

The following iron finds were not recognisable as any artefact:

***156/1954** Tapering strip, roughly triangular in plan, length 73.3mm., width from 4.6mm. to 15mm. Kitchen, topsoil. *Fig.* 68.

***157/1954** Fragment of iron sheet, 2mm. thick, 56mm. by 70mm. Kitchen, topsoil. *Fig.* 68.

158/1960-63 Amorphous lump of partially forged iron/slag 40mm. by 75mm. X-ray plate 44, no. 10. Kitchen Yard, KY 10.

159/1958 Eight small fragments of sheet iron and one amorphous lump of partially forged iron/slag (length 60mm.).
Structures south of Kitchen Yard, WR 10, topsoil.

160/US Curved fragment of sheet iron, 50mm. by 115mm. X-ray plate 45, no. 13. No provenance.

161/1960-63 Amorphous lump of partially forged iron/slag. Infirmary, I 18, topsoil.

162/1963-64 Badly damaged iron rod of rectangular section, broken in two pieces, length *c.* 115mm. X-ray plates 44, 49, no. 11. Structures south of Kitchen Yard, WRB 3.

163/1957 Portions of three badly damaged rods of rectangular section, lengths 98mm., 54mm., 55mm. Drain Dl, MKA 7 2.

164/1959 Iron object, badly damaged and corroded. Possibly a rod, but it is too corroded to be certain, length 83.4mm. Infirmary, I 5 2.

The following iron finds consisted of only small amorphous iron lumps:

165/1958 WR 12 1A

166/1959 I 5, topsoil

167/1959 I 8 2

168/1959 I 9 1

169/1959 I 9 2

170/1959 I 10 1

171/1962 LR V1 3

Copper alloy objects

Belt fittings

***172/1963-64** Incomplete frame of bronze spectacle or double buckle. Roughly oval in section and plan. Dimensions 43mm. by 39mm. Structures south of Kitchen Yard, WR H, topsoil. No longer extant. *Fig.* 69.

***173/1951** Bronze belt fitting, two rectangular plates, 17mm. by 30mm., held together by four large headed rivets; both plates are centrally perforated, diameter 5mm. Upper plate decorated with rocker tracer floral pattern. Warming House Courtyard. *Fig.* 69.

***174/1955** Bronze strap end, 9mm. by 55mm., with three rivet holes situated between three small depressions, all with incised or stamped rings around them. Refectory, unstratified adjoining Main Drain. No longer extant. *Fig.* 69.

***175/1960-63** Damaged strap end plate of bronze sheet, 9mm. by 40mm., with rivet hole at one end and rouletted zig-zag decoration. Kitchen Yard, KY 10, topsoil. No longer extant. *Fig.* 69.

***176/1956** Two very small strap ornaments, both 10mm. long, with a rivet at each end and central perforation diameter 2mm. ? Meat Kitchen, MK II 6. No longer extant. *Fig.* 69.

***177/1956** Bronze ? strap end, length 45mm., width 21mm., one end pointed, other end straight, showing parts of three possible rivet holes on broken end. Drain Dl, BD XI 1. *Fig.* 69.

***178/US** Bronze strap end, 23mm. by 45mm. decorated with parallel incised lines with one rivet in position near formed end and rivet hole at the other end. No provenance. No longer extant. *Fig.* 69.

***179/1956** Bronze stud, 12mm. by 13mm., slightly domed with central rivet hole, diameter 4mm., decorated with incised lines. Drain Dl, BD XI 1. *Fig.* 69.

***180/1955** Strap fitting consisting of a bronze strip 14.2mm. by 28.6mm., with two rivets in place at diagonally opposite corners. One end appears to retain half of an oval perforation. Refectory, R 3. *Fig.* 69.

Pins

***181/US** Bronze pin, damaged hexagonal head, length 49mm. No provenance. No longer extant. *Fig.* 69.

***182/US** Bronze pin damaged circular head, diameter 2mm., broken, but total length 43mm. No provenance. No longer extant. *Fig.* 69.

***183/1956** Bronze pin, with looped-over head, length 82mm. Drain Dl, BD XIV 1, 'Broken flag floor and make-up'. No longer extant. *Fig.* 69.

Toilet implements

***184/1959** Ear scoop or unguent spoon, length 59mm., spoon bowl at one end, the opposite end is forked with out-turned 'blades'. The shaft has a fine coiled wire wrapped around it. Infirmary. No longer extant. *Fig.* 69.

***185/1963-64** (?) Ear scoop or unguent spoon, two joining fragments, total length 52mm., twisted rectangular section, with one end flattened and spoon-shaped. The opposite end is flattened and broken off. Structures south of the Kitchen Yard, WR G/H north 1. *Fig.* 69.

***186/US** One arm of a pair of tweezers, thin sub-retangular strip, tapering toward one end which has a slightly curved end. Edges are bevelled. No provenance. *Fig.* 69.

Taps

***187/1953**
*1 Lower portion of a hollow bronze tap handle, height 75mm.
*2 Complete solid bronze tap handle, crook-shaped with leaf and ball terminal. Height 115mm.
Both Refectory, FR 1. *Fig.* 69.

***188/1960** Upper portion of a solid bronze tap handle terminating in a zoomorphic head with a ball grasped between its jaws. The handle is curved at an acute angle, height 46.5mm. (surviving only as a cast). Kitchen Yard, KY A 1. *Fig.* 69.

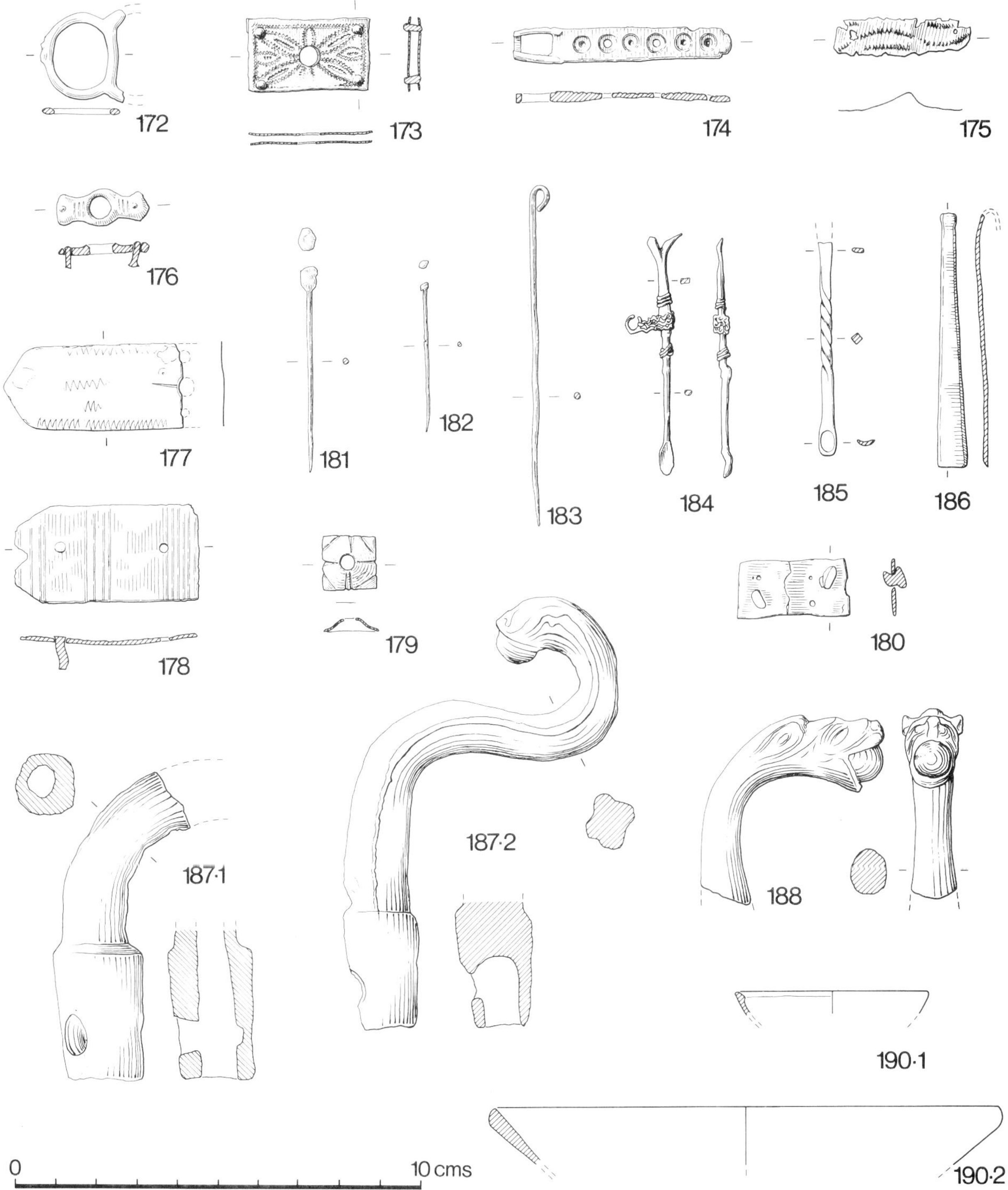

Fig. 69. Bronze material.

Vessel fragments

189/1960-63 Fragment of bronze vessel rim, 16mm. by 30mm. Kitchen Yard, KY 5. No longer extant.

***190/1950** Two fragments of bronze vessel rim, not from same vessel. ? Kitchen Yard, 'under sand of east drain'. *Fig.* 69.

191/1959 Bronze vessel foot, rectangular section, length 47mm. Structures south of Kitchen Yard, WR 13A 1.

Rings

***192/1951** Bronze ring, oval section, diameter 24mm. Possible harness ring. Warming House Courtyard. No longer extant. *Fig.* 70.

***193/1952** Bronze ring, diameter 25mm., flattened D-shaped section, with five links of bronze chain attached. Warming House, sand layer over charcoal, WH 4. No longer extant. *Fig.* 70.

***194/1960** Copper alloy annular ring, diameter 37mm., formed of three groups of five plaited bronze wires of circular section, each 0.4mm. dia. Kitchen Yard, KY 9 1. *Fig.* 70.

Miscellaneous fittings and objects

195/1952 Three fragments of thin, curved bronze sheet, smallest fragment 8mm. by 10mm., with suspension loop, 2mm. by 4mm., attached. Two other fragments, 10mm. by 12mm., 11mm. by 12mm. Probably a small bell. Warming House, WH 4, sand over charcoal.

196/1960-63 Decorative edging; 1 large and 1 small fragment of very thin copper alloy foil sheet, width 13mm. Large fragment forms three sides of rectangle 22mm. by 140mm. by 68mm. Smaller fragment length 53mm. Both with impressed leaf decoration in narrow band along inner edge. (?) Modern. Kitchen Yard, KY 2.

***197/1960-63** Large fragment of flat bronze strip, 32mm. by 76mm., one end rounded with three punched holes, other end broken off, with three punched holes closely grouped in one corner. A second group of three punched holes may have been situated in the opposing corner. Red substance, probably paint, adhering in patches on both sides, (?)Modern. Kitchen Yard, KY 5, topsoil. *Fig.* 70.

***198/1960-63** Folded bronze strip, rectangular in plan and section, length 25mm. by 6mm., with rivet hole in one end. Kitchen Yard, KY 8 2. *Fig.* 70.

***199/1962** Object of thin sheet bronze, length 38mm., tapering to a fine point, maximum width 5mm. The opposite end is filleted with a central circular perforation. Structures south of Lay Brothers' Reredorter, LR V 2. No longer extant. *Fig.* 70.

***200/1962** Fragment of flat bronze sheet 32mm. by 48.5mm., with two opposing pairs of punched holes. One end regular, the opposite has been cut on the diagonal. Rectangular in section. Structures south of Lay-Brothers' Reredorter, LR X, topsoil. *Fig.* 70.

***201/1956** Copper alloy wire of rectangular section curved round to form a circle; one end is broken, the opposite end has been flattened, diameter 12mm. Drain D1, BD VII 1. *Fig.* 70.

***202/1956** Oval loop of bronze wire 5mm. by 10mm., square sectioned with rounded edges with two ends crossed over and small fragment of sheet bronze adhering to them. ?Suspension loop. Drain D1, BD XI 1. *Fig.* 70.

203/1959 Bronze nail or tack, rounded head, square section and wedge-shaped tip, length 34.4mm. Structures south of Kitchen Yard, WR 14, topsoil.

***204/1952** Thin sub-rectangular plate of bronze sheet, 60mm. by 90mm., with four rivet holes along each end, damaged. ?Warming House. *Fig.* 70.

***205/1958** Bronze chain, length 160mm. Structures south of Kitchen Yard, WR 13, topsoil. *Fig.* 70.

***206/1958** Two-piece hinged object consisting of a lower, flat plate of roughly tear-drop plan. A decorative stud, mushroom shaped, is attached to the centre of the obverse face by a cylindrical iron rivet which pierces its centre. The reverse face is partially covered in iron corrosion. The upper piece of plate is bent at a 45 degree angle and is a domed bell shape. The upper stem of the 'bell' appears to have been horizontally perforated. Both plates taper as they approach the hinge, length 28mm. ?Modern. Structures south of Kitchen Yard, WR 13, topsoil. *Fig.* 70.

207/US Tapering rod of circular section, both ends broken and one end curved. The rod consists of rolled thin sheet with a longitudinal join, length 82mm., diameter 2mm. No provenance.

***208/1956** Bronze tombstone letter, upper portion missing, probably an 'A', thickness varies between 3.2mm. and 4.4mm. Present height 26.8mm., present breadth 25.1mm. Dr J. Blair writes that the letter is a north eastern imitation of the main group pattern series of tombstone letters and is most closely paralleled by two letters presently displayed at Fishlake Church, Yorkshire. Drain D1, BD XI 2. *Fig.* 70.

Miscellaneous fragments

209/1960-63 Fragment of curved bronze sheet, length 45mm., width tapering end to end from 35mm. to 25mm. Wider end has rectangular piece cut out from edge and score mark, (?) offcut. Kitchen Yard, KY 5, topsoil.

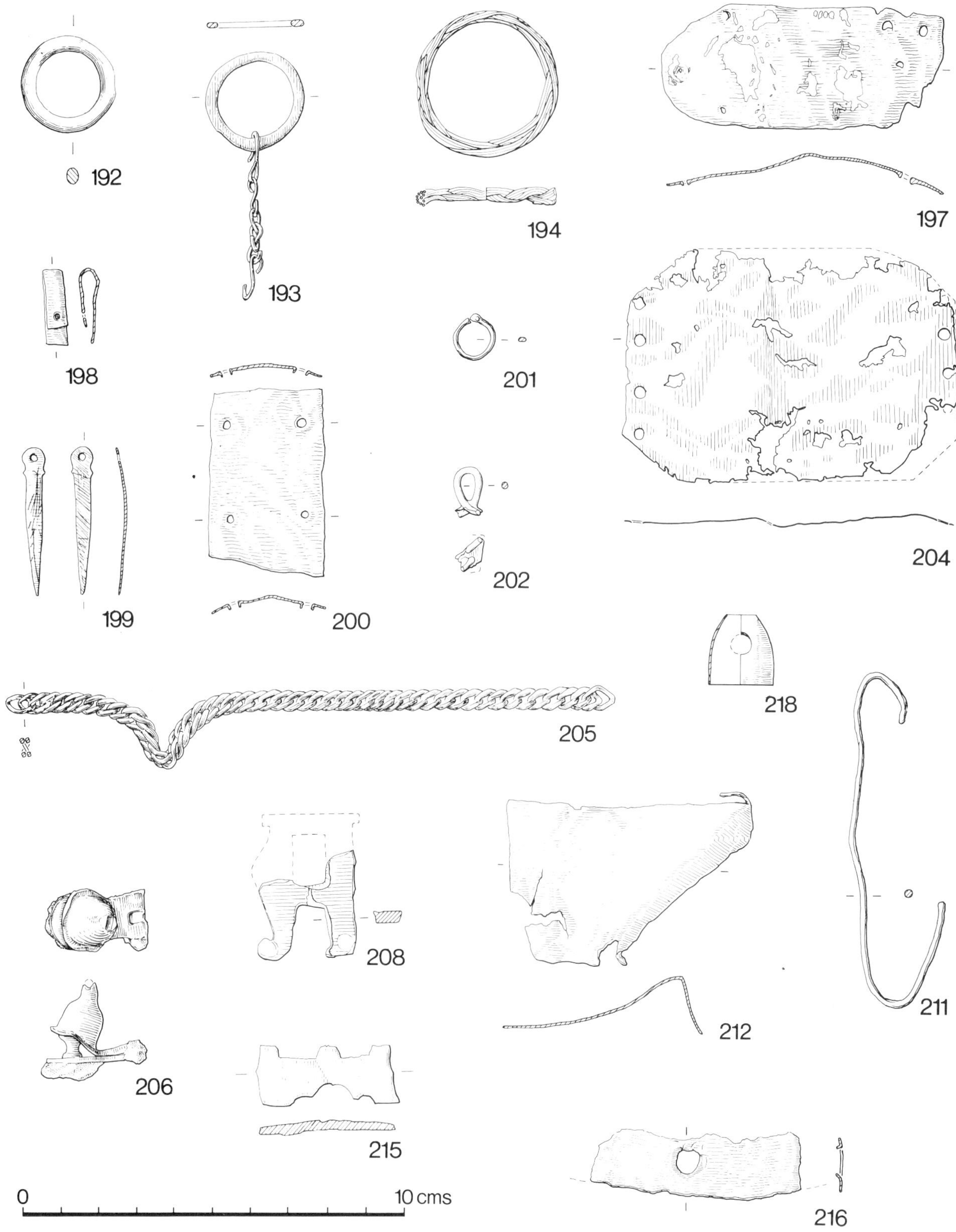

Fig. 70. Bronze material.

210/1960-63 Four fragments of thin bronze strips all of rectangular section. (a) Lengths 18mm. by 70mm., (b) 11mm. by 80mm., (c) 23mm. by 42mm. (with one corner folded over), (d) rectangular fragment 18mm. by 30mm. Fragment (c) has the remains of a circular perforation along one edge (possibly strap fitting). Kitchen Yard, KY 5.

***211/1960-63** Fragment of bronze wire, length *c.* 135mm., with both ends bent over, circular section diameter 2mm. Kitchen Yard, KY 8 2A. *Fig.* 70.

***212/1960-63** Trapezoidal fragment of thin copper alloy sheet, 65mm. by 60mm. by 50mm., with longest edge folded over at right angles to main body. Kitchen Yard, KY 9. *Fig.* 70.

213/1960-63 Fragment of bronze strip, with one edge bent at an acute angle, 9.5mm. by 43mm. Kitchen Yard, KY 10 1.

214/1952 Slightly curved fragment of bronze sheet, one straight side, length 50mm., others irregular, width varying from 17mm. to 32mm. Structures south of Lay-Brothers' Reredorter, LR X 2.

***215/1956** Fragment of (?) scrap bronze from casting. (?)Drain D1, BD XIV 1 'Broken flag floor and make-up'. No longer extant. *Fig.* 70.

***216/1958** Fragment of bronze strip, length 57.6mm., width 16.2mm., with hole diameter 5mm., punched through 20mm. from broken end. Structures south of Kitchen Yard, WR 9 3. *Fig.* 70.

217/1964 Two small fragments of bronze sheet, 5mm. by 5mm., 5mm. by 3mm. Infirmary, I 16 2.

***218/US** Fragment of bronze sheet length *c.* 25mm., curled round, one end straight width 9mm., other end broken off with remains of circular hole diameter *c.* 7mm. on edge. No provenance. *Fig.* 70.

219/US One fragment of bronze strip, length 74mm., width 7mm., with one end twisted. No provenance.

220/US Sub-rectangular fragment of flat, rectangular sectioned bronze sheet, length 61mm., width 13mm. to 15mm. Spoilheap.

221/1959 Fragment of flat bronze sheet, sub-rectangular in plan, length 66mm., width from 24mm. to 40mm. Structures south of Kitchen Yard, WR 14 1.

222/1959 Large fragment of bronze sheet, irregular edges, *c.* 40mm., by 146mm. Structures south of Kitchen Yard, WR 14 1.

223/1956 Fragment of bronze waste, 24mm. by 33mm. Drain D1, BD XI 1.

224/1960-63 Irregular fragment of bronze waste, *c.* 15mm. by 30mm. Kitchen Yard, KY 4.

225/1964 Fragment of bronze waste, 15mm. by 20mm. Infirmary, I 17 1.

226/1964 Three small lumps bronze waste. Infirmary, I 14, north baulk 1 A.

227/1964 Small fragment of waste bronze and silver/lateen?, 7mm. by 13mm. Infirmary, I 15 2.

228/1960-61 Small fragment of bronze, miscast or clipping, roughly rectangular in plan and section, 16.8mm. by 12mm. Kitchen Yard, KY 4 1.

Lead and lead alloy objects

Weights

***229/1956** Oval lead weight (37.7mm. by 35.7mm.), rectangular in section, height 22.7mm. Reverse surface slightly convex. Weight 8oz. 6gr. Meat Kitchen. *Fig.* 71.

***230/1956** Roughly cylindrical lead (?) clock weight (one oz. 86gr.), with pierced, rectangular sectioned tab for suspension. Total height 34.8mm., diameter 14.4mm. Meat Kitchen, MK III 1. *Fig.* 71.

Plumb bob

***231/US** Lead plumb-bob of sub-triangular plan, tapering sharply to a point. The opposite end is semi-circular in plan and has a roughly circular perforation, 3mm. in diameter. Rectangular in section, length 37.7mm., width 15.4mm., thickness 3mm. Unknown context, SD I 1. *Fig.* 71.

Token

***232/1955** Lead (?)token, roughly circular, diameter 21mm. with striations on obverse face, forming shell-like pattern. Refectory, topsoil. No longer extant. *Fig.* 71.

Spoon

***233/1958** Pewter spoon bowl, length 65mm., post-medieval. Structures south of Kitchen Yard, WR 11, topsoil. No longer extant. *Fig.* 71.

Window came

234/1960-63 Fragment of H-sectioned lead came, length 102mm., internal width 2.5mm.
Twisted fragment of H-sectioned lead came, length 55mm., internal width 2.5mm.
Both Kitchen Yard, KY 10 1.

235/1960-63 Twisted fragment of H-sectioned lead came, indeterminate internal width, length 55mm. Kitchen Yard, KY 8.

236/1960 Twisted and folded fragment of lead came, length 50mm., internal width 3mm. Cloister, WC I 1.

237/1960-63 Seven fragments of H-section lead came, lengths from 35mm. to 85mm., measurable internal widths 2.8mm., 3.6mm., 4.2mm., 2.7mm.
Fragment of a V-shaped lead came joint, height 35mm., internal width 3.7mm.
Damaged fragment of H-sectioned lead came, bent, flattened and partially split.
All Kitchen Yard.

238/1958 Fragment of H-sectioned lead came, length 60mm., internal width 3mm.
Fragment of badly damaged lead (?)came, length 45mm., internal width indeterminate.
Both structures south of Kitchen Yard, WR.

239/1963-64 Fragment of H-sectioned lead came, partially split, twisted and folded in half, length 56mm., internal width indeterminate. Structures south of Kitchen Yard, WR A-H.

240/1959 Fragment of lead came, distorted, length 35mm., internal width indeterminate. Structures south of Kitchen Yard, WR 14 2.

241/1959 Lead (?)came fragment, internal width indeterminate, length 45mm. Structures south of Kitchen Yard, WR 14 2.

242/US Five fragments of H-sectioned lead came, three flattened and distorted, measurable internal widths 2.8mm., 2.6mm. No provenance.

243/1956 Fragment of split came, length 86mm.
Fragment of split came, folded in half, length 43mm.
Both Drain D1, 'Bath drain'.

244/1960 Lead came joint, H-shaped cross section (internal width 3.4mm.). The joint is at a 100 degree angle. Kitchen Yard, KY 3 1.

245/1960-61 Piece of lead came, originally H-shaped cross-section, now partially flattened, estimated internal width 3.8mm. Kitchen Yard, KY 4 1.

Miscellaneous objects

246/1956 Lead alloy ?stylus, length 49mm., width 11.5mm., sub-rectangular in plan with one end tapered off to form a narrow shaft, end missing. The opposite end tapers in thickness forming a wedge. Purpose uncertain. Meat Kichen, MK III N2.

***247/1958** Lead (?) washer, irregular shaped piece of lead sheet, *c.* 20mm. by 30mm., with a roughly rectangular perforation. Structures south of Kitchen Yard, WR Baulk 9/10, topsoil. *Fig.* 71.

***248/1958** Lead caulking plug, length 27mm., diameter 13mm. Probably for a D-shaped glazing bar. Structures south of Kitchen Yard, WR I 1. *Fig.* 71.

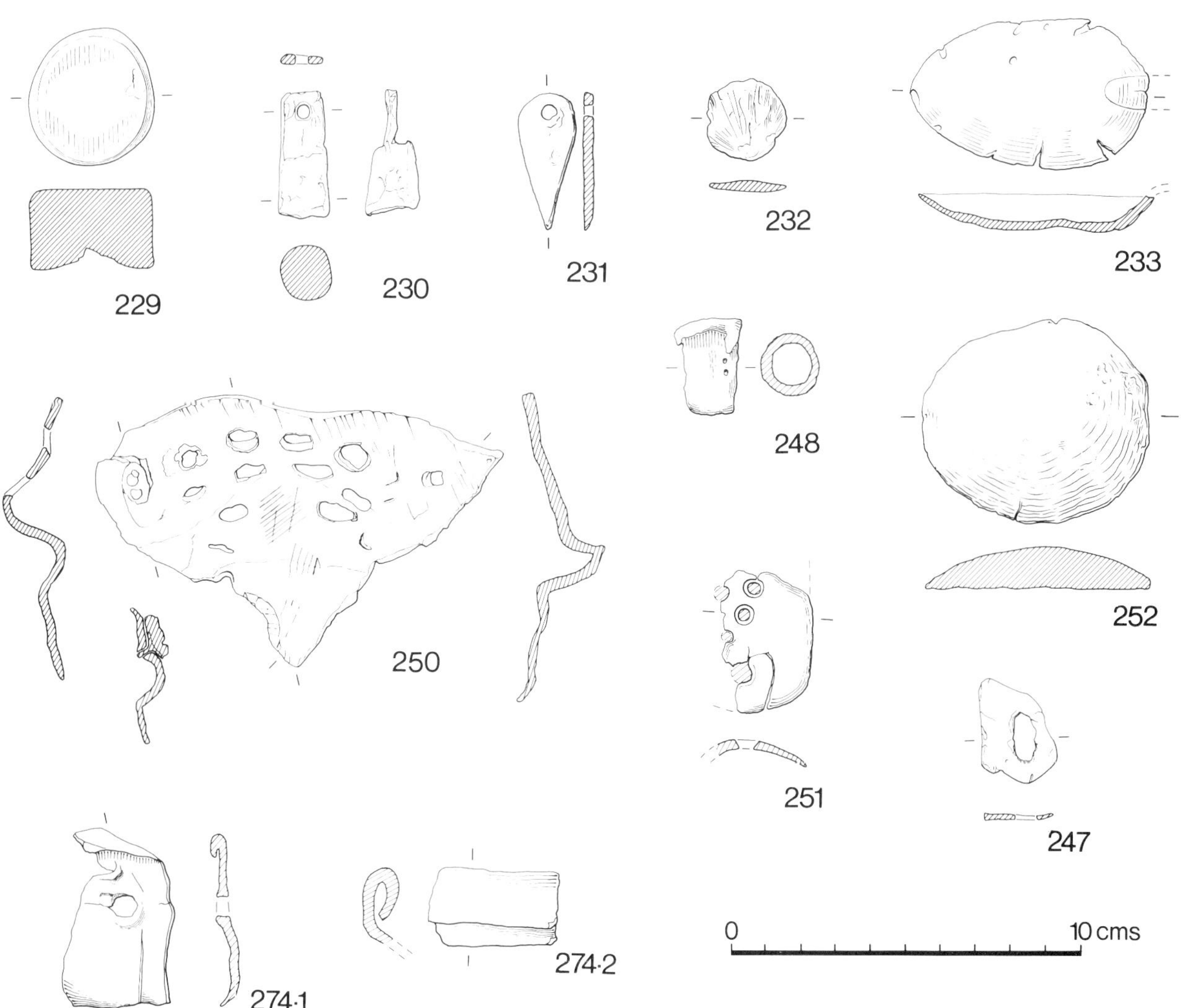

Fig. 71. Lead objects.

249/1962 Flattened tube of thin lead sheet, length 50mm., one end open, roughly rectangular in shape, and folded back. The opposite end is flattened. Pipe (?). Structures south of Lay Brothers' Reredorter, LR IV 1.

***250/US** Lead sheet, roughly triangular in plan, perforated by ten oval holes (two rows of 4 and one of 2). Near the edges of the sheet are four nail holes, two on each side, one retaining the remains of an iron nail *in situ*. Gutter filter or sink fitting? Cloister cistern. *Fig*. 71.

***251/1953** Portion of lead sheet with curving outline, rectangular in section. Only portions of two original edges survive. The sheet has two whole, and portions of six other, oval perforations (4mm. by 3.6mm.). Part of a drain cover, strainer or filter? Length 38mm. Cloisters, CL III, south extension. *Fig*. 71.

***252/1957** Roughly oval plano-convex lead lump, possibly from a hearth bottom, 66mm. by 55.8mm. Meat Kitchen. *Fig*. 71.

253/1953 Plano-convex lead ball, shot (?) or weight(?). Dimensions 13mm. by 13mm., height 11mm. Refectory, FR I, topsoil.

Lead sheet

254/1963 Nine fragments of thin lead (?) alloy sheet. Largest fragment 65mm. by 95mm., with five roughly rectangular holes punched through. Other fragments measure between 35mm. by 80mm., and 15mm. by 15mm. Malt House, K 1(a) 1.

255/1960-63 Slightly curving triangular fragment of lead sheet, length 46.5mm., 17mm. at widest point. Kitchen Yard, KY 4 2A.

256/1960-63 Triangular fragment of lead sheet, length 61.4mm., 27.5mm. at widest point. Kitchen Yard, KY 4 2A.

257/1960-63 Large, irregular fragment of folded lead sheet, scoring marks visible, off-cut/scrap, length 100mm. Kitchen Yard, KY 10 1.

258/1959 Irregular shaped fragment of thin lead sheet, 20mm. by 35mm. Infirmary, I 11 1.

259/1960-63 Fragment of folded lead sheet. Kitchen Yard, KY 8.

260/1957 Large fragment of lead sheet *c*. 74mm. by 80.8mm. Portions of five perforations survive along the edges of the fragment. Meat Kitchen: rooms at south end, MKA 5 1.

261/1957 Fragment of bent and folded lead sheet, *c*. 55mm. by 65mm., with curving outline. Meat Kitchen: rooms at south end, MKA 5 2.

262/1957 Large fragment of folded and twisted lead sheet, length 100mm., width 10mm. to 30mm. Irregular in plan and section.
Two fragments of lead sheet *c*. 30mm. by 30mm., 20mm. by 30mm.
Meat Kitchen: rooms at south end, MKA 5.

263/1962 Irregular fragment of lead sheet, folded, *c*. 70mm. by 50mm. Scrap/off-cut. Structures south of Lay Brothers' Reredorter, LR II 1.

264/1962 Irregular fragment of lead sheet folded, *c*. 50mm. by 100mm., with iron corrosion attached to upper surface. Off-cut/scrap. Structures south of Lay Brothers' Reredorter, LR I 1.

265/1959 Irregular folded and twisted fragment of lead sheet *c*. 40mm. by 80mm. Infirmary. I 12 2.

266/1964 Sub-rectangular fragment of lead sheet, 25mm. by 25mm. Infirmary, I 16 2A.

267/1953 Sub-rectangular fragment of lead sheet, 25mm. by 27mm., with remains of (?)nail hole in one side. Cloister, CL II 5.

268/1953 Rolled and twisted fragment of lead sheet, *c*. 40mm. by 60mm., with scoring marks on one edge. Cloister, CL II 2A.

269/1953 Rectangular fragment of lead alloy (pewter?) sheet, 30mm. by 36mm. Refectory, FR II, topsoil.

270/1960 Sub-rectangular fragment of lead sheet, 58mm. by 44.4mm., with scoring mark along one edge. Cloister, WC 1 1.

271/1960-63 Fragment of crumpled lead sheet, *c*. 50mm. by 60mm., with circular nail hole in centre. Kitchen Yard, KY 4 7.

272/1960-63 Sub-rectangular fragment of lead sheet 40mm. by 90mm., with three irregular punched holes. Kitchen Yard, KY 1 1.

273/1960-63 Rectangular fragment of folded lead sheet *c*. 50mm. by 70mm., with one circular punched hole.
Sub-rectangular fragment of lead sheet, 40mm. by 60mm., heavily scored with circular hole near one end.
Fragment of folded lead sheet, 30mm. by 45mm., with one rectangular perforation near one edge.
All Kitchen Yard.

***274/1958**
- *1 Sub-rectangular fragment of lead sheet, 30mm. by 50mm., with circular hole near the centre. *Fig*. 71.
- *2 Rectangular fragment of lead sheet folded in half, 20mm. by 35mm. *Fig*. 71.
- *3 Rectangular piece of lead sheet, 51mm. by 103mm., with nail fragment in position on one end and circular hole adjacent. The opposite end is folded over. *Fig*. 72.
- *4 Rectangular piece of lead sheet 51mm. by 105mm., with two pairs of nail holes in one end and other end folded over. *Fig*. 72.
- 5 Triangular fragment of lead sheet, 45mm. by 25mm.

All structures south of Kitchen Yard, WR.

275/1963-64 Very large rectangular fragment of lead sheet folded in half, 80mm. by 130mm. Scoring marks visible along edges.
Fragment of lead sheet, folded twice, 50mm.

by 70mm., two incised lines visible along one edge.

Sub-rectangular fragment of twisted and folded sheet, *c.* 60mm. by 70mm.

Fragment of lead sheet folded in half, 35mm. by 40mm.

All structures south of Kitchen Yard, WR A-H.

276/1963-64 Pentagonal fragment of lead sheet, length 42mm., width 25mm. Structures south of Kitchen Yard, WR A/B 1.

277/1956(?) Large fragment of sub-rectangular lead sheet, one edge cut and twisted, 77mm. by 80mm. Rectangular fragment of lead sheet, 55mm. by 70mm., partially cut along one edge. Both Drain D 1, 'Bath drain'.

278/1956 Fragment of lead sheet, 40mm. by 60mm., with two rectangular nail holes in one edge. Fragment of lead sheet, *c.* 35mm. by 45mm., with a cut lengthwise.

Two small irregular fragments of lead sheet with strips partly cut off the sides. Off cuts. All Drain D 1, BD XI 2.

279/1956 Sub-rectangular fragment of lead sheet *c.* 40mm. by 65mm., with one notch each along two edges. Structures south of Kitchen Yard, BD 20 7.

280/1956 Very large sub-rectangular piece of lead sheet, two sides cut and crumpled, with round nail hole in upper edge, 135mm. by 170mm. Drain D1, BD XI 1.

281/1956 Large fragment of sub-rectangular lead sheet, *c.* 85mm. by 140mm., with roughly oval nail hole near one edge. Drain D 1, BD XI 1.

282/1956 Rectangular fragment of lead sheet with one edge rolled over, *c.* 40mm. by 50mm. Drain D 1, BD XI 1.

283/1956 Fragment of lead sheet, with strips partly cut off and rectangular nail hole, *c.* 25mm. by 50mm. Off-cut/scrap. Drain D 1, BD XI 1.

284/1959 Roughly triangular fragment of crumpled lead sheet, 40mm. by 85mm., at widest point. Structures south of Kitchen Yard, WR 8, topsoil.

285/1963 Rectangular fragment of lead sheet, 24mm. by 55mm. Kitchen, K (NE?) 1.

***286/1959** Lead sheet, *c.* 102mm. by 67mm., with one end folded over and two nail holes in opposite end. Structures south of Kitchen Yard, WR 8 1. *Fig.* 72.

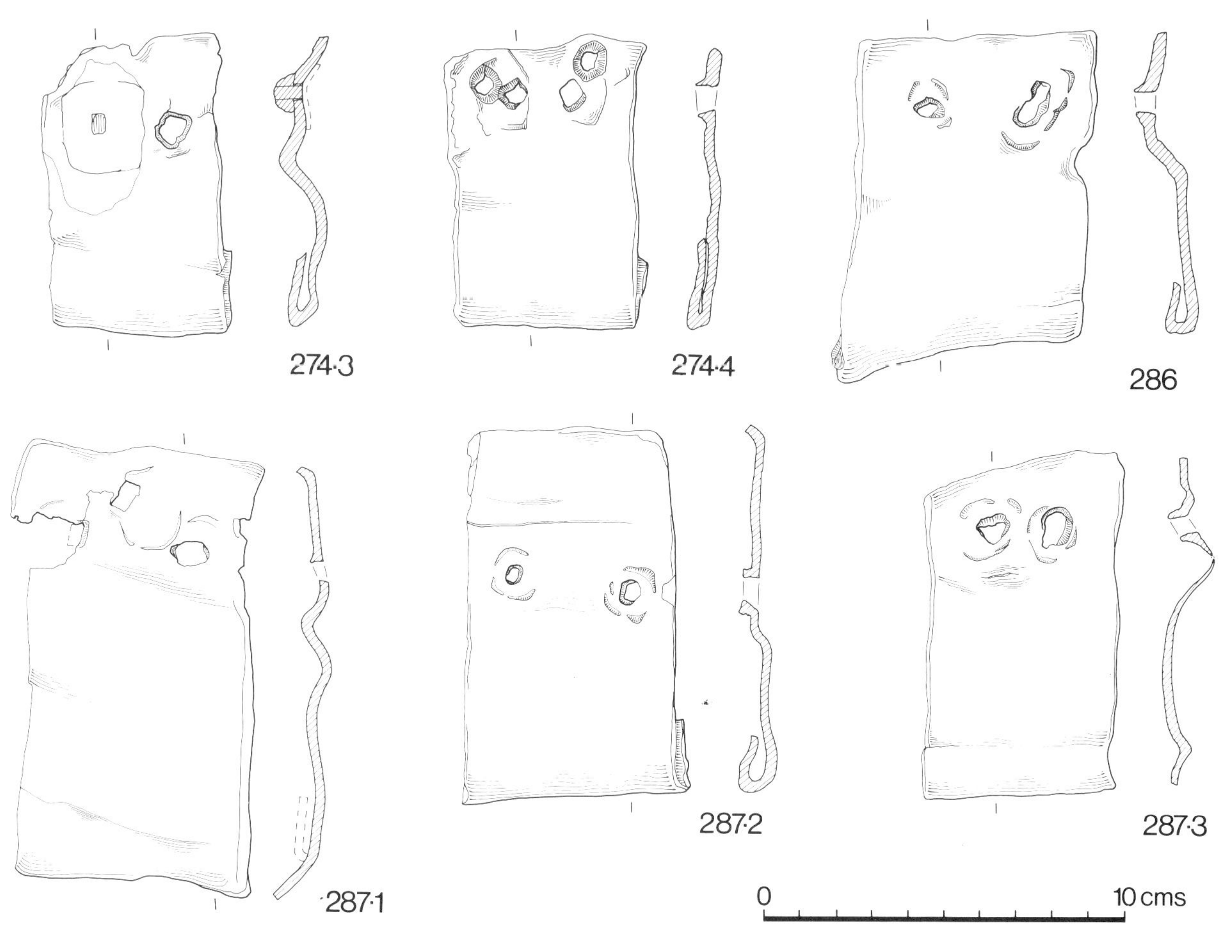

Fig. 72. Lead roof fittings.

***287/US** Three pieces of lead sheet, two with two nail holes and one piece with three holes in one end, 120mm. by 63mm., 118mm. by 58mm., 95mm. by 55mm. No provenance. *Fig.* 72.

288/1960 Rough irregular lead sheet, bent in half, *c.* 25mm. by 75mm., with oval perforation along one edge. Scrap. Kitchen Yard, KY 8.

289/1956 Fragment of lead sheet, 18mm. by 58mm., with piece partly cut off one side.
Fragment of lead sheet, 15mm. by 50mm., with piece partly cut off one side.
Fragment of lead sheet, 5mm. by 54mm.
All Drain D 1, BD XI 2.

290/1960-61 Irregular shaped fragment of lead or lead alloy sheet, with the remains of a circular perforation along one broken edge. Length 23.8mm. Kitchen Yard, KY 4.

Lead strips

291/1960-63 Fragment of folded lead strip, length 40mm., width 9mm., tapering to a point. Kitchen Yard, KY 10 1.

292/1956 Fragment of lead strip, length 35mm., width 8mm., with one end rounded. Structures south of Kitchen Yard, WR 9 6.

293/1958 Fragment of lead strip, 8mm. by 45mm. One end is split. Structures south of Kitchen Yard, WR baulk 9/10, topsoil.

294/1959 Fragment of bent lead strip, 3mm. by 25mm. Structures south of Kitchen Yard, WR 14 2.

295/1959 Irregular fragment of lead strip, 10mm. by 55mm. Infirmary, I 5, topsoil.

***296/1959** Curving piece of lead strip, length 85mm., square section, width tapering from 6mm. to 3mm., with the other end splayed and tapered. ?Stylus. Infirmary, I 9 2. *Fig.* 73.

297/1957 Bent fragment of irregular lead strip, width from 10mm. to 25mm., length 80mm. Edges slightly inturned, ends damaged. Meat Kitchen: rooms at south end, MKA 5.

298/US Fragment of tapering lead strip, one end folded over, length 70mm., width from 20mm. to 30mm. Abbot's Lodging, T 1, topsoil.

299/1959 Rectangular lead strip, one end bent over, length 58mm., width from 23mm. to 24mm. Structures south of Kitchen Yard, WR 13A.

300/1959 Fragment of lead strip, length 88mm., tapering in width from 35mm. to 20mm. One end rolled over and one edge partially cut. Infirmary, I 4 1.

***301/1959**
*1 Tapering fragment of lead strip, length 62mm., width from 1mm. to 11mm. Remains of a small, circular perforation along one edge. Possibly re-shaped piece of waste lead for use as a stylus. *Fig.* 73.
2 Curved fragment of rectangular lead strip, length 35mm., width 5mm.
Both Infirmary, I 12 2.

***302/1953** Rectangular lead strip, 20mm. by 74mm., with two rectangular nail holes. Iron corrosion surrounds one perforation, with the impression of the nail head in the other. Cloister, CL, topsoil. *Fig.* 73.

***303/1953** Rectangular lead strip, 14mm. by 62mm., with two rectangular nail holes. The faint impression of the square nail heads is visible Cloister, CL II, topsoil. *Fig.* 73.

***304/1953** Lead strip, length 38mm., width tapering from 20mm. to 12mm., with two rectangular nail holes. The impression of one nail head is visible. Cloister, CL IV 1. *Fig.* 73.

305/1953 Fragment of lead strip, L-shaped, with long sides bevelled, length 70mm., width 10mm. to 20mm. Off-cut. Cloister, CL II 1.

***306/1959** Fragment of lead sheet folded in half, 23mm. by 28mm., with nail in position through one half. Nail has rectangular sectioned shank; the head is corroded but appears to be thin and about 12mm. by 16mm. Lead strip has been folded over to protect iron nail head. Infirmary, I 4 1. *Fig.* 73.

***307/1960-63**
*1 Folded rectangular lead strip, 20mm. by 23mm., with iron nail *in situ*, strip folded over to protect iron nail head. *Fig.* 73.
2 Thin rectangular strip of lead, length *c.* 40mm., width 0.9mm.
*3 Twisted and bent fragment of lead strip, length 105mm., width from 5mm. to 20mm. *Fig.* 73.
All Kitchen Yard.

308/1960-63 Fragment of bent and twisted lead strip, length *c.* 65mm., width 3mm. to 5mm. Kitchen Yard, KY 6, topsoil.

309/1960-63 Six fragments of twisted and folded lead strip, lengths between 15mm. and 40mm. Kitchen Yard.

310/1958 Large fragment of lead strip, tapering at both ends, and one end folded, length 190mm., width 3mm to 20mm.
Damaged fragment of twisted and folded lead strip, length 100mm., width 13mm. to 15mm.
Two fragments of folded lead strip, one strip has two rectangular perforations, 15mm. by 81mm., 20mm. by 76mm.
Two tapering fragments of lead strip, lengths 50mm., 70mm. One has a hook-shaped end.
All structures south of Kitchen Yard, WR.

311/1963-64 Fragment of lead strip, one end folded over, 30mm. by 158mm.
Two fragments of narrow curved, tapering lead strip, lengths 33mm., 34.
All structures south of Kitchen Yard, WR A-H.

312/1956 Fragment of lead strip 15mm. by 55mm., with edges inturned. Lead caulking for fixing iron into stonework.
Lead strip, length 80mm., one end rounded,

width 25mm. to 27mm. Lead caulking for fixing iron into stonework.

Both structures south of Kitchen Yard, BD 25 4.

313/1956 Two fragments of irregular lead strip *c.* 30mm. by 100mm., *c.* 20mm. by 100mm. Drain D1, BD XI 1.

314/US Lead strip, oval section, broken at one end, flattened and broken at other, one end melted, 74mm. by 13mm., width 20mm. Function unknown.

Lead strip, length 79mm., width tapering from 12mm. to 3mm.

Fourteen fragments of thin lead strip, lengths between 13mm. and 35mm., widths all 3mm. to 4mm.

All no provenance.

315/1959 Lead strip, 94mm. by 4mm. by 2mm. Infirmary, I 6, topsoil.

316/1959 Lead strip, length *c.* 75mm., width tapering from 11mm. to 7mm. Structures south of Kitchen Yard, WR 14 2.

317/1960-61 Portion of a fairly thick rectangular sectioned strip, tapering at one end. Offcut. Two deep V-shaped channels indicate attempts at cutting the strip. Length 51mm., width 10.9mm., thickness 4.2mm. Kitchen Yard, KY 4 2.

318/1960-61 Two narrow, irregular strips of lead, possibly split came. Lengths 23.5mm. and 38mm. Kichen Yard, KY 4 2A.

Lead piping

***319/US** A length of lead piping made from a rolled sheet of lead; the seam is clearly visible. A joint, roughly rounded in section, is located about a third of the way along its length. The pipe is oval in section and one end is flattened. Length 484mm. Dimensions: external 32.8mm. by 29.8mm., internal 26.2mm. by 23.2mm; No provenance. *Fig.* 74.

***320/1963** A length of piping made from a rolled sheet of lead, the seam is clearly visible, oval in section. One end of the pipe has been bent (upwards) and flattened. The opposite end has a plano-convex section joint, indicating that the joint was sealed after the piping had been laid in the ground. Length 238mm. Dimensions: external 40.6mm. by 32.7mm., internal 32mm. by 27.1mm. Kitchen, K NE 2. *Fig.* 74.

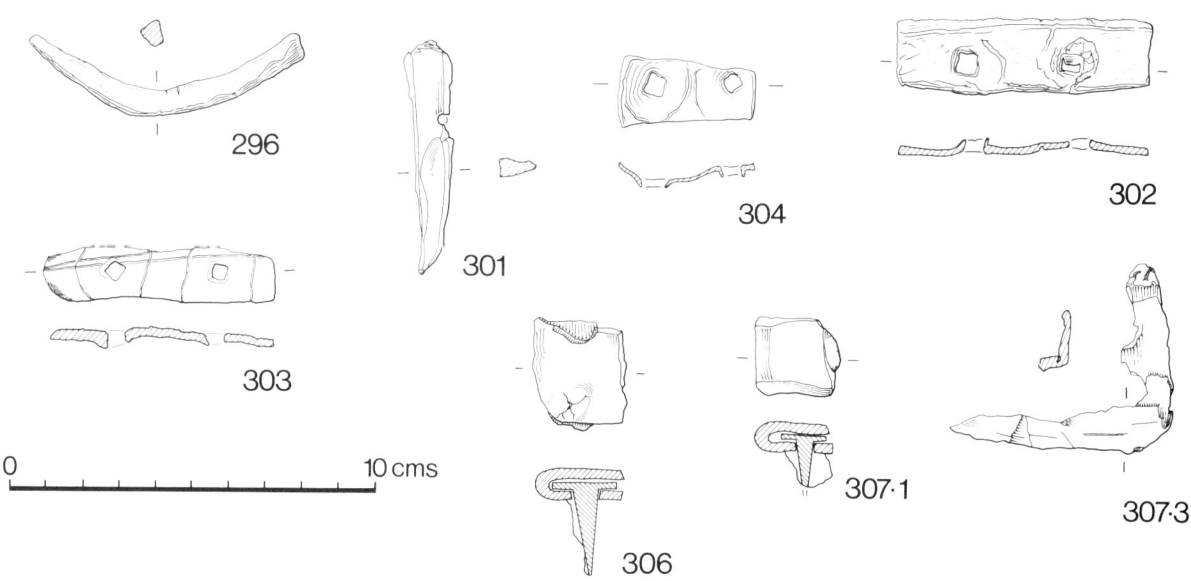

Fig. 73. Lead objects.

***321/US** Length of piping made from a rolled sheet of lead; the seam is clearly visible. Oval in section. One end has been flattened, the opposite end has a joint and a very damaged portion of piping leading from it. Length 421mm. (excluding damaged end). Dimensions: external 44mm. by 38.3mm. No provenance. *Fig.* 74.

322/1952 Length of fairly broad piping made from a rolled sheet of lead, the seam is clearly visible. Roughly oval in section, length 825mm. Dimensions: external 56.5mm. by 55mm., internal 48.5mm. by 43.6mm. Warming House, WH.

***323/1952** Length of fairly broad piping made from a rolled sheet of lead, the seam is clearly visible. One end is flattened. Oval in section. Length 927mm. Dimensions: external 63.1mm. by 47mm., internal 56.3mm. by 40.2mm. Warming House, WH. *Fig.* 74.

***324/US** Length of fairly narrow pipe made from a rolled sheet of lead, the seam of which is visible. One end has been flattened. Oval in section. Length 587mm. Dimensions: external 27mm. by 25.5mm., internal 20.3mm. by 17.3mm. No provenance. *Fig.* 74.

325/US Length of fairly narrow lead pipe made from a rolled sheet of lead, the seam of which is visible. Both ends have been flattened. Oval in section. Length 1007mm. Dimensions: external 27.6mm. by 25.7mm. No provenance.

***326/1952** Length of fairly broad pipe made from a rolled sheet of lead, the seam of which is clearly visible. An irregular shaped joint, with two faces flattened, occurs about a third of the way along the length of the pipe. Length 755mm. Dimensions: external 53mm. by 56mm., internal 44.1mm. by 46.3mm. Warming House, WH. *Fig.* 74.

Lead waste

327/1959 Two small lumps. Infirmary, I 10, topsoil.

328/1960-63 Two lumps. Kichen Yard, KY 8.

329/1960 Three small fragments. Cloisters, WC 1 1.

330/1963-64 Two fragments. Structures south of Kitchen Yard, WR A-H.

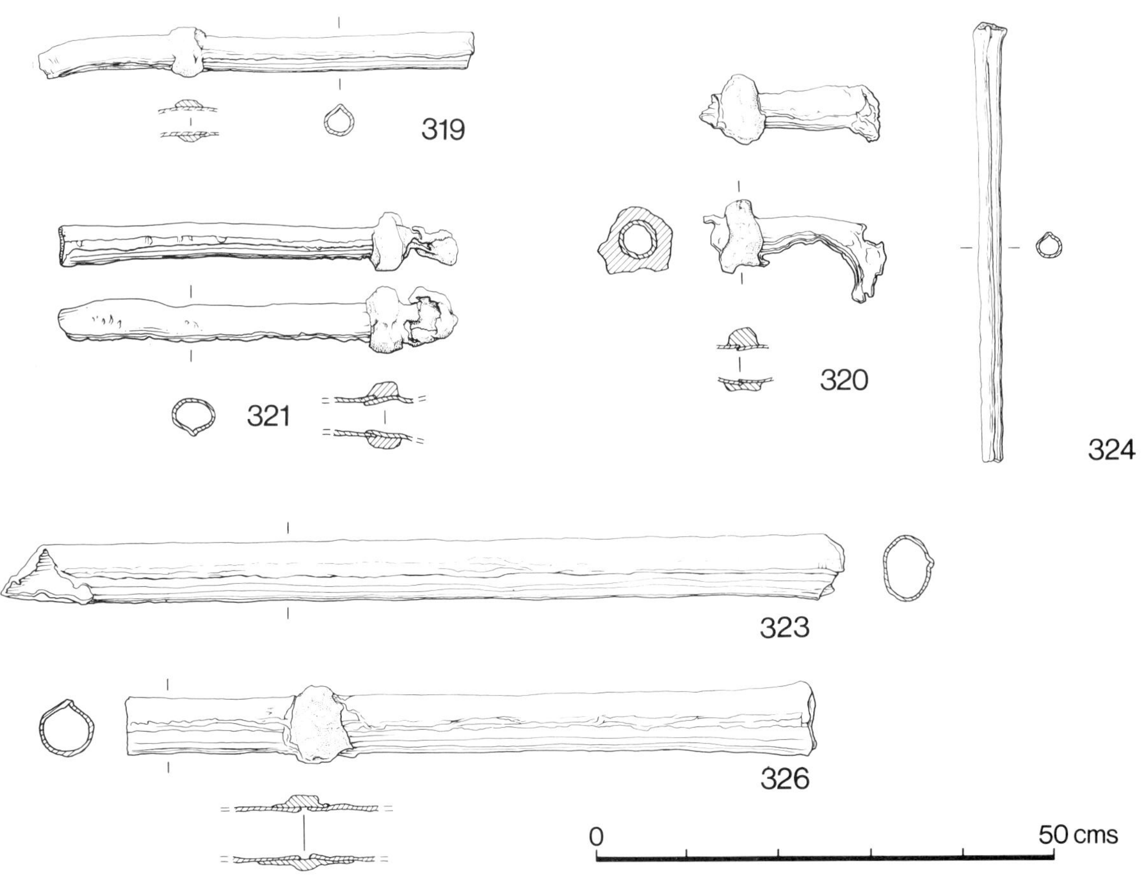

Fig. 74. Lead piping.

Worked bone

***331/1952** Bone ? skewer, made from a long bone split lengthwise and tapering to a point. Areas of polish survive. Length 172mm. Warming House, WH 7-8. *Fig.* 75.

***332/1952** Bone handle, made from a long bone split in half, length 102mm. Outer edges squared off and polished, hollow sub-rectangular section, 20mm. by 25mm. Warming House, WH 7-8. *Fig.* 75.

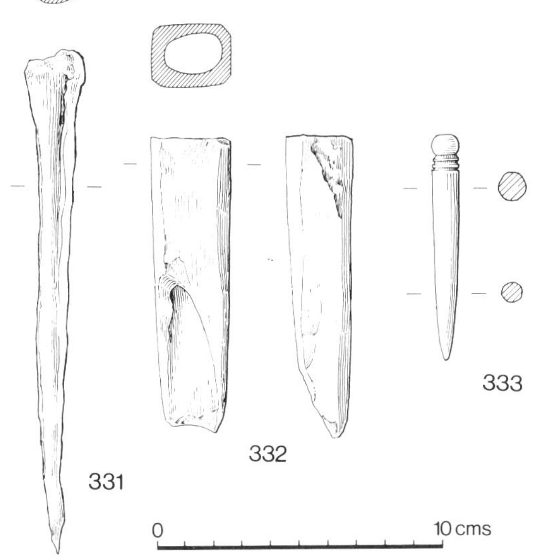

Fig. 75. Bone objects.

***333/US** Bone pin or parchment pricker, length 78mm., circular section, diameter 10mm., tapering to a point. The head is ball-shaped with two parallel grooves encircling the junction of the head and shank. No provenance. No longer extant. *Fig.* 75.

Window glass

All the potash window glass excluding three cobalt blue fragments, which may be soda-lime-silica composition, are badly corroded, some to an extent where the original colour has become impossible to detect.

Translucent colourless panes

334/1960-63 Five fragments with opaque matt black surfaces, in a sandwich containing colourless glass, between 6mm. and 17mm. across, thickness 2.2mm. Kitchen Yard.

335/1960-63 Five fragments with opaque matt black and silvery corrosion products. Interior layer of translucent pitted colourless glass, thickness: 1.4mm., 1.5mm., 1.5mm., 1.85mm. Kitchen Yard, 23 1.

***336/1960-63** Single fragment, length *c.* 45mm; with translucent and silvery corrosion products. Hydration layers visible in section. Surface possibly painted in a red-brown colour, though may be a corrosion product. Three grozed edges survive, suggesting a rectangular quarry Thickness 3.1mm. Kitchen Yard 2 extension, drain fill. *Fig.* 76.

337/1963-64 Totally disintegrated, mainly opaque granular devitrified panes containing three badly pitted translucent colourless fragments. Up to *c.* 10mm. across, thickness 4.1mm. Structures south of Kitchen Yard, WR E, topsoil.

338/1958 Totally opaque pale brown black outer surface with sandwich of opaque yellow and translucent colourless glass, thickness 3.2mm. A portion of one grozed edge survives. Structures south of Kitchen Yard, WR 9 N2.

339/US Fragment 35mm. long, black corrosion around outside, sub-rectangular with translucent colourless interior, thickness 2.1mm. No provenance.

Translucent green panes

***340/1955** Five fragments of window panes up to 55mm. long, of pale apple green tint. All are covered with patches of silvery corrosion. Thickness 2.2mm., 2.3mm., 2.6mm., 3.2mm. One fragment retains three grozed edges. Refectory, topsoil. *Fig.* 76.

341/1956 One pane *c.* 65mm. long, pale green colour covered with opaque matt black corrion, thickness 4.6mm. Abbot's Lodging, AH VI 1.

***342/US** Two panes both of translucent apple green tint, with opaque brown surface corrosion. Both up to 30mm. across, the longest (45mm. long), retains three grozed edges suggesting a rectangular quarry, thickness 3.6mm. No provenance. *Fig.* 76.

***343/US** Sub-triangular shaped fragment with a weak green hue covered with opaque black corrosion layers. May approximate to original window pane shape, thickness 2.45mm. Portions of two grozed edges survive. No provenance. *Fig.* 76.

344/US Three joining fragments of pale green window panes which appear to form a portion of a sub-rectangular quarry, estimated 8.4mm.×6.4mm. Corrosion products of silvery and opaque brown. Thickness 1.8mm. No provenance.

345/1956 Pane *c.* 45mm. long, of weak green tint and translucent pale brown corrosion. Thickness 0.9mm. Abbot's Lodging, I, topsoil.

346/1953 Three panes of weak apple green glass containing small air bubbles of up to 1mm. diameter. Translucent silver and black surface corrosion. The larger pane, 48mm. long, may have originally been a square or sub-rectangular quarry; portions of two grozed edges survive. Cloister, CL II, topsoil.

347/1953 A single broken triangular shaped pane *c.* 35mm. long, of very weak pale green hue and covered with silver and opaque black corrosion products, thickness 1.4mm. Cloister, CL II 1.

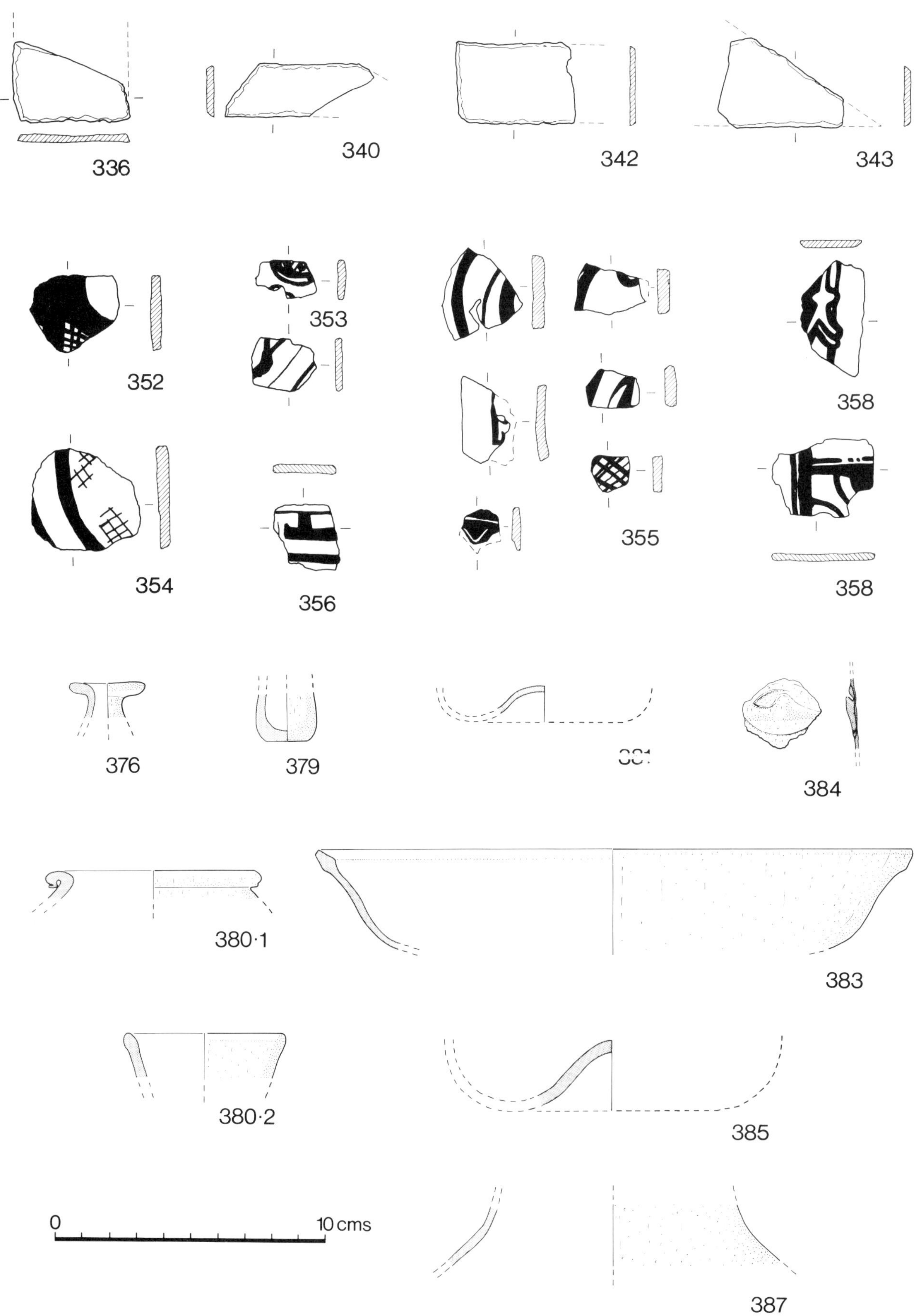

Fig. 76. Glass: nos 336-358, window glass; nos 376-387, vessel glass.

348/1960 Well preserved fragment, perhaps soda composition, full of air bubbles. Pale green colour, with no discernable original edges, thickness 1.3mm. Cloister, CL II 6.

Translucent blue panes

349/1956 Cobalt blue fragment. Visible surface of surviving glass is pitted by corrosion. The other side has an accretion of opaque black corrosion, thickness 2.4mm. Abbot's Lodging, III, topsoil.

350/1961 Three joining fragments of translucent cobalt blue window panes. All are in extremely good condition with little surface deterioration. This suggests that the glass is of soda-lime-silica composition and not of the potash-based glass which has probably been used to make those described so far. The longest side of the smallest fragment (35mm.), has a rounded edge, which evidently fitted into a lead window came. The largest of the three fragments also has this feature and it is *c.* 5mm. in length. Similar cobalt blue soda glass, of twelfth-century date, has come from York. Thickness 2.7mm; Kitchen Yard KY 8, topsoil.

351/US Translucent cobalt blue pane with one smoothed rounded pane edge. Well preserved. Thickness 2.65mm. No provenance.

Painted glass

***352/1953** A black, badly weathered fragment *c.* 30mm. long with a red-brown coating of paint over *c.* 60% of one surface in no particular pattern. Before the glass became weathered the ground colour of the glass was probably translucent and colourless, the evidence for this being a thin colourless core. Thickness 3.5mm. 1953, topsoil. *Fig.* 76.

***353/1955** Three fragments, part of one and possibly part of a second cut edge remain on the largest fragment. It has a core of colourless glass and one surface has two parallel stripes of opaque, fired-on red paint as well as a third branching strip. Two smaller joining fragments are also on one face with fired-on paint. Thickness 2.8mm., 2.2mm. Refectory, R5 9. *Fig.* 76.

***354/1953** Sub-rectangular fragment of 37mm. maximum length. Original flat edge, length 12mm. remains. Decorated with a lattice pattern of fired-on opaque red paint apparently overlaid by a swirling design in paint. It is impossible to determine the original ground colour. Thickness 4.2mm. Refectory, FR II 2. *Fig.* 76.

***355/1956?** Twenty-four fragments of painted glass panes with a colourless translucent ground colour visible in the section of one fragment. Opaque red-brown paint forms a combination of criss-crossed lattice pattern and a more random wavy pattern on one surface. One fragment has a rounded-off original edge consistent with its use within lead window cames. Thicknesses range from 3mm. to 4.8mm. Drain D 1, BD XI 1. *Fig.* 76.

***356/1956?** Two fragments with opaque red-brown paint on one face. The smaller fragment *c.* 15mm. across, has a discernible pale green ground colour. The painted pattern on the larger fragment incorporates three parallel lines, two of which are joined with a single transverse line. Thicknesses 3.6mm., 3mm. Drain D 1, BD XI 2. *Fig.* 76.

357/1963-64 Colourless translucent pane fragment with traces of red-brown paint on one face in no discernible pattern. Opposite face has opaque black corrosion products. Thickness 2.2mm. Structures south of Kitchen Yard, WR D 1.

***358/1956?** Two fragments with traces of red-brown fired-on painted patterns on one side. One fragment has a colourless translucent ground colour although both are opacified by black corrosion products. Thickness 3mm., 2.8mm. Drain D 1, BD XI 2. *Fig.* 76.

359/1960-63 Small sub-triangular fragment of totally laminated glass with traces of reddish-brown paint, possibly a portion of a lattice work design. No original edges survive. Thickness 2.4mm. Kitchen Yard, KY 10 1.

Wholly or partially devitrified window pane fragments

Most of these fragments have formed crystalline silicates as a result of devitrification, occasionally with traces of a glassy substance sandwiched at the centre between black layers of corrosion.

360/1950 Two fragments. Kitchen Yard 1950, below sand layer under flags.

361/1956 Three fragments. Meat Kitchen, MK III 1.

362/1958 Four fragments, two of which have original straight edge preserved. Structures south of Kitchen Yard, WR 9 N 2.

363/1956? Single fragment with opaque silver surface devitrification. Thickness 3.4mm. Drain Dl, BD X1.

364/1955 Four fragments. Refectory R 2 4.

365/1958 Five fragments, thickness 4.4mm. One fragment retains portions of two grozed edges. Structures south of Kitchen Yard, WR 14 1.

366/1958 Six fragments. Structures south of Kitchen Yard, WR 14 1.

367/1963-64 One fragment, thickness 4.6mm. Structures south of Kitchen Yard, WR A/B 1.

368/1962 Three fragments, thickness 4.9mm. Structures south of Lay Brothers' Reredorter, LR X 1.

369/1962 Four fragments, many smaller. Structures of Lay Brothers' Reredorter. LR X 1.

370/1962 One fragment with associated powder. Structures south of Lay Brothers' Reredorter, LR.

371/1960-63 Sixteen fragments, thickness *c.* 3.8mm. Kitchen Yard, KY 4 2.

372/1960-63 One fragment with opaque yellow ?corrosion, thickness 3.8mm. One fragment with black corrosion. Both Kitchen Yard, KY 4 2A.

373/1960-63 One fragment, thickness 3.6mm., retaining rounded pane edge. Kitchen Yard, KY 23, topsoil.

374/US Fourteen fragments: two fragments have portions of rounded pane edges while a third fragment retains portions of two grozed edges at right angles. Thicknesses between 1.8mm. and 5mm. No provenance.

Vessel glass

375/1958 Very pale green moulded wall fragment from a modern octagonal vessel. Structures south of Kitchen Yard, WR 13A, topsoil.

***376/1958** Rim in apple green glass, possibly from one half of an hour glass, 27mm. diameter, of medieval date. Structures south of Kitchen Yard, WR 14, topsoil. *Fig.* 76.

377/1960-63 Two fragments, both badly corroded and opaque. The larger is a base sherd *c.* 30mm. long, possibly from a flask of uncertain date. Kitchen Yard, KY 10 1.

378/1960-63 Cylindrical, curved fragment, originally colourless glass with silver corrosion. Possibly part of a spout from a glass ewer, distorted. Post-medieval. Kitchen Yard, KY 8 2.

***379/1956** Totally devitrified, but consolidated, fragment of the base and wall of a hanging lamp. Base *c.* 15mm. diameter. Abbot's Lodging, AH VI 1. *Fig.* 76.

***380/1953** Two fragments. One opaque devitrified rim sherd, form unknown, but possibly a rim from a small alembic. The second fragment is badly weathered, possibly a rolled-over rim sherd from a vessel. Refectory, FR I 3. *Fig.* 76.

***381/1953** Pale light green with silvery corrosion from the centre of the base of a glass vessel of late medieval date, form uncertain. Cloister, CL I, topsoil. *Fig.* 76.

382/1953 Colourless curving sherd of clear, colourless glass from a modern glass vessel, scratched outer surface. Cloister, CL IV, topsoil.

***383/1953** Five totally devitrified fragments of a vessel, possibly a bowl. Four of the fragments are rim sherds. No provenance. *Fig.* 76.

***384/1959** Single body piece, possibly from a beaker in clear colourless glass, with light green hue to the applied prunt. Late medieval, possibly English. Infirmary, I 9, topsoil. *Fig.* 76.

***385/US** Translucent green portion from the base of a flask, late medieval, English. No provenance. *Fig.* 76.

386/US Ribbed translucent colourless wall of a hexagonal bottle, modern. No provenance.

***387/1953** Weathered opaque yellow core and black outer corrosion, curved, possibly the shoulder of a flask. Cloister, CL II, brown clay. *Fig.* 76.

388/US Large translucent green sherd, covered with opaque black corrosion. Possibly from the base of a large jar of nineteenth-century date. No provenance.

Coins and jettons

389/1 Richard I, 1190-94. Short-cross cut halfpenny, Class IIb. Bath drain (Dl) trench in Meat Kitchen.

390/1959 John 1199-1216. Short-cross halfpenny, Class V. Infirmary south aisle, 2.

391/1953 John-Henry III, 1205-18. Short-cross York penny, Class V, *Tomas*. Refectory, FR.

392/1953 Henry III, *c.* 1218-23. London penny, Class ?VI, *Rauf*. Refectory, FR.

393/1951 Henry III, 1223-42. Canterbury penny, Class VIII, *Roger*. Unstratified in north-west corner of Warming House Courtyard.

394/1952 Henry V, 1413-22. London Groat. In sand layer beneath drain in Warming House.

395/1950 Alexander III, 1249-85. Scottish long-cross penny. Unstratified, in south-west corner of Kitchen courtyard.

396/1952 Charles the Bold of Burgundy, 1467-77. Double patard struck in Burgundy. Inside drain in Warming House.

397/1958 Mary, 1553-54. Penny. Structures south of Kitchen Yard, WR 12, topsoil.

398/1962 Edward II? (1307-1327). Canterbury Penny. Structures south of Lay Brothers' Reredorter.

399/1959 Anglo-Gallic jetton. Infirmary, 1.

400/1959 French jetton ? Infirmary.

401/1964 Anglo-Gallic jetton. Infirmary, I 16 1.

402/1952 French jetton, late fifteenth century. Below cobbles north of Meat Kitchen.

403/1956 Netherlands jetton *c.* 1490-1520. In rubble below flags in Meat Kitchen,

404/1961 Nuremberg jetton, sixteenth century. Kitchen Yard, topsoil.

405/1957 ?Imitation jetton. Drain Dl, MKA 7 1.

406/1950 Rochdale halfpenny, 1792. Kitchen courtyard, unstratified.

407/1963 Edward IV, 1464. M. Dolley reports: 'Coin weight for the half rose-noble issued in 1464. Theoretical weight 60 grains, actual weight 58.8 grains'. Cloister, WC 2 2 (mortar over wall footings).

Stone

Domestic objects

***408/1960-63** Sandstone disc, roughly circular in plan, *c.* 50mm., thickness 12mm., edges unfinished. Kitchen Yard, topsoil. *Fig.* 77.

***409/1962** Sandstone spindle whorl, disc diameter 27.7mm., with central hole, diameter 5.6mm., and rectangular section, thickness 7.6mm. Structures south of Lay Brothers' Reredorter, LR IX 2. *Fig.* 77.

***410/1956?** Curving fragment from the body of a marble mortar with the edge of one side handle surviving. Thickness 32.6mm. expanding at handle to 41.6mm. Drain Dl, BD XI. *Fig.* 77.

***411/1958** Portion of a small, perforated whetstone, originally of rectangular cross section. The perforation was initially bored from one side and appears to have split when the perforation began to be bored from the opposing side. Present length 36.7mm., thickness 6.2mm. Structures south of Kitchen Yard, WR 9 3. *Fig.* 77.

Architectural pieces

***412/1958** Fragment of magnesian limestone column base or capital, diameter *c.* 156mm., with compass-drawn circle, diameter 115mm., divided into four quarters incised on one face, presumably for the placing of the column shaft. Structures south of Kitchen Yard, WR 13 1. *Fig.* 78.

***413/1957** Fragment of magnesian limestone column base or capital, broken in half, diameter *c.* 157mm. Structures south of Kitchen Yard, WR I 1. *Fig.* 78.

414/1963 Fragment of magnesian limestone column shaft, split in half, diameter *c.* 110mm., length 70mm. Cloister Lane, WC 6 1.

Fig. 78.

***415/1956?** Fragment of gritstone window or door moulding, length 8mm. Drain, Dl, BD XI 1. *Fig.* 78.

***416/US** Thackstone of sub-rectangular plan and section with off-centre perforation. The perforation has first been chiselled and then bored. Length 330mm., width 194mm., tile size 11 inches. No provenance. *Fig.* 78.

417/1956 Small portion of a sandstone thackstone retaining approximately half of a bored and chiselled perforation. Thickness 16.2mm. Drain D 1, BD VII 1.

Mortar and plaster

418/1955 Two lumps mortar, *c.* 50mm. by 60mm. Refectory.

419/1960-63 One lump pinkish plaster, length 80mm., width 50mm., thickness 30mm. Kitchen Yard, KY 5, topsoil.

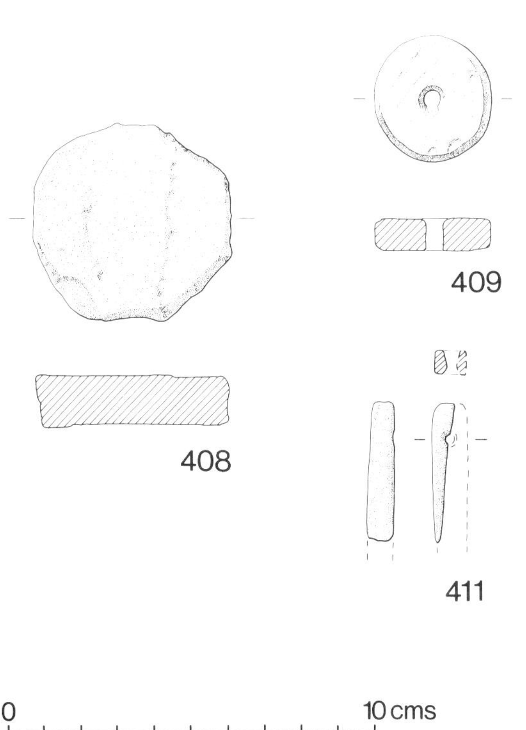

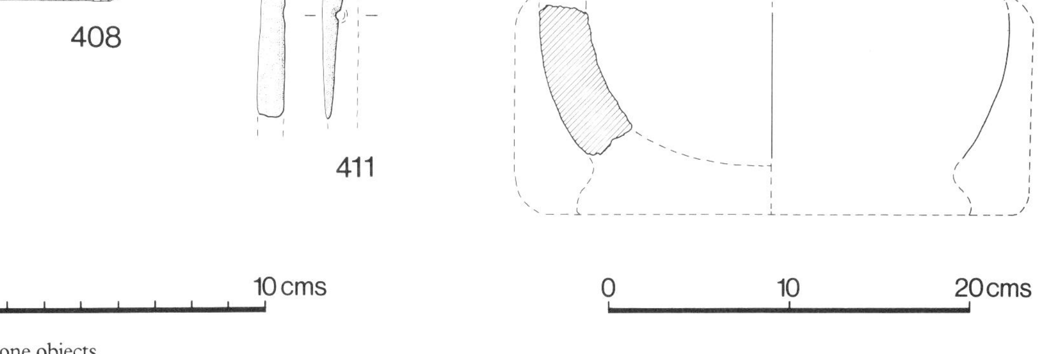

Fig. 77. Stone objects.

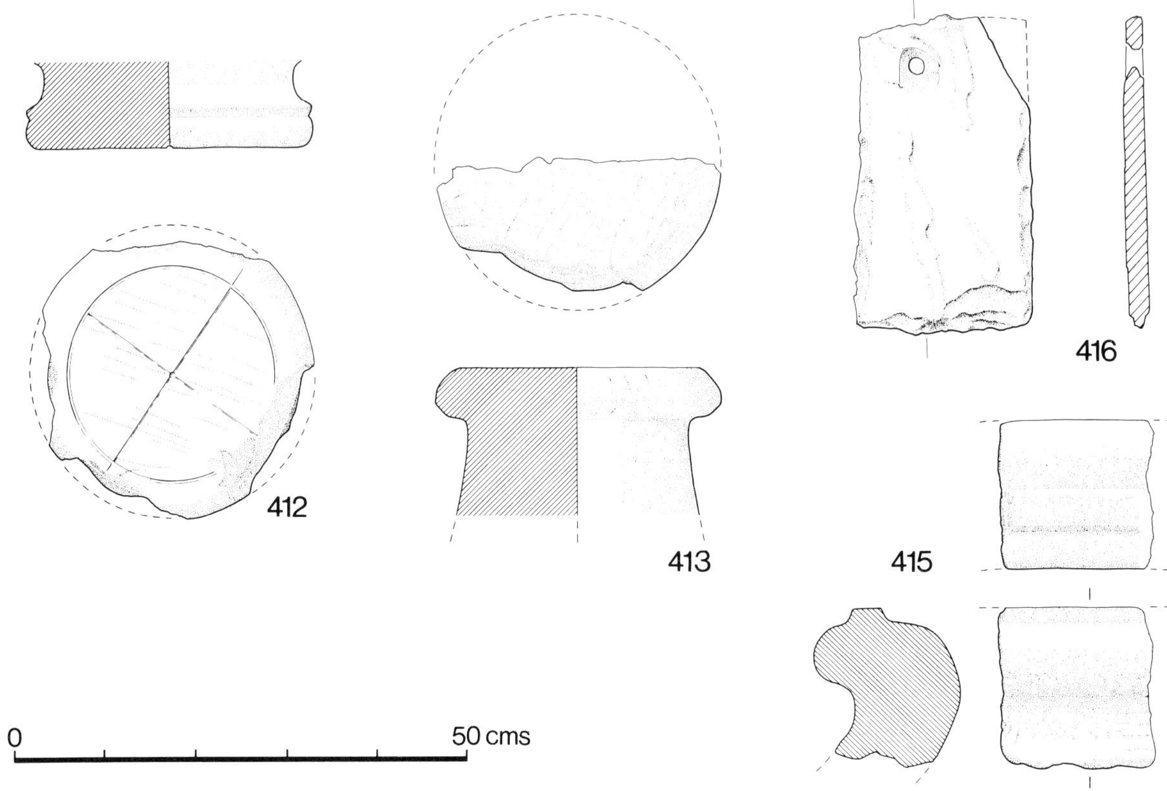

Fig. 78. Architectural stonework.

Chapter 17
The Evidence of Metal Working

Introduction

The surviving assemblage of site finds contains only a small amount of slag, yet it is clear from the published reports that some parts of the Abbey produced considerable quantities of metal-working debris. Immediately after excavation, some of this material was subjected to chemical analysis, and the resulting reports on slag composition must remain the definitive account.[194] The interpretations based on these analyses are, however, reassessed here; as is the metal-working pit in the Kitchen (p. 25). A list of contexts recorded as containing slag is also appended.

The most significant concentration of slag was found around the Cloister cistern (Chapter 3), intermixed with a spread of charcoal. It was undoubtedly derived from metal working either within or immediately outside the excavated area. Dr E. Simister analysed some of the slag, and suggested that the lumps were scrapings from a furnace bottom, derived perhaps from a cleaning-out operation.[195] The slag and charcoal deposit was stratigraphically earlier than the Cloister cistern, which was itself probably (though not certainly) a feature of the primary water-supply system (see Chapter 3, p.9). The metal working may therefore have been associated with the initial building operations.

The slag found elsewhere in the excavations was recovered mainly from two contexts which indicated redeposition. Both groups may, in fact, have been derived from the Cloister metal-working site. The first came from the make-up layers of the early thirteenth century Refectory floor.[196] A more varied collection was found in the backfill of the Warming House water-pipe trench, a deposit which can also be dated to the early thirteenth century.[197] Samples from these groups were analysed by Dr R. Haynes.[198] He concluded that iron ore had been smelted directly with charcoal to produce metal and slag; and he suggested that local ores may have been worked.[199] Copper was found in the slag, and Haynes suggested that they have been smelted in the same furnace.[200]

Comments on the metal-working evidence

by P. N. Cheetham

It should be noted that copper smelting slags are similar to iron-smelting slags of the bloomery period, the only distinctive feature being the copper and sulphur content.[201] Haynes notes that 'the presence of copper is unusual' in his analysis of the iron smelting slag.[202] In a more detailed report of the analysis,[203] sulphur is also shown to be present at a low concentration. The iron content of 5.78% is very low for medieval iron smelting slags and cinder,[204] and equally low for a copper smelting slag,[205] although the copper content is comparable.[206] The composition of the slag is similar to crucible slags formed in smelting or melting operations,[207] the comparative analysis being (by percentage):

Composition	York[208] (Roman or 12th-13th century) crucible slag	Meare, Somerset[209] (early Iron Age) slaggy glaze	Kirkstall Abbey[210] (13th century) cindery mass
SiO_2	57.1	66.8	73.58
Fe_2O_3	8.6	7.3 (Fe 0)	5.78 (Fe 0)
Al_2O_3	19.6	14.5	14.28
Cu 0	2.0	2.0	3.16
Ca 0	3.0	6.2	1.66
Mg 0	1.73	2.0	1.08
Pb 0	6.70	trace	0.22
S	—	0.3	0.018

This suggests that we may be dealing with a crucible residue from copper smelting operations, an interpretation re-inforced by the association of some partially smelted copper alloy charge in the same deposits.[211] Piaskowski argued against Haynes' interpretation of the 'iron smelting slag', suggesting that it represented a crucible or foundry furnace lining. This was based on the evidence of similar material derived from a sixteenth-century bronze foundry in Cracow, Poland.[212] In his reply, Haynes maintained that there was strong evidence of iron founding, if not unequivocally smelting, at the site of the Abbey.[213]

Haynes' suggestion that tin ore was smelted with copper or copper ore may be supported. Recent work on the possibilities of the method,[214] and the identification of a medieval (1300-1700AD) tin mine producing only dressed ore,[215] combined with the lack of evidence for tin smelting sites of the period in Cornwall,[216] suggest that both ores could have been smelted together. Piaskowski, however, stated that 'this method was unknown', apparently basing his argument on negative documentary evidence; and he considered the partially smelted charge to be a bronze melting slag.[217] The evidence presented by Haynes, in reply, suggested this was not the case.[218]

Thirteenth-century 'tap cinder' is reported from Kirkstall but the results presented do not apparently represent a complete analysis.[219] Although the composition is more comparable with iron slag and cinder, as opposed to a copper smelting slag, this may not represent conclusive evidence of iron smelting at the site of the Abbey.

Haynes also proposed from the results of his analysis of the lead residues that the lead had been desilvered by cupellation.[220] This was based on the silver content of 0.0085% (2.8oz per ton). Analysis of the silver yields of Yorkshire and Derbyshire ores, however, gives a range of 1-4oz per ton typically.[221] The low silver content of the Kirkstall lead cannot therefore be used to provide evidence of the cupellation of lead at Kirkstall or elsewhere. High yield veins did exist in the region: the Rimington Lead and Barytes is reported to have yielded 416oz per ton, and was worked illicitly during the reign of Elizabeth I.[222] For the majority of ores, however, the extraction process, which was expensive in terms of time, fuel and significant losses of lead, would not have been attempted.

The smelting of lead in the vicinity of the Abbey[223] would at first seem unlikely owing to the toxic and unsocial nature of the fumes, and to the more practical considerations of transporting ore rather than metal. In the post-medieval period the smelting of lead was invariably performed at the ore source.[224] A find of galena in the excavation (unfortunately unprovenanced) and finds of barytes (a lead gangue mineral) in medieval contexts of the Guest House site are, however, hard to explain unless some small-scale smelting operations were carried out in the vicinity of the site, or unless the material was deposited by natural agencies.

On balance the evidence presented would therefore suggest that bronze smelting did take place in the vicinity of the Abbey; but that the smelting of iron and lead needs further evidence before it may be confidently asserted.

Bell founding remains from the Abbey Kitchen

by Holly B. Duncan and Stuart Wrathmell.

During the 1954 excavation in the Kitchen area a pear-shaped pit was uncovered, cut down against the west side of the second-phase hearth.[225] In the bottom of the pit was an annular object of fired clay centrally placed on a hearth of flagstones. This was identified as the up-turned rim of a crucible.[226] The pit itself was filled with rubble, charcoal, bronze debris, fragments of fired clay and fifteenth-century pottery.[227]

The crucible as reconstructed in the drawing by Mr C. M. Mitchell[228] had iron suspension lugs, a lid and an inverted rim. It was the last feature in particular which led Dr Tylecote to question its identification.[229] The rim, although complete, lacked a pouring lip and would have presented difficulties if the crucible were used in casting. An analysis of the metallic waste indicated melting rather then smelting; and the high proportion of tin was consistent with the manufacture of bells or mirrors.[230]

In the light of these findings, and in view of more recent discoveries of similar remains at Cheddar, Somerset,[231] Thurgarton, Nottinghamshire,[232] and the Kirkstall Abbey Guest House,[233] the remains of the crucible were re-examined. This resulted in the identification of two sets (A and B) of bell mould fragments. Only one set (A) was substantial. This has been used to reconstruct the lower portions of the mould, and has enabled some details of manufacture to be established.

The various mould fragments comprising set (A) were found to belong to the lowest parts of both core and cope moulds (Fig. 79). Their curvature indicates a bell rim diameter of 34cm. The most significant feature of these remains is the skin of clay which extends beneath the mould, uniting the bases of the core and the cope. This feature suggests that manufacture was by the *cire perdu* method as described by Theophilus: the skin would have prevented the separation of the moulds to allow removal of a clay pattern.

The core of the mould is comprised of black loam with fibrous inclusions, presumably organic matter. This would have been applied, in successive layers, to a spindle former and shaped by turning. Once the bell was modelled in wax, further layers of loam were applied to form the cope. Two distinct layers were identified within the cope, marking a pause in the application, for drying. A series of iron rods were inserted into these layers during formation: they would appear to have been positioned, at bell rim level, around the mould at approximately 230mm. intervals and were probably ties for an iron binding strap. Evidence for only two of these rods survives, one largely as a void, the other more complete with a 'washer' embedded in the first layer of loam. Both the core and the cope extended well below the wax bell rim, ensuring a better seal for casting. In addition, once the former was removed, a clay skin was applied to the base of the outer wall of the cope, and was continued beneath both parts of the mould, lapping upwards over the inner face of the core.

Once the mould was completed, it was placed on the hearth stones in the pit and heated to liquify the wax and to remove any moisture from the clay. With the mould still in place, the pit was backfilled and the casting took place. After casting the pit was re-excavated to retrieve the bell. The mould was not, however, completely removed: the cope was broken just above bell rim level; and during extraction the outer clay skin ensured that not only the bottom part of the cope, but also the lowest layer of core remained intact and *in situ*.

Three further fragments of baked clay were found in the Kitchen pit (set B). These did not belong to set (A) and were presumably remains from an earlier casting. These fragments were identified in the 1954 excavation report as pieces of crucible lid. They are in fact part of the outer clay skin which united the core and cope. The diameter of the rim of this bell is estimated to have been about 30cm.

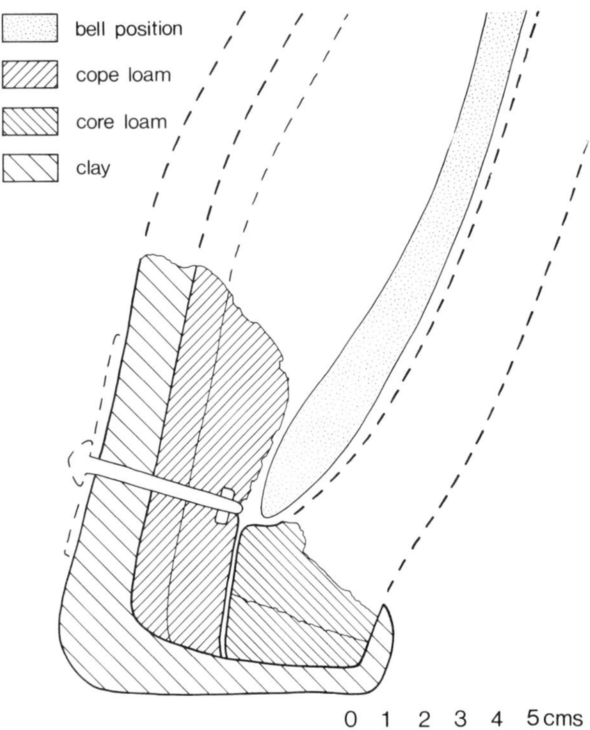

Fig. 79. Pieces of bell mould from the Abbey Kitchen pit, restored to their relative positions for casting.

Contexts recorded as producing slag

Iron slag finds came from the following contexts:

KY 4 4	19 2
KY 5 A	19 2
KY 8 2a	DSK unknown context
WR 9 2	BDX 1 drain construction trench under wall
WR 9 3	I 17 1 1
WR 9 5	KY 9 2a
WR 13 topsoil	KY 4 2a
WR 13 1B	KY 6 topsoil
WR 13 A topsoil	KY 5 1
WR 13 A topsoil	KY 6 6
WR 14 topsoil	MKA 5
WR 14 2	CL II 3 west
15 topsoil	WH 8

Lead slag finds came from the following contexts:

KY 4	KY 4 2
KY 4 8	I 4 1
KY 4 2a	MK III 2

Bronze slag came from the following contexts:

KY 10 1	KY 10 1a
KY 4 2a	MKA 5
KY 4 2	WH 8
KY 6 topsoil	

Chapter 18
The Animal Remains

The excavated animal bones and shells were largely discarded on site after examination. Fortunately, a series of detailed studies, with supporting quantification tables, was published in the Thoresby Society reports by Dr M. L. Ryder.[234] These are valuable, particularly, for their analysis of the large quantities of animal bone which were recovered from the so-called 'bone layer' around the Meat Kitchen (see Chapter 9).

Until the fourteenth century, the Cistercians adhered strictly to the rule of St. Benedict which prohibited the consumption of flesh meat, except by the sick. Thereafter, a series of relaxations in the rule allowed meat to be eaten by others in specific locations: first in the Infirmary and the abbot's lodging, and later in a separate refectory, the misericord.[235] At Kirkstall, the Misericord was built in the late fifteenth century on the ground floor of the old Refectory; and it was provided with its own Kitchen at the south-east corner of the dining hall block.

The 'bone layer' was located immediately to the west and south of the Meat Kitchen. It was a spread of dumped food refuse containing the remains of an estimated 5000 animals.[236] The 'bone layer' was not generally sealed by anything earlier than the nineteenth-century park levelling layer,[237] but some of the lowest pockets of bone lay beneath the drain which served the Meat Kitchen Scullery sink (Chapter 9 and Fig. 22).[238] The sink and therefore the drain may have been secondary features of the Meat Kitchen. On the other hand it may be that the animal bones began to accumulate before the surviving Meat Kitchen was erected, perhaps in association with the timber building which preceded it. Most of the bones had been chopped, but some were clean-cut as if sawn.[239] There is no need here to reproduce in full Dr Ryder's analysis; but we may note the overwhelming preponderance of ox bones.[240] Many bones were from relatively old animals, perhaps draught oxen grown too old to work.[241] Other animals represented were pigs, sheep and domestic fowl. There were also red, roe and fallow deer, wild duck, rabbit and fish including sea-water fish, perhaps cod.[242]

Elsewhere, an absence of monastic-period animal bones was to be expected, since the Infirmary Kitchen, which presumably served also the Abbot's Lodging, and adjacent areas were not investigated. The pig and sheep molars and fish vertebrae from the thirteenth-century Refectory floor make-up were presumably redeposited there along with the dumped earth.[243] The bones of a horse beneath the floor make-up represented a straight-forward burial.[244]

Oysters, cockles, mussels and whelks were all found in the bone layer, and both oysters and cockles were represented beneath the Meat Kitchen floor.[245] Large quantities of oyster and mussel shells were also found in and around the monastic Kitchen: they were numerous enough to form layers several inches in thickness.[246]

NOTES

1. Hope 1907, pp. 3-4.
2. *Report 11,* fig. 20.
3. *Report 1,* p. 2; *Report 2,* p. 13.
4. *Report 4,* p. 56.
5. *Report 6,* pp. 14-20.
6. Hope 1907, pp. 53, 58.
7. *Report 11,* pp. 1-5.
8. *Report 4,* fig. 14.
9. *Report 4,* p. 62.
10. *Report 4,* p.52.
11. *Report 4,* p. 51.
12. Hope 1907, pp. 40-1.
13. *Report 5,* pp. 68-70.
14. *Report 5,* p. 68.
15. *Report 3,* pp. 30-38.
16. Hope 1907, p. 43.
17. Hope 1907, p. 44, note 1.
18. Hope 1907, p. 44.
19. *Report 2,* pp. 13-18.
20. *Report 6,* pp. 11-13.
21. *Report 11,* pp. 60-65.
22. *Report 3,* fig. 10.
23. *Report 4,* p. 60; see p. 22.
24. *Report 11,* p. 60.
25. *Report 3,* p. 35.
26. *Report 6,* p. 11.
27. *Report 2,* p. 18.
28. *Report 3,* p. 33.
29. *Report 3,* p. 30.
30. *Report 3,* p. 33.
31. *Report 3,* p. 30.
32. *Report 2,* p. 16.
33. Hope 1907, pp. 46-9.
34. *Report 4,* p.58.
35. *Report 6,* p. 2.
36. *Report 6,* p. 2.
37. Hope 1907, p. 4.
38. *Report 6,* p. 2.
39. *Report 4,* p. 58.
40. *Report 4,* p. 61.
41. *Report 6,* fig. 2.
42. Hope 1907, p. 48.
43. Eames 1980, pp. 132, 138-9.
44. Wall A: *Report 4,* p. 49.
45. *Report 4,* p. 60.
46. *Report 4,* p. 60.
47. Hope 1907, pp. 51-53.
48. Hope 1907, p. 59.
49. *Report 1,* pp. 2-7.
50. *Report 5,* pp. 67-75.
51. *Report 11,* pp. 5-20.
52. *Report 11,* p. 6.
53. *Report 11,* pl. IIa.
54. *Report 11,* pp. 9, 11.
55. *Report 11,* p. 9.
56. *Report 11,* pl. IIIa.
57. *See Report 11,* pls IIIa and IIIb.
58. Hope 1907, p. 52.
59. Hope 1907, p. 51.
60. *Report 5,* p. 72.
61. *Report 5,* p. 74.
62. *Report 11,* p.15.
63. Hope 1907, p. 51.
64. Floor C in *Report 1,* p. 5.
65. *Report 11,* p.12.
66. *Report 1,* p.7.
67. *Report 1,* pp. 8-9.
68. Society of Antiquaries Correspondence File for 1893.
69. *Report 11,* pp. 20-9.
70. *Report 11,* pl. VI.
71. *Report 11,* p. 25, and pl. VIIa.
72. *Report 11,* p. 11.
73. *Report 11,* pl. VI.
74. See *Report 11,* pl. VIIa.
75. *Report 11,* p. 27.
76. *Report 11,* p. 27.
77. Hope 1907, p. 59.
78. Hope 1907, pp. 49-50.
79. *Report 7,* p. 34; *Report 8,* p. 56.
80. Burton 1758, pl. facing p. 288.
81. *Report 8,* p. 57.
82. *Report 8,* fig. 16.
83. *Report 8,* p. 57.
84. Burton 1758, pl. facing p. 288.
85. *Report 8,* p. 57.
86. *Report 8,* p. 64.
87. *Report 8,* p. 64.
88. *Report 9,* p. 85.
89. *Report 9,* fig. 20.
90. *Report 8,* p. 58.
91. *Report 7,* p. 32.
92. *Report 8,* p. 58.
93. *Report 7,* p. 34.
94. *Report 8,* p. 57.
95. *Report 9,* p. 80.
96. *Report 9,* p. 79.
97. *Report 9,* pl. X.
98. *Report 9,* p. 81.
99. *Report 9,* pp. 80 and 98.
100. *Report 3,* p. 37.
101. *Report 7,* pp. 41-54; *Report 8,* pp. 67-77; *Report 9,* pp. 98-100.
102. *Report 11,* fig 12.
103. *Report 11,* p. 32.
104. Hope 1907, plan.
105. *Report 10,* p. 105.
106. *Report 10,* p. 102.
107. *Report 9,* p. 93.
108. *Report 10,* p. 104.
109. *Report 11,* p. 32.
110. *Report 11,* p. 31.
111. Hope 1907, fig. 44.
112. Brakspear 1905, p. 50.
113. Willis 1869, pl. I.
114. Hope 1903, p. 301 and pl. XXII.
115. At Lewes it lay beneath a circular laver: Godfrey 1952, p. 94.
116. Hope 1903, pp. 453-56 pl. XXXVII.
117. Willis 1869, p. 168 and pl. I.
118. Brakspear 1905, p. 50.
119. *Report 11,* p. 19, note.
120. *Report 11,* p. 11.
121. *Report 11,* p. 17.
122. *Report 11,* pp. 16-20.
123. Hope 1907, plan.
124. Brakspear 1905, p. 90.
125. Brakspear 1905, p. 50; see also Hope 1900, p. 364.
126. Hope 1907, p. 46.
127. Hope 1903, p. 446.
128. Brakspear 1905, p. 56.
129. Hope 1900, p. 386.
130. Brakspear 1905, p. 48.
131. Hope 1907, pp. 34-38.
132. *Report 7,* p. 28.
133. *Report 7,* p. 28.
134. Hope 1907, pp. 38-43.
135. Hope 1907, p. 40.
136. *Report 10,* p. 101.
137. *Report 11,* pp. 33-36.
138. *Report 11,* fig. 13.
139. *Report 10,* p. 118.
140. *Report 10,* p. 118.
141. *Report 10,* p. 118.
142. *Report 10,* fig. 30A.
143. *Report 10,* fig. 30, section A-A .
144. *Report 11,* p. 34.
145. *Report 11,* pl. XII.
146. e.g. *Report 11,* fig. 14.
147. Hope 1907, p. 38.
148. Brakspear 1905, p. 58.
149. Brakspear 1905, p. 58.
150. *Report 7,* p. 36.
151. *Report 6,* p. 23.
152. *Report 5,* p. 82.
153. Owen n.d., pp. 73-4; *Report 2,* p. 20, note 3.
154. We are grateful to Peter Bolam and Stephanie Ratkai for allowing us to examine this material.
155. Moorhouse 1983a, p. 135, fig. 27, nos 285-94, defined at Sandal as Type 14i.
156. e.g. Moorhouse 1983a, pp. 162-73, figs 62-4; Moorhouse 1983b, p. 47.
157. Owen n.d., pp. 71-81.
158. *Report 9,* p. 96, fig. 25, no. 2.
159. Moorhouse 1983a, p. 183 with references.
160. Moorhouse 1983a, pp. 191-94, fig. 80.
161. Moorhouse 1983b, pp. 47, 48; fig. 23.
162. We are grateful to David and Evelyn Baker for allowing us to look through the material in advance of their own publication.
163. We are grateful to John Allan for this information.
164. Moorhouse 1984, pp. 49-50, fig 2.
165. Moorhouse 1983a, p. 130.
166. *Report 10,* pp. 115, 121.
167. Manby 1973.
168. Moorhouse 1983b, p. 314, fig. 31, no. 25.
169. Dunning 1969, p. 311.
170. Moorhouse 1983b, p. 315.
171. Goodall 1981a, p. 53.
172. Salzman 1967, p. 330.
173. Perkins 1940, p. 61.
174. Salzman 1967, pp. 342-3.
175. Salzman 1967, p. 333.
176. Goodall 1981a, p. 54.
177. Perkins 1940, p. 135, fig. 42, Type III.
178. Perkins 1940, pp. 141-2.
179. Salzman 1967, p. 286.
180. Salzman 1967, pp. 304-6.
181. Salzman 1967, p. 311.
182. Hunter 1981, p. 143.
183. Hunter 1981, p. 150.
184. Salzman 1967, p. 175.
185. Dunning 1968, p. 311.
186. Micklethwaite 1892, p. 168, fig. 7.
187. Dunning 1968, p. 311.
188. Goodall 1981b, p. 67.
189. Perkins 1940, p. 278.
190. Goodall 1981b, p. 67.
191. Goodall 1981b, p. 68.
192. Goodall 1981b, p. 67.
193. Goodall 1981b, p. 67.
194. Haynes 1956, pp. 359-61.
195. *Report 4,* p. 62.
196. *Report 6,* p. 13.
197. *Report 3,* p. 39.
198. *Report 3,* pp. 45-48.
199. *Report 3,* p. 45.
200. *Report 3,* pp. 46-48.
201. Tylecote 1962, p. 34.
202. *Report 3,* p. 46.
203. Haynes 1956, p. 361.
204. Tylecote 1962, p. 262, table 85.
205. Tylecote 1982, p. 61.
206. Tylecote 1962, p. 36.
207. Tylecote 1962, p. 131, table 52.
208. Tylecote 1962, p. 131, table 52.
209. Tylecote 1962, p. 131, table 52.
210. Haynes 1956, p. 361.
211. *Report 4,* pp. 39, 48.
212. Piaskowski and Haynes 1957.
213. Piaskowski and Haynes 1957.
214. Rostoker, McNallen and Gebhard 1983, p. 25.
215. Greeves 1980, p. 105.
216. Tylecote 1980, p. 1.
217. Piaskowski and Haynes 1957.
218. Piaskowski and Haynes 1957.
219. *Report 4,* p. 62.

220. Haynes 1956, p. 163.

221. Tylecote 1962, p. 75, table 10; personal communication from M. Gill, of the Northern Mines Research Group, who quotes 3-4 ounces per ton from ores in the Grassington area.

222. Watson 1800, pp. 313-14, quoting Webster 1671; personal communication from M. Gill, who considers the reported yield 'truly incredible'. Webster never located the ore source of his assayed sample.

223. *Report 4,* p. 35; Haynes 1956, p. 395.

224. Personal communication from M. Gill of the Northern Mines Research Group.

225. *Report 5,* pp. 72-73.

226. *Report 5,* p. 79.

227. *Report 5,* pp. 73-74.

228. *Report 5,* fig. 23.

229. Tylecote 1962, pp. 138-39.

230. Tylecote 1962, p. 139.

231. Rahtz 1979, pp. 212-16.

232. Gathercole 1955, pp. 181-82.

233. Duncan and Wrathmell, forthcoming.

234. *Report 8,* pp. 67-76; *Report 9,* pp. 98-100; *Report 10,* pp. 130-32.

235. Brakspear 1905, p. 69.

236. *Report 8,* p. 75.

237. *Report 7,* pp. 41-42.

238. *Report 8,* p. 75.

239. *Report 8,* p. 67.

240. *Report 10,* pp. 131-32.

241. *Report 7,* p.48.

242. *Report 7,* p.42; *Report 8,* pp. 67-68; *Report 9,* p. 99.

243. *Report 6,* p. 14.

244. *Report 6,* p. 14.

245. *Report 7,* p. 35.

246. *Report 1,* p. 7.

Appendix A: Site Records in the Archive

Compiled by A. N. Smith

It will be evident from comments in the main text that for some areas and years the surviving excavation records are fairly extensive; whilst for others, nothing at all has been found. The following list of records, arranged by area and, where necessary, by year and trench code (see Figs 9, 37) is intended as a comprehensive index to the site archive. The records are now held by Leeds City Museums.

Cloister Lane
Plans: WC1, WC2, WC5, WC7.
Sections: WC7.

Cloister cistern
Site notebook, with tracings of plans and sections.

East Room
Site notebook, with tracings of plans and sections.

Warming House
No original records were available from the excavations in 1951 or for the trenching in the courtyard in 1955.
Sections: 1952, north-south and east-west through Warming House.

Refectory
No original records were available for the excavations in 1953. Three 1955 site notebooks survive covering the following excavated squares: R1, R2, R3; R4, R5, R6; R7, R8. There are tracings of plans and sections.

Kitchen
No original records are available for the excavations of 1950 or 1954 and only one plan of K2 survives.

Kitchen Yard

Site Notebooks:	1960 KY1, KY5; 1960 KY2, KY3, KY6, KY7.
Plans:	KY1, KY2, KY3-4, KY5b, KY5d, KY7, KY8-9, KY9, KY9a, KY10, KY22.
Sections:	KY1, KY2, KY3, KY4, KY5, KY5b, KY5d, KY6, KY7, KY8-9, KY9, KY10, KY22.

Area south of Lay Brothers' Reredorter

Plans:	LRII, LRIII, LRV, LRVI, LRX.
Sections:	LRI, LRII, LRIII, LRIV, LRV, LRVI, LRX.

The Meat Kitchen and area to south
No original records are available for any of the years, with the exception of a general plan which shows trenches and structures south of the Meat Kitchen.

South of Kitchen Yard
Site Notebook for 1957 covering: WR1, WR2, WR4, WR9, WR10, WR11, T1, T2.

Plans:	WR8, WR 8-9, WR9, WR 9-10, WR10, WR10-11, WR11, WR 11-12, WR12, WR 12-13, WR13, WR13a, WR14; SJH1=WR9N; WRA, WRB, WRC, WRd, WRF, WRA-E, WRG-H.
Sections:	WR 8-9, WR9, WR9N, WR 9-10, WR10, WR11, WR12, WR13, WR13A, WR14; WRA-D, WRE.

Abbot's Lodging
Site Notebook; plans and sections of areas I to IV.

Infirmary

Plans:	1959, I1, 2, 5, 6, 7, 10, 11, 12; IKY1, 2; IS.
Sections:	1959, I1, 2, 3, 4, 5, 7, 8, 9, 10, 11, 12.
Plans:	1964, I14, 15, 16-17, 18, 19, 20, 21, 22.
Sections:	1964, I14, 15, 16.

Appendix B: Photographic Archive

Compiled by A. N. Smith

The photographs listed below are all black-and-white prints. The archive contains few negatives. For each print the following information is recorded: the excavation area code (if any); the year of excavation; the feature and the direction from which it has been photographed. The concluding index number appears on the back of the print.

Cloister cistern

CL II/III	1953	Cistern	looking NE	1
CL II/III	1953	Cistern	looking SW	2
CL II/III	1953	Cistern (interior)	looking E	3
CL I	1953	Cistern outlet	looking NE	4
CL I	1953	Cistern outlet	looking NE	5
CL I	1953	Cistern outlet	looking E	6
CL I	1953	Cistern outlet	looking W	7
CL I	1953	Cistern outlet	looking NE	8
CL IV	1953	Cistern inlet	looking W	9
CL I	1953	Disturbance cutting drain	looking SW	10
CL I 3	1953	Charcoal layer	looking ?	11
CL I	1953	Cistern outlet	looking NW?	12

Warming House and Courtyard

	1951	Foundation of E wall of Refectory	looking N	1
	1951	Drain S of S wall of Warming House	looking N	2
	1951	Soakaway S of Warming House	looking N	3
	1951	Soakaway S of Warming House	looking NW	4
	1951	Soakaway within Warming House	looking S	5
	1951	Warming House Courtyard cistern	looking E	6
	1951	Warming House Courtyard cistern	looking SE	7
	1951	Warming House Courtyard cistern	looking NE	8
	1951	Warming House Courtyard cistern floor	looking N	9
	1951	Warming House Courtyard cistern	looking N	10
	1951	Warming House Courtyard cistern	looking W	11
	1951	Drain S of Warming House	looking N?	12
	1951	Medieval jug *in situ* in courtyard	looking ?	13
	1951	Soakaway under S wall of Warming House	looking N	14
	1951	Drain S of Warming House	looking N	15
	1952	Drain in Warming House	looking N	16
	1952	Soakaway below N wall of Warming House	looking N	17
	1952	Mortar floor in Warming House	looking NE	18
	1952	Soakaway	looking N	19
	1952	Twelfth-century floor	looking E	20
	1952	Soakaway in trench in courtyard	looking ?	21
	1952	Flag floor and fireplace (back to front?)	looking N	22

Refectory

FR II	1953	S wall of first Refectory	looking E	1
FR II	1953	Wall A on footings of Wall B	looking S	2
FR II	1953	Wall A on footings of Wall B	looking N	3
FR I	1953	Stairbase and lead pipe	looking NE	4
FR II	1953	Tiled floor	looking NE	5
FR II	1953	Tiled floor	looking SW	6
FR II	1953	Tiled floor over footings of first S wall of Refectory	looking SW	7
	1955	Patterned floor tiles and flags *in situ*	looking ?	8
	1955	Patterned floor tiles and flags *in situ*	looking ?	9
	1955	Patterned floor tiles and flags *in situ*	looking ?	10
	1955	Patterned floor tiles and flags *in situ*	looking ?	11
	1955	Patterned floor tiles and flags *in situ*	looking ?	12
	1955	Patterned floor tiles and flags *in situ*	looking ?	13
	1955	Patterned floor tiles and flags removed	looking ?	14

Kitchen

	1954	Crucible		1
	1954	Crucible		2
	1954	Crucible hearth		3

Kitchen Yard

	1950	Drain 15 below S wall of Kitchen	looking S	1
	1950	Drain 14 in courtyard	looking NE	2
	1950	Drain 14 in courtyard	looking S	3
	1950	Drain 14 in courtyard	looking N	4
	1950	Drain 15 in Kitchen	looking N	5
	1950	Drain 15 in courtyard	looking E	6
	1950	Drain 15 in courtyard	looking E	7
	1950	Drain 15 in courtyard (close-up)	looking E	8
	1950	Drain 15 and Refectory W wall foundations	looking E	9
	1950	Drain 15 in courtyard	looking N?	10
	1950	Floor A S of Kitchen S wall	looking NW	11
	1950	Wall contiguous to Vat and lead pipe trench	looking W	12
	1950	Floors B and C, S of Kitchen S wall	looking NE	13
	1950	Floors B and C, S of Kitchen S wall	looking NE	14
	1950	Wall 25 marking edge of floor levels	looking NE	15

	1950			16
	1950	Wall foundation (W25?) in courtyard	looking ?	17
	1950	Floor A	looking NE	18
	1950	Floor levels and curb	looking NE	19
	1950	Broken flags adjacent to curb in courtyard	looking W	20
K1B	1960-64	Lead pipe below E wall of *Cellarium*	looking W	21
K1A	1960-64	Drain (D10A) by E wall of *Cellarium*	looking W	22
KY5b	1960-64	Junction of drains D10 and D11	looking E	23
KY5b	1960-64	Junction of drains D10 and D11	looking W	24
KY5b	1960-64	Junction of drains D10 and D11	looking SW	25
KY5b	1960-64	Junction of drains D10 and D11	looking E	26
KY5b	1960-64	Junction of drains D10 and D11	looking E	27
KY5b	1960-64	Junction of drains D10 and D11	looking E	28
KY5b	1960-64	Junction of drains D10 and D11	looking E	29
KY10	1960-64	Drain D15	looking NE	30
KY10	1960-64	Drain D15	looking SE	31
KY6 or 7	1960-64	Main Drain and drain D7	looking NW	32
KY6 or 7	1960-64	Main Drain and drain D7	looking S	33
KY6 or 7	1960-64	Main Drain and drain D7	looking NE	34
KY9	1960-64	Drains D10A and D12	looking W	35
KY9A	1960-64	Drains D10A and D12	looking S	36
KY9A	1960-64	Drain D12	looking S	37
KY9A	1960-64	Drain D12	looking N	38
KY1	1960-64	After removal of turf and topsoil	looking W	39
KY1	1960-64	After removal of turf and topsoil	looking W	40
KY1	1960-64	After removal of turf and topsoil	looking SE	41
KY1	1960-64	Wall 23 and Main Drain	looking W	42
KY1	1960-64	Wall 23 and Main Drain	looking S	43
KY5	1960-64		looking W	44
KY5	1960-64		looking SW	45
KY5	1960-64		looking S	46
KY5	1960-64		looking W	47
KY5	1960-64		looking E	48
KY5	1960-64	Flags of D10?	looking E	49
KY5	1960-64	Flags of D10?	looking S	50

South of Lay Brothers' Reredorter

LRV, IX, X	1962	Before baulks removed	looking N	1
LR general	1962	Wall W20, drain D10, hearth C	looking W	2
LRVI, X	1962	Wall W21 and rubble areas A and B	looking NW	3
LRII, III	1962	Drain D11, wall W20	looking	4
LRV, VI, X	1962	Wall W21, drain D10, rubble areas A and B	looking W	5
LRIV	1962	Hearth C	looking E	6
LRIV	1962	Hearth C	looking S	7
LRII	1962	Drain D11 (corner)	looking NW	8
LRII	1962	Drain D10 in early stage of excavation	looking E	9
LRVI	1962	Drain D10, walls W20A and W21A	looking S	10
LRVI	1962	Drain D10, walls W20A and W21A after removal of rubble area A	looking S	11
LRV, II	1962	Drain D11, wall W20	looking N	12
LRIV	1962	Hearth C	looking E	13
LRX	1962	Wall W21	looking N	14
LRII, III, VI	1962	Drain D11 and wall W20	looking E	15
LRII	1962	Drain D11 and wall W20	looking NE	16
LRVI	1962	Wall W21A	looking S	17
LRII	1962	Corner of Drain D11	from above	18
LRV	1962	Rubble foundation of wall W20	looking W	19
LR	1962	?		

Meat Kitchen

MK?	1956	Drain D3, walls W2 and W3	looking SE	1

Area south of Kitchen Yard

WR13A	1958-59	Drain D7	looking S	1
WR14	1959	Walls 16 and 17, doorway (back to front)	looking	2
WR14	1959	Doorway	looking SW	3
WR14	1959	Doorway	looking S	4
WR14	1959	Doorway and drain D9	looking W	5
WR14	1959	Doorway and drain D9	looking SE	6
WR14	1959	Doorway, drain D9 and wall W18	looking W	7
WR14	1959	Drain D9 and wall W8, partially excavated	looking W	8
WR14	1959	Drain D9 partially excavated	looking SW	9
WR14	1959	Drain D9 partially excavated	looking SW	10
WR14	1959	Drain D9 partially excavated	looking SW	11
WR14	1959	Drain D9 and wall W18	looking SW	12
WR14	1959	Drain D9 and wall W18	looking SE	13
WR14	1959	Drain D9 and wall W18	looking S	14

Infirmary

I	1959	S aisle, showing early wall	looking E	1
I	1959	S aisle, paving at E end	looking S	2

Appendix C: Small Finds by Context

Compiled by Holly B. Duncan

Cloister Lane Wall (1963)

Context	Material	Description	Small finds no.
WC 1 1	Lead	came	236
	Lead	sheet	270
	Lead	waste (3pieces)	329
WC 2 2		coin weight-1464	407
WC 6 1	Stone	column shaft	414

Cloister cistern (1953)

Context	Material	Description	Small finds no.
CL topsoil	Lead	strip	302
CL I topsoil	Vessel glass	1 sherd (centre of base)	381
CL II topsoil	Lead	strip	303
	Window glass	3 sherds (green)	346
CL II 1	Lead	strip	305
	Window glass	1 sherd (green)	347
CL II 2a	Lead	sheet	268
CL II 3	Iron	slag	
CL II 5	Lead	sheet	267
CL II 6	Window glass	1 fragment (green)	348
CL II brown clay	Vessel glass	1 sherd-shoulder flask	387
CL III S. ext.	Lead	?strainer	251
CL IV topsoil	Vessel glass	1 fragment (modern)	382
CL IV	Lead	strip	304

Warming House

Context	Material	Description	Small finds no.
WH	Bronze	sheet-perforated	204
	Lead	pipe	322
	Lead	pipe	323
	Lead	pipe	326
WH 3	Iron	awl	21
WH 4	Bronze	ring and chain	193
	Bronze	bell?	195
WH 7-8	Bone	skewer	331
	Bone	handle	332
WH 8	Iron	slag	
	Bronze	slag	
In sand layer beneath drain		coin-Henry V	394
Inside drain		coin-Charles the Bold	396

Warming House Courtyard

Context	Material	Description	Small finds no.
Unstrat.	Bronze	belt fitting	173
Unstrat.	Bronze	harness ring	192
Unstrat. in N.W. corner		coin-Henry III	393

Refectory (1953)

Context	Material	Description	Small finds no.
FR		coin-John or Henry III	391
		coin-Henry III	392
FR I topsoil	Iron	knife (post-medieval)	17
	Lead	?weight	253
FR I	Bronze	2 tap handles	187
FR I 3	Vessel glass	2 rim sherds	380
FR II topsoil	Lead alloy	sheet	269
FR II 2	Window glass	1 painted fragment	354

Refectory (1955)

Context	Material	Description	Small finds no.
R	Mortar	2 lumps	418
R topsoil	Lead	token	232
	Window glass	5 pieces-green	340
R 2 4	Window glass	4 sherds	364
R 3	Bronze	strap fitting	180
R 5 9	Window glass	3 painted pieces	353
Unstrat.-adjoining main drain	Bronze	strap end	174

Malthouse (1963)

Context	Material	Description	Small finds no.
K 1 (a) 1	Lead alloy	sheet	254
K 1 B topsoil	Iron	2 nails	65
K 1 B 1	Iron	nail	66

Kitchen (1954)

Context	Material	Description	Small finds no.
K topsoil	Iron	wedge	43
	Iron	rod	51
	Iron	8 nails	64
	Iron	strip	156
	Iron	sheet	157

Kitchen (1963)

Context	Material	Description	Small finds no.
K NE 1	Lead	sheet	285
K NE 2	Lead	pipe	320
K 2 1	Iron	nail	67

Kitchen Yard

Context	Material	Description	Small finds no.
KY	Iron	2 nails	68
	Lead	9 pieces came	237
	Lead	3 sheets	274
	Lead	3 strips	307
	Lead	6 strips	309
	Window glass	5 sherds-colourless	334
KY A 1	Bronze	tap handle	188
KY topsoil		jetton-Nuremberg	404
KY 1 1	Lead	sheet	273
KY 2	Copper alloy	decorative foil edging	196
KY 2 ext.	Window glass	1 sherd-colourless	336
KY 3 1	Lead	came joint	244
KY 4	Bronze	waste	224
	Lead alloy	sheet	291
	Lead	slag	
KY 4 topsoil	Stone	disc	408
KY 4 1	Bronze	miscast/clipping	228
	Lead	came	245
KY 4 2	Bronze	slag	
	Iron	3 nails	69
	Iron	slag	
	Lead	strip	317

Context	Material	Description	Small finds no.
	Lead	slag	
	Window glass	16 sherds	371
	Charcoal		
KY 4 2a	Iron	shears blade	20
	Iron	2 nails	70
	Lead	sheet	255
	Lead	sheet	256
	Lead	2 strips	318
	Lead	slag	
	Window glass	2 sherds	372
	Charcoal		
KY 4 4	Iron	slag	
KY 4 7	Lead	sheet	271
KY 4 8	Lead	slag	
KY 4-8 baulk 1A	Iron	horse shoe-modern	62
	Iron	4 nails	71
KY 5	Bronze	vessel rim	189
	Bronze	4 strips	210
KY 5 topsoil	Bronze	perforated strip	197
	Bronze	sheet	209
	Plaster	1 lump	419
KY 5 A	Iron	slag	
KY 5 1	Iron	slag	
	Bronze	slag	
	Charcoal		
KY 6 topsoil	Lead	strip	308
	Charcoal		
KY 6 6	Iron	7 nails	142
	Iron	slag	
KY 8	Iron	2 nails	72
	Lead	came	235
	Lead	sheet	259
	Lead	sheet	289
	Lead	waste	328
KY 8 topsoil	Iron	5 nails	73
	Window glass	3 blue sherds	350
KY 8 1	Iron	oval link	36
	Iron	9 nails	74
KY 8 2	Iron	3 hooks	34
	Iron	nail	75
	Iron	3 nails	76
	Bronze	perforated strip	198
	Vessel glass	spout of ewer (post-med.)	378
KY 8 2a	Iron	6 nails	77
	Iron	7 nails	78
	Bronze	wire	
	Iron	slag	
KY 9	Copper alloy	sheet	212
KY 9 1	Copper alloy	ring of plaited wire	194
KY 9 2a	Iron	2 nails	141
	Iron	slag	
KY 10	Iron	nail	79
	Iron	amorphous lump	158
KY 10 topsoil	Bronze	strap end plate	175
KY 10 1	Iron	2 nails	80
	Iron	2 nails	81
	Iron	nail	82
	Bronze	strip	213
	Lead	2 pieces came	234
	Lead	sheet	257
	Lead	strip	291
	Window glass	1 painted sherd	359
	Vessel glass	3 sherds	377
	Bronze	slag	
KY 10 1a	Iron	12 nails	144
	Bronze	slag	
KY 10 B 13	Iron	20 nails	83
KY 23 topsoil	Iron	strap hinge	6
	Window glass	1 sherd	373
KY 23 1	Window glass	5 colourless sherds	335
KY 1950-below sand layer under flags	Window glass	2 sherds	360
KY SW corner: U/S		coin-Alexander III	395
KY under sand of east drain	Bronze	2 vessel rims	190
KY Unstrat.		coin (1792-Rochdale)	406

Structures south of the Lay Brothers' Reredorter

Context	Material	Description	Small finds no.
LR	Window glass	1 sherd	370
		coin-Edward II	398
LR I 1	Lead	sheet	264
LR II 1	Iron	door stud	15
	Iron	rod	52
	Lead	sheet	263
LR III 2	Iron	spade shoe	30
LR IV 1	Lead	tube or pipe?	249
LR V 2	Bronze	filleted sheet	199
LR VI 2	Iron	nail	84
LR VI 3	Iron	amorphous lump	171
LR IX 2	Stone	spindle whorl	409
LR X topsoil	Bronze	perforated sheet	200
LR X 1	Window glass	3 sherds	368
	Window glass	4 sherds	369
LR X 2	Bronze	sheet	214

Meat Kitchen

Context	Material	Description	Small finds no.
MK	Lead	weight	229
	Lead	hearth bottom	252
MK II 6	Bronze	strap ornaments	176
MK III 1	Lead	weight	230
	Window glass	3 sherds	361
MK III 2	Lead	slag	
MK III 2N	Lead	object	246
In rubble below flags in MK		jetton-Netherlands	403
Bath drain in MK		coin-Richard I	389
Below cobbles N. of MK		jetton-French	402

Meat Kitchen: rooms at south end

Context	Material	Description	Small finds no.
MKA	Iron	ring staple	33
MKA 5	Lead	3 fragments of sheet	262
	Lead	strip	298
	Iron	slag	
	Bronze	slag	
MKA 5 1	Lead	perforated sheet	260
MKA 5 2	Lead	sheet	261

Trench for Drain D1

Context	Material	Description	Small finds no.
BD	Lead	2 pieces came	243
	Lead	2 fragments sheet	277

BD VII 1	Copper alloy	wire	201
	Stone	thackstone	417
BD VIII topsoil	Iron	key	3
BD X 1	Iron	nail	88
	Window glass	1 sherd	363
BD XI	Stone	mortar of marble	410
	Iron	slag	
BD XI topsoil	Iron	nail	89
BD XI 1	Iron	2 nails	90
	Bronze	strap end	177
	Bronze	stud	179
	Bronze	suspension loop?	202
	Bronze	waste	223
	Lead	perforated sheet	280
	Lead	perforated sheet	281
	Lead	sheet	282
	Lead	perforated sheet	283
	Lead	2 strips	313
	Window glass	24 painted sherds	355
	Stone	window/door moulding	415
	Charcoal		
BD XI 2	Bronze	grave letter	208
	Lead	4 fragments of sheet	278
	Lead	3 fragments of sheet	289
	Window glass	2 painted sherds	356
	Window glass	2 painted sherds	358
BD XII 1	Iron	nail	91
BD XIV 1	Bronze	pin	183
	Bronze	miscast	215
MKA 7 1		imitation jetton	405
MKA 7 2	Iron	horseshoe (post-med.)	60
	Iron	3 rods	163
MKA 7 5	Iron	chisel	27
	Iron	nail	85
MKA 7 6	Iron	key	2
	Iron	2 strips	49
	Iron	10 nails	86
MKA 8 6	Iron	nail	87

Structures south of Kitchen Yard

Context	Material	Description	Small finds no.
WR	Iron	2 nails	92
	Iron	2 nails	149
	Lead	2 came fragments	238
	Lead	5 sheet fragments	274
	Lead	6 strips	310
WR 1 1	Lead	cylinder or spout	248
	Stone	column base or capital	413
WR 8 topsoil	Iron	3 nails	93
	Lead	sheet	284
WR 8 1	Lead	sheet	287
WR 9 topsoil	Iron	strip	47
	Iron	buckle	57
	Iron	2 nails	94
WR 9 1	Iron	nail	95
WR 9 2	Iron	3 nails	96
	Iron	slag	
WR 9 3	Iron	?buckle frame	59
	Iron	2 nails	97
	Bronze	perforated strip	216
	Stone	whetstone	411
	Iron	slag	
WR 9 5	Iron	nail	98
	Iron	slag	
WR 9 6	Lead	strip	292
WR 9 ext. E 1	Iron	3 nails	102
	Iron	3 nails	150
	Charcoal		
WR 9 N 2	Window glass	1 colourless fragment	338
	Window glass	4 fragments	362
WR 9/10 baulk topsoil	Iron	4 nails	99
	Lead	washer (?)	247
	Lead	strip	293
	Charcoal		
WR 9/10 baulk 1	Iron	nail	100
WR 10 topsoil	Iron	end plate of padlock	1
	Iron	strap hinge	10
	Iron	wedge	44
	Iron	4 nails	101
	Iron	8 fragments of sheet	159
WR 10 1A	Iron	2 nails	103
WR 10 A1	Iron	nail	104
	Iron	nail	148
	Iron	nail	153
WR 10/11 1	Iron	strip	50
	Iron	rod	55
	Iron	2 nails	155
WR 11 topsoil	Iron	file	23
	Iron	3 nails	105
	Lead alloy	pewter spoon bowl	233
WR 11A topsoil	Iron	7 nails	106
WR 11A 1	Iron	3 nails	107
WR 11 B1	Iron	12 nails	143
WR 11/12 baulk topsoil	Iron	clench bolt	46
WR 12 topsoil		coin-Mary	397
WR 12 1A	Iron	12 nails	108
	Iron	amorphous lump	165
WR 12/13 baulk topsoil	Iron	3 nails	109
WR 12/13 baulk 1	Iron	4 nails	110
WR 13 topsoil	Iron	washer	37
	Iron	5 nails	111
	Bronze	chain	205
	Bronze	hinged object	206
	Iron	slag	
	Charcoal		
WR 13 1	Stone	column base or capital	412
WR 13 1B	Iron	6 nails	112
	Iron	slag	
WR 13A	Lead	strip	299
WR 13A topsoil	Iron	10 nails	113
	Iron	2 nails	114
	Vessel glass	1 modern sherd	375
	Iron	slag	
WR 13 A1	Iron	11 nails	115
	Bronze	vessel foot	191
	Charcoal		
WR 14	Iron	axehead	24
WR 14 topsoil	Iron	strip	48
	Iron	sheet	56
	Iron	2 nails	116
	Iron	3 nails	117
	Iron	8 nails	118
	Iron	nail	154

	Bronze	tack	203
	Vessel glass	hour-glass fragment	376
	Iron	slag	
WR 14 1	Bronze	sheet	221
	Bronze	sheet	222
	Window glass	5 fragments	365
	Window glass	6 fragments	366
WR 14 2	Iron	7 nails	119
	Iron	4 nails	120
	Lead	came	240
	Lead	came	241
	Lead	strip	294
	Lead	strip	316
	Iron	slag	
WR A/B 1	Lead	sheet	276
	Window glass	1 fragment	367
WR A-H	Lead	came	239
	Lead	4 fragments of sheet	275
	Lead	3 strips	311
	Lead	2 lumps, waste	330
WR B 3	Iron	hooked rod (latch lifter?)	35
	Iron	bucket handle	53
	Iron	rod	162
	Charcoal		
WR D 1	Window glass	1 painted fragment	357
WR E topsoil	Window glass	3 colourless fragments	337
WR GH north 1	Bronze	ear scoop	185
WR H topsoil	Bronze	buckle	172
BD 20 7	Lead	sheet	279
BD 25 4	Lead	2 fragments of strips	312

Abbot's Lodging

Context	Material	Description	Small finds no.
AH I topsoil	Window glass	1 green sherd	345
AH III topsoil	Window glass	1 blue sherd	349
AH VI 1	Window glass	1 green sherd	341
	Vessel glass	base sherd of hanging lamp	379
T 1 topsoil	Lead	strip	298

Infirmary

Context	Material	Description	Small finds no.
I	Bronze	ear scoop	184
		jetton-French	400
I 1		jetton-Anglo-Gallic	399
I 4 1	Lead	sheet	306
	Lead	strip	300
	Lead	slag	
I 5 topsoil	Iron	5 nails	121
	Iron	amorphous lump	166
	Lead	strip	295
	Iron	slag	
I 5 2	Iron	strap hinge	8
	Iron	2 nails	122
	Iron	object (rod?)	164
I 6 topsoil	Lead	strip	315
I 7 1	Iron	nail	123
I 8 2	Iron	18 nails	124
	Iron	amorphous lumps	167
I 9 topsoil	Vessel glass	1 sherd of English forest	384
I 9 1	Iron	5 nails	125
	Iron	amorphous lumps	168
I 9 2	Iron	9 nails	127
	Iron	5 nails	151
	Iron	amorphous lumps	169
	Iron	slag	
	Lead	strip	296
I 10 topsoil	Lead	waste	327
I 10 1	Iron	4 nails	126
	Iron	amorphous lump	170
I 11 1	Iron	nail	128
	Lead	sheet	258
I 12 2	Lead	sheet	265
	Lead	2 strips	301
I 14 1A	Iron	collar	41
I 14 north baulk 1A	Iron	3 nails	129
	Bronze	waste	226
I 15 1	Iron	11 nails	130
I 15 2	Iron	3 nails	131
	Bronze and lateen waste		227
I 16 1	Iron	collar	39
	Iron	buckle	58
	Iron	2 nails	132
	Iron	nail	152
		jetton-Anglo-Gallic	401
I 16 2	Iron	5 nails	133
	Iron	3 nails	134
	Bronze	2 fragments of sheet	217
I 16 2a	Lead	sheet	266
I 16/17 baulk 1	Iron	2 nails	135
I 17 1	Iron	nail	136
	Iron	nail	137
	Iron	slag	
	Bronze	waste	225
I 18 topsoil	Iron	amorphous lump	161
I 18 1	Iron	nail	138
I 20 1	Iron	nail	139
I 24 topsoil	Iron	2 nails and 1 nut (modern)	140
I south aisle 2		coin-John	390

Unknown Contexts

Context	Material	Description	Small finds no.
SD I 1	Lead	plumb bob	231

Appendix D: Catalogue of X-rayed Iron Objects

Small finds no.	**X-ray plate and number**	**Small finds no.**	**X-ray plate and number**				
2	*pl.* 49, no. 25	33	*pl.* 43, no. 8	15	*pl.* 46, no. 18	61	*pl.* 48, no. 22
4	*pl.* 42, no. 1	53	*pl.* 48, no. 21	17	*pl.* 42, no. 2	62	*pl.* 43, no. 7
6	*pl.* 47, no. 19	54	*pl.* 48, no. 23	18	*pl.* 42, no. 5	158	*pl.* 44, no. 10
7	*pl.* 42, no. 3	55	*pl.* 49, no. 24	20	*pl.* 42, no. 4	160	*pl.* 45, no. 13
9	*pl.* 42, no. 1a	60	*pl.* 45, no. 14	26	*pl.* 44, no. 12	162	*pls* 44, 49, no. 11